White Market Drugs

White Market Drugs

Big Pharma and the
Hidden History of
Addiction in America

DAVID HERZBERG

The University of Chicago Press

Chicago and London

The University of Chicago Press, Chicago 60637
The University of Chicago Press, Ltd., London
© 2020 by The University of Chicago
Published 2020
Printed in the United States of America

29 28 27 26 25 24 23 22 21 20   1 2 3 4 5

ISBN-13: 978-0-226-73188-9 (cloth)
ISBN-13: 978-0-226-73191-9 (e-book)
DOI: https://doi.org/10.7208/chicago/9780226731919.001
.0001

Library of Congress Cataloging-in-Publication Data

Names: Herzberg, David L. (David Lowell), author.
Title: White market drugs : big pharma and the hidden
    history of addiction in America / David Herzberg.
Description: Chicago ; London : The University of Chicago
    Press, 2020. | Includes bibliographical references and
    index.
Identifiers: LCCN 2020017334 | ISBN 9780226731889
    (cloth) | ISBN 9780226731919 (ebook)
Subjects: LCSH: Pharmaceutical policy—United States—
    History. | Drug control—United States—History. |
    Narcotics—United States—History. | Drug addiction—
    United States—History. | Pharmaceutical industry—
    United States—History.
Classification: LCC RA401.A3 H47 2020 | DDC 362.17/82—
    dc23`
LC record available at https://lccn.loc.gov/2020017334

⊚ This paper meets the requirements of ANSI/NISO
Z39.48-1992 (Permanence of Paper).

Contents

Introduction

At the turn of the twenty-first century, America faced two seemingly contradictory drug crises. The first began with an unprecedented increase in opioid addiction, especially in rural white areas such as Maine, Appalachia, and parts of the Midwest. Most observers traced this crisis to the aggressive marketing of OxyContin, a long-acting opioid introduced by Purdue Pharma in 1996.[1] The second was an unprecedented increase in incarceration, especially among racial minorities. Most observers agreed that harsh drug sentencing contributed significantly to a crisis so severe, and so racially disparate, that some called it the "new Jim Crow."[2]

There was a brutal irony in this moment of twin social catastrophes: American drug control was too weak to restrain Purdue Pharma, but so strong that it sent countless people to prison. How was it possible for drug laws to have both problems at the same time?

The answer is all too obvious. In early twenty-first-century America, "pharmaceuticals" were not "drugs." Regulating the pharmaceutical industry was seen as separate from controlling drugs, and the crisis of addiction to pharmaceutical opioids was not seen as connected in any way to the crisis of mass incarceration driven in part by drug arrests. Pharmaceuticals and drugs belonged to separate stories, involving different people and different challenges, and calling for different solutions.

This assumed difference provided cultural fuel for one of the most relentlessly sensationalized narratives about the opioid crisis:

1

that addiction had left its traditional home among poor, urban racial minorities and was, for the first time, invading largely white suburbs and small towns, transforming wholesome children into "a new breed of addict," supplied by a "new breed of dealer."[3] The crux of the typical media story on OxyContin was the defilement of white innocence: suburban cheerleader to sex worker, rural honors student to criminal.

To see the opioid crisis as new and unprecedented in this way required a radical act of forgetting. During the last 150 years, small town and suburban white communities have suffered repeated crises of addiction to pharmaceuticals. Indeed, they have been home to far more drug use and addiction than poorer communities with less access to the medical system. These previous crises were no carefully held secret; medical and popular media have been covering them breathlessly for over a century. Yet eerily, year after year, decade after decade, this coverage has recounted the same story of addiction appearing for the first time in places and people where it did not belong.

Why has addiction to pharmaceuticals been so widespread, for so long? How is it possible to continually "discover" it as if it were something new? What purposes are served by this bizarre, long-running national surprise?

This book answers these questions by remembering the story of what I call "white markets": legal and medically approved social institutions within which the vast majority of American experiences with psychoactive drugs and addiction have taken place. White markets, I show, have been home to three major addiction crises in the modern era, far larger than any crises associated with illegal drugs. The first, at the turn of the twentieth century, began with sharp increases in medical sales of opioids and cocaine. The second, from the 1930s to the 1970s, came during a historic boom in sales of pharmaceutical sedatives and stimulants. The third, at the turn of the twenty-first century, grew from dramatic increases in medical use of all three classes of white market drugs—sedatives, stimulants, and opioids. These crises, I argue, all happened for the same reason: a presumption of therapeutic intent that left white markets with insufficient consumer protections. They were also all resolved through a similar set of policies, quite different from (and significantly more effective than) the punitive prohibitions of America's drug wars. These policies involved a combination of strong regulation of large commercial suppliers and continued provision of safe, reliable drugs to people who needed them, including people who were addicted.

The story of these three crises challenges us to rethink our basic assumptions about drug use, drug addiction, and drug policy. First and foremost, it reminds us that despite its famous drug wars, America has never tried to prohibit the use of addictive drugs. Instead, vast resources have been marshaled to enable and promote use of these drugs in contexts defined as medical. For over a century, providing sedatives, stimulants, and opioids to patients has been one of the single most common therapeutic acts in American medical and pharmacy practice. This has been so consistently true, for so long, that it cannot be written off as an accident or aberration; it has been a primary function of the medical system. The driving question in American drug history has not been how to prohibit use of addictive drugs, but how to define the medical—that is, how to determine who should have access to drugs, under what circumstances.

In theory, at least, the medical is simple to define: use that heals rather than harms. Seemingly simple terms like "heal" and "harm" are actually quite complex, however, and have been the subject of intense political conflict. Then too, since white markets have been home to the majority of addiction and drug-related harms, it would make little sense to characterize them as free of harm. Medical status did not confer special protection against addiction to the privileged type of consumer known as "patients"; it did not immunize pharmaceutical companies against the lure of profit; and it did not prevent physicians and pharmacists from being swept up by unwarranted enthusiasm for new drugs. For much of American history, privileged access to the medical system has meant heightened exposure to addiction and related risks.

Of course, access to white markets was not all bad. Far from it.

Even during the three great crises, the majority of white market drug use did not lead to addiction or harm but was unproblematic or even beneficial. It often treated rather than caused addiction. For untold numbers of Americans, sedatives, stimulants, and opioids have been highly desirable tools for easing suffering and pursuing pleasure. In this sense, white markets have indeed been a social privilege, not a century-long conspiracy by Big Pharma or an ongoing therapeutic error by physicians and pharmacists.

The history of white markets thus challenges us to take seriously not just the dire risks but also the irreplaceable benefits of addictive drugs. It also, I argue, provides us with rarely consulted tools for doing so: an alternate history of drug policy driven by the goal of consumer protection rather than "free markets" or prohibition.

Free markets and prohibition are usually thought of as opposite policies, but in practice they lead to the same end result: poorly regulated markets designed to serve sellers' profits rather than consumers' interests. White markets were an attempt to establish a middle ground. They were designed to enable extensive use rather than to quash it, and they did so by protecting consumers from inevitable drug risks such as addiction. True, protections were almost always insufficient—this is why white markets were in crisis for so much of the past 150 years. But the crises also provoked political creativity, leading reformers to build stronger and more effective regulations. Flawed as they were, these white market reforms were the closest approximations of successful drug policy that America has ever seen. Given the disastrous track record of the nation's drug wars, they are models that merit serious attention.

The mixed track record of white market drug policy highlights an important point that is sometimes forgotten in today's obsession with neuroscience: the biology of addiction may not change over time, but the extent of addiction, and how harmful addiction is to those who experience it, do change over time—quite a lot. These are fundamentally social issues that wax or wane in response to collective political action. The balance of drug risks and benefits at any given time has been determined more by the social configuration of markets than by the chemical interactions between substances and brains. Political economy, not pharmacology, encourages or prevents individual risks from becoming public health crises.

White market history thus offers an invaluable toolbox of past efforts to regulate rather than to prohibit America's most dangerous and desirable consumer goods. Yet this history is rarely remembered or consulted during debates around drug policy. Instead it is considered a medical story, relevant only for the supposedly distinctive world of therapeutics. This distinctiveness is overdrawn. The history of white markets reveals that their participants, like most humans, have also been motivated by profit and desire. White market policies, I argue, should be understood as what they actually are: a set of rules designed to maximize the benefits and minimize the harms of addictive drug use. Their failures and admittedly rarer successes offer much-needed history lessons about how (and how not) to approach drug policy more broadly, not just for pharmaceuticals but for all psychoactive drugs.

The people in the markets

Politics is a process, not a result. It is not enough to know the content of good policies; we must also know how they were achieved—or not achieved. White markets are vast and vastly complex social institutions. Many different people have a stake in them for many different reasons. A central goal of this book is to understand those people, their ideas, and their goals, and to trace how their interactions shaped white markets over time.

A particularly important set of characters in the story are four broad, overlapping types of reformers who directly fought to influence drug policy. The first were what historians call "therapeutic reformers." These were primarily elite physicians and pharmacists who believed that empowering professional experts—that is, themselves—was the best way to ensure that psychoactive drugs would be used safely.[4] In contentious alliance with therapeutic reformers were a second group, consumer advocates. This diverse coalition of politicians, journalists, and activists believed that strong government regulation was needed to protect consumers from a profit-hungry pharmaceutical industry.[5] The third group were moral crusaders. These were law-and-order activists, often native-born white evangelical Protestants, who saw addiction as one of many threats posed by poor, uneducated urban ethnic and racial minorities. They favored punitive policing to protect society from what they considered to be a criminal menace.[6] Finally, the fourth group, addiction medicalizers, were a specialized strand of therapeutic reformers. They opposed nonmedical drug use but believed that addiction was an illness to be handled by medical experts rather than the criminal justice system.

Through a shifting and often surprising series of coalitions and conflicts, these four types of reformers played central roles in defining and redefining white market drug policy over time. They did not do so alone, however; they interacted dynamically with others also seeking to influence the nature and extent of white markets.

All reformers, for example, had to contend with one of the most powerful actors in the story: the pharmaceutical industry. With endlessly deep pockets, drug companies battled against white market regulations, often deflecting blame for drug harms onto "addicts" and criminals. Meanwhile they marketed their drugs with aggressive creativity, downplaying addiction and other risks while expanding the definition of medical conditions (or inventing new ones) to justify increased prescribing and sales. No matter how dire the crisis, they did not relinquish profitable sales without a fight. Addictive drugs have inherent dangers, but the drug industry was central in escalating those dangers into public health crises.

A focal point of both reformers and industry were the government regulators tasked with implementing American drug policy: the Food and Drug Administration (FDA) and the Federal Bureau of Narcotics (FBN). A focus on white markets casts these familiar agencies in a new light. Historians typically portray the FDA, for example, as a hard-won and pioneering, yet limited and often outmaneuvered, bulwark of the regulatory state—a marquee, if imperfect, liberal accomplishment.[7] The FBN and its longtime chief Harry Anslinger, on the other hand, are usually portrayed as an illiberal and malign force, using punitive powers more to racially stigmatize foreigners and the urban poor than to prohibit or even reduce dangerous drug use.[8] White market history definitely does not debunk this binary opposition. It does, however, complicate it in important ways. Rather than being separate agencies pursuing entirely different missions, the FDA and the FBN appear in this book as twin stewards of the line dividing pharmaceuticals and drugs.

Political reformers, business executives, and government regulators saw themselves as uniquely responsible for the fate of white markets (and American drug policy more generally). These powerful figures, however, actually spent much of their time reacting to, and bemoaning their limited control over, the people they were supposed to be leading: workaday physicians and pharmacists and—perhaps most important—drug consumers. The daily decisions and experiences of these ordinary people drove white market history as much as the more dramatic battles over federal policy.

Physicians and pharmacists, for example, did not always behave as therapeutic reformers wished them to. Most were motivated by the desire to provide patients with comfort and relief, but there was no universal agreement on how to do this. Practices varied widely, from limited or no use of addictive drugs to large scale, overtly commercial "pill mills" that sold prescriptions to all comers. This variability was possible because of the hard-won professional autonomy physicians and pharmacists enjoyed in America. For the most part they were governed not by distant federal regulators but by state medical and pharmacy boards, composed of their colleagues and often more devoted to professional advocacy than to enforcing the latest federal dictates. To understand white markets, then, means understanding the thinking and decisions of physicians and pharmacists who do not usually appear in the history books except, perhaps, as maddening problems to be fixed by therapeutic reformers.

Finally, the most important and, I believe, misunderstood group of all: drug consumers. They are the ones in whose name all the other people claimed to be acting, and they are the ones whose experiences are the ultimate arbiter of success or failure in policy and practices. Yet they are rarely cast as central figures in histories of pharmaceuticals or drugs; they appear instead as ciphers—as passive pawns of the drug industry or of their own misguided desire for easy solutions to life's problems.[9]

Consumers are not always central to this book either. Often the story veers far from their experiences and focuses on more powerful figures who did not see themselves, or at least did not portray themselves, as drug consumers. But when consumers do enter the story—and even when they remain at its edges, invoked as justifications by others—they do so not as ciphers but as people with their own lives and agendas, pursuing relief and pleasure as best they could with the information and markets available to them. More often than not, they got what they were looking for. The great majority of white market drug use, after all, did not lead to addiction or death. To desire and to use drugs under such circumstances was not foolish or aberrant; it did not require having been tricked by an evil industry or misled by physicians. White markets thrived, in part, because of the perfectly understandable, human decisions of countless consumers.

To be respectful of consumers, however, also means acknowledging the very real risks they faced. Using addictive drugs can be dangerous, and drug markets have often been set up in such a way as to magnify those dangers unnecessarily. Reformers, drug companies, physicians, and federal regulators may have claimed to be acting on behalf of consumers, but their understanding of who consumers were and what they needed was strongly colored by self-interest. White markets were designed to serve the needs of these powerful groups as well as—perhaps more than—the agendas of consumers. One result was sales that careened out of control thanks to dangerous but hyper-marketed "wonder drugs." Another result was the opposite: the exclusion of many consumers, especially those with addiction, from accessing white markets at all. In pursuing pharmaceutical relief and pleasure, consumers had to contend not just with inherent drug risks but with the asymmetries of power and knowledge within (and outside of) white markets.

To write respectfully about drug consumers means writing with care and respect about addiction. This is not an easy task. Take the word "addiction" itself: over the course of the twentieth century, it has become so stigmatized, so packed with moral associations, that it seems almost impossible to use safely. For good reason, many thoughtful observers urge us to use different terms that better emphasize the humanity of people who use drugs. While I fully agree with their goals, I have chosen not to do so in this book. This requires an explanation.

Two main strategies are used for replacing or revising the term "addiction." One is to adopt a medical term such as "substance use disorder," which highlights addiction's status as an illness like other illnesses, deserving of sympathy and care rather than judgment and punishment. These are worthy goals. Yet as a historian, I resist using this term because it casts addiction as a timeless, unchanging individual condition rather than as an experience that has changed significantly over time in response to social, political, and cultural factors. It also obscures the political struggles that produce diagnostic categories and the medical logic behind them. In a book devoted to uncovering and understanding just such political struggles, it does not make sense to endorse a particular era's medical model of addiction—even if that era is my own.

The second strategy is to distinguish "dependence" from "addiction."[10] Dependence refers to a state of physical adaptation in which a drug is required for normal functioning, whereas addiction refers to compulsive use despite negative consequences. The goal of making this distinction is to acknowledge healthy, functional, long-term drug consumers and to protect them from the stigma and policing associated with addiction. Drawing these kinds of distinction can be a risky endeavor for a historian, however. Since the 1870s, safe drug use—"dependence" rather than "addiction"—has been challenging for the socially marginalized consumers forced to navigate unregulated, unreliable, and punitively policed informal markets. Dependence has been far easier to achieve for white market consumers with access to a stable, regulated supply. In other words, historically, dependence has not been an inherent quality of a person's relationship to drugs, but a contextual quality determined at least partly by the social circumstances of purchase and use. Terms like "dependence" (and earlier concepts such as "habituation") have mostly been used to obscure this fact—to dignify and legally protect the drug use of privileged people in explicit contrast to the drug use of marginalized people. I am already reluctant to act as arbiter of who was truly addicted and who was simply dependent; the political implications of doing so make me even warier.

In the end, I found no way to avoid or transcend the politics attached to "addiction," especially since those politics are the subject of this book. There are, however, ways to minimize the harms. Insofar as possible, I use "addiction" to refer to the broad phenomenon— as a risk associated with certain drugs or as a public health phenomenon—rather than applying it to particular people. Instead of emphasizing differences between people with dependence and people with addiction, I emphasize differences between consumers with access to more or less safe drug markets. This acknowledges both the gravity of addiction and the possibility of safe long-term drug use. It also emphasizes that drug consumers' safety has been determined as much by social and political forces as by consumers' own inherent qualities.

Thinking past the medicine-drug divide

White markets are an open secret of American history, widely acknowledged but rarely examined in depth. This is, in part, because they fall into a scholarly gap between historians who study medicines and historians who study drugs. These are different people, who belong to different scholarly societies, each with their own journals and conferences, and who organize their research around their own distinctive questions. Addictive medicines sit directly in the gap between these groups and fit only awkwardly into either. Not all historians respect this boundary between medicines and drugs; a number of excellent works tell key parts of the story.[11] Yet much of the story has not been told. Pharmaceutical opioids do not yet have their historian, for example, and despite good biographies of individual classes of drugs, the broader significance of white markets as a whole has not been explored.

From the vantage point of white markets, medicines and drugs appear not as separate things but as parts of a single, complex whole. America has not really had one set of "pharmaceutical regulations" and another set of "drug controls"; instead, it has had a single, divided regulatory system that unequally governs access to psychoactive substances. This system was built in the wake of the first white market crisis in the late nineteenth century and was consolidated with the establishment of the FDA and the FBN in the early twentieth century. Since then their stories have marched together in lock step, with major developments on one side nearly always echoed by major developments on the other.[12] This is because the dividing line between medicines and drugs is not a premise but a product of their history, continually renewed and renegotiated. Many drugs, and many types of drug use, have been dragged back and forth across the line—or maybe the dividing line has been dragged back and forth across them. How the line has been drawn at any given point was a social construction—the product of political struggle—but one with real and sometimes life-or-death consequences for consumers both within and outside of white markets.

A central argument of this book is that, most of the time, the division between medicines and drugs has not been effective. It has been an obstacle rather than an aid in protecting the public health. The presumption of therapeutic intent, fiercely promoted by drug companies and the health professions, has protected white markets from the robust regulation needed for such addictive, dangerous, and profitable products. The result has been a boom-bust sales cycle accompanied by a series of devastating public health crises. Meanwhile, the presumption that all nonmedical drug use is illegitimate and harmful has encouraged a long-running punitive anti-drug war with similarly devastating consequences on communities already hard hit by social inequality and, often, by the harms associated with illegal and thus unregulated drug sales. The twenty-first century's twin crises are just the most recent, severe manifestation of this recurring problem with America's divided approach to drugs and addiction. To repair and prevent this destructive cycle, I argue, requires knowing and then transcending the history that has built it. I hope this book can be part of that project.

The First Crisis

Opioids, 1870s–1950s

1

Drug wars and white markets

The distinction between "medicines" and "drugs" is central to the way Americans think about, regulate, sell, and use psychoactive substances. Both law and custom are designed to promote access to medicines while prohibiting use of drugs. This binary mission is so basic, so fundamental, that it seems obvious.

Yet as countless critics have pointed out, this seemingly obvious mission does not withstand even casual scrutiny. For one thing, drugs and medicines are very nearly the same substances. Heroin, the drug, differs little from opioid medicines; amphetamine, the drug, is the main ingredient of many medicines used to treat attention deficit hyperactivity disorder; and so forth. Nor does it help to shift from pharmacology to context—to define medicines as substances used in treatment of an illness and drugs as substances used in the absence of illness. The types of suffering considered to be illnesses have changed dramatically over time and are also contested at any moment. In practice, the question ultimately comes down to whether a person's suffering receives a diagnosis—a decision fraught with social, cultural, economic, and political influences. Unsurprisingly, such decisions do not map neatly onto health outcomes. Addictive medicines help ease suffering, true, but they also cause significant harm; fatal overdose of medicines causes many deaths. Meanwhile, addictive drugs cause harm, but only for a (very visible) minority of consumers, and virtually no one asks whether there are also benefits to their nonmedical use—a seemingly crucial area of inquiry if health were indeed the crux of the question.

The distinction between medicines and drugs does not simply reflect reality. It is a human accomplishment, built and rebuilt at particular times and in particular circumstances. Its configuration at any historical moment has resulted from purposeful political action, from conflict, collaborations, and compromises, all in response to now-forgotten challenges and crises. This is why the elegant conceptual simplicity of the medicine-drug divide does not easily map onto any similarly elegant or simple divide in lived experiences. The binary simplicity is achieved, not found. It is a call for more questions, not an answer.

For a historian, the most important question is also the most obvious: if the medicine-drug divide is not a simple reflection of reality, where did it come from? Who built it, why, and how has it been maintained despite its many contradictions?

An opioid crisis in industrializing America

The medicine-drug divide was born as the solution to a crisis. It was the late nineteenth century, an era of industrialization when advances in manufacturing, transportation, and corporate organization led to rapid increases in the production and circulation of a wide range of commodities and consumer goods. Among these commodities and consumer goods were derivatives of the opium poppy and the coca plant. These derivatives were stronger and purer than ever thanks to the isolation of active principles like morphine (from opium) and cocaine (from coca), and new inventions such as the hypodermic syringe. Consumption of these stronger drugs rose rapidly: opioid use more than tripled from 1870 to the mid-1890s, and cocaine use jumped by nearly tenfold in the decade after its introduction in 1883.[1] This wild growth was possible because of a relative lack of state regulation. Drug consumers, like consumers of other goods, faced a bewildering variety of new and often dangerous products. One result was a sharp increase in a distinctive and disturbing pattern of harmful, compulsive use that eventually came to be identified as "addiction." Fearful authorities declared an epidemic and implemented a variety of market reforms to deal with it. The most important of these reforms was the medicine-drug divide.

The idea of distinguishing between medicines and drugs did not come out of nowhere. It was built out of a range of informal existing practices that already structured opioid and cocaine markets.[2] The largest market for opioids involved morphine sold by physicians and pharmacists. Physicians had few ways to ease pain (physical or psychological) during an era when suffering of all types was a near-universal aspect of life. Aside from the devastating impact of the Civil War, workplace injuries, dental problems, and contagious illnesses were common.[3] Faced with all this suffering, physicians found "St. Morphine" indispensable. The US *Dispensatory*, an official almanac of pharmaceutical preparations and their uses, noted as early as 1858 that opiates were "more frequently prescribed than perhaps any other article of the *materia medica*," useful "in all cases where the object is to relieve pain, quiet restlessness, promote sleep, or allay nervous irritation in any shape."[4] Physicians reported prescribing opiates for neuralgia, headache, "female complaints," respiratory disorders, diarrhea, syphilis, rheumatism, insomnia, anxiety, overwork, masturbation, photophobia, nymphomania, and violent hiccough.[5] By 1870, a physician observed, morphine injections had reached "the height of fashion."[6] Cocaine expanded from its initial use as a surgical anesthetic to wide application as a treatment for ubiquitous nervous diseases and hay fever.[7]

These medical markets were not equally accessible to all Americans. They mostly served what we might call the doctor-visiting classes: people who were white, native born, Protestant, middle aged, and middle class.[8] Women were the primary consumers of morphine, and men, especially professional men, were the primary consumers of cocaine.[9]

People with less access to physicians also suffered, and also desired the relief and pleasure that drugs could bring. They too could purchase opioids and cocaine, but through smaller, informal mar-

18   CHAPTER ONE

kets outside of medical channels. These informal markets were typically located in poorer, racially mixed urban neighborhoods where municipal authorities segregated the trade in other disapproved goods and services such as sex work, gambling, and alcohol. Drug consumers in these so-called vice districts tended to be poorer and more racially diverse than medical market consumers, although their ranks also included many adventurous middle-class whites.[10]

Informal markets for smoking opium grew from complex origins to become particularly important by the late nineteenth century. In the midcentury Opium Wars, Britain, unhappy about a trade imbalance with China, had forced China to allow imports of opium from British colonial India. Unrestricted imports led to a dramatic expansion of opium smoking in China, including among laborers, whose global diaspora helped spread the practice. By the late nineteenth century, a backlash had developed against Chinese laborers, with many political and cultural figures in the West characterizing them as dirty, criminal, and unsuitable for citizenship. In the United States, Chinese workers found themselves segregated into or near urban vice districts. This spatial arrangement was important because, unlike medical opioid use (but similar to Euro-American alcohol consumption), opium smoking was typically social. Consumers used the drug together in the public or quasi-public businesses where they purchased it. Informal markets for smoking opium, in other words, required physical spaces as well as customers. In the United States, those spaces tended to be in or near the urban neighborhoods where Chinese immigrants lived.

Despite their differences, both medical and informal drug markets became hazardous in the late nineteenth century for the same reason: dramatic commercial growth that outpaced consumers' traditional strategies for recognizing and navigating risks. In both markets, more powerful drugs had suddenly become more easily and more cheaply available. This was not a development unique to drugs; industrialization brought hosts of new products manufactured and sold by distant, unfamiliar concerns whose risks consumers could no longer reliably assess through the era's traditional mechanisms of contract law (*caveat emptor* or let the buyer beware).[11] Drug addiction and fatal overdoses were no more shocking than, say, babies starved to death on "swill milk" or women disfigured by toxic cosmetics.[12] And in addition to their shared dangers, medical and informal markets overlapped significantly: many drugs sold informally had been purchased at less reputable drugstores, and drug consumers (especially if addicted) moved between the two markets as opportunities or needs arose.[13]

Authorities at the turn of the twentieth century, however, did not recognize an underlying unity to the crisis. Instead they believed they faced two fundamentally different problems calling for very different solutions. Opium smoking and other informal-market drug use attracted the attention and zeal of moral crusaders and anti-immigrant activists, who incorporated addiction into their broader campaign to govern urban vices, especially by policing white women's sexuality. Morphine and other medical-market drugs, on the other hand, were tackled by a slowly emerging coalition of consumer advocates and therapeutic reformers who saw addiction as one more example of the need to protect the public by regulating commerce. Together, these two campaigns built the legal and cultural architecture of the medicine-drug divide.

Opium smoking and racialized vice: Building the moral state

Most nineteenth-century Americans saw opium smoking as a distinctively Chinese practice, linked to supposed Oriental qualities such as irrationality, weakness, and emasculation.[14] "There is something in the very character of those vast Asiatic populations," ran a typical newspaper account in 1866, "with their corrupt and effeminate manners, and their decided tastes for negative enjoyments and a dreamy and contemplative life, which seems to draw them peculiarly toward the stimulus supplied by opium."[15] There was a dark irony to this belief: it blamed the Chinese for a practice driven by British profit seeking and Western hunger for cheap, exploitable labor. But it made perfect sense to nativists who already saw Chinese laborers as a threat to be closely policed and excluded from full citizenship or even barred from immigrating altogether. It thus circulated widely in Europe and America through elite texts such as Thomas de Quincey's 1821 classic *Confessions of an English Opium Eater* and in popular media such as the newspaper quoted above.[16]

As America's Chinese immigrant population grew, nativists found so-called opium dens a perfect focal point for their campaign to cast the Chinese as an immoral and unsanitary infestation.[17] In truth, informal markets for smoking opium served a variety of urban consumers. Nativists, however, described the "vile, pernicious dens of debauchery" as uniquely Chinese—an inevitable manifestation of innate Oriental qualities.[18] As the editors of the *Journal of the American Medical Association* warned, "wherever the Chinese go . . . the curse of opium smoking goes with them. It is a phase of the 'yellow peril' that we may have to meet nearer our homes than we have anticipated."[19] A journalist writing for the well-regarded national literary magazine *Scribner's Monthly* put it more directly: "Just now," he wrote after describing a "den" visit, "we were practically in China."[20]

Central to the popular appeal of "opium den" scare stories was their focus on the supposed sexual vulnerability of white women to the lure of opium.[21] The *New York Times*, for example, regularly reported on opium den raids in which "pretty" or "fashionable" young women were found entwined with Chinese lovers.[22] In *How the Other Half Lives*, influential photojournalist Jacob Riis described the "wives" of Chinatown as "all white girls hardly yet grown to womanhood, worshipping nothing save the pipe that has enslaved them body and soul."[23]

As a social problem, then, smoking opium did not stand on its own; instead, it was understood as one aspect of a multifarious racial threat posed by Chinese immigrants, symbolized by the sexual enslavement of white women. So when reformers took action, they did not campaign against smoking opium itself. Rather, they banned opium dens. The first such bans were passed in California: in San Francisco in 1875 and statewide in 1881.[24] Chicago's 1881 ban was typical. It made it illegal to "keep or maintain or become an inmate of, or in any way contribute to the support of any place, house or room where opium is smoked or where persons assemble for the purpose of smoking opium."[25] The right for cities to pass such ordinances was usually specified in state code alongside the right to outlaw sex work, vagrancy, gambling, disorderly conduct, and other criminal behaviors.[26]

Anti-opium-den laws should thus be understood as belonging to white moral crusaders' broader fight against Chinese immigration, similar to the Page Act of 1875 (limiting Chinese women's immigration) and the Chinese Exclusion Act of 1882. Enforcement targeted Chinese American opium smokers, especially those caught intermixing with whites.[27] The first national smoking opium law, passed as a supplement to the 1881 treaty excluding Chinese immigration, forbade Chinese nationals—but not US citizens—from importing smoking opium into the United States.[28]

It is obvious but still worth noting that these were not efforts to protect opium smokers. The laws were not designed to improve the safety and reliability of opium as a consumer good. Almost none of them applied to opium sales that did not take place in "dens."[29] These were anti-vice campaigns that drew a racialized boundary through America's emerging opium markets, defining who counted as legitimate consumers and who did not. People buying opium in dens were not consumers, and the people selling to them were not vendors; both were criminals, like gamblers and sex workers. They needed policing, not protection.

Morphine and white innocence:
Building the regulatory state

Addiction to morphine also became increasingly common as medical sales and use of the drug rose in the 1870s. Like opium smoking, morphine addiction became a subject of popular fascination thanks to avid coverage by newspapers and magazines. And also like opium smoking, morphine addiction became useful to reformers as a way to dramatize the importance of a broader agenda they were already pursuing. Morphine addiction, however, drew the attention of a different, more sympathetic set of journalists and reformers. Rather than portraying it as a racialized vice, they treated it as a tragedy visited on innocent consumers. Rather than calling for prohibition, they called for consumer protection.

The basis of this approach was the popular and professional perception of morphine use as a phenomenon distinctive to white, respectable Americans. As the *New York Times* put it in 1877, morphine habitués were rare among "the laboring classes," "the negro and Indian races," or "tramps." Rather, they were "the highest, worthiest, and best educated people in the country—those whose social and intellectual status gives them a certain pre-eminence over the masses."[30] Physician and early addiction popularizer H. H. Kane similarly described them as belonging to "the higher orders, in point of intellect and culture."[31] To a sympathetic physician writing in the *Journal of the American Medical Association*, those who turned to morphine "for relief of the pains of existence" were "those who dwell among us: our fathers, mothers, brothers, sisters and friends." (A few paragraphs later this same physician delivered far harsher views of opium smokers: they were "wholly given over to evil ways and the sooner they end their days the better for themselves and mankind at large.")[32]

When the physician mentioned "relief of the pains of existence," he was referring to a common explanation for why addiction was rearing its head among America's "best" people. Much as opium smoking had been ascribed to Chinese racial characteristics, morphine addiction was attributed to the supposedly advanced characteristics of well-to-do native-born whites. According to prevailing racial myths, these whites' highly evolved nervous systems were too refined and delicate to withstand the ubiquitous stresses of the modern society their intelligence had created.[33] According to eminent neurologist George Beard, for example, excessive morphine use was a variety of "neurasthenia," a form of nervous depletion supposedly rampant among educated whites in modernizing America.[34] As popularizer H. H. Kane explained, "A higher degree of civilization, bringing with it increased mental development among all classes . . . seems to have caused the habitual use of narcotics, once a comparatively rare vice among Christian nations, to have become alarmingly common."[35]

Unlike opium smokers, who were seen as having consciously chosen to engage in vice by visiting opium dens, morphine users were seen as having been innocently exposed through medical treatment.[36] "The vast majority of Anglo-Saxon opium-eaters," *Harper's Magazine* explained, "first learned its seductions . . . through a medical prescription."[37] The *New York Times* agreed, saying that "far from being a vice," the morphine habit "is actually a disease, produced not through the culpability of its victims, but in consequence of their physical and mental ailments, and chiefly through the instrumentality of their physicians."[38]

Because morphine users were understood to be pursuing health rather than indulging in vice, both popular and medical observers were sympathetic if they became addicted. Habitués (as they were often called at the time) may have lost control over their drug use, but they continued to be seen as moral, upright people. As the *New York Times* explained in 1877, "opium habituates . . . contract the habit in spite of their intelligence, their desire, and their will." They were not threatening criminals but rather "pitiable" victims with an "earnest longing to be free." In the end, the *Times* argued, "To no class of unfortunates should our floodgates of pity, sympathy, and commiseration be wider opened than to the victims of opium."[39] The *Journal of the American Medical Association* similarly offered nothing but sympathy for people whose "enslavement" had occurred thanks to "circumstances over which they have no control," and who suffered not only from the drug but from "the goadings of [their own] outraged moral nature."[40]

A habitué's loss of self-control remained a source of horrified fascination, but popular accounts often domesticated it in a way that softened the threat: morphine users were a danger to themselves, not to others. In one *New York Times* story, for example, the narrator told of a friend who had recently died after many years of compulsively injecting morphine. The injections had left her entire body disfigured by puncture marks and scars, but her behavior during those years had been anything but fearsome. She would, the narrator wrote, "leave the table in the middle of a meal when the terrible craving for the drug came upon her. Her husband would excuse himself also, to accompany her. She would go to her room, administer the drug, and return again apparently all right."[41] In another *Times* story, a morphine-addicted banker secretly visited a physician so that he could be cured without his wife ever knowing; unbeknownst to him, his wife had previously done the same thing. "Neither suspects to this day that the other was ever a victim," their physician noted of the devoted couple.[42]

Since individual immorality had not caused their addiction, blame fell elsewhere: on the physicians and pharmacists who had carelessly facilitated their state. "Whose was the sin?" asked *Arthur's Illustrated Home Magazine*. "If it was [the doctor's] ignorance, was it not in his case sinful ignorance? Are they not supine and careless about the matter?"[43] Many others agreed that physicians were "too lavish," "careless," "weak," and "almost criminal" in their quick recourse to morphine and their willingness to allow patients to continue the treatment themselves.[44] Pharmacy critics too complained of "careless" sales and warned that druggists had "no moral right to sell indiscriminately."[45]

These criticisms intensified with the popularity of cocaine after it was introduced by Parke, Davis in 1883. Cocaine was the first local anesthetic, offering dramatic advantages over general anesthesia in eye, nose, throat, and other surgeries that required patients to be conscious. But physicians also prescribed it widely as a "tonic," especially for nervous or neurasthenic patients. Perhaps the most dangerous of its applications was as a treatment for hay fever and other sinus problems because it called for "snuffing" the drug nasally. As nonsurgical uses became more and more common, cocaine addiction spread. Critics again blamed careless prescribing and sales for what many saw as an even more terrible habit than morphine.[46]

By the late nineteenth century, therapeutic reformers had coalesced around a simple and restrictive set of guidelines for the sale of morphine and cocaine. Up-to-date physicians and pharmacists, they argued, had little need for the drugs thanks to public health advances such as clean water, medical progress in diagnostic and surgical techniques, and the discovery of safer pain relievers such as aspirin and novocaine.[47] They urged great caution in the rare instances that morphine or cocaine had to be prescribed. Physicians should personally oversee morphine use to ensure that patients used the minimum amount necessary, for example. Prescriptions should not be refilled without a physician's order, and, to avoid self-medication, patients should not be given their own hypodermic syringe or be told what drug they were using.[48] Pharmacy reformers, meanwhile, urged "knights of the mortar and pestle" to protect "weak-minded men and women" by selling only to those in clear medical need.[49]

Reformers thus cast America's morphine (and cocaine) problem in radically different terms than opium smoking. Those ensnared by morphine were innocent victims, insufficiently protected from a dangerous product by incompetent or greedy physicians and pharmacists. Just as fears of opium smoking helped justify already existing campaigns to exclude and police Chinese immigrants, morphine addiction helped justify already existing campaigns to reform the professions of medicine and pharmacy.[50] In the late nineteenth and early twentieth centuries, therapeutic elites sought to improve healthcare while also enhancing their own professional authority—indeed, they saw these goals as one and the same. They pushed for stronger state licensing laws; increased educational standards; and more robust enforcement of ethical codes for physicians, pharmacists, and the pharmaceutical industry.[51] An addiction crisis blamed on poorly educated physicians and pharmacists dramatized the need for such reforms, casting them as a noble social good rather than an elite's selfish grab for power.[52]

Ironically, despite their universalist rhetoric, therapeutic reformers, like moral crusaders, trafficked in the politics of race, class, and gender. They were unsubtle in portraying themselves as benevolent patriarchs putting their intelligence and education to work protecting a public they portrayed as feminine or childlike. As one physician explained, "the laity" should be treated as "undisciplined and untutored children" when it came to morphine. "If you treat them otherwise," he warned, "they will look upon you as an ignorant, opinionated, willful and dangerous bungler in medicine—and you will deserve it all."[53] Such reasoning helped therapeutic reformers portray themselves as men of science nobly intervening to protect an infantilized (or sometimes feminized) public.[54]

Therapeutic reformers' goals extended beyond the medical and pharmacy professions. They also set their sights on the pharmaceutical industry. Here they joined consumer advocates whose longstanding campaigns had already achieved some of America's first federal consumer protections. As early as 1848, for example, the Drug Importation Act outlawed the importation of adulterated pharmaceuticals.[55] Already in 1870, twenty-five states and territories had laws governing the sale of poisons, typically requiring clear labeling, additional precautions in selling, and sales records. Opium and morphine were usually included in these laws, although they were designed to prevent murders and did not mention habit or addiction.[56] Consumer advocates had also succeeded in categorizing poisons as one of the "ultrahazardous" products exempt from the nineteenth century's general rule of *caveat emptor*; consumers injured by poisons could sue manufacturers.[57]

By the time the late nineteenth-century morphine crisis hit, American pharmaceutical companies had divided themselves into two sectors. The vast majority of companies were manufacturers of so-called patent medicines: premixed, prepackaged, brand-named medicines whose exact composition was kept secret to protect them from competition.[58] Many patent medicines contained alcohol, opium derivatives, or cocaine. Backed by raucous, ubiquitous advertising, they were among America's most recognizable and profitable products.[59] In contrast, a much smaller group of companies styled themselves as "ethical" and catered to physicians. They sold only established, clearly labeled medicines of guaranteed purity, and promised to abide by the Code of Medical Ethics. Among other things, this meant that they did not advertise to the public. In effect, these companies sold pure ingredients to druggists, who then mixed those ingredients into drugs according to a physician's prescription.[60]

Therapeutic elites had long favored the ethical drug industry and had been openly critical of what they called "quack" remedies. Indeed, the Code of Medical Ethics forbade physicians from employing patent medicines. But no laws, state or federal, backed the Code; compliance was voluntary, and it was routinely ignored in practice. The morphine crisis offered therapeutic reformers an opportunity to change that, at least for a few of the most dangerous ingredients. Thanks to their efforts, as states passed stronger medical licensing laws in the 1870s and 1880s, many also imposed the first prescription-only requirements for the sale of narcotics (a term that included both opium derivatives and cocaine).[61]

These nineteenth-century prescription-only laws were notable but also limited. Each state's law differed in strictness and coverage, often focusing on whatever drug happened to be a local problem at the time (for example, many early laws in the South included only cocaine). Some laws did not even require a prescription, only honest labeling. Almost all had exemptions of one sort or another: for opium used for diarrhea, for example; for Dover's Powder (a mixture of ipecac and opium often explicitly exempted by name); or for premixed patent medicines with relatively small narcotic content.[62] Enforcement was underfunded and weak, and because there was no federal law, restrictions applied only to transactions within a single state.[63]

Despite their many loopholes, the laws set a precedent for protecting consumers by enhancing the authority of medical and pharmacy professionals—"learned intermediaries" better equipped to navigate market risks. Yet, as we have seen, therapeutic reformers could be quite pessimistic about the educational and ethical standards of their not-so-learned colleagues when it came to morphine and cocaine. Perhaps with this pessimism in mind, approximately half the state laws passed in the late nineteenth century included what would later be called "good faith" clauses restricting the prescription of narcotics to the treatment of a legitimate illness.[64] This gave real power to reformers because, according to the new licensing laws, they were the ones who got to define good faith practice. Unlike smoking opium laws, which were enforced by police, licensing laws were enforced by state medical and pharmacy boards— bodies created and controlled by therapeutic reformers.[65]

It is worth pausing to consider the irony of therapeutic reformers' stance. Despite their professions' dubious track record of having quickly and passionately embraced not one but two addictive drugs at the same time, they were confident that they were the best stewards for morphine and cocaine. As they saw it, physicians had overprescribed only out of ignorance—very different, supposedly, from opium den owners who purposefully preyed on their victims. When the ignorance was cured, the addiction crisis would be over. This was peculiar logic indeed. Opium's habit-forming powers had already been quite well known in the 1870s when physicians began their twenty-year romance with the hypodermic, and physicians were among the many portraying opium smoking as an existential threat. To freely use morphine in this context, and then to continue to do so for years as addiction spread, suggests a willful rather than an accidental ignorance. Physicians purposefully continued to use a profitable and patient-pleasing treatment while stubbornly denying any linkage between their hypodermics and opium den "kits." The irony is captured perfectly by a *New York Times* article criticizing "the Chinese" for "resort[ing] to opium smoking for any slight ailment" and for regarding opium "as a panacea for all their ills."[66] The article was published in 1876, as the boom in casual morphine prescribing was well underway.

Flawed, ironic, and paternalistic as state and local laws were, however, they still represented a very different approach to regulating drugs than moral crusaders' smoking opium bans. Rather than criminalizing sales and use, they sought to protect consumers. Rather than prohibiting markets, they sought to make them safer. They were, in short, the troubled beginnings of the white market tradition in American drug policy.

The medicine-drug divide goes federal

THE PURE FOOD AND DRUG ACT OF 1906

The reformist ferment bubbling at the state and local levels in the late nineteenth century broke into national politics in the early twentieth century with the rise of the Progressives, a diverse coalition that prominently included both moral crusaders and consumer advocates. Consumer advocates were the first to pay attention to the drug issue, arriving at it through their concern about adulteration of food. A central figure was Harvey W. Wiley, the energetic head of the Department of Agriculture's Bureau of Chemistry. Wiley, a zealous reformer and clever politician, drew public attention (and federal funding) with his Poison Squad, a group of scientific men who examined food products microscopically to reveal adulteration and who tested the toxicity of commercially used preservatives. Drugs were a consistent, but minor, element of Wiley's anti-adulteration campaign until the ingenious lobbying of the patent medicine industry drew his ire. Starting in the early 1900s, he threw his considerable weight into the battle to regulate them.[67]

Patent medicines were a ripe target for a consumer advocate like Wiley. Sales were still growing rapidly, in part because the patchwork of state and local regulations were riddled with loopholes and exemptions. Moreover, patent medicines illustrated the consumerist argument perfectly: because they did not reveal their ingredients on the label, even the savviest consumers could not protect themselves. In actuality, patent medicines did not cause many new cases of addiction, and given the relatively small quantities of narcotics they contained, they were probably not very useful for people with addiction.[68] But this did not affect their value as a rallying point for reform.

Patent medicine companies were highly profitable and devilishly clever opponents. For example, as some of the highest-volume purchasers of newspaper advertising, patent medicine companies negotiated a "red clause" that would cancel contracts if the paper's home state passed laws restricting patent medicines.[69] Such "muzzle clauses" and other tactics stymied reform for years, helped by a prevailing laissez-faire reluctance to regulate markets.

At the turn of the century, however, political winds were shifting, aided in part by a new generation of investigative journalists commonly known as muckrakers. Muckrakers energized reform with popular and shocking exposés of corporate monopolies, corrupt political machines, and urban poverty. Patent medicines were a favorite target starting as early as the 1890s, when the *Ladies' Home Journal* stopped accepting their ads and ran occasional criticisms of the "Patent-Medicine Curse."[70] The most influential exposé was probably Samuel Hopkins Adams's 1905 series "The Great American Fraud" in *Collier's* magazine. Adams took aim at a rogues' gallery of remedies: those marketed to teetotalers that secretly contained alcohol; those fraudulently promising cures for dreaded diseases; and "subtle poisons" that "create enslaving appetites."[71]

Adams's characterization of "enslaving appetites" perfectly embodied the consumer protection approach to addictive drugs. Two things stand out. First, it cast consumers as innocent, but also ignorant, victims of profit-hungry companies. Adams dramatized this dynamic by forefronting the tragic stories of respectable white women—symbols of innocence who were also supposedly weak and in need of male protection.[72] Defining consumers as damsels in distress was a shrewd cultural strategy to counteract laissez-faire resistance to state regulation of markets. Laissez-faire ideology assumed that markets rewarded rational, benefit-maximizing individuals. Women, however, were supposedly ruled by emotion and piety; they needed and deserved male protection from the brutal machinery of markets. This was why laws protecting women and child workers were among labor reformers' earliest and most impressive legislative wins. Perhaps the same logic would work to achieve consumer regulations.[73]

Second, Adams's series grouped habit-forming drugs along with other poisons. He assigned no unique moral drama to addiction, instead categorizing it as just one of many manifestations of the true evil: unregulated commercial greed. Indeed, Adams's language about the narcotic habit was relatively restrained compared to his withering denunciations of other patent medicine crimes. He was particularly offended by fraudulent cures for sexually transmitted diseases, for example, which he regarded as "the most degraded and degrading . . . reeking of terrorization and blackmail."[74] For Adams, as for other consumer advocates, addiction was horrifying but not uniquely so; it was just one example of the terrible damage wreaked by unrestrained greed.

The idea that innocent consumers, often portrayed as white women, needed protection from the dangers of unregulated drug commerce powered patent medicine debates all the way to the halls of Congress in 1906. Addiction was not ignored in these debates, but again it played a relatively minor role—just one horror among many.[75] It was, however, particularly useful in dramatizing a central focus of reformist anger: secret or falsely labeled ingredients. As one prominent reformer told the House of Representatives, addiction resulted from "the innocent use of secret remedies containing these beguiling elements" by "good conscientious people who would recoil and avoid it if they knew what they were doing." This was particularly a problem for "our women," he said, because their "nervous constitution" made them vulnerable to advertisers' promises of relief. "They begin the use unknowingly of 'dope' . . . and are lost."[76]

Their focus on secret ingredients reminds us that reformers were not trying to prohibit sales of addictive or otherwise dangerous medicines. Quite the opposite: their goal was to make commerce possible by enabling consumers to make rational decisions.[77] One representative was met with rousing applause when he told the chamber that "we cannot undertake to prevent the man who is an opium fiend from obtaining opium, but we can undertake to prevent the man who never wishes to take opium from taking it without knowing that he is taking it."[78] Wiley himself repeatedly emphasized that reformers' only goal was that "the innocent consumer may get what he thinks he is buying."[79]

The law that passed, the Pure Food and Drug Act of 1906, was relatively modest. It required that all drugs be labeled honestly, and it created a new federal enforcement agency: initially Wiley's Bureau of Chemistry, and later the Food and Drug Administration. Labels did not have to list all ingredients but had to be accurate about any that were listed. Ten habit-forming drugs considered to be especially dangerous, however, had to appear on the label: alcohol, morphine, cocaine, heroin, opium, eucaine, chloroform, cannabis indica, chloral hydrate, and acetanilide.[80]

Out of the welter of weak and varied state laws, the Food and Drug Act carved a new domain of commerce: a white market for medically approved, legal sales of addictive substances. This white market was to be governed by the principle of consumer protection, under the assumption that native-born white consumers were innocent (they had no desire to experience pleasure from drugs and wanted to avoid addiction) but also ignorant (they needed expert guidance to avoid drug dangers).

THE SMOKING OPIUM EXCLUSION ACT OF 1909

When reformers built white markets to serve health-seeking innocents in need of protection, they made an implicit (and sometimes explicit) contrast with the supposedly immoral consumers who purchased drugs outside of formal medical channels. Smoking opium remained a primary frame for thinking about this type of drug user, and moral crusaders continued to spearhead the effort to police them. Here too reforms jumped from local and state to the national stage, in this case thanks to developments in international diplomacy. Hungry to expand global markets for American goods but facing a world largely carved up by European empires, many in the US foreign policy establishment saw China as a crucial potential trading partner. But how to gain favor after the recent offense of excluding Chinese immigrants from US shores? America's domestic crusades against smoking opium offered an intriguing option. After the Opium Wars, China was flooded with British opium and eager to regain the right to restrict or even eliminate the trade. The United States, home to prudish campaigns against alcohol and sex work, and fresh from an anti-opium campaign in its newly won colony in the Philippines, could credibly proclaim itself an ally in China's fight against opium.[81]

Toward this goal, the US government invested in global anti-opium campaigns by Protestant moral crusaders such as Bishop Charles Henry Brent and Hamilton Wright. These efforts led to a diplomatic summit in Shanghai in 1909 where Wright proposed a seemingly simple approach modeled on America's potpourri of state and local laws: nations should limit sales of opium to legitimate medical purposes.[82] Because smoking opium did not have a medical use (at least in America or Europe), this would enable China to protect itself against British imports.

There was one problem, however: America itself had no national law against smoking opium. Despite their best efforts, moral crusaders had been unable to overcome fierce resistance by the medical and pharmacy professions and the drug industry. On the eve of the Shanghai conference, however, they gained a new and powerful ally in the US State Department, whose support finally propelled them past the lobbying gauntlet. A new law was passed that banned imports of opium prepared for smoking and restricted imports of other opioids to "medicinal purposes only."[83] For most forms of opium the law had little effect because once a drug got past customs, it faced no further federal restrictions. Smoking opium, though, had no formal medical uses in the United States and could thus be prevented from crossing the border.[84]

Smoking opium thus provided an opportunity to draw a seemingly bright, clear line in the otherwise hopelessly messy terrain between medicinal and nonmedicinal drugs and drug use. Together with the Pure Food and Drug Act, the smoking opium ban offered a federal template for the medicine-drug divide: white markets would be regulated to protect innocent consumers, while informal markets would be prohibited and their participants punished.

THE HARRISON ANTI-NARCOTIC ACT OF 1914

The ban on smoking opium did have an impact on informal markets, but it was the kind of ironic impact for which prohibition efforts have since become infamous. With smoking opium illegal, informal-market consumers slowly shifted to a more powerful opium derivative, heroin, that was easier to smuggle because it had no odor and was less bulky.[85] Heroin was often injected, meaning that from a public health standpoint this was a step in the wrong direction; it was far more dangerous than smoking opium. The switch to heroin also accelerated an expansion of informal markets from their original base in Chinese immigrant neighborhoods to a broader network of disreputable druggists and illicit street peddlers. (The informal cocaine trade, begun within a few years of the drug's introduction in 1883, had already helped to establish this new market infrastructure.[86]) Moral crusaders continued to blame these informal markets on the low morals of the racialized poor, since illicit sales usually flourished where formal medical care was least available: the poor urban neighborhoods where a turn-of-the-century wave of immigration had brought hosts of Catholics, Jews, and other southern and eastern Europeans considered inferior by native-born white Protestants.[87]

Existing law offered few tools to rein in informal markets. Smoking opium was no longer an important product, so the 1909 federal ban on it was largely irrelevant. Neither the Pure Food and Drug Act nor most state or local codes prevented druggists from selling properly labeled drugs, especially on a physician's prescription. It was difficult for local authorities to stop even fully illicit street sales if the sellers had bought the drugs legally. Authorities did not ignore informal-market consumers; local police harassed and arrested them for a range of other behaviors increasingly criminalized as part of anti-"vice" crusading such as vagrancy, gambling, sex work, and petty crime.[88]

These were unsatisfying responses to a phenomenon depicted for years as a national crisis, and the situation quickly drew the attention of both moral crusaders and therapeutic reformers. Moral crusaders saw medically unapproved use of heroin and cocaine as a particularly virulent example of racialized vice. Therapeutic reformers were aghast at the participation of wayward physicians, pharmacists, and the pharmaceutical industry (whose too-free sales supplied the whole enterprise).

On their own, neither group of reformers had been able to achieve a strong federal law over the objections of the many powerful interests who profited handsomely from unregulated drug markets. The continuing diplomatic campaign to establish the United States as a global anti-drug leader opened a window of opportunity, however, and in the 1910s a coalition of moral crusaders and therapeutic reformers finally gathered the political clout to win robust federal regulation.

The 1914 Harrison Anti-narcotic Act spoke to both of the political constituencies that had pushed for it. Its central approach was familiar, building on state and local precedents. All sales of narcotics would be illegal unless they were part of a good faith treatment of a legitimate illness. Moral crusaders applauded an end to the legal confusion and patchwork loopholes that had allowed informal markets to thrive. Therapeutic reformers saw two benefits: it gave the professions a monopoly on an important but dangerous trade good, while also augmenting reformers' power by formally recognizing their preferred definitions of good faith medical practice. The drug industry and other naysayers had won minor concessions (for example, premade remedies with small amounts of narcotics were exempted, and physicians retained special rights to administer narcotics in person), but overall, the law appeared to have met everyone's goals.[89]

The Harrison Act was an early and remarkable achievement in

federal consumer protection. It imposed strong regulation over an important and profitable commercial sector at a time when the Constitution was widely interpreted as forbidding such actions. (In comparison, for example, similar controls over alcohol required a constitutional amendment five years later.) To accomplish this feat, Harrison was written as a tax law. It levied a tax on all narcotics transactions, from manufacture to retail sale. To implement the tax, all market actors including importers, manufacturers, distributors, physicians, and pharmacists had to register with the federal government and record all their transactions. A new federal agency (first the Narcotics Division and then, starting in 1929, the Federal Bureau of Narcotics) would share those records with state and local governments, thus allowing multiple levels of oversight. Every transaction would be exposed to surveillance and regulatory discipline by multiple state bodies. This was strong medicine indeed for the drug industry, especially as compared to the weak tea faced by virtually every other type of drug.

The Harrison Act met moral crusaders' goal of prohibiting nonmedical drug use in a more convoluted fashion. Congress did not have the constitutional authority to simply ban a particular product. So the law criminalized nonmedical sales through a complex regulatory jujitsu. Harrison was a tax act. People who had not registered— that is, the general public, who were not permitted to do so—could not pay the tax. Possession of narcotics without evidence of having paid the tax was automatically a federal crime. Thus, the general public could not legally possess narcotics. The law provided only one exception: the general public was exempt from paying the tax if the narcotics had been prescribed in the good faith treatment of an illness by a licensed physician properly registered with federal narcotics authorities. Through this circuitous route, the Harrison Act established the first clear, unambiguous prohibition of informal market sales and possession. The number of actual federal agents enforcing the law was never very large, but it provided new tools for state and local police, especially as states adopted their own versions of the Harrison Act.

Although it offered something to all constituencies, the Harrison Act was more of a consumer protection law than a moral policing law. Wiley noted, in disappointment, that "we are not asking for prohibition, which is what I would like to ask for if I had my way, but regulation."[90] Even so, the act owed its existence to significant support from moral crusaders like Wright, and it definitely contained prohibitionist elements as well. Perhaps most important, it consolidated, formalized, and nationalized the basic distinction reformers had been building between white market medicines and their consumers (to be protected through regulations) and informal-market drugs and their consumers (to be prohibited through criminal punishments).

From drug policy to drug war

The Harrison Act walked a fine line in balancing the demands of therapeutic reformers and moral crusaders. There was one area, however, where these two constituencies clashed directly: whether physicians could provide opioids as a treatment for people with addiction. Moral reformers were absolutely opposed. Therapeutic reformers were less unified on the question, but all agreed that medical professionals, not moral crusaders or government bureaucrats, should get to answer the question. While most of the Harrison Act was implemented without a hitch, this conflict became a central, definitional struggle over the soul of America's new drug policy. By the 1920s, moral crusaders had won this struggle decisively.

Therapeutic reformers had reason to believe that the Harrison Act was on their side. After all, the law's central purpose was to give the medical and pharmacy professions a legal monopoly on narcotics. As a 1915 *JAMA* editorial explained, the act merely permitted authorities to "trace these drugs from the importer to the ultimate consumer" so as to more effectively limit them to "their proper medicinal purposes." Ethical and competent physicians would barely notice the law other than registering and keeping records. "So long as he complies with the law of his own state," the editorial continued, a physician "can prescribe whatever he sees fit," including to "old habitués" as well as to any others for whom, in their judgment, "opium in some form is absolutely necessary."[91] Since "the law of his own state" typically just required that a prescription be "necessary for professional treatment," and since necessity was determined by state medical boards, the Harrison Act represented no federal intrusion on medical decision making.[92]

Therapeutic reformers did not oppose limits on opioid prescribing. Indeed, as we have seen, no one was harsher than they were in denouncing ignorant or profit-hungry physicians and pharmacists who prescribed or sold too freely. And prescribing opioids to treat addiction remained controversial. Some experts, like Charles B. Towns and Alexander Lambert, believed addiction was relatively easy to cure through some form of phased withdrawal. Others, like Charles Terry and Ernest Bishop, saw addiction as a chronic illness best managed by the provision of maintenance doses, regulated either through state law or through municipal clinics like Terry's in Jacksonville, Florida.[93] Both sides, however, agreed that addiction was a disease and, as such, belonged under medical purview.

Treasury Department authorities charged with administering the Harrison Act, however, sided with moral crusaders. They saw prescribing to people with addiction not as therapy but as the criminal act of a so-called dope doctor. So when Treasury wrote regulations for enforcing the Harrison Act, they declared such prescriptions illegal unless they were part of a phased withdrawal with the goal of abstinence.[94] This went much further than earlier state "good faith" clauses since it did not leave the definition of treatment up to medical authorities. Physicians would not be free to exercise professional judgment when faced with a case of addiction. Nor would state medical boards be the ones to determine whether a physician's prescription was legitimate. Whether intentionally or not, the Treasury Department was asserting America's first federal control over the practice of medicine, which had previously been regulated entirely at the state level.[95]

Courts were not initially sympathetic to Treasury's bold assertion of power. As early as June 1915, for example, a Tennessee federal district court overturned the conviction of a physician for prescribing large amounts of morphine to an addicted patient. The court held that the physician had kept proper records and had prescribed "in the course of professional practice," which a tax law like the Harrison Act had no authority to define.[96] The Supreme Court did not immediately address the question of legitimate prescribing, but in the 1916 case *Jin Fuey Moy* did even more damage to the law by striking down the criminalization of possession without a prescription. Since consumers were not permitted to register, the Court reasoned, they could not be charged with failing to pay the tax. The Court also explicitly sided with therapeutic reformers, declaring the Harrison Act "a revenue measure" that could achieve its intended "moral end" only within those constraints.[97] *JAMA*'s editors applauded the decision but, in keeping with their own campaign to police narcotics prescribing, called on states to enforce what the federal government could not.[98]

Judges' initial deference to professional authority quickly reversed after World War I, when a series of events buoyed moral crusaders and led to a greater acceptance of federal policing power. A postwar panic over immigrant radicals, for example, helped produce the nation's first immigration restriction and further fueled a boom in eugenics campaigns to restrict the fertility of the "unfit." Racial segregation was refined and formalized in both its southern and northern versions. Meanwhile, Prohibition of alcohol was passed after many decades of struggle led by evangelical Protestants. Each of these were substantial expansions of the federal state.[99] Importantly, these powers were won under the aegis of moral policing, not professional reform or consumer protection.

The expansion of federal police powers came at a key moment, when addiction was increasingly understood as a racial and class threat. By making it more difficult to purchase narcotics without a physician's prescription, the Harrison Act made informal-market consumers more visible as they were arrested or, if addicted, were forced to seek prescriptions or hospital treatment. The social status of these newly visible consumers was precarious. They were often working class or poor, and faced racial stigma as the children of immigrants from southern and eastern Europe or China.[100] Their new prominence made it easier for moral reformers to paint addiction as one of the many racialized social threats that the federal government was increasingly being tasked with handling. The regulatory state had stopped growing with the postwar political shift; not so the moral state.[101]

Freed to ramp up the campaign against "dope fiends," Congress amended the Harrison Act in 1919 to more definitively outlaw nonmedical possession as well as nonmedical sales. That same year narcotics enforcement was transferred to a new and better-funded home in the Treasury Department's new Prohibition Unit. Under new chief Levi C. Nutt, funding nearly doubled, and the Narcotics Division fielded half again as many agents.[102] Perhaps most important, in 1919 the Supreme Court upheld the convictions of two physicians who had prescribed narcotics to addicted patients without even pretending the purpose was medical care.[103]

The Court's decision did not materially change the tense balance of power between medical and federal authorities. This was because the convicted physicians' behavior had been so egregious that therapeutic reformers scorned them too—no one came to their defense at trial.[104] Since the Narcotics Division and medical professionals agreed, the Supreme Court's decisions did not actually answer the question of whose judgment would have won the day.

Aware that many people—including many physicians and at least some judges—still believed that addiction was a dreadful disease, the Narcotics Division worried that courts might be sympathetic to addicted consumers if they were suddenly deprived of narcotics by the strengthened Harrison Act. So the Division briefly partnered with the US Public Health Service in 1919 to encourage cities to establish narcotic clinics to provide treatment for people with addiction. About a dozen cities complied, including New York (which had the largest clinic) and New Orleans and Shreveport (which had the longest-lasting clinics). The clinics provided narcotics but were usually required to taper the doses until a patient was "cured," that is, had completed the withdrawal process.[105]

The narcotic clinics heightened tensions within the medical profession because they exposed more physicians to poorer, urban, and racially diverse patients with addiction.[106] Confronted by people they found culturally alien and immoral, many physicians—including addiction specialists—began to abandon their belief in addiction as a disease or, at least, a physical disease that could strike anyone.[107] Instead they began to focus on questions of individual character and morality. When clinic clients repeatedly returned to drug use even after having been "cured" (i.e., withdrawn from opioids), it was the last straw for many physicians. Here was definitive evidence that people with addiction did not want to be or could not be cured. The only real solution was to prevent them from buying drugs.[108] In 1920, internal debates among physicians officially came to a close as the AMA formally opposed ambulatory (noninstitutionalized) treatment of addiction. This significantly narrowed the distance between punishment (jail) and treatment (forced hospitalization and weaning from drugs).[109]

By the early 1920s, the transformation of addiction from a medical to a criminal matter appeared to be complete. When the Narcotics Division decided to shut down the narcotics clinics, few therapeutic reformers protested; the last clinic shut its doors in 1923. The Narcotics Division began revising the Harrison Act's enabling regulations to more restrictively define legitimate medical use of opioids. Such use, new language specified, included only the treatment of acute pain or incurable diseases. Physicians should be wary even in those cases, the regulations warned, "because such persons may use the narcotics wrongfully, either by taking excessive quantities or by disposing of a portion of the drugs in their possession to other addicts or persons not lawfully entitled thereto."[110] The Narcotics Division also ruled that a physician's intentions were no protection if a prescription diverged from their guidelines.[111] And finally, the Division took the radical step of refusing to allow physicians to register to pay the narcotics tax if they were themselves addicted or if they had a felony narcotic conviction within the past year. The Supreme Court struck this last rule down in 1922, but Nutt signaled his determination by asking Congress to explicitly give his Division these and other powers.[112]

Therapeutic reformers were appalled at what they considered federal overreach and lobbied vigorously against Nutt's request. The AMA warned its members that Nutt had not proposed a mechanism for determining whether a doctor was in fact addicted, and there would be no right to notice or to a hearing, and no appeal of the decision. The ban on registration for a year after a narcotics conviction, they pointed out, "denies the right of the states to determine who is and who is not qualified to use narcotics professionally within their respective borders."[113] The AMA's efforts finally bore fruit in 1926 when Congress rejected Nutt's request. Two years earlier in 1924, the Supreme Court had also given medical authorities a boost in the *Linder* case, declaring that not every prescription to a person with addiction was necessarily illegal, and that medical, not federal, authorities were the ones to make the determination.[114]

By the mid-1920s a precarious settlement had been reached. On the one hand, virtually everyone agreed that providing opioids to a person with addiction was not a legitimate form of medical therapy—a win for moral crusaders. On the other hand, therapeutic reformers had tenuously established their right to make and enforce that rule. This appeared to be a distinction without a difference, but as we will see, it was actually quite significant because it allowed leeway for ordinary physicians who did not agree with the new approach.

This leeway mattered because, despite therapeutic reformers' decision that providing opioids was no treatment for addiction, many physicians continued to believe in that approach in at least some cases. The persistence of such beliefs can be discerned in what has generally been seen as a major consensus statement defining addiction as a crime rather than a disease: the 1930 report by Charles Lambert and the municipal government of New York City. In it, Lambert called for an end to opioid maintenance and expressed pessimism about the possibility of a true cure for addiction. The only way forward, he claimed, was prohibition: preventing addiction in the first place. This was a harsh judgment, essentially abandoning medical responsibility (and hope) for people with addiction. Yet even this uncompromising report did note, almost as an aside, that, based on a physician's professional judgment, a small minority of "well-adjusted addicts" could be maintained.[115]

This tiny bit of wiggle room did little to change the overall fact of moral crusaders' decisive victory in the battle to define the Harrison Act, nor did it alter the most important of the law's accomplishments: the formal division of opioid commerce into medical and nonmedical markets. If there was yet some ambiguity as to whether physicians could treat a person with addiction by supplying him or her with opioids, there was no ambiguity at all about whether opioids (or cocaine) could be bought or sold without medical approval.

Conclusion

Two overlapping but distinct groups of reformers organized responses to the late nineteenth century's opioid crisis: moral crusaders campaigning against racialized urban vices, and therapeutic reformers seeking to strengthen the medical and pharmacy professions. Both sets of reformers faced the daunting task of expanding state regulatory capacity during an era of laissez-faire opposition to government regulation of markets. To overcome this reluctance, each set of reformers called on proven cultural traditions rife with racial and gendered appeals: policing vice and regulating poisons to protect consumers. Both campaigns can be seen as part of a single effort to rationalize markets for opioids by excluding irrational buyers and sellers while empowering medical and pharmacy professionals to safeguard legal sales.[116] With informal markets criminalized and eliminated, what remained, practically and metaphorically, would be white markets connecting a largely white, respectable consumer base with largely white, professional sellers.

This is not what happened. The Harrison Act did not eliminate nonmedical buyers and sellers; it just defined them as criminal

and pushed them ever more firmly into the informal urban economy. Quick-prescribing physicians and willing pharmacists moved
further and further from main streets into back alleys, eventually
giving way to smuggled heroin that had never seen the inside of a
pharmacy. This evolving informal market for drugs was as much a
product of early drug reform as were white markets for medicines.

The practical effect of the Harrison Act, then, was not to unify
all opioid sales in a single, safe market, but to formalize the existing division between white and informal markets. This structure
reinforced and even intensified the racial and class politics that had
helped create the medicine-drug divide in the first place. Informal
markets flourished in dense urban "vice districts" near major ports
that already housed a well-developed illicit commercial infrastructure. Thanks to ethnic and racial segregation, these neighborhoods
were largely populated by second- and third-generation immigrants
and then, starting in the 1920s, by African Americans. These communities had little access to medical care, which was also segregated, but were surrounded by informal drug markets offering easy
purchases (and employment opportunities). Meanwhile, only the
most persistent white Americans knew how to find and patronize
ever more carefully guarded illicit markets.[117] The medicine-drug
divide, in other words, was a self-fulfilling prophecy, creating the
categories of consumer it had supposedly been built around.

It is important to emphasize, again, that like other forms of segregation, the divisions between these markets were the products of
active efforts and not a natural boundary between two essentially
different types of activity. Both markets had been flooded with more
powerful and less expensive opioids (and cocaine), assisted by sellers happy to profit from consumer enthusiasm. Consumers in both
markets actively sought to buy and use drugs for their psychoactive
effects. True, there was a difference between a direly ill person using morphine to stave off intense pain and a healthy person trying
morphine or heroin for a "kick." But many, many consumers fell
somewhere in between these two ideal types. Some white market
consumers received morphine for relatively minor ailments or con-

tinued to purchase morphine on their own after their illness ended. Some informal-market consumers had never visited a physician but had begun using opioids to ease undiagnosed but no less real physical or psychological suffering. No one in either market set out to become addicted. Once addiction set in, however, no matter where someone had initially purchased opioids, they now bought where they could, often moving back and forth between "medical" and "nonmedical" markets as the need or opportunity arose.[118] That white and informal markets looked so different owed more to their divided governance than to any clear distinction between the intentions, hopes, and worthiness of their consumers.

Indeed, if you squint, the Food and Drug Act and the Harrison Act look much like other reforms in an era marked by enormous political investment in the segregation of consumer markets by race, class, and gender. People continued to buy (and sell) opioids, as they did other goods and services, in the markets to which their social status gave them access.

As we have seen, this binary division between medicines and drugs had a profound impact on how authorities responded to addiction as a social problem. By the 1920s, there was an almost universal consensus that addiction was a crime, not a disease, and that "dope fiends" needed policing and punishment, not treatment (or perhaps treatments so punitive that there was essentially no difference). Not everyone would be subjected equally to the punitive approach, however. One founding assumption of the medicine-drug divide, after all, was that white markets were fundamentally innocent affairs: errant sellers could be educated, and ignorant consumers could be protected. This, combined with the small bit of wiggle room built in to Harrison Act enforcement, left open the possibility that "medical addicts" might be spared the punitive machinery designed for "dope fiends."

2

"Legitimate addicts" in the first drug war

Henry D. was a traveling salesman who, when he was home, lived in the tiny town of Smithers, West Virginia. He had begun using morphine in 1904 during treatment for gallstones, and despite his "strong opposition to being a slave to the drug," he was unable to stop using it after the gallstones were gone. Twenty-one years later, in 1925, D. was evaluated by Lawrence Kolb, a physician with the US Public Health Service and America's leading expert on addiction. Pronouncing him in decent health, Kolb concluded that there was no "physical reason . . . why he should continue with narcotics."[1] He was not, in other words, using morphine to treat an illness—a key distinction under the Harrison Act. According to both legal and medical authorities, D. was simply an "addict" and should not be eligible to buy white market opioids in medical markets.

But Kolb was not finished. Despite the nonmedical status of D.'s opioid use, he observed, D. showed "no moral or mental deterioration from the use of morphine." Instead "the patient seems to have been a fairly useful citizen—he has supported a family and kept out of trouble except in relation to his narcotic habit."[2] (D. had been arrested once for an illegal morphine purchase.) Limited 1920s terminology did not make it easy, but Kolb appears to have been reaching for what in the twenty-first century would be seen as a distinction between addiction and dependence. D. was addicted, Kolb found, but did not act "like an addict."

Based on this assessment, Kolb recommended that D. should

receive special permission to purchase morphine in the medical market. "He will be a better citizen as a legitimate addict," he wrote to the Narcotics Division, "than he will be if his legal supply is cut off."[3] Despite the Division's campaign to forbid medical mainte-nance, Division chief Levi Nutt accepted Kolb's recommendation and permitted D.'s physician to continue prescribing morphine. Also following Kolb's advice, however, he insisted that D.'s supply be re-duced from 15–17 grains per day to 10 grains of morphine per day and eventually even less.[4]

Even with the lowered dose, this was a remarkable decision. Both federal and medical authorities had soundly rejected maintenance as a treatment for addiction; it was not the legitimate practice of medicine, but rather gratifying an immoral appetite.

D.'s case suggests that such official pronouncements may not have been applied equally to white and informal markets as physi-cians grappled with the aftermath of the nineteenth century's opioid crisis. For informal-market consumers, authorities no longer recog-nized any treatment for addiction other than forced institutional-ization and withdrawal. Repeated moral panics and punitive polic-ing beginning in the 1920s demonized nonmedical consumers as "addicts" and "dope fiends," establishing an enduring link between addiction and crime, immorality, and urban racial minorities.[5] The opioid crisis had also left a large population of addicted white mar-ket consumers in its wake, however. They too faced growing stigma, but not all of them were cut off from medical care. Like D., many of them were recognized as what Kolb called legitimate addicts and were permitted to continue purchasing relatively safe, regulated morphine via a physician's prescription.

The Harrison Act meant that such purchases were not easy. D.'s physician, for example, felt it necessary to ask permission from fed-eral narcotics authorities before prescribing. But the Harrison-based system of drug control was far better at cracking down on large-scale, commercialized "dope doctors" than it was at catching indi-vidual physicians maintaining a few trusted or sympathetic patients. Conflict between the Narcotics Division and professional medical authorities left legal loopholes and made for weak oversight, which, combined with the rudimentary state of surveillance technologies, allowed a clandestine and often unpredictable space for medical maintenance. This was not an easy space for consumers to navigate. It was a disconnected, disorganized, and largely secret archipelago, dependent on individual physicians' judgments and thus profoundly unequal in its availability. Even more than for most sectors of the white market, one needed both luck and, in most cases, the proper social attributes (white, employed, etc.) to gain access.

Despite these very substantial constraints, morphine maintenance was a much more important and extensive part of America's response to the turn-of-the-century opioid crisis than was understood by authorities at the time—or by historians since. The number of people with addiction being treated this way probably rivaled the number of "dope fiends," and almost certainly represented the majority of addiction outside of a few big-city informal markets.

The hidden history of white market maintenance sheds new light on what would otherwise be a mystery: how did authorities decrease the legal opioid supply so sharply in the early twentieth century without overdose deaths surging as addicted white market consumers moved to unfamiliar and riskier informal markets? This is one of the most basic dilemmas of drug policy. How is it possible to prevent new cases of addiction by restricting drug supply, while caring for already-addicted people by ensuring safe and predictable access to drugs? Historian David Courtwright has influentially argued that conservative prescribing practices successfully ended America's first opioid crisis.[6] This chapter shows that continued morphine maintenance was also a crucial part of that success. Even as authorities cracked down on opioids, many people able to portray themselves as "medical addicts" were able to access a relatively safe white market for morphine. Telling their story recovers a forgotten but sorely needed policy precedent: a consumer protection version of "supply side" policies that focused not on prohibition but on consumers' health, even those who had become addicted.

Beyond its policy implications, the disorganized white market experiment with morphine maintenance also invites us to rethink our conceptions of addiction itself. Early twentieth-century experts built a highly stigmatized concept of addiction by studying consumers in informal urban markets—people whose experiences were shaped by poverty and anti-vice policing, and whose daily lives were further distorted by the perception and moral judgments of experts and authorities. They provided the clinical material for a "junkie" paradigm that incorporated poverty and criminality as elements of addiction itself.[7] That paradigm made it seem surprising to discover a "fairly useful citizen" like D. among the ranks of the addicted. But people like D. were not the exception; they were the rule. Our ideas of addiction should include their experiences too. Remembering their stories can help us disentangle the realities of addiction from a century of inherited stigma.

Addiction to pharmaceutical opioids after the Harrison Act

The anti-maintenance interpretation of the Harrison Act had been made possible, in part, by an apparent shift in the demographics of narcotic use and narcotic addiction. According to a series of epidemiological studies and anecdotal reports, opioid users in the 1910s and 1920s were no longer predominantly white, native-born, middle-class, middle-aged women who had begun using morphine under a physician's care. Instead they had given way to a new generation of young working-class men, either immigrants or children of immigrants, who had begun using heroin (or cocaine) because of "bad association."[8]

To experts at the time, this demographic shift confirmed the hardening distinction between medical and nonmedical consumers. In the nineteenth century, they reasoned, medical overuse had exposed innocent, health-seeking patients to morphine, leading to a spike in so-called medical addiction. But then two reforms had seemingly solved the problem. First, voluntary professional and market reforms had reduced careless sales and thus reduced the number of new cases of addiction. Second, the Harrison Act ended sales to people with addiction, leading most law-abiding medical consumers, even addicted ones, to stop using morphine. As Lawrence Kolb put it, "the social and personal urge to cure has successfully eliminated many of the more normal members" of the "medical addict" class.[9]

When these medical experts looked at informal markets, however, they saw no such positive developments. Instead, they saw consumers switching to more powerful drugs such as heroin and remaining purposefully committed to drug use. These consumers did not seem to want to be "cured" and, indeed, openly resisted any effort to protect them from addiction.

Experts at the time believed, in effect, that they had witnessed what amounted to a large-scale *in vivo* experiment, with what appeared to them to be very clear results. Medical drug consumers had quit when required by law, whereas nonmedical consumers had not. This supported their prior assumption that the two groups differed in key ways. In one group, addiction was a hated illness; in the other, it was a purposeful vice. Kolb best captured this interpretation with his influential theory that people who suffered from seemingly incurable addiction were unstable or even "psychopathic." Kolb was actually being sympathetic; like many early twentieth-century psychiatrists, he saw psychopathy as a mental illness distinct from criminality, and he rejected the idea that addiction actually turned people into criminals.[10] But moral crusaders blurred Kolb's painstaking distinction and used his psychopath theory to stigmatize people with addiction as deranged criminals.[11] Even the relatively sympathetic Kolb agreed that people unable to stop using drugs were psychologically defective in some way.

This too-neat interpretation of the *in vivo* experiment, however, was almost certainly wrong. Differences in behavior between white and informal-market consumers reflected not innate moral or psychological differences, but the differential impact of drug reform. White markets became both safer and less publicly visible, while informal markets became both more dangerous and more visible.

Informal markets first. Sales and consumption figures for these markets are obviously not available, and estimates from the time are notoriously unreliable. Nonetheless, historians have persuasively argued that the primary impact of nonmedical drug prohibition was not to shrink these markets but to make them more dangerous, and to embed them ever more deeply into the ethnically and racially segregated urban demimonde.[12] The Harrison regime proved better at segregating and policing illicit consumers than stopping the flow of easy-to-smuggle powders into major port cities. Police harassment (and, eventually, police corruption) reconfigured informal markets, encouraging hidden locales, secret passwords, and other gatekeepers. Importantly, these gatekeepers were not there to protect consumers from exposure to opioids. Their goal was to avoid trouble with the authorities. In particular, they were designed to prevent sales to youths from respectable families whose outrage might elicit a response. For the marginal populations of many poor urban neighborhoods (and for especially persistent outsiders), however, the gatekeepers offered no protection at all—just an alluring invitation to unregulated commerce.[13] Because of the geographic overlap between urban segregation and urban vice policing, many poor families belonging to ethnic or racial minorities had little choice but to raise their children—those most at risk of addiction—in neighborhoods with easiest access to informal drug markets.

None of these developments boded well for informal-market consumers. For generations of marginalized young men and women in America's large port cities (especially New York City), the nineteenth-century opioid crisis did not end in the twentieth century. Instead it grew worse. As noted earlier, prohibition encouraged informal markets to shift from bulky, smelly, but relatively safe smoking opium to odorless, easy-to-smuggle, and dangerous heroin for injection. The consumers harmed by these new risks had virtually no access to treatment. Quite the opposite: they faced stigma and punishment as "dope fiends" that only worsened their plight. There were other problems, too. Injected heroin lasts just a few hours, meaning that addicted consumers were on a nearly constant quest to make purchases from unpredictable suppliers while being harassed by police. Maintaining a supply under such circumstances made it difficult to hold down a job with regular working hours, but opened new opportunities for employment in the informal economy through drug sales, property crime, and sex work. Treating consumers like criminals, in other words, was a self-fulfilling prophecy. And a vicious cycle too: as informal-market consumers were arrested or approached charity hospitals for treatment, moral crusaders pointed to them as a frightening and highly visible spectacle of the horrors of addiction.

White markets were very different. They were not subjected to the blunt instrument of prohibition. Instead reforms made white markets safer for consumers, in part by reducing casual or unnecessary exposure to morphine and cocaine. Physicians replaced morphine and cocaine with nonaddictive alternatives such as aspirin and novocaine, for example, and offered narcotics only as a last resort, under careful supervision, and in smaller quantities.[14] The result was a steep decline in opioid prescribing and pharmacy sales. Pharmacy surveys estimated that the proportion of prescriptions containing morphine fell from nearly 13 percent in 1885 to 6 percent in 1909.[15] Although the proportion rebounded in the 1930s, by then codeine had supplanted morphine as the most common opioid (codeine, in fact, was the most common prescription ingredient of all, second only to distilled water).[16] Since codeine is only a tenth as strong as morphine and is far less addictive, this switch must be counted as a genuine public health improvement. Meanwhile the total supply of opioids moving through white markets also decreased, with per capita imports plummeting from their mid-1890s peak of twenty morphine-equivalent ounces. On the eve of the Harrison Act, they had already declined by half; by the mid-1920s, they settled to a new low of about two ounces (see fig. A.1 in the appendix). The reduction in casual prescribing combined with the turn to codeine almost certainly led to a corresponding decline in the number of new cases of white market addiction.

Even as they became smaller and safer, white markets remained substantial enough to provide morphine maintenance to a large number of consumers. A large portion of the overall decline in imports, for example, reflected the exclusion of smoking opium, not a reduction in morphine supply. Then, too, per capita import figures were driven down by a very large increase in the number of poor and marginalized immigrants who had little access to white markets. And finally, overall importation and sale figures do not specify the purposes for which the remaining opioids were used. Half of the decline in white market opioids occurred before the Harrison Act—a time when physicians still widely accepted that morphine maintenance was a reasonable addiction treatment, and a time when the loudest reform rhetoric focused on casual prescribing, not maintenance. By the time the AMA formally rejected maintenance in the 1920s, the largest import declines had already taken place.

Even when per capita sales reached their nadir in the 1930s, the overall size of opioid white markets remained substantial. At the lowest point, enough opioids were still imported to support a maximum of about 60,000 people with addiction. Obviously not all of the imports were used for this purpose. It is impossible to know with certainty how much went to addicted consumers, but it is possible to make an educated guess. Sales of opioids, like sales of most consumer goods (including most psychoactive drugs), probably fell along what is called a pareto distribution. In a pareto distribution, a relatively small proportion of heavy users make the vast majority of purchases—typically, 20 percent of consumers are responsible for 80 percent of sales. For opioids, the high-purchase 20 percent were likely to be people with addiction. If we estimate that 80 percent of white-market opioids went to them, that would be enough opioids to support a maximum of 48,000 people. By the 1950s, this pareto-derived number climbed back up to a maximum of 80,000.[17] This was less than the nineteenth-century peak despite a much larger national population, so white market opioid addiction clearly had declined over time. It was still quite a significant number, however—higher, for example, than the FBN's admittedly questionable 1955 estimate of 60,000 people addicted to informal market opioids.[18]

Statistics allowed for morphine maintenance, but cannot prove that it was occurring. And as noted earlier, a host of epidemiological studies seemed to prove that medical addiction had disappeared even as nonmedical addiction was rising. On closer inspection, however, those studies are far from definitive. For one thing, they suffered from inadvertent selection bias. All were conducted in the wake of the Harrison Act, a time when informal-market consumers became unusually visible because of arrest or need for charity treatment. Epidemiological researchers, apparently taking advantage of this development, sited their studies in jails or large municipal hospitals. This made it more likely that their subjects would be the urban, racialized poor who could not avoid these stigmatized locales.[19] Other kinds of research—surveys and physicians' impressionistic accounts of their own practices—suffered from a similar unintentional selection bias during a period when federal authorities fulminated against "dope doctors." Physicians willing to answer surveys honestly or to publish an account of their own prescribing practices were unlikely to be ones breaking the law.[20] One of the only studies that used actual prescribing and sales records told a somewhat different story: in 1919, one out of twenty-four physicians in Pennsylvania were prescribing large quantities of opioids to people with addiction. This was a small minority of the profession, true, but it was still nearly 500 physicians who, together, prescribed almost half of all Pennsylvania's opioids.[21]

So how extensive was morphine maintenance? We will never have concrete statistics about an activity that was technically illegal and that was kept secret by its practitioners. It is possible, however, to stitch together surviving scraps of evidence to reconstruct a general sense of their extent over time. They were quite expansive through the 1930s, during the aftermath of the opioid crisis when white market addiction was still plentiful and a relatively sympathetic generation of physicians was still practicing. As white market addiction shrank from epidemic to endemic levels in the 1930s and 1940s, white market maintenance shrank as well. Medical maintenance was, in some ways, an emergency response that was gradually abandoned as the opioid crisis abated. Importantly, however, it never fully disappeared. A declining population of people who could claim to be "medical addicts" were able to access it well into the 1950s.

The early ubiquity of white market maintenance can be seen in two studies by researchers who swam against the grain in studying medical opioids rather than fearsome "dope fiends." The first was the 1919 survey of Pennsylvania mentioned previously.[22] The second was a major study of Detroit in the mid-1920s that identified over 500 regular morphine users supplied by physicians. Over half of them had received no diagnosis or had been diagnosed simply as "addicted."[23] Intriguingly, an earlier study by the same researchers had examined six smaller cities, and two of them (Elmira, New York, and Montgomery, Alabama) had had much higher rates of opioid use and of self-reported medical maintenance, apparently because "special provisions had been made" by "narcotic law enforcement officials and the local medical societies" for "locally supplying cases of addiction resulting from incurable or painful maladies." If those special provisions had been implemented nationally, the researchers calculated, white market maintenance would have been serving between 150,000 and 300,000 addicted consumers.[24]

These strikingly high numbers did not last. Surveillance and policing did slowly tighten up as the crisis-born wave of addiction dwindled and sympathetic physicians retired or died. One turning point may have been 1935, when a federal prison/hospital for people with addiction opened in Lexington, Kentucky. While "Narco" offered only abstinence treatment rather than maintenance, it still gave sympathetic physicians an alternative to prescribing morphine. Perhaps for this reason, medical authorities slowly began to be more cooperative in narcotics enforcement. By the late 1940s, the AMA began to publish the names of Harrison Act violators in the Medical News section of *JAMA*, and standardized its communications with state boards about opioid cases. By 1957 it was sending a mimeographed form with blanks for state boards to report actions taken against transgressing physicians.[25]

These developments were slow, however, and suggest a decline rather than a disappearance of white markets for morphine maintenance. The AMA's more efficient communication was primarily informational, for example, and did not encourage any particular disciplinary action. The most common response by state boards was to report that they had taken no action. (Florida's board, for example, responded to one query "P.S., all agreed this came under the heading of a 'stupid mistake.'"[26]) It was not until 1963 that the AMA officially committed to formally reporting all revoked narcotics licenses to state boards.[27]

Meanwhile, on the rare occasions when researchers looked for white market maintenance, they continued to find it. In 1954, a report commissioned by California's attorney general claimed to have found 32,000 consumers using legal opioids, as compared to only 20,000 using illicit opioids.[28] In 1957, an FBN report on Virginia claimed that "to date, almost without exception, the traffic in narcotics in Virginia's Western District stems from diversion from registrants," that is, sales by physicians. The problem apparently stemmed from the state's many addicted physicians, who, the agent complained, still received support from their local medical peers. (Two area physicians did have what the agent considered to be a "refreshing view towards members of his profession," but neither was willing to release his name publicly as supporting even a mild crackdown on addicted physicians.)[29] As late as the 1960s, a federal study of Kentucky—the only large-scale study conducted outside a major urban setting—found that the state's addiction rate was among the highest in the nation, and that people with addiction were largely "white, Anglo-Saxon Protestants" from "long-established families" who saw themselves as ill and who used morphine provided by physicians. This type of morphine use had declined somewhat after the Lexington prison/hospital opened in 1935, the researcher found, but it obviously remained quite common.[30]

Buttressing these admittedly scant studies is the overarching fact that per capita legal opioid sales stopped falling in the mid-1920s and then remained relatively steady for nearly seven decades (see fig. A.1 in the appendix). It is impossible to know how physicians were using these opioids. For example, cigarette smoking, and thus lung cancer, increased significantly during the period, and late-stage cancer was one of the indisputably legitimate uses of opioids. Rising use for cancer might have masked declining use for maintenance.[31] On the other hand, during those same years physicians grew increasingly conservative about using opioids to treat medical problems other than cancer; this may have balanced out any cancer-related increases.

All told, archival records, survey research, and sales figures provide an incomplete but compelling body of evidence that opioid maintenance continued during a time that historians have described as a "classic era of narcotics control" devoted wholly to punitive prohibition. Based on these numbers, it is quite likely that before World War II—the crucial decades when addiction experts built the "junkie" paradigm by studying addicted informal-market consumers—the majority of people with addiction in the United States were actually white market consumers being maintained by sympathetic physicians. At the very least, such consumers were a majority outside of the major port cities where most informal markets were located. Even in the heyday of the so-called junkie, in other words, the street-hustling style of addiction was the exception rather than the rule.

Physicians and narcotics controls after Harrison

The difficulty of compiling accurate statistics, and the impossibility of knowing the health circumstances of those prescribed narcotics, are a form of evidence in their own right: they demonstrate the relatively weak surveillance and policing of physicians during this period. True, the Harrison Act gave federal authorities a say in judging whether a prescription for narcotics was written in "good faith," and they prohibited prescribing for people with addiction. Also true, at least some physicians complained loudly about tyrannical intrusions of federal power into their sacred professional duties.[32] Yet these complaints should not necessarily be taken at face value; like professional complaints about "socialized medicine," they were not simple descriptions of reality but signs of political complexity and conflict. In practice, the definition of good faith treatment remained in the hands of medical authorities for a variety of reasons.

To begin with, the Narcotics Division's legal power over physicians was far less fearsome than one might expect. The Division's own regulations implementing the Harrison Act, for example, gave physicians surprisingly wide latitude to make decisions about prescribing for people with addiction. The earliest versions did not even define good faith medical practice at all; instead they focused solely on distinguishing between medical and nonmedical use.[33] Clashes between medical and federal authorities later in the 1910s (see chapter 1) produced ambiguous changes in the regulations. On the one hand, they became stricter: in May 1919 the regulations clarified for the first time that prescribing to a person with addiction was against the law. Yet this restriction was accompanied by exceptions for anyone who was diagnosed with an incurable disease and for "an aged and infirm addict whose collapse would result from the withdrawal of the drug."[34] The editors of the AMA saw the 1919 revisions as making the rules "more liberal" and "plac[ing] the responsibility on the physician where it rightly belongs."[35]

Narcotics Division rules permitted even more flexibility in response to the Supreme Court's 1924 decision in *Linder v. United States*. In *Linder*, the Court held that providing opioids to a person in withdrawal must be legitimate medical practice because "it is the business of physicians to alleviate the pain and suffering of patients." Such provision had to be made in good faith, the Court warned; the law would not permit purely commercial transactions of the sort that both therapeutic reformers and Narcotics Division authorities opposed.[36] Nevertheless, the decision forced the Narcotics Division to add a new rule in 1927 permitting physicians to "accord temporary relief for an ordinary addict [i.e., one who was not ill or aged] whose condition demands immediate attention."[37]

Linder was the best known, but hardly the only, court decision

to limit the Narcotics Division's legal authority over medical practice. Tennessee's Supreme Court, for example, ruled in 1925 that
violating the Harrison Act was not, on its face, proof of "moral turpitude" (for which medical licenses could be revoked) because the
only crime possible under the act was tax evasion. Moral turpitude
would have to be proved separately.[38] And in 1934, a federal court
overturned the conviction of a Seattle physician caught providing
morphine to multiple people with addiction, ruling that the physician was innocent because he had honestly believed this to be a legitimate medical treatment. "Since this time," *Northwest Medicine*
reported the next year, "morphine addicts under arrest in Seattle
have been discharged by the police court judge on the grounds that
the jail is no place for them."[39]

Adverse court decisions were not the only legal obstacles to Narcotics Division power. State laws, too, placed limits. The Division
was required to allow any licensed physician to register to pay the
Harrison tax and receive a narcotics permit; only when a state medical board revoked a license could the Division refuse to give a permit.[40] Yet in 1926, only nine states allowed a physician's license to be
revoked solely for a Harrison Act conviction (thirty-one allowed, but
did not require, licenses to be pulled if a physician was addicted).
Only six states had their own specific law against prescribing opioids
to an addicted patient; in all other states Narcotics Division agents
bore the full brunt of enforcement, and revoking a license was extremely difficult.[41] State laws could be problematic in other ways as
well. In Wisconsin, for example, medical licenses could be revoked
only for convictions under state law—federal convictions, Harrison
Act or other, did not count. Wisconsin's law was not amended to include federal convictions until 1947, and even then it did not include
convictions in other states.[42] State-level variations of this sort did
decline over time as more states adopted the Uniform State Narcotic
Law, but this was a slow process: by 1935 only nine states had passed
the uniform act; by 1946 the tally had reached forty-two.[43]

These legal constraints were particularly important because
the Narcotics Division, and the Federal Bureau of Narcotics that

replaced it in 1930, were relatively small agencies charged with a very large job. The United States had more than 150,000 practicing physicians; federal authorities had to police them with fewer than 300 agents employing a rudimentary surveillance system.[44] This was a Herculean task when, for example, records of prescriptions and sales were kept on premises, meaning that agents had to undertake in-person audits to discover transgressions.[45]

In theory, state and local cooperation would make up for the many shortcomings of federal authorities. Indeed, the Harrison Act had been billed as a minor expansion of federal power whose central purpose was to provide states with the information they needed to enforce their own laws. Yet as we have seen, even if they had been zealously enforced, state laws were inconsistent at best. And there was no certainty that they would be enforced zealously or even at all, at least when it came to the treatment of people with addiction. Therapeutic reformers may have opposed morphine maintenance, but they also opposed giving the federal government the power to ban the practice. Persistent conflict over this jurisdictional question caused friction between federal authorities and the state and local medical institutions whose cooperation they desperately needed.

To begin with, opioids were simply not a priority for most state medical boards. Massachusetts and Wisconsin were two of the few states whose full disciplinary records are available from these years, and they paint a picture of boards only fitfully active on the opioid front. Of more than 100 convictions for violations of Massachusetts's Medical Practice Act between 1920 and 1932, for example, only four were related to opioids. Of these four, only one was for an illegal prescription of morphine to a person with addiction—and that physician was found not guilty.[46] Opioid offenses did not even rate their own category on a list of more than 300 "complaints and charges made against registered physicians" between 1925 and 1938. More than a third were related to alcohol Prohibition; another tenth were for abortion.[47] Even during what appear to have been sporadic crackdowns—there were ten opioid cases in 1931 and another nine in 1936—Massachusetts physicians were rarely punished. Those nineteen cases were the bulk of state disciplinary action related to opioids, and most of them resulted in "no action taken." Only one, involving a physician also diagnosed with "insanity," led to a revoked license.[48] In Wisconsin, meanwhile, the medical board investigated only eight physicians for opioid infractions from 1920 to 1946, and six of these were addicted physicians illegally supplying themselves. Only one physician was convicted, although several others had their licenses temporarily suspended.[49]

Even when state boards did pursue opioid cases, it appears that they were often doing so as a means to get at a physician already under suspicion for other causes. In Wisconsin, for example, a disproportionate number of opioid investigations through the 1950s involved physicians who were suspected of providing abortions. In one case, a physician was convicted after prescribing morphine for his abortion patient—he was unable to explain the legitimate medical condition for which he had prescribed.[50] A number of non-abortion issues also could trigger investigation. One physician had been accused of rape and of promising cures for incurable illnesses[51]; another was a public drunk who had tried to shoot his wife and family with a shotgun[52]; another was reputed to have been homosexual.[53] California, which preserved partial disciplinary records from this era, has similar examples. Of four extensive case files available, two were abortionists and one had been diagnosed with a mental illness. There may also have been a racial dimension to authorities' suspicions. Two of Wisconsin's several dozen cases involved African American physicians, as did one of California's four cases. The California investigator warned the state board that "if the colored physicians of Los Angeles continue to get into trouble as they have in the past few months there will be a shortage of colored doctors in Los Angeles."[54]

Federal narcotics authorities were not happy about this state of affairs. The top lawyer for the Federal Bureau of Narcotics, Alfred Tennyson, vented frustration by berating a national conference of medical associations in 1930. He singled out Missouri's state medical board, which, he claimed, had refused to revoke the license of

a St. Louis physician even after two convictions for opioid violations; the physician was now, Tennyson claimed, writing more than
1,000 prescriptions per month to as many as twenty-five addicted
people per day. He also pointed to Georgia, where, he complained,
a thrice-convicted physician had continued to practice medicine despite having lost his license; "astoundingly," the board "fixed" the
problem be reinstating his license. Tennyson's audience was skeptical. The AMA's representative, for example, asked to hear from the
Missouri and Georgia boards before accepting the FBN's version of
events.[55]

The FBN was determined, however. Bureau chief Harry J. Anslinger railed to Congress in 1935 about "over-tolerant medical
boards" that "spared . . . dope peddling physicians" and asked that
the FBN be granted "the power to jail and un-license" them.[56] Anslinger also wanted the power to revoke the narcotics licenses of
addicted physicians, who he claimed were common and "responsible . . . for the prevalence of the narcotic vices."[57] The AMA fought
back fiercely. If Anslinger could deny or revoke a physician's narcotics permit, it would in effect constitute a second, federal licensing system—an intolerable government intrusion into professional
autonomy. It should be "competent, disinterested" experts in the
AMA, not bureaucrats at the FBN, who evaluated evidence of addiction and determined whether a physician could still practice.[58]

The AMA won this round: Anslinger, like Levi Nutt before him,
failed to get the power to refuse permits. But the push had rattled
the AMA, which internally acknowledged the problem of pervasive "inaction" on narcotics and sent a warning to all state medical
boards that their reluctance to enforce narcotics laws might invite
federal interference.[59] Even this relatively minor action was novel
for the AMA. Previously, when the organization received reports of
physicians convicted on narcotics charges (either from federal authorities or from newspapers), the AMA had forwarded the information to state medical boards but done little else. Between 1925
and 1944, they sent out nearly eighty such letters, the overwhelm-

ing majority of them circulating California cases reported by that state's unusually energetic medical board. The AMA did not use the occasion to suggest that boards take any particular action; the letters were informational only.[60]

Insufficient as they were, the AMA's letters probably were useful given the rudimentary state of surveillance available to authorities at the time. In 1924, for example, the Narcotics Division informed Michigan's medical board about a physician who was still practicing despite having recently served a year in federal prison for a narcotics violation. The board's secretary was grateful: "I want to thank you," he wrote back, "for calling this to our attention, as this is practically the only way we have of checking up on these convictions—by the newspapers or by some one reporting them to us."[61] Of necessity, even with a cooperative medical board, the vast majority of white market opioid transactions, ordinary or suspicious, went unobserved unless something else unusual happened to draw authorities' attention.

The Michigan board's gratitude was not universally shared, particularly when it came to enforcing the rule against providing opioids to addicted patients. The archival record is quite incomplete, and certainly nothing like a statistical portrait can be reconstructed. But the sheer volume of anecdotal reports in state, professional, and federal archives is quite compelling in its own right: many physicians continued to prescribe for people with addiction, and even when they were caught they often benefited from their social status and faced little or no punishment.

A Wisconsin case from the 1940s illustrates the dynamics well. Acting on a tip from suspicious pharmacists in the miniscule town of Siren, the FBN sent an opioid-addicted informant to make a "sting" purchase from a local physician, Dr. T, in 1943. The informant told Dr. T that he was a "carnie" with an addiction but no other medical problems. Dr. T replied that he regularly treated people with addiction and offered to sell him morphine or dilaudid, whichever he preferred. After the informant had made three purchases on three different days, narcotics agents arrested Dr. T and charged him with a federal crime.[62] A federal judge, however, threw out the case, claiming that the physician had been entrapped.[63]

There the matter appeared to end since, remarkably, the state medical board was unaware of the FBN's investigation and prosecution. But as it turns out, the board was separately pursuing a case against Dr. T for criminal abortion. That case also failed, but in the process the board discovered the FBN's case and realized that Dr. T could still be charged with state narcotics violations.[64] Armed with a full report from the FBN, which included not only the original sting purchase but also information about a handful of other addicted people Dr. T had been providing with opioids, the board indicted Dr. T in 1945.[65] The county district attorney had to be instructed on how to file the charges since, in his two decades on the job, he had never used the state narcotics law against a physician.[66] He was also somewhat reluctant. "In fairness," he wrote to the medical board, "I should state to you that I am sympathetic with Dr. T. I have known him for years and like him. I intend to recommend a short suspension of his licenses if the Judge asks me for a recommendation."[67] In the end the judge followed this suggestion, and Dr. T's license was suspended for a significant—but not devastating—sixty days.[68]

Dr. T's case was not representative. But this is partly the point: no case was representative. Harrison-era drug reforms had successfully brought an end to any systematic approach to providing opioids to people with addiction. What remained were idiosyncratic instances of physicians choosing, for any number of reasons, to provide for one or perhaps a small handful of patients. What made these idiosyncratic cases significant was their extent: they may not have been systematic, but they added up, providing a version of maintenance treatment to a substantial number of people.

Dr. T, for example, was not the only morphine-providing physician to escape discipline in Wisconsin. In addition to many other similarly lenient cases collected in the state board's records, one observer in the 1940s counted more than two dozen physicians in Madison, the state capitol, who regularly provided opioids to people with addiction.[69] Nor was the phenomenon limited to Wisconsin. What follows are just four of many archival sources, from the 1920s to the 1950s, showing that physicians continued to prescribe for people with addiction, and that they often did not lose professional support for having done so. In Cooper, Texas, a parade of physicians testified on behalf of a physician accused of prescribing for people with addiction in 1928; according to a local observer, no one believed the accused was "guiltless," but they were angry over what they perceived as entrapment and motivated to respond out of "pride in their profession."[70] (Informed of the situation, the AMA agreed that the "entrapment of a man of good repute" should be "received reluctantly, if at all, by the courts."[71]) In Ely, Minnesota, a physician who had served time in a federal prison for a narcotics violation was not only still practicing in 1933 but was receiving patients steered his way by a friendly state senator; the state medical board informed the AMA that "there was nothing [it] could do in the matter."[72] In 1944, a federal narcotics agent in the Miami region observed that "a number of physicians have prescribed [Demerol] for their so-called medical addict cases (and there are entirely too many of that class) who have heretofore been getting morphine."[73] Finally, a North Dakota physician who admitted to "selling morphine sulfate to numerous addicts for years" in 1954 received only a brief suspension of his license "because of his many years of faithful service to the Hettinger area."[74]

The difficulty of enforcing the anti-maintenance rule is particularly well illustrated by the example of California. In the half century after the Harrison Act, California was well known for being unusually eager to root out narcotics violators. The California state medical board undertook dozens of investigations and showed a precocious zealousness in reporting every one of them to both the FBN and the AMA (as noted earlier).[75] As early as 1926, the board started publishing in its newsletter the names of physicians whose license had been revoked.[76] "Ours has been one of the most active Boards in the United States in disciplining those guilty of narcotic derelictions," the secretary treasurer rightly boasted, especially as compared to "some of the Medical Examining Boards [that] are de-cidedly remiss."[77] Anslinger went out of his way to praise California even as he complained bitterly about other states.[78]

Yet even in California, where policing was relatively energetic and consistent, physicians clearly had plenty of leeway. The vast majority of the cases the state board so assiduously reported to the AMA were addicted physicians who had checked into a medical institution for treatment, or "notorious" physicians whose misbehavior was plainly visible (and, as noted earlier, often also involved infractions other than opioids).[79] Even physicians caught red-handed were only lightly disciplined. A Bakersfield physician, for example, was arrested in 1937 after prescribing for a "notorious drug addict" who happened to be a federal agent. The state medical board had been unaware of the physician, even though local police knew that he had been prescribing widely to people with addiction for years. The board revoked the physician's license, but a judge ruled that the crime had not involved "moral turpitude" and reinstated it.[80] In Sacramento, Dr. W, a "well known physician," was caught selling opioids to informers in 1934 after developing a reputation as "the source of supply for the so-called 'de luxe' element among Sacramento's narcotic drug users." After his arrest, "many of Sacramento's leading citizens rallied in his defense" and a US district court acquitted him.[81] As late as 1948, a maintenance-prescribing physician was spared after a friend of the governor intervened on his behalf.[82]

Perhaps the most astonishing, and revealing, California case occurred in 1934. That year, an FBN informant visited Dr. L's office in Los Angeles, claiming to be addicted to morphine and asking for help. Dr. L told him that if he could provide a letter from his employer stating that he was "honest and industrious," she would "register him with the squad" (the local narcotics police unit) and prescribe for him. She asked "what diseases other doctors had noted on narcotic prescriptions" and did not balk when he listed a variety ("some had stated gall stones," he said, "some had stated asthma, and still other physicians had stated other diseases"). When he returned with a letter from his supposed employer, Dr. L wrote him a prescription and warned him not to drive, which, she said, was against state law. She then handed the FBN informant her business card(!), on which she wrote, "This is to certify that Mr. [C. F.] is under my professional care and has been registered." Later, in court, Dr. L admitted she had been prescribing for over a dozen people with addiction. Ultimately, however, the judge instructed the jury that physicians could prescribe "in good faith" even to addicted patients; Dr. L was found not guilty.[83]

As late as 1964, California authorities remained concerned enough about lenient judges such as Dr. L's that the deputy attorney general considered forbidding informants from requesting drugs from a suspected physician altogether; it was too easy for a physician to claim he or she had sincerely believed the informant to be ill.[84] Ultimately, the deputy settled on a lesser, although still quite constraining, approach. According to formal state guidelines, agents attempting sting purchases should "request a specific dangerous drug by its trade or common name"; should claim to be "perfectly healthy" with "no symptoms of any kind (he should not even say that he gets sleepy at parties)"; should literally say that they "only want the medication for kicks"; should "refuse any physical examination no matter how cursory in nature"; and should tell the physician that the sought-for prescription is "in part at least for a friend."[85] Only fully commercial prescribers could be caught with such ham-handed tactics. Certainly a physician quietly maintaining one or a few people with addiction would not.

Given all the obstacles faced even in a state as enthusiastic about enforcement as California, it will not be surprising to learn that, nationally, relatively few physicians were successfully disciplined for narcotics violations. From 1930 to 1935, 1,362 physicians were reported to state boards for narcotics violations, but boards only revoked or even suspended 184 licenses.[86] The FBN had a similarly poor record. From 1931 to 1935, the Bureau convicted only 11 percent of the registrants (physicians but also pharmacists, wholesalers, etc.) reported for violations, in contrast to the nearly 70 percent of nonregistrants (i.e., "street" peddlers and consumers) reported for violations during the same time period.[87] Between 1920 and 1935, this amounted to 1,100 physicians, or an average of 75 per year.[88]

That is certainly enough to have made others watchful of their narcotics prescribing.[89] But on closer inspection, the numbers are slightly less intimidating. During these years there were, on average, slightly fewer than 150,000 physicians in the United States, meaning that in any given year only 0.05 percent of physicians (one in 2,000) were convicted. Three hundred of the convictions were of addicted doctors who supplied only themselves, reducing the yearly average of physicians convicted for illegal prescribing to 53—0.03 percent or one out of every 3,000. Even this paltry number is likely inflated because the physicians most likely to have been convicted were the most egregious transgressors or were already in trouble with authorities for other reasons (such as abortion). A relatively respectable physician prescribing or dispensing discreetly to a handful of patients would have little reason to fear. And finally, even convicted physicians did not necessarily face harsh penalties. The FBN's *Annual Reports* typically listed fines of $200 and brief license suspensions, and we have already seen how lenient many state boards were.

Consumers and physicians in a clandestine world of medical maintenance

So far we have seen evidence that physicians continued to flout the maintenance prohibition, often without incurring punishment. But this does not tell us much about what maintenance looked like during these years that it was (mostly) illegal. Information about this is not easy to find. Because it was illegal, provision of opioids to people with addiction tends not to show up in the obvious places in the archival record. Unfortunately, the best records were those produced by narcotics authorities, and these are not overly useful for reconstructing the experiences of addicted white market consumers. Some records, however, contain more information, although it must be parsed carefully and often read against the grain. This final section of the chapter explores two such unusually revealing archival sources: the records of Dr. Lawrence Kolb, mentioned earlier as the nation's leading expert on addiction, who examined and judged the "legitimacy" of dozens of people with addiction in the 1920s; and letters written to the FBN from the 1920s to the 1950s by people with addiction or their physicians requesting a (nonexistent) "narcotics permit" to legalize their treatment. Both records provide a similar portrait of white market maintenance as a practice that followed at least some of the principles of what later came to be called harm reduction. Both suggest that people with addiction who had access to maintenance were able to lead stable and productive lives—that contrary to stereotypes, they did not become dangerous criminals. And both confirm that maintenance was an exclusive phenomenon, open primarily to native-born, respectable white Americans living far from the urban contexts associated with "dope fiends."

Kolb's records from the 1920s provide some of the most detailed information about medical maintenance. Kolb began his career as a physician at Ellis Island in the 1910s, and turned his attention to addiction in 1923 from a new post at the US Public Health Service, where he produced influential studies on the relationship between drug addiction and crime.[90] The ambiguities and internal conflicts that run through Kolb's work convey the torments of therapeutic reformers during an era of criminalization. On the one hand, Kolb was arguably most influential in claiming that only abnormal people became addicted—the psychopath theory of addiction that moral crusaders pressed into service to justify punitive prohibition. On the other hand, Kolb was remarkably sympathetic to people he saw as "medical addicts." Since addiction did not produce criminality, but was rather a sign that a person suffered from preexisting psychological defects, in the rare cases where a "normal" person became addicted, he argued, the person would not deteriorate into a deranged criminal.[91]

Because of Kolb's prominence and his easy availability for Washington authorities, the Narcotics Division appears to have relied

on him regularly for expert guidance in the early years of Harrison
Act enforcement. In particular, in several dozen cases when federal
agents caught a physician providing morphine to a person with addiction, Kolb was called in to evaluate the legitimacy of the case.[92]
His records of these evaluations provide a rare glimpse of the thinking and practices behind maintenance.

The first thing that stands out in Kolb's records is the way social
bias meshed inextricably with medical judgment. To receive Kolb's
stamp of approval—and thus a legal supply of morphine—required
certain racial and class markers of respectability. The value of these
characteristics was immediately evident: to be evaluated by Kolb
usually required travel to Washington, DC, at one's own expense (including travel, hotel, and lost work time).[93] To even make it that far
a person had to earn the sympathy of the arresting narcotics agent
and the agent's superiors, even before having to succeed again with
Kolb himself. Legally such sympathy could be given only to people
with illnesses other than addiction. And indeed, most (but not all)
of the people Kolb examined had been diagnosed with a variety of
conditions. In many cases, however, the originally diagnosed condition was long gone, and in any case, Kolb seemed equally or even
more interested in assessing whether the person had lived what he
considered to be a moral life.

Gender-appropriate work was a particularly important aspect of such a life. Kolb's case notes are peppered with approving
comments about patients' employment: "has been a fairly useful
citizen—he has supported a family," he remarked of one man[94]; he
noted that another "has not missed a day of work in ten years."[95]
Kolb described a physician as "a successful man . . . regarded as a
good citizen in the community . . . making twelve thousand dollars
a year in practice."[96] Case notes on women assessed domestic labor.
One women "seems devoted to her family and has worked hard"[97];
another "has always been a moral woman and a useful citizen."[98]
Kolb was particularly impressed by a third woman who "has a serious outlook on life and is presumably morally normal as shown by
her care of her mother."[99]

In keeping with his published philosophy about addiction, Kolb usually noted that addiction itself had not inflicted further moral damage on people whose morals were good to begin with. He often remarked specifically that, as in the case of a World War I veteran, "the patient is not believed to have suffered any moral deterioration from the drug,"[100] or as in another case, that addiction had not "injured him physically, morally, or mentally."[101]

Kolb's ability to see the humanity of people with addiction, so rare among experts and authorities of his class and cultural background, still hinged on social prejudices. It was no accident that the employed and moral people he approved were overwhelmingly native-born, rural or small-town whites. According to his intake sheets (which noted nationality, race, religion, and occupation), every person he examined was what at the time would have been called an "un-hyphenated American."[102] The sole exception was a middle-age African American couple who won Kolb's approval because of their "sobriety and industry."[103]

The importance of class and race markers of respectability can be seen in cases where Kolb bent over backwards to understand and forgive behaviors that might otherwise have seemed clear evidence of characterological defects. For example, Kolb approved a World War I veteran, addicted since 1923, who was "the black sheep of the family." He may have "raised hell," Kolb concluded, but he "never did anything disgraceful."[104] Even in one of the few cases he rejected for long-term maintenance (he approved six months' worth), Kolb offered a strikingly sympathetic portrait of a man with quite a checkered past. The man had become addicted after the Harrison Act, in 1918, and had what Kolb called "shady spots in his history" including gambling and embezzlement. But, Kolb argued, "it is very likely that the useless life he has led during the past 3 years has been in part due, as he says, to the fact that he could not get drugs conveniently and had to travel around for them and that he spent so much money to secure them that little was left for his family."[105] Few people, even Kolb himself, would have been so generous in explaining the behavior of informal-market "dope fiends."

Many of the people appealing to Kolb were aware of the need to present themselves as respectable. The letters from one farmer and itinerant laborer, for example, were rambling and unfocused except for a repeated insistence on his commitment to work. Pointing to his long and reliable work record, the man described himself as a "straight, honest man, wishing to do what is right" who "attended to my business and was a good and valuable citizen," and promised that if Kolb would "send a man here" he would "see what sort man I am and what esteem I am held in this community."[106] Kolb approved him. In another case, an addicted Louisiana physician's wife claimed that "his integrity and standing are above question in this neighborhood," while the physician himself appealed to class and professional values he shared with Kolb. He asked for the "courtesy" of being allowed to write his own narcotics prescriptions for himself and closed with a gentlemanly wish: "I hope you are having as good golf weather as we are here."[107]

It is important not to draw too elevated a portrait of the people Kolb approved for maintenance. Most were far from rich. His approved case records include itinerant farmers, salesmen, tobacco buyers, sign painters, and gas station managers. Racial background, small-town pedigree, and evident effort to meet the demands of respectability appear to have been more important than social class.

Kolb's notes suggest that white markets, like informal markets, had gatekeepers allowing some people in and keeping some people out. As in informal markets, these gatekeepers were more attuned to social hierarchies of class and race than to consumer protection. Yet Kolb's notes also show that the consumers who did make it past the gatekeepers gained access to something genuinely valuable: a humane and pragmatic approach to addiction treatment dramatically different from the prevailing punitive model. Kolb did not assume that abstinence from drug use should be the goal for every person with addiction. Instead, he evaluated abstinence from a range of practical perspectives. Was abstinence possible? Would it actually improve the person's overall well-being? If abstinence was desirable, how could it be implemented so that it would cause the least suffering?

Kolb always considered whether abstinence was a realistic possibility. So, for example, one of Kolb's first cases was a professional musician who had at one point served as director of the Chicago Conservatory of Music. She had begun taking morphine while recuperating from a teenage hysterectomy after her first child, and during her entire career physicians had continued to prescribe her morphine based on "some [unspecified] lung condition." Kolb recommended enough morphine to "keep her comfortable for the rest of her life" because, he said, her case seemed unlikely to result in a successful "cure" (abstinence). To justify his decision, he explained that "she has been taking morphine for about twenty-five years" and so quitting would be hard under any circumstances, but especially for a "temperamental" musician in poor health. Without morphine, Kolb concluded, she would be "confined to bed as an invalid for the rest of her life" whereas with it, "it will be possible for her to enjoy some periods of comfort."[108]

Similar judgments run through Kolb's records. Kolb recommended against "cure" for a middle-aged stenographer from Charlotte, for example, because "it is impossible for her to get rid of the financial worries that would go along with any attempt at cure," and "worry is one of the most frequent causes for relapse of drug addicts."[109] Kolb also approved morphine for a fifty-nine-year old assistant manager of an "amusement place" in Washington, DC, who had been addicted for decades after treatment for rheumatic pains. Withdrawal would "bring on extreme suffering," Kolb wrote, and "even if a cure were accomplished the recurrence of these chronic pains would make relapse certain."[110] The physician who inquired about "golf weather" got approved too because Kolb assumed he would just relapse after the "inevitable accentuation of the nervous condition . . . that would follow withdrawal."[111]

Even in cases where abstinence was a realistic possibility, Kolb often advised against it on the grounds that it would lead to an overall reduction in quality of life or social "usefulness." A salesman from Narrows, Virginia, provides a good example. Addicted during treatment for a shrapnel wound and nerve gas exposure in World War I, the salesman later contracted gonorrhea and rheumatism, which provided a medical justification for continued morphine prescribing. Kolb was impressed by his "morality and seriousness of purpose" and by the fact that he worked hard to support himself and his mother. Kolb believed it might be possible to "get him away from it after a long period of time," but ultimately decided against withdrawal because "he will be physically depleted over a long period" and "in the end he will resort to the underworld channel," leaving him to be "socially a much less useful individual than he otherwise would be."[112]

In multiple other cases Kolb used similar logic to approve a patient for maintenance. Kolb approved of the "black sheep" mentioned earlier, for example, because "he is now working and his work will doubtless be done better if he receives a regular supply of morphine."[113] Recall that Henry D., whose story opened this chapter, was approved because "he will be a better citizen as a legitimate addict than he will be if his legal supply is cut off." Kolb approved a middle-aged Mt. Solon, Virginia, man because, he said, "It is plain that he does not intend to do without this drug for a year . . . [and] more would be lost in an attempt to force a cure upon this man than could possibly be gained."[114] In one case, Kolb recommended that a physician be encouraged to prescribe extra morphine for a man who "uses up what is prescribed for him a little quicker than is intended and runs short before the end of the week. He is then unable to work."[115]

It is particularly fascinating that Kolb was willing to apply such logic not just to matters of employment, but also to alcoholism, which he evidently judged to be worse than opioid addiction in at least some cases. He approved a Richmond, Virginia, man who had become addicted because of "sprees" (i.e., nonmedical use), for example, because the man had unsuccessfully attempted four "cures" within the past year, indicating "a constitutional psychic defect that will impel him to take something like alcohol or morphine." Given those choices, Kolb reasoned, "the history seems to indicate that morphine would be the lesser of the two evils." Given that decision, he concluded, "the interest of society as well as his own interests would be better served if he is allowed to have three grains a day so that he can attend to his business and be spared the demoralizing effect of dealing with peddlers."[116] Another man who had been "addicted through dissipation" (i.e., not medical treatment) "probably would have been a drunkard if he had not contracted the addiction when quite young." The man was now respectably married and employed, but any attempt at cure, Kolb warned, would bring "irritability, discontent and restlessness and make him a much less acceptable citizen than he now is."[117]

Even in the relatively few cases where Kolb rejected maintenance, he extended a consideration to the addicted consumer unheard of in informal markets, subordinating abstinence to other more important life goals such as employment. Thus, for example, he acknowledged that a physician "can be cured easily" but called an immediate withdrawal "inadvisable" because "this is the season in which he makes money"; instead, he should wait until the summer.[118] He was similarly flexible with a perfectly healthy and recently addicted Maryland physician, who, Kolb said, could wait half a year "in order that certain arrangements can be made which will doubtless take some worry off his mind."[119] He advised that a hardscrabble rural woman who had been taking morphine for only three months should be maintained temporarily until her physicians developed a treatment plan for her migraines.[120] The man Kolb judged to have led a "useless life" because of his difficulty securing drugs (mentioned previously) needed to be withdrawn eventually, but was allowed six months more maintenance "so as to set up his family right" first.[121] Kolb also approved three months' additional morphine for a healthy but addicted machinist to align his "cure" with a period during which his workplace would be closed.[122]

A fascinating example of the trouble Kolb's role could produce for narcotics authorities, and thus perhaps an explanation for why his type of examination was never expanded or institutionalized, came in an unusual sequence of events in the town of Bristol, located on the border of Virginia and Tennessee. In 1923, physician E. D. Rollins moved to Bristol and was asked to serve as the town health officer. Rollins agreed and soon discovered that the previous officer had been "looking after the morphine addicts, in addition to the regular duties." Rollins had already been caring for one bedridden person with addiction, but he now received a list of others that, he understood, were to be his responsibility according to town tradition. His understanding of his duties were confirmed when Lawrence Kolb visited Bristol later that year, examined his addicted patients, and, in similar language to the cases we have already seen, declared all but one to be legitimate medical cases.[123] Rollins continued to prescribe and also accepted new patients if they met what he understood to be Kolb's standards.

So things went until, six months later, federal narcotics agents visited Bristol and discovered an outsized population of people with addiction—as many as sixty. A great many of them, they found, were patients of the same physician, and at least some of them did not appear to be legitimately ill.[124]

Rollins was in trouble but unrepentant. "When an agent admits in one breath that he knows nothing about medicine, and in the next breath tells me that so-and-so does not need morphine," he complained to the Narcotics Division, "he is presuming [too] much."[125] Rollins angrily vowed to stop prescribing morphine for anyone, even to ease suffering "pitiful to the extreme."[126] This left people with addiction desperate and pleading with other local physicians. One woman wrote to the Narcotics Division: "pleas help me, I am sick, and you can see by the enclosed papers [Kolb's evaluation of her case] that I am entitled to morphine."[127]

Narcotics authorities had a decision to make. On the one hand, Rollins and two other local doctors had been supplying dozens of people with addiction, a good number of whom were later arrested for selling morphine. On the other hand, most of the patients were definitely ill (even some of those who had been arrested for selling morphine on the street), and the physicians involved were eminently respectable practitioners who also had large general practices—one had even been mayor of Bristol for three terms.

In the end, the Narcotics Division determined that it would be impossible to get a conviction and so dropped the case. The Division's postmortem on Bristol included one revealing moment, when the Nashville area narcotics chief commented bitterly that, in the future, physicians like Kolb should not be allowed to meddle in narcotics policing.[128] And yet, if physicians were to be excluded from decision making, what did "therapeutic" even mean? The question was easy to answer when the drug consumers were opium-smoking Chinese or heroin-injecting Italian immigrants; the racist presumption of their pathology allowed authorities to sidestep questions of medical merit. For people with access to physicians—legitimate, well-intended physicians—the story was more complicated.

It is not clear how much weight to place on Kolb's records. He was just one person, after all, and he was increasingly out of step with other medical authorities in his views on addiction and maintenance. Not all physicians agreed with medical authorities on any given issue, however. It is not unreasonable to assume that at least some of them shared Kolb's mixture of sympathy and prejudices.

There is one other body of evidence that supports this hypothesis: hundreds of letters from physicians, drug users, and their family members to the FBN requesting a nonexistent "narcotics permit" that would allow a physician to prescribe morphine to a person with addiction. Two-thirds of the letters were written in the 1930s, but they continued through the 1940s and the 1950s; in fact, there were more letters in the 1950s than in the 1940s.

One of the most important aspects of these letters is that they existed at all—that, despite the anti-opioid messages promulgated at every level of American society, so many people still believed that "narcotic permits" were available. It is particularly telling that so many physicians shared this belief, and so confidently. A Roanoke Rapids, North Carolina, physician, for example, brusquely demanded a permit in 1937 for a patient suffering from asthma.[129] As late as 1955, a physician from Middlebourne, West Virginia, wrote to confirm that the permits "were still being done" and to register a "medical addict."[130]

It is not clear where these physicians had heard about narcotics permits. A physician in small-town Appleton, Wisconsin, cited radio newsman Walter Winchell, and a Mansfield, Louisiana, physician cited the US district attorney in Shreveport.[131] A lawyer in Stillwater, Oklahoma, claimed in 1954 that a "competent authority" (probably a physician) assured him that narcotic permits existed.[132] Knowledge was obviously murky; as one person with addiction wrote from Lima, Ohio, in 1932, "every Dr I talk to seems to understand narcotic law different . . . please tell me way [sic] to do, and be on the laws side."[133]

Some letters from addicted consumers did complain about physicians afraid to prescribe morphine even in dire circumstances. A Cairo, Georgia, man, for example, claimed to be "dying by degrees" but was still unable to convince frightened physicians to prescribe.[134] A Jackson, Mississippi, woman found physicians so fearful that she asked Senator James Eastland to request a permit from the FBN so that she could buy enough morphine to bring her terminally ill son home for his last days.[135]

Such letters made up a tiny minority of the collection, however. Far more came from people whose long-established morphine supply had been disrupted when their physician died or moved.[136] A Tarboro, North Carolina, man, for example, wrote in 1933 that his "former physician who had verbal permission from your department to furnish me necessary amount, committed suicide several days ago," and the new physician "will gladly prescribe" but "wishes permission from your office in order to avoid any possible embarrassment from some smaller agent."[137] A Fulton, Ohio, woman explained in 1940 that her mother had been addicted for a mind-boggling fifty-six years, supplied by a physician with a "special permit." When this physician died, his replacement would prescribe only temporarily until she received a new FBN permit.[138] A man writing in 1951 was actually able to produce a letter from the

Veterans Administration "certifying that he was a disabled veteran and used Dilaudid."[139]

Even under the best of circumstances, their reliance on a particular physician placed significant limits and constraints on addicted white market consumers. It was particularly onerous for people whose jobs required travel. As one contractor wrote in 1936, "I am not able to have xray pictures made to show my troubles and to walk into a strange Dr. office the first thing you are branded as a dope addict."[140] An itinerant peddler from Lepanto, Arkansas, asked a lawyer to request a "permit to buy morphine or other opiates from drug stores any where that he might be."[141]

It is fascinating, and also revealing, that the most common type of letter was from people with a stable supply who wrote to complain about the cost of visiting a physician to get a prescription. Mostly dating from the Great Depression years, these letters did not ask for government permission—they believed they already had it—but in effect requested a government subsidy by allowing them to bypass the doctor's office and go straight to the pharmacy. A Mendota, Wisconsin, man, for example, requested a permit in 1936 because prescriptions are "a heavy draw on my income."[142] A Watertown, New York, man warned the FBN in 1935 that the high costs of seeing a physician were driving him to "become a public charge, which is any thing but desirable."[143] In 1933, a woman from Campbell, Ohio, wrote

> Sir: We were requested to write to you. Cause I am a morphine addict. Sir I have been using them for the last eleven years. Now cannot receive them from the doctors we use to because we don't have the money to pay for the prescription and morphines.[144]

One letter featured different reasoning toward a similar goal: a physician described a woman as "a pauper and quite a bit of trouble to the doctors," and pleaded for her to get a permit so as to limit her bothersome office visits.[145]

All letter writers were aware of the need to emphasize their respectability and their distance from stereotypical "dope fiends." For many, this meant emphasizing their desire to obey the law. "I am a law abiding citizen and I don't want to do anything against the law," a Brooklyn woman wrote in 1942; a Johnson City, Tennessee, man pleaded for a permit to avoid "the illegal under ground."[146] Perhaps the most intriguing letter of this type came from the sheriff of Alma, Georgia, who wrote, on office letterhead, of his need for morphine ("lord knows that if anyone needs it it is me," he claimed, because of angina), and of his desire to avoid buying from "peddlers" because that would be "a violation of the Law."[147]

Other writers played up their social respectability to differentiate themselves from "dope fiends." One man, pleading on behalf of his addicted wife, wrote that "she is a College Graduate, a fine penman, graduated book-keeper, and business woman, who for, thirty five years, taken great interest in her home. [Her] reputation is beyond dispute with the leading physicians of Zanesville, Ohio."[148] A Corpus Christi, Texas, physician described an addicted patient as "a high class gentleman in every respect and tries to support his family in a decent way."[149] Sometimes such claims were supported by name dropping. An Osceola, Florida, man, for example, claimed to know Lawrence Kolb personally.[150] A Dubuque, Iowa, writer told the FBN that "as to my character, I refer you to Senator Louis Murphy of this city [Dubuque], whom I have known personally all of his life.[151]

Finally, letter writers were also clearly aware that authorities valued employment and productivity. A Shreveport, Louisiana, woman, writing on behalf of her husband, explained that he "works all the time and has done so all his life." Because he "does not mix or associate with other addicts," she continued, "he is the victim of many dirty tricks and always has to pay the very highest prices."[152] A narcotics agent in Bethlehem, Pennsylvania, urged the FBN to approve of a married couple because "neither one is what could be styled an underworld character, both to all appearances being respectable and sincere business people"[153] A Columbus, Ohio, man identified himself as a "head Blacksmith" in asking for a permit for his wife, who, he said, "is and always has been a good Christian woman a hard worker has made a happy home I love her beyond words . . . we are nice people in good standing."[154]

Conclusion

The period from the 1920s to the 1950s is remembered as the "classic era of narcotics control" in America—a time when authorities favored prohibition and punishment over treatment. This characterization is certainly correct. Repeated moral panics over "dope fiends" during these decades led to harsh stigmatization of informal-market consumers and an apparently endless appetite for punishing them. Nearly a third of federal prisoners were serving time for narcotics convictions as early as 1928, and in 1930, the Public Health Service opened a special hybrid jail/prison/farm in Lexington, Kentucky, to house them—in part a "New Deal for drug addicts" predicated on reforming urban "toughs" by exposing them to wholesome farm work, but also a place to warehouse people that even prison wardens did not want.[155]

The anti-drug frenzy reached a peak in the 1950s, during one of the periodic surges in informal heroin markets. Increased global trade after the Depression and World War II expanded the heroin supply in major cities just as the number of young people segregated into "urban vice districts" had grown dramatically thanks to the Great Migration of African Americans from the south to industrial centers. The result was a spike in addiction in neighborhoods whose residents were slowly shifting from European ethnics to African Americans and Latinos. Authorities did not see these consumers as people in need of protection and help, but as criminals who society needed to be protected against. Congress passed two new draconian laws in the 1950s that included America's first mandatory minimum jail sentences (and, technically, even the possibility of a death sentence).[156] It was a devastating blow to communities already grappling with rapidly growing and poorly regulated informal heroin markets.

This familiar story of American drug policy is accurate but, as this chapter has shown, it is also incomplete. When federal and medical authorities opened the "classic era" by closing the narcotics clinics in 1921, they were rejecting a public health response based on systematically providing opioids to people with addiction. They did not entirely succeed in stamping out maintenance as an individual treatment, however. Rudimentary policing tools and tensions between medical and federal authorities allowed an informal and clandestine archipelago of opioid maintenance to survive despite the anti-narcotic crusade. Access to maintenance hinged on the sympathy and judgment of individual physicians, and was thus highly variable, unreliable, and profoundly unequal. With few exceptions, consumers had to be white, native born, employed, or otherwise "respectable," and live outside of major cities. Drug prohibition, like alcohol Prohibition, targeted a certain type of person (urban, immigrant), not just a psychoactive substance.

The continued availability of medical maintenance clarifies the results of the *in vivo* experiment of America's first national drug control regime. White markets and informal markets were not, in fact, subjected to the same policies. Informal markets faced full prohibition; no distinctions were drawn between addicted and nonaddicted consumers. With few consumer protections, those markets continued to generate new cases of addiction at a relatively steady pace, dependent primarily on the vagaries of global commerce (declining during the Depression and World War II, rebounding in the 1950s, etc.). People who developed addiction faced intense social disabilities and punishments on top of any harms they already suffered from their drug use.

White market consumers faced a very different situation. Consumers were shielded from unnecessary exposure to opioids but were still permitted access in times of need; at those times, their purchases were carefully regulated to minimize the possibility of addiction. New cases of addiction still cropped up, but at a significantly lower rate than in the nineteenth century. And when white market consumers developed an addiction, they had a chance of being treated through morphine maintenance—with all its limits and constraints, still a relatively safe supply. Addicted white market consumers still faced challenges and serious constraints, but they fared better than their peers in informal markets.

Authorities at the time explained the different outcomes in white and informal markets by pointing to the different moral character of consumers in each market. Socially respectable "patients," they believed, had obediently stopped using drugs because they valued their health, while urban "dope fiends" purposefully flouted the law in pursuit of immoral pleasures. But good policy, not good people, explains white market success. And bad policy, not bad people, explains why informal markets went so wrong. Robustly regulated availability, combined with medical maintenance for those who became addicted, proved a successful way to handle a drug crisis. This historical precedent has been obscured, however, by the relative invisibility of medical maintenance during an era dominated by sensationalist images of "dope fiends."

Like maintenance itself, robustly regulated availability was partly a professional responsibility; after the nineteenth-century crisis physicians grew more conservative in their use of opioids (and pharmacists more careful in their sales). Yet it also required grappling with another important and powerful force: the pharmaceutical industry. Dramatic declines in white market opioid sales meant dramatic declines in opioid profits. The industry did not take this setback lying down. How it pushed back, and how regulators contended with its efforts, is another story altogether and the subject of the next chapter.

3

Preventing blockbuster opioids

Fixing the opioid crisis required more than reforming medical practice. It also required reining in the massive commercial market for opioids that had produced such widespread addiction in the first place. And just like policing physicians, restraining commerce would not be easy. Therapeutic reformers and consumer advocates had successfully established the Food and Drug Administration (FDA), but the federal regulatory state remained relatively small and limited. Meanwhile, powered in part by revolutionary drug discoveries such as antibiotics, the once-tiny "ethical" drug industry grew by the 1950s into a behemoth known as much for its ingenious marketing as for its miracle medicines. Federal regulators and therapeutic reformers were aghast but unable to prevent a string of scandals and public health crises resulting from massive, marketing-driven overuse of potentially dangerous drugs.[1]

Opioids were a very different story. There were no new fads or crazes for hypermarketed miracle opioids, and no major scandals or public health crises. Historians have tended to take this for granted, ignoring pharmaceutical opioids in favor of informal markets and drug-war policing. To do this, however, is to ignore a very mysterious historical phenomenon. Opioids did not disappear after the 1920s; they continued to be important and widely prescribed medicines. Moreover the pharmaceutical industry did not simply give up on them. Companies continually tried to introduce and market new opioids as revolutionary, nonaddictive wonder drugs, using all the tools that had helped them to inflate the use of so many other medicines. Yet somehow, these efforts all failed. No opioids appear on the twentieth century's long list of infamous drug brand names. Per capita prescribing and sales of pharmaceutical opioids remained relatively flat for nearly seven decades starting in the 1920s. How did this happen? The boom-bust cycle for new drugs is such a consistent feature of pharmaceutical markets that its absence in opioids demands an explanation.[2]

The answer is strong federal regulation. It came from unexpected quarters: not the FDA, where we would usually look for it, but the Federal Bureau of Narcotics (FBN). The FBN is mostly remembered as prosecutor of a punitive and racialized drug war. Yet it was also appointed by Congress to govern pharmaceutical opioids. And here, unlike its destructive governance of informal markets, the agency and its bullying chief Harry J. Anslinger demonstrated genuine concern for consumers. Through close collaboration with elite pharmacological researchers, Anslinger battled furiously against marketing hype while encouraging the development of genuinely safer opioids. To do so he pioneered new powers unavailable to the FDA and governed every step of the opioid commodity chain from research, to formal and informal marketing, to postmarketing surveillance. Ironically, America's fiercest moral crusaders at the FBN came closer than anyone else in the twentieth century to realizing therapeutic reformers' vision of a rational medical market.

This was truly a remarkable achievement, especially in an era when the pharmaceutical industry regularly thwarted regulators' efforts. Yet the regulatory regime also had serious flaws. For one thing, like other good policies explored in this book, it was entirely limited to white markets and their relatively privileged consumers. Informal-market consumers received no similar care or protection. Then, too, Anslinger had won his extraordinary power over the drug industry by stirring public fear of the racial minorities and foreign agents he blamed for the "dope" menace. The kind of authority won in this manner differs from that achieved through other means. Driven by moral ferocity as much as by its scientific collaborators, the FBN overshot the mark, preventing hype but also limiting access to those in genuine need—those in dire pain and those with addiction. And ironically, its battle-hardened skepticism of opioid manufacturers also prevented it from recognizing or eventually accepting the transformative potential of methadone, the era's most potentially revolutionary opioid.

Despite these serious problems, for decades the FBN oversaw a regulatory regime that prevented new opioids from inflating a harmful boom-bust cycle while encouraging real and meaningful innovation. This is not a zero-sum game; the achievements do not erase the harms. But neither do the harms negate the achievements. In a century of failed policies, even partial successes deserve careful attention.

A founding drug policy disaster: Bayer's Heroin, 1898–1924

In 1898, just as therapeutic reformers' campaign to persuade physicians to prescribe less morphine had finally begun to bear fruit, the German pharmaceutical giant Bayer introduced a new opioid, diacetylmorphine. It was twice as powerful as morphine, and to suggest its heroic therapeutic qualities the company named it Heroin.

Compared to its later notoriety, Heroin's launch was a surprisingly minor affair. It attracted relatively little medical notice and virtually no public attention. Despite Bayer's optimistic trade name, few hailed it as a wonder drug, and it was never widely prescribed by physicians. It was, in short, a forgettable entry in the annals of opioid white markets. But Heroin was anything but minor or forgettable in the history of drugs and addiction in America. If informal markets are included, in fact, it should be considered one of the most spectacular "blockbuster" drugs in the modern era. As early as the 1920s, Heroin had become practically synonymous with "dope" and addiction, and in 1924 Congress took the astonishing step of passing a special law just to outlaw it, making it America's second entirely criminalized drug (after smoking opium). Nonetheless it remained an informal market staple, one of the most enduringly successful drug products of the twentieth century. Altogether, Heroin's story was a dramatic, founding moment in American drug and pharmaceutical policy, revealing the weakness of the early regulatory state and the challenges reformers faced in trying to build a stronger one.

When it launched Heroin in 1898, Bayer faced no federal restraints on marketing or sales. Rather, the company's behavior was governed by its carefully nurtured status as an "ethical" pharmaceutical house, that is, one that catered to the medical profession and promised to abide by the code of medical ethics. So Bayer did not advertise Heroin to the public and was fairly restrained in its medical advertising, promoting Heroin primarily in low-dose products for the treatment of respiratory ailments such as asthma, bronchitis, pneumonia, and tuberculosis.[3] Some observers did initially believe that Heroin was nonaddictive, but Bayer does not appear to have capitalized on this in its American marketing.[4] Nor is there evidence that the company pushed back when medical authorities confirmed that it could indeed be addictive. Addictiveness did not yet have any legal ramifications, and it did not affect Heroin's status as a relatively minor white market opioid.

Legal ramifications were coming via the Food and Drug Act (1906) and the Harrison Act (1914), but at least initially these had little impact on an "ethical" company like Bayer. The FDA was established to combat fraud and adulteration, not to restrict the sale of honest goods. Its sole power was to require that drug labels be truthful in listing contents and, after 1912, in making therapeutic claims. It also required that labels include ten particularly dangerous ingredients, including opioids and cocaine. These requirements did help the FDA build a federal regulatory infrastructure. The agency formalized the US Pharmacopeia and the National Formulary, for example, establishing standard names, ingredients, and purity so that a newly appointed Bureau of Chemistry could test products and, if necessary, levy fraud charges. But none of these requirements caused a problem for Bayer, which as an "ethical" company already labeled its products honestly; indeed, by forcing competitors to do so as well, the FDA probably helped Bayer.[5]

Drug marketing remained almost entirely unregulated. The FDA's powers ended with the label; advertisements did not fall under its purview. The Federal Trade Commission (FTC), established in 1914, did require truth in advertising—but only advertising directed at the public. Ads that appeared in medical journals or were mailed directly to physicians had been carved out of the FTC's jurisdiction in deference to physicians' claims that they, not bureaucrats, were most qualified to evaluate medical claims.[6] Moreover, the FTC's mandate was to prevent unfair competition between businesses, not to protect consumers.[7] Unless a false advertisement could be shown to harm a competitor, the FTC could not pursue it.

The primary restraints on drug advertising lay not with the government but with the American Medical Association. The AMA had long sanctioned anyone who advertised a medicine (or medical services) directly to the public, and the campaign against frauds and quackery intensified in 1905 with the establishment of a Council on Pharmacy and Chemistry. The Council centralized and formalized therapeutic reformers' efforts to rationalize pharmaceutical markets, but their powers remained relatively limited: they were given a regular column in *JAMA* to influence practitioners; they developed an official list of approved products, *New and Nonofficial Remedies*, to guide physician prescribing; and they could exclude offending advertisements from AMA-sponsored journals. Like most voluntary regulations, the AMA's efforts worked best in the most respectable quarters of the market; those willing to risk ill repute (or those who already had it) faced little constraint.[8]

Of course, Bayer represented just such respectable quarters, and again, the company had no problem complying with the AMA's requests. Bayer, however, was not the only player in Heroin markets. Heroin was an ingredient, one that Bayer also sold to other companies to incorporate in their own products. There was no legal obligation to sell only to "ethical" firms, or even a voluntary promise to do so. Indeed, there was no responsibility to engage in what would later be called protecting the supply chain—to ensure that Heroin was sold only to legitimate medical businesses. Moreover, Bayer had no patent, just a trademark on the brand name Heroin. Other companies could also manufacture and sell it. In other words, Heroin could travel multiple pathways on its way to market. There is no telling which one resulted in "Craig's Heroin Compound," a drug advertised in 1906 in the local paper by Craig's Drug Store in Stanford, Kentucky, with a tagline advising use "When baby first begins to sneeze" (see fig. 3.1).[9] Neither the FDA nor the AMA had tools to prevent such advertising or sales.

Heroin's relatively free availability came at a critical moment of change in informal markets. The most common opioid in those markets, smoking opium, was slowly being prohibited, first by states and municipalities, and then in 1909 by the federal government. Smoking opium was bulky and smelly, making it relatively easy to police imports; prohibition decreased its availability dramatically. Heroin was well positioned to take its place. Physicians and pharmacists were growing more cautious about prescribing and selling morphine, but Heroin's addictiveness took years to establish definitively. While reduced risk of addiction had not been a major selling point in white markets, it did weaken professional restraints on sales and allow freer circulation into informal markets via products like "Craig's Heroin Compound." By the early 1910s, many informal-market consumers were already familiar with and partial to Bayer's Heroin, especially in cities like New York and Philadelphia near where the drug was manufactured.[10]

It was to stop such popular sales that the Harrison Act was passed in 1914. The act limited sales to legitimate medical purposes and required companies to keep records on all narcotics they made, transported, or sold. Informal market sales of Heroin and other opioids shifted from being disreputable to being outright illegal. Prohibition did not reduce demand, however, and informal markets excel at providing illegal goods and services. Here Heroin's natural advantages (it was odorless and potent, easy to conceal) helped it flourish friends of the work in that community are urged to be present as important matters are to be attended to.

Judge Wm. Myers, John D. Burton and T. L. Carpenter were elected members of the board of education without opposition. The opponents of the school on former occasions made a bitter fight without satisfactory results and for the present at least, have withdrawn from the field. The work of repairing and adding to the old school building will begin as soon as the material can be gotten on the grounds.

Frye & Greening were awarded the contract for erecting the People's Bank building at $3,650, same to be ready for occupancy July 1st. Work has commenced and the building will be a two-story brick 50x26 feet with all windows and doors arched with Bedford stone. The plan for the second story is a model of the modern flat and when completed will indeed be a credit to the town.

Rev. George O. Barnes, the famous evangelist, has been preaching in Alcorn's Opera House since last Wednesday to large audiences. On Sunday morning by invitation he filled the pulpit at the Christian church. He will probably not continue the meeting here longer than Wednesday evening. No one can hold an audience more spellbound than this distinguished octogenarian, who has traversed the globe in his work.

No Quarter.

The evils which always follow after indigestion, biliousness or constipation will give no quarter. Better fight them to a finish with Dr. Caldwell's (laxative) Syrup Pepsin. It is a weapon against these dangerous diseases, which will give you quick relief and permanent cure. Sold by Penny's Drug Store, Stanford; C. W Adams, Hustonville, at 50c and $1 Money back if it fails.

A pension examiner reports that an old Richmond darky refused to identify a former member of his company who had lost his discharge papers, on the ground that "I done got in an application myself sah fo' loss er mem'ry."

Deaths from Appendicitis

decrease in the same ratio that the use of Dr. King's New Life Pills increases They save you from danger and bring quick and painless release from constipation and the ills growing out of it. Strength and vigor always follow their use. Guaranteed by Penny's Drug Store, Stanford, and Lyne Bros., Crab Orchard. 25c. Try them.

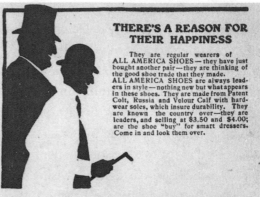

Figure 3.1. No legal restrictions prevented popular marketing of Heroin, a potent opioid, in the early twentieth century. *Interior Journal* (Stanford, KY), May 8, 1906, 1. Chronicling America: Historic American Newspapers.

and eventually replace all competitors.[11] Its increasingly unsavory reputation as "dope," however, did nothing to help its already lagging medical sales. By 1924, Heroin had become so fully associated with nonmedical use that even medical authorities were willing to wash their hands of it. Few protested when Congress took the radical step of forbidding importation of opium to manufacture it.[12] Heroin's days as a medicine were over; it had become a wholly illicit substance, heroin, which served for a century as an archetype—*the* archetype—of addictive "dope."

Heroin's fate was a worst-case scenario of drug policy failure. White markets lost access to a useful, if minor, product. Meanwhile, prohibition did not eliminate informal market sales but simply ensured that those sales went relatively unregulated—or at least, not regulated with the goal of protecting consumers. Stuck buying an unreliable product sold by criminals, and punished rather than treated if caught by authorities, heroin consumers faced risks far beyond those associated with almost any other product. This unhappy outcome cast a long shadow over American drug policy for decades to come, highlighting in sharp relief the failure of early regulation. As reformers and the drug industry battled over the structure of opioid markets, neither forgot Heroin's saga, although both drew very different lessons from it.

Building capacity to regulate opioids: Dilaudid and Pantopon, 1914–1945

The first major test of opioid governance after Heroin's demise came in 1932 when the Bilhuber-Knoll Corporation introduced Dilaudid, a semisynthetic derivative of morphine first produced by Merck in Germany in 1924. Unlike Bayer, Bilhuber-Knoll did not leave assessments of their drug's addictiveness to chance. Instead they launched it with a marketing campaign built around the claims of prominent Mayo Clinic physician Walter C. Alvarez, who described Dilaudid as an "ideal analgesic" that "no one has yet become habituated to."[13]

The company reprinted Alvarez's sunny take—originally published in the *Proceedings of the Staff Meetings of the Mayo Clinic*—in its first marketing pamphlet.[14] They also managed to land Alvarez's report in Edwin Scripps Science Service newswire, which led to widespread coverage in popular magazines like *Collier's* and the *Literary Digest*, and even found its way into obscure local papers like the *Montgomery Advertiser*. Most of this coverage quoted Alvarez and described Dilaudid as "five times stronger than morphine" but "not habit-forming" because it lacked morphine's "pleasurable sensations."[15] Bilhuber-Knoll also ramped up direct marketing to physicians, mailing one circular to 5,000 physicians citing German animal studies as evidence that the drug did not produce tolerance, "dangerous euphoria," or a "habit" (see fig. 3.2).[16] Smaller postcard and medical journal advertisements urged physicians to send away for free sample tubes.[17]

While they had not been applied to an opioid before, this full-court marketing press was not unusual for a new "ethical" pharmaceutical. Recall that "ethical" pharmaceutical companies were the respectable, perhaps even reformist, wing of the drug industry—companies that catered to physicians and promised to abide by the AMA's code of medical ethics. Despite their supposed commitment to noncommercial virtues, however, ethical companies were not immune to the lure of profit, and they were skilled in obeying the letter while flouting the spirit of FDA and AMA rules. Many companies turned drug research into a form of marketing by collaborating with practicing physicians to produce favorable medical studies. Public relations campaigns skirted restrictions by attracting (or even co-producing) friendly science journalism rather than formal advertisements. And ethical companies avoided AMA censure through the technicality of advertising themselves and their commitment to medical ethics rather than touting a particular product.[18]

Dilaudid's marketing was an archetypal example of this corporate art form. As an ethical drug, it was properly labeled and thus safe from the FDA. To assuage the AMA, Bilhuber-Knoll advertised

Figure 3.2. Bilhuber-Knoll Corporation's advertising promised "better analgesic action" but less "euphoria" and thus less addiction (n.d.; probably 1933). Sterling Drug, Inc. Records, Archives Center, National Museum of American History, Smithsonian Institution.

only to physicians and only used therapeutic claims based on the carefully curated conclusions of eminent medical authorities. The orchestrated media blitz, meanwhile, technically qualified as journalism and thus fell outside the purview of not just the FDA and the AMA but also the FTC.

For most drugs, these tactics would have effectively tied regulators' hands. Thanks to the Harrison Act, however, opioids were not most drugs. In addition to the FDA, opioids were also governed by another regulatory agency, originally the Narcotics Division of the Treasury Department's Prohibition Bureau. While therapeutic reformers and consumer advocates battled furiously to win relatively meagre powers for the FDA and the FTC, supporters of the Narcotics Division found it much easier to navigate the congressional gauntlet. This was in part because they represented a broader political coalition, drawing from not just therapeutic reformers and consumer advocates but also moral crusaders—powerful enough to win the prohibition of alcohol—and State Department diplomats still pursuing a global anti-narcotics agreement. They also did not need to invent new federal powers: narcotic plants were not grown domestically, and so commerce could be controlled through the government's traditional power over imports and exports.[19]

Thus even as reformers despaired at addressing FDA weaknesses in the business-friendly 1920s, narcotics campaigners won what turned out to be an extraordinarily important new law: the Jones-Miller Act of 1922. This act outlawed the importation of all narcotics except for crude opium and coca leaves in quantities "necessary to provide for medical and legitimate purposes only," and established a Federal Narcotics Control Board to determine those quantities.[20] The Board immediately restricted imports to twelve major cities, imposed strict recordkeeping of all transactions, and required special approval before any narcotics could be removed from customs warehouses after entry into the United States.[21] A few months later entry ports were reduced to four, and rules clearly stated that no narcotics could enter the United States without written approval of the Board.[22]

Narcotics controls grew even stronger with the 1929 Porter Act. In part to rescue it from the demise of Prohibition, the Narcotics Division was pulled out of the Prohibition Bureau and recreated as a stand-alone Federal Bureau of Narcotics in the Treasury Department. The act also abolished the Narcotic Control Board and handed its powers over to the FBN's new chief, Harry J. Anslinger.[23] This gave Anslinger quite a free hand in judging import quotas. Aside from the overall question of estimated medical need, he could decide whether a shipment of opioids was likely to be misused and was permitted to base decisions on his assessment of the "character and standing of the applicant." He could also distribute imports between companies in the way he believed would best ensure the "efficient administration" of the law.[24] Combined with the Harrison and Jones-Miller Acts, the Porter Act gave the FBN powers well beyond anything enjoyed by the FDA.

A final, fortuitous development gave the FBN something it sorely needed: a source of definitive scientific information about opioids. Unlike the FDA, the FBN had no scientists on staff to expose weak or fraudulent drug company claims. But the agency gained a direct line to this kind of expertise in 1928, when the National Research Council gathered the nation's leading addiction researchers to explore the physiology and pharmacology of addiction in hopes of discovering a nonaddicting painkiller. The Committee on Drug Addiction, as the group was called, built and tested new morphine-like molecules in a small network of university laboratories, systemizing knowledge of narcotics and developing research protocols to evaluate them. In 1929, the Committee also gained access to the US Public Health Service's new quasi-prison, quasi-hospital at Lexington, Kentucky, where, in keeping with that era's dubious research ethics, inmates being treated for addiction were available as research subjects.[25] They were the perfect group to evaluate new opioid products—and by invitation, Anslinger sat on their governing board.

Thus when Bilhuber-Knoll launched Dilaudid, it faced not a relatively toothless FDA but a fearsome new FBN allied with America's most distinguished opioid experts. Anslinger set the tone immediately, demanding that Bilhuber-Knoll provide all its Dilau-did medical research and marketing materials to the Committee for evaluation.[26] Working at the federal prison/hospital in Lexington, Kentucky, Committee researchers followed their usual proto-col, switching actively addicted inmates/patients from morphine to Dilaudid. If the new drug prevented the test subjects from ex-periencing withdrawal symptoms, it could be substituted for other opioids and was thus addictive. After these tests, the Committee re-turned a quick and unequivocal appraisal: Dilaudid was a "compar-atively simple type of change in the morphine molecule" similar to others they had tested and found addictive. It would be wise, they advised, to treat the drug as cautiously as morphine itself and "delay the too rapid spread of clinical use."[27]

Armed with this evaluation, and angered by a letter sent to the FBN from a physician recounting how a colleague had accidentally become addicted after believing Bilhuber-Knoll advertising, An-slinger summoned Dr. Knoll to discuss Dilaudid in person. Knoll assured Anslinger that his company was not "pushing" sales but just "seeking to interest physicians in the substance which they believed to possess certain advantages."[28] In any case, the doctor pointed out, they were only circulating direct quotes from prominent authorities such as Dr. Alvarez. Who was a federal bureaucrat to second-guess medical expertise?

This might have been the end of the story had Knoll been dealing with the FDA, but Anslinger did not budge. He insisted that the ad-vertising was "misleading" and had to be changed, and that all revi-sions must be submitted to the FBN for approval.[29] That approval, in turn, depended on two factors: compliance with therapeutic reform-ers' restrictive guidelines for opioid use as outlined in the *JAMA* se-ries on "indispensable" uses of narcotics, and forthright acknowl-edgment of addiction risk.

The Committee also raised red flags about Bilhuber-Knoll's list of potential uses for Dilaudid, which, they said, went beyond *JAMA*'s recommendations. In a move that would have been the envy of ther-apeutic reformers elsewhere, Anslinger took the Committee's critique and turned it into an order: future advertising must eliminate claims that Dilaudid would be useful in childbirth, tabes dorsalis, renal cholic, and gynecological lesions; must change "intractable" to "inoperable" cancer; and must add "terminal stage of" before tuberculosis.[30] Bilhuber-Knoll did not fold immediately. Since the concern was that the advertisements might increase overall prescribing of opioids, the company reasoned, what about simply claiming that "the use of Dilaudid is suggested in place of morphine for the control of pain in tabes, etc."?[31] Anslinger, however, judged this to be even worse because it implied expanded uses for morphine as well as Dilaudid. After asking the Committee for advice, Anslinger made a final determination: Bilhuber-Knoll should delete the list of uses altogether and simply make the blanket claim that "Dilaudid may be used as a substitute for morphine for the relief of severe pain."[32]

Anslinger was particularly zealous in denying Bilhuber-Knoll's claim that Dilaudid was less addictive than morphine—a central part of their marketing that the company stubbornly clung to despite the Committee's judgment. Hoping to play the time-honored game of accepting the letter while violating the spirit of the Committee's findings, the company proposed that its advertisements should urge "caution" because "the relation of Dilaudid to morphine in regard to the habit forming property has not been determined definitely."[33] Anslinger acknowledged that this as "an unobjectionable statement of fact," but he still rejected it because "a casual reading" might give the impression that "the habit-forming quality of Dilaudid is as yet undetermined." This was remarkable: the FBN rejected an advertising claim not because it was false but because readers might misunderstand it. In the diplomatically threatening language that he was quickly becoming adept at, Anslinger continued:

> Believing, as I do, that you have suggested this in contemplation of assisting the enforcement authorities and not for any value it may have in inducing a trial of dilaudid by the medical profession, I feel that you will have no special objection to the omission of the sentence. Without wishing to make what

> may be considered an offensive comparison, I have been given
> to understand that certain unwisely chosen representations
> were made with respect to the effects of heroin [when it] was
> introduced, even to the point, if I am correctly informed, that
> this derivative was less habit-forming than morphine.[34]

This was no small threat, given Heroin's fate. Protesting that the language had been intended "solely as a warning," Bilhuber-Knoll quickly capitulated, agreeing that "of course there is no point in . . . including it."[35]

The FBN's close policing of Dilaudid's launch established the basic principles that would govern the federal approach to opioids for more than half a century: companies could compete for existing market share, but they could not try to expand total medical opioid use. Voluntary professional reforms had put the genie back in the bottle after the nineteenth-century crisis, and barring some truly revolutionary advance, no company would be allowed to take out the stopper again. Claims of reduced addiction risk and suggestions of new uses for new opioids—the two most obvious strategies for expanding sales—came under particularly strict scrutiny.

This scrutiny did not end with a drug's launch; it was a daily slog to oversee the never-ending creativity of pharmaceutical marketing. In the case of Dilaudid, for example, the FBN continued to monitor advertisements for years, demanding line-by-line and even word-by-word revisions when errant claims crept in, as they seemed to do with some regularity.[36] The Bureau also performed a sort of ad hoc form of postmarketing surveillance—another regulatory innovation—by keeping close tabs on sales and instructing district chiefs to look for and compile cases of addiction to Dilaudid along with several other "unusual drugs of addiction."[37] This would help catch any opioid booms before they caused too much trouble, while also collecting potentially damning information about a company to use as leverage during negotiations.

The development of postmarketing surveillance highlights another aspect of the FBN as a regulatory agency: the way it matched industry creativity by continually finding new ways to wield its powers. This creativity was enabled, in part, by the strengthening of the regulatory state in the New Deal era of the 1930s—the FDA, too, won important (but still comparatively weak) new powers in these years, as we will see in chapter 4. But the FBN could also rely on its successful popular campaign to demonize narcotics and narcotics users, which gave it both a public bullhorn and an opportunity to make credible threats against recalcitrant drug companies.

The FBN's growing regulatory creativity was on full display in the story of another early twentieth-century opioid, Pantopon. Pantopon, an injectable form of opium that contained all of opium's alkaloids in naturally occurring proportions, had been introduced by Hoffman-La Roche Chemical Works in Switzerland in 1908 and appeared in the United States several years later. By the 1920s, Roche was advertising extensively, mass-mailing offers of free samples to American physicians and circulating brochures depicting Pantopon as a historic achievement that married the science of alkaloids with the "full therapeutic value of the mother drug, opium" (see fig. 3.3).[38] The Narcotics Division did little about the drug in the 1920s, despite complaints from Roche's competitors about the "propaganda."[39] The marketing was "not unlawful and represents a practice indulged in by drug manufacturers generally," explained Division chief Levi C. Nutt.[40] The AMA did not agree: the Council on Pharmacy and Chemistry dropped Pantopon from the approved *New and Nonofficial Remedies* list in 1931, making it ineligible for advertising in *JAMA* and other journals.[41] But this only freed Roche to make even more extravagant claims in other marketing materials such as mass-mailed letters to American physicians.[42]

By 1931, however, the FBN was up and running, and Roche unexpectedly found itself sparring with a much more powerful force. As he had done with Dilaudid, Anslinger referred the offending mailers to Committee experts for evaluation and tasked FBN agents with collecting cases of Pantopon addiction.[43] Perhaps because he believed that Roche had already demonstrated bad faith, however, Anslinger did not stop there. Instead he found new ways to

Better than Morphine

Pantopon 'Roche' is definitely superior to morphine because it provides the corrective and harmonious action of all the opium alkaloids. It has a valuable antispasmodic effect which morphine lacks. With Pantopon there is not so much excitation, or "let-down," or nausea, or constipation. Won't you, next time, write for Pantopon 'Roche' instead of morphine?

Packages: *Ampuls, 1.1 cc (1 cc. contains ⅓ gr), cartons of 6 and 12 . Hypodermic Tablets, ⅓ gr., tubes of 20, and bottles of 1000 for hospitals . . Oral Tablets, ⅛ gr., vials of 20 . . . Powder, vials of 1, ½, ¼, ⅛ oz.*

HOFFMANN - LA ROCHE, Inc., Nutley, N. J.

Figure 3.3. Hoffmann-La Roche advertised Pantopon as a more natural ("harmonious") alternative to morphine (n.d.; probably 1934–35). "Pantopon," FBN Papers, National Archives.

coerce the company. For example, just a few months later he used technicalities to deny Roche's repeated request to use Pantopon in "exempt" products, that is, medicines such as cough syrup with so little narcotic content that they were exempted from Harrison Act requirements.[44]

The ban on "exempt" Pantopon products was just the first of many clever new tactics that gave the FBN far more leverage over drug marketing than the FDA. Take, for example, the FBN's success in quashing or at least massively reducing "sampling," the traditional pharmaceutical industry practice of offering of free samples of a drug to physicians. Roche's offer of free Pantopon samples included instructions on how to fill out narcotics forms. This, Anslinger decided, suggested a goal of drumming up new business rather than persuading current morphine prescribers to switch.[45] There is "grave doubt," he wrote the company, that free samples represented a "definite medical need"; rather, they were "an artificial demand" created by the manufacturer.[46] This was important language because Anslinger determined the size of each company's allotment of imported opium each year based on medical need. He was, essentially, threatening the company's access to raw materials—his strongest statutory power.

When Roche defended what was, after all, a nearly universal practice, Anslinger turned to another lever of power. Free samples of Pantopon, he suggested, might be considered illegal drug trafficking under the Harrison Act. This is because they might tempt a physician to order narcotics "not because he is in immediate need for narcotics or even, perhaps, that he has intention to make any immediate use thereof, but because the tablets are free."[47] This would not be a sale for legitimate medical need—the only kind of sale permitted under the Harrison Act. Roche got the message and quickly promised to "cooperate . . . in every way possible."[48] The anti-sampling policy intensified even further in 1949, when the FBN issued a ruling that "detail men" (sales reps) and their pharmaceutical company employers would be held "jointly responsible" for any abuses stemming from free samples they provided.[49] While there is no evidence that this policy was ever put into effect, even the threat of arrest and imprisonment as a "dope peddler" was a notable escalation of regulatory pressure.

Perhaps the most innovative FBN use of this pressure was to insist that opioid advertising be—for lack of a better word—boring. In the early 1950s, the FBN issued a ruling specifying that such advertising could be used only to inform physicians in a restrained manner about new drugs.[50] In at least one case, the Bureau interpreted the policy to disallow the use of colorful images: when a 1951 Pantopon advertisement with "a colored poppy and other illustrations" came to Anslinger's attention, he demanded the company retract it.[51] Roche protested, but Anslinger explained that Pantopon was "well-known and established" and must thus follow "the same advertising restrictions as are applied to opium and morphine." He was blunt about the consequences: "if this advertising is repeated we will be compelled to take it into consideration when establishing opium quotas for future manufacturing of the drug."[52] An unhappy Roche agreed to cancel the ad.[53]

The "miracle drug" test: Demerol, 1940–1947

Both Dilaudid and Pantopon were older drugs already included under the Harrison Act. A truer test of the opioid regulatory system came with a new drug discovered by German researchers in 1939: Demerol (meperidine). Demerol was the first entirely synthetic opioid, and Winthrop Chemical Company, a subsidiary of Sterling Pharmaceuticals, used it to mount a frontal challenge to the FBN's restrictive regime. Claiming they were selling a scientific miracle that had conquered old problems of addictiveness, the company launched Demerol with the full range of industry marketing strategies and the intention to sell it outside the FBN's opioid controls. This posed a real challenge. Demerol was a genuinely new drug, not derived from opium, so the FBN could not immediately dismiss claims that it was nonaddictive. But the Bureau could not blindly accept these claims either; they required real investigation. How to insist on such investigation was unclear. The Harrison Act covered only derivatives of opium, so the FBN would be without its most powerful regulatory tools. Meanwhile, Winthrop was moving full speed ahead to launch what it hoped would be a bestselling product.

This was a key, decisive moment in the history of commercial narcotics: how would the system handle the introduction of a truly innovative product? The history of pharmaceuticals is full of such moments, and most have followed a depressingly predictable path. Based on these precedents, we would expect Winthrop to ride a highly hyped story of scientific breakthrough to achieve medical enthusiasm and record sales; to obscure risks and problems as long as possible even as public health harms grew; then at long last, usually after competitor drugs had entered the market, to finally accept new regulatory restraints. For Demerol, however, as for opioids more generally, the story played out very differently. The new drug was incorporated into medical markets without igniting a sales craze. Overall per capita sales of pharmaceutical opioids remained flat.

This accomplishment owed nothing to any voluntary restraint on Winthrop's part. Rather, the FBN and experts at the Committee persistently and vigorously debunked the hype while creatively pioneering new regulatory powers that furthered the spirit, rather than the letter, of the opioid regulatory system: enable innovation, but only on regulators' terms, and never in such a way as to significantly expand overall medical use of opioids.

The story began in 1942, when Winthrop first applied for licenses to manufacture meperidine under the trade name Demerol.[54] To spearhead the campaign, Winthrop brought in Theodore Klumpp, a physician and savvy regulatory insider who had just finished a five-year stint as the chief of the FDA's drug division.[55] Under Klumpp's able leadership, the company secured the necessary licenses and launched Demerol in early 1944.[56]

The FBN was not idle during these years. Anslinger had first heard about meperidine in 1940 and, perhaps wary after his expe-

riences with Pantopon and Dilaudid, had immediately asked the
Committee to test the drug's addictiveness. Early tests showed that
addicted inmates/patients switched to Demerol did not experience
withdrawal—enough to warrant caution.[57] The Committee advised
that "some means of protecting the public should be provided."[58]
Armed with their findings, Anslinger warned Winthrop well before
it was ready to launch that the FBN would take "drastic actions" if
the company allowed "any careless distribution" of Demerol.[59]

Anslinger had far less leverage than he was accustomed to, however, both because Demerol was excluded from the Harrison Act
and because the early medical literature was actually quite incon-
clusive. Experiments at Lexington had proved that people with
preexisting addictions could also become addicted to Demerol,
but prevailing medical wisdom held that addiction resulted from
underlying psychological flaws; it was not necessarily clear what
would happen when "normal" people used the drug. Even if you accepted that Demerol was addictive, the experiments had not shown
how addictive it was. It had been relatively difficult to establish a
new Demerol addiction in previously addicted inmates/patients
at Lexington, and addiction had not yet been observed in opioid-
naïve subjects. Demerol was definitely addictive, in other words,
but its addictiveness appeared to depend on the circumstances of
use and the psychological makeup of the user.[60] As one Committee
member warned Anslinger, the drug "may be mildly habit-forming,
but the extent of this cannot be known until it gets to be generally
used."[61] This was good news for Winthrop, which happily quoted the
FBN's own research in response to Anslinger's bluster about "drastic
actions."[62]

Winthrop also produced its own favorable medical literature by
cultivating relationships with cooperative physicians, who published
seemingly independent reports of the drug's beneficial qualities for
the company to reprint and circulate.[63] One such connection was Dr.
Robert Hoffman of Indiana, who obligingly produced several highly
favorable reports in 1943.[64] In *Anesthesia and Analgesia*, for example,
he described physicians as waiting with "hopeful expectancy" for

the government to "release" Demerol, which he described as ideal for chronic pain because "our own studies never encountered either habituation, or dependence." In a startling move, Hoffman even provided a personal testimonial: "the writer self-administered demerol for one year constantly, both by mouth and by injection [for a spinal injury] . . . but never did he experience euphoria, or allied symptoms. Three times it was stopped abruptly with no need for gradual discontinuance."[65] In an earlier article in the Indiana state medical journal, Hoffman called Demerol "relatively harmless" because "it seldom creates *desire* leading to addiction."[66]

Hoffman even became a sort of lobbyist for Demerol once it came on the market in 1944. He wrote the FBN directly, describing himself as "among the pioneer investigators of the drug in this country" and advising the Bureau not to label it a "narcotic" because the "stigma" might convince "literally millions of sufferers [to] refrain, even from judicious use of this most amazing discovery." He did acknowledge that two of his patients developed "a vaso-motor dependency . . . requiring injections of it in the morning," but, he argued, they were not addicted; they rather "resemble[d] individuals, who depend upon coffee or Coca Cola to 'get going' in the morning."[67] He described himself as having "no connections of any sort with the Winthrop Company," just a physician concerned that "the salvation of the millions of chronic pain sufferers" might be "socially stigmatized."[68] Hoffman later recanted his views after watching a patient and his own brother-in-law develop addictions to Demerol. Even so, he told the FBN that he was not prepared to go public because he did "not wish to do anything that might be construed as being unfriendly to the Winthrop Chemical Company."[69]

In addition to building relationships with physicians like Hoffman, Winthrop pursued another standard industry tactic: an informal popular marketing campaign based on principles of public relations.[70] Thus, for example, the company placed two stories in the widely circulated Hearst newspapers Sunday magazine, *American Weekly*, timed to run just as Demerol was launched. One article, written by Pulitzer Prize–winning science journalist Gobind Behari Lai, was ostensibly about the dangers of prescription morphine, but it discussed Demerol as a possible alternative. "No addiction has been found" to Demerol, Lai wrote; the drug was only "habit-forming," which, he reassured, meant only that some users developed "a yearning which can be conquered."[71] The other article, attributed to the magazine's science editor, opened with a large-font headline: "The Use of Morphine to Relieve Suffering Patients Has Started Thousands of Them on the Road to Drug Addiction, But Now a New and Effective Pain-Killer Will Exact No Such Pitiful Price." Demerol is "available for everyone," the article assured, and as a result, "the morphine menace . . . is on the run" (see fig. 3.4).[72] Less sensational but still positive articles also appeared in the newswire Science Service and popular weeklies *Time* and *Newsweek* (whose article was titled "Drug without Addicts").[73]

In all, then, Winthrop exploited Demerol's pharmacological

Figure 3.4. Winthrop Chemical Company successfully generated media hype around its synthetic opioid Demerol even before it was brought to market. *Sunday Times-Herald*, October 24, 1943. "Demerol," FBN Papers, National Archives.

novelty and the lack of Harrison Act controls with all the marketing machinery in its arsenal. For its part, the FBN did what it could with its uncharacteristically limited authority to constrain the marketing hype. Anslinger continued to seek help from a network of his own experts to refute Winthrop's claims. He asked for assistance from *JAMA*'s editor, for example, telling him that "I fear that [the company's] attitude with respect to its addiction properties is not what it should be."[74] He urged the Committee to publish more definitive statements of the drug's addictiveness—"similar to that caused by morphine"—and circulated them as a pamphlet just before Demerol became commercially available.[75] He also developed what would become a lasting relationship with Argentinian physician and researcher Pablo O. Wolff, sending Wolff's damning research report on Demerol to anyone and everyone, and relying on him to rebut Winthrop claims that Demerol was sold freely in Mexico and South America "in competition with aspirin."[76]

Meanwhile, Anslinger explored ways to enhance his leverage over Winthrop. First he tried, and failed, to have Demerol declared a chemical derivative of morphine or cocaine because it shared certain chemical similarities with them.[77] He also tried to prevent the FDA from approving the drug, but discovered—as Winthrop's Klumpp surely already knew—that the FDA's powers were far weaker than the Bureau's. The FDA could not reject a drug if it had been proven safe to use and was honestly labeled, nor could it even require a warning label about addiction. (Winthrop was willing to allow such a label, apparently; it cared only that Demerol not be formally classed as a "narcotic.")[78]

Even as he pursued these efforts, Anslinger was already hard at work at what would be a much more successful tactic: getting Congress to pass a new law that would add Demerol to the Harrison Act. The effort had actually begun earlier, in mid-1942, with a campaign to have Demerol added to international treaties administered by the League of Nations (it succeeded in April 1944).[79] Meanwhile the FBN drafted a US control bill in October 1943 and urged Congress to pass it as soon as possible.[80] The FBN-provided talking points included Committee experts' findings, other nations' strict legal controls, seven case histories of Demerol addiction, letters of support from the medical and pharmacy professions, and pointed critiques of Winthrop as "none too ethical" and as a former subsidiary of the German industrial giant I. G. Farbenindustrie.[81]

Outraged, Winthrop sent Klumpp to the FBN to complain in person in February 1944. Klumpp insisted Demerol was nonaddictive, accused Anslinger's expert Dr. Wolff of being a German agent, and generally "appeared to resent any Federal interference." Anslinger replied with a challenge: since Demerol was not habit-forming, "I asked him whether he would submit himself to having the drug administered over a reasonable period to test out his theory." When Klumpp did not take him up on this, Anslinger proposed a second possibility: he would permit "free distribution of the drug in New Orleans" and observe the results. If Winthrop was not "afraid of the drug," he reasoned, "why hesitate on a simple proposition of this kind"?[82] Accepting that Anslinger was unmovable, Klumpp shifted tactics, agreeing to help pass federal Demerol legislation so as to avoid having to face variable state laws.[83]

With Winthrop's opposition muted, Congress added Demerol to the Harrison Act with relatively little debate in June 1944. Even before passage, the FBN had already organized a full-throttle campaign to get the amendment added to state Uniform Narcotics Acts.[84] District supervisors were tasked with visiting at least two states per month during their legislative sessions and were advised on strategy such as finding a legislator with a medical or pharmacy background to "actively sponsor" the amendment.[85] By 1947, their efforts had been successful in twenty states.[86]

The passage of these laws gave the FBN the tools it needed to grapple with Winthrop, and, as usual, Anslinger was not shy about using them. He immediately circulated an announcement to all Harrison registrants (commercial and medical) that also ran in *JAMA*.[87] He sent FBN agents on a triumphant tour of Winthrop's factories to acquaint the company with the Harrison Act's many requirements.[88] Meanwhile he gave Demerol what had already become the standard treatment: he demanded that Winthrop submit all marketing materials for approval and instructed FBN agents to collect instances of Demerol addiction for his files.[89] Telling the company that the FBN disapproved of "widespread advertising" that "forced" opioid sales, he discouraged use of bright colors and imagery or taking out full-page ads in medical journals.[90] He even went so far as to contact the FTC to ask whether it would force a retraction of "misleading advertising" (it would not).[91]

The FBN was particularly zealous in preventing Winthrop from making unwarranted claims about Demerol's addictiveness. Winthrop's strategy on this front was clever. Drawing on the latest research—including some commissioned by the FBN itself—the company warned that Demerol could be addictive, but only for people who were or previously had been addicted to some other opioid (see fig. 3.5). For example, one pamphlet characterized the addiction risk in this way: "in the absence of pain, physical dependence has been produced experimentally in former or active morphine addicts when daily amounts in excess of therapeutic dosages were administered for prolonged periods of time (upwards of 2 months)."[92] Shorter advertisements simply claimed that Demerol was less addictive than morphine because "the majority of patients do not acquire tolerance" and because fewer than one in ten patients being treated for pain experienced euphoria.[93] With the Committee's help, Anslinger went through such language with a fine-toothed comb, catching "partial quotations," "significant omissions," and quotes "printed out of context" that, he charged, "minimize the real addiction liability of Demerol."[94]

Negotiations with Winthrop could get quite technical, but it is worth examining one of them in detail to show both the company's shrewd tactics and Anslinger's equally shrewd rebuttals. In this case, Winthrop downplayed addiction risk by claiming that "physical dependence resulting from the bona fide use of Demerol hydrochloride has not yet been encountered in normal persons." No doubt assisted by Committee experts, Anslinger protested that the advertisement had subtly misquoted the cited research. In the original

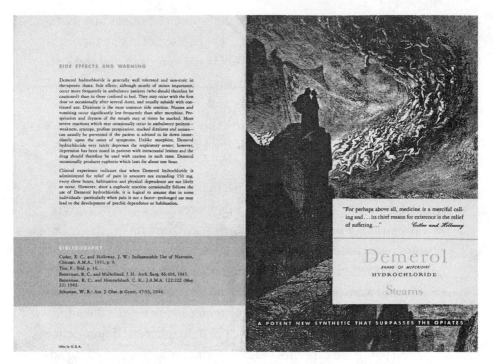

Figure 3.5. Stearns's Demerol advertising reminded physicians that "medicine is a merciful calling" whose "chief reason for existence is the relief of suffering," and reassured that "habituation and physical dependence are not likely to occur" except after "prolonged use" by "some individuals" when "pain is not a factor" (n.d.; probably late 1940s or 1950s). Sterling Drug, Inc. Records, Archives Center, National Museum of American History, Smithsonian Institution.

article, researchers had said that "[w]hile physical dependence on Demerol has not yet been encountered in 'normal' persons, it has been produced in former addicts." The researchers had used scare quotes around the word "normal," Anslinger explained, to signify "some special or restricted meaning of the term." Specifically, they meant "persons whose normality consisted in not having been theretofore addicted." Since the study in question had been in an institutionalized population of people who had formerly been addicted, no "normal" persons would have been tested.[95]

In addition to its unparalleled scrutiny of formal advertising to physicians, the FBN also broke new regulatory ground by battling against the informal public relations campaigns that had become so commonplace in the pharmaceutical industry. Masquerading as

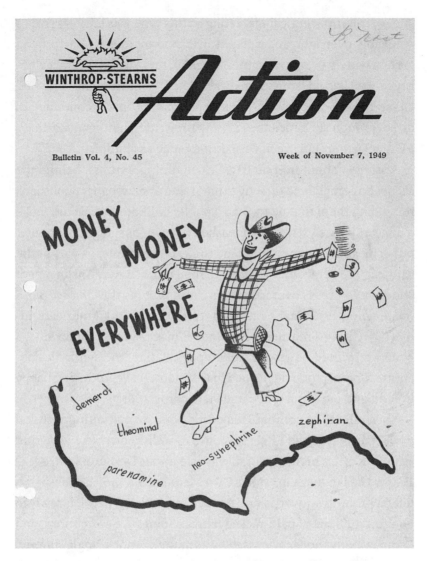

Figure 3.6. In the company newsletter for sales representatives, Winthrop-Stearns celebrated "money money everywhere." Note that Demerol is one of the rainmakers (as is Theominal, which contained the barbiturate sedative Luminal). *Winthrop-Stearns Action* 4, no. 45 (1949). Sterling Drug, Inc. Records, Archives Center, National Museum of American History, Smithsonian Institution.

"news," pharmaceutical marketing of this type was entirely free of regulatory oversight, and it played an important role in transforming certain widely used drugs into "blockbusters" with cultural celebrity as well as widespread medical sales.[96] Winthrop had launched Demerol with exactly such popular puff pieces, and it continued to do so through such means as issuing prewritten newspaper articles touting Demerol in specific conditions such as childbirth.[97]

Anslinger countered such tactics on multiple fronts. Behind the scenes he complained directly to magazine or newspaper publishers, reminding them that he too had a public bullhorn and would make a dangerous foe.[98] He also unleashed his own onslaught of popular publicity about Demerol. In May 1944, for example, as part of the campaign to get Demerol added to the Harrison Act, Anslinger got widespread press coverage for his claim that (as the *Chicago Sun*'s headline put it) "Nazi's Ersatz Morphine Sold [to] American Addicts."[99] Citing Treasury Department "disclosures," meanwhile, a widely reprinted newswire story reported that "the synthetic substitute for morphine developed in Germany . . . is producing happy dreams and euphoria for United States drug addicts."[100]

Such efforts to combat Demerol's popular marketing were on perfect display in the FBN's response to well-known science writer Paul de Kruif's highly favorable article about Demerol in *Reader's Digest*. The language in "God's Own Medicine—1946" closely paralleled Winthrop's advertising. "A new chemical, Demerol, is ready to comfort millions of pain-racked human beings," it announced, and "among many thousands eased by its magic . . . not a single sufferer, who has not previously taken opiates, has been recorded as becoming addicted to it." De Kruif admitted that in some cases the drug's "relaxing action" could produce a "desire to continue its use," but, he assured, "*this does not mean addiction*, for if the Demerol is withdrawn there are no bad results" (emphasis in original).[101]

Anslinger was livid. "This is dangerous propaganda to push sales of this drug," he wrote; "I shall arrange to have the article answered."[102] This was no idle threat. Anslinger began with a press release and a signed rebuttal that he successfully published in *JAMA* and other medical and pharmacy journals, as well as a host of popular venues like Science Service newswire, *Time* magazine, and even smaller niche publications such as the leftist *Daily Worker*.[103] When de Kruif wrote a letter to *JAMA* angrily defending himself, Anslinger turned it into a new opportunity. He published a second rebuttal in the same issue, which was accompanied by a brief supportive "Comment" by *JAMA*'s editors and by a substantive article refuting de Kruif point by point written by one of the Committee's experts. The article concluded with fifteen case histories of Demerol addiction drawn from the FBN's files.[104] Then Anslinger got yet another anti-Demerol editorial published in *JAMA*, and with the help of the FBN's district supervisors, got that editorial—and others based on it by locally prominent physicians—published in local and regional medical journals across the country.[105] Finally, and most unusually, Anslinger also fought fire with fire. Mirroring the pharmaceutical industry's own practices, he collaborated with journalists to produce popular articles on the drug, most significantly Roland Berg's "The Not So Wonderful Wonder Drugs" in *Everybody's Digest*, which castigated "sensational typewriter scientists" who "endanger a gullible public" by promoting new drugs.[106]

Behind the scenes, Anslinger was just as active. He wrote an angry letter to *Reader's Digest*, but the periodical did not back down. It published a two-part article praising de Kruif as a "Fighter for the Right to Live," which dismissed Anslinger as "short on facts" but "long on insinuation." Anslinger then ordered the FBN to stop cooperating with the magazine even in small matters such as confirming facts about drugs or drug policy.[107]

Amid the onslaught, Winthrop distanced itself from de Kruif's article, protesting that it had provided the journalist with information only on request. Anslinger extracted a promise to consult with him personally if Winthrop was ever approached to provide information for any other magazine article.[108]

Klumpp was clearly unhappy about Anslinger's bare-knuckled

tactics, and a few months later he organized a campaign at the American Pharmaceutical Association to raise questions about the FBN's behavior.[109] Anslinger privately raged at what he claimed was a "transparent effort to take Demerol out of the Federal narcotics laws" and publicly took to the media to denounce both Demerol and the Association's campaign.[110] Dozens of newspapers ran Anslinger's article under headlines like "U.S. Battles Killing Grip of New Narcotic," lionizing the FBN's "bitter struggle" against what it described as a German-controlled drug so pernicious it had dethroned even the dreaded heroin.[111] Anslinger even reached out to the FTC again, advising it that articles like de Kruif's were an especially "subtle and powerful form of advertising" because they masqueraded as unbiased science journalism. Therefore, he continued, the author and publisher of such articles should be held liable for false advertising.[112]

Anslinger's crusade against Winthrop's public relations campaign is either shocking or routine, depending on how it is viewed. In the context of white market regulation, it was unprecedented. FDA authority was limited to formal labeling and did not cover advertising to physicians until 1962, and therapeutic reformers complained without noticeable effect about public relations campaigns to market drugs to the general public. No one had a popular media megaphone as powerful as Anslinger's and the FBN's.

What was groundbreaking in pharmaceutical regulation, however, was standard procedure in the policing of informal markets. In those markets, where the FBN could impose no effective commercial bottlenecks and had little practical capacity to govern traffic, maintaining public terror of "dope" was a central strategy. To accomplish this, Anslinger built and perfected a public relations operation rivaling any pharmaceutical company's. He circulated sensationalized and sexually titillating scare stories and savagely attacked any voices who dared disagree.

Here was the paradox of the FBN in a nutshell: the agency wielded unmatched regulatory power to protect white market con-

sumers, but only because of its unmatched police power to demonize and harm informal-market consumers.

Institutionalizing opioid control: Metopon, 1946–1951

Even as the FBN was battling Demerol, the next would-be miracle
opioid was already teed up for launch. Like other opioid hopefuls,
Metopon was touted as less addictive than morphine—significant
in this case because its painkilling power was stronger.[113] But there
was something odd about Metopon's marketing when it was introduced in 1947. For one thing, there was so little of it. There were no
advertisements and no popular media splash. What did exist was
strangely restrained, advising use of the drug solely for end-stage
cancer patients. This odd campaign reflected Metopon's unusual
origins: it had been discovered and patented not by a pharmaceutical company but by the Committee, with full support from Harry J.
Anslinger.

The brief and medically unremarkable life of the FBN's own opioid represented a high-water mark of centralized white market regulation and, in many ways, of therapeutic reform as a whole. This
may at first be hard to believe. Anslinger is remembered, among
other things, for regularly ignoring (or inventing) science and facts
to support his prohibitionist war against "dope fiends." It would be
hard to imagine an approach more directly opposed to therapeutic
reformers' program of remaking American medicine along scientific lines. Yet the anti-science portrait of Anslinger is drawn almost
entirely from his policing of informal markets; in white markets,
where his agenda and therapeutic reformers' overlapped, he actively supported cutting-edge scientific research and built federal
policy around its findings. Although Metopon itself was unsuccess-
ful, its story shows how fully the FBN and the Committee were able
to implement a program of scientific rationalization of opioid research, development, and marketing—an unparalleled level of regulatory control.

The centerpiece of this system was the FBN's collaboration with the Committee on Drug Addiction. The Committee's survival after World War II was no sure thing; many other centralized planning efforts were quickly disbanded. Early casualties included such wartime successes as the National Resources Planning Board, the War Production Board, the Office of Price Administration, and, closer to home, centralized control over antibiotics.[114] But the war's end coincided with Anslinger's struggle with Bilhuber-Knoll over Demerol, which left him deeply concerned about future commercial opioids and acutely aware of the value of the Committee's expertise in reining them in.[115] With Anslinger's support, the Committee survived the postwar winnowing and was reconstituted with a slightly new name (the Committee on Drug Addiction and Narcotics) as one of the National Research Council's fifteen medical advisory committees.[116]

With its existence secure, the Committee moved to insert itself in the process of commercial opioid development. The first step was to request that companies share full information about new opioids and submit samples for addiction testing. While this merely formalized what Anslinger had already been doing, it was still an assertive move given the traditional resistance of both industry and organized medicine to what they saw as government interference. The Committee had a compelling sales pitch, however. To industry, it offered to take over the practical challenges (and costs) of testing new drugs for addictiveness—a step Anslinger and the FDA already required of them. As a central clearinghouse for information on the new drug pipeline the Committee could help companies avoid duplicating efforts on substances already tested and abandoned by competitors. The AMA went along in the spirit of therapeutic reform because the involvement of the nation's leading addiction pharmacologists would ensure that research was done by "competent and trustworthy authorities" and thus be protected from the biases and conflicts of interest inherent to commercial research.[117]

Having successfully inserted itself into the drug approval process, the Committee went to work developing procedures to rationalize opioid development. One key move was to define how addictiveness was to be measured: by seeing whether a drug eased the withdrawal symptoms of a person addicted to opioids. The Committee, of course, could undertake such tests easily thanks to its exclusive access to a captive population of inmates/patients at the US Narcotics Farm in Lexington, Kentucky. Its near-monopoly on addictiveness testing gave it leverage to impose another, even more intrusive requirement. For fear of creating a bottleneck, the Committee would test a substance only if a company could prove that it was at least as good as standard opioids like morphine in terms of effectiveness, toxicity, side effects, and duration of action. In other words, the Committee defined what would count as "innovation" in the commercial development of opioids.[118]

With the essential elements of its role established just a few years after World War II, the Committee, with Anslinger's full support, spent the next decade—a decade of retrenchment in other areas of the regulatory state—strengthening and formalizing its de facto role as a centralized planner of opioid research and development. In 1957, for example, the Committee added a new prescreening step, requiring that opioids be tested for addictiveness in monkeys before being sent to human subjects at Lexington.[119] The next year it issued a policy defining the level of addictiveness that would trigger Harrison Act controls (equivalent to codeine or greater).[120] The year after that it declared that full Harrison controls should be applied to any substance convertible to an addictive drug, whether or not the original substance was itself addictive.[121] By that time, the Committee had codified these and other requirements into an official protocol for testing new opioids and making recommendations to the FDA and FBN.[122] This outcome was, in many ways, therapeutic reformers' ultimate dream: the nation's leading medical experts devising policy guidelines and implementing them directly, without even requiring a buildup of the hated regulatory state.

It was in the context of such heady successes that the Committee dared an even more ambitious dream: developing its own opioid that would conquer the market not because of advertising gimmickry but because of genuine superiority. Before reconstituting itself as the testing arm for new opioids, the Committee's main research agenda had been to discover a nonaddictive painkiller. Toward this goal, its own researchers had regularly synthesized new opioids and tested their addictiveness.[123] While they failed to find a nonaddictive opioid, they did find some that were—or at least seemed to be—less addictive. One of these, discovered during the war, was Metopon.[124]

After large-scale wartime tests by the US Army and Navy showed that Metopon was more effective against pain than morphine, Anslinger and the Committee decided to patent the drug and shepherd it to market themselves.[125] They would have to contract with commercial firms to manufacture the drug, of course, but otherwise their plan was to follow principles of science and therapeutic reform rather than to hunt for profit. Despite industry skepticism, for example, they insisted that Metopon would at least initially be restricted to people suffering from end-stage cancer—appropriate, they felt, given its potency. They also decided not to advertise. Instead, they proposed, the National Research Council would issue a statement and place announcements in *JAMA* and state medical journals.[126]

Ironically, the Committee at least considered deploying its own version of a public relations campaign in addition to these sober scientific announcements. Someone, at any rate, wrote a magazine puff piece on Metopon that rivaled any that had ever enraged Anslinger for other drugs. The Committee participated by providing extensive interviews with the (unnamed) author; the draft was also sprinkled with questions for the Committee to answer, for example, a request for a list of "pains which are now difficult to control." The article began with a teary look at a young boy "writhing in agony with a shattered leg" whose pain was not relieved by "shot after shot of morphine." Once given Metopon, however, it was "as if some kind fairy had touched the boy with a magic wand—his pain was gone and he was sound asleep." It went on in the same vein, interviewing and offering romantic portraits of key Committee members as trail-blazing scientific heroes. But its highest praise was reserved for Metopon itself, which it described as "the greatest painkiller known to man," a miracle drug that could "banish the sufferings of millions" even while "wip[ing] out the dread, horrible curse of drug addiction."[127]

It is easy to imagine why the Committee never used this embarrassing piece of puffery, especially in light of the pains it took to control the drug's clinical use. It decided to license just two pharmaceutical houses to sell the finished product, for example, after the FBN's legal counsel pointed out this arrangement would maximize the Committee's power to ensure that the drug was sold only for terminal cancer cases. Wary of the "great many 'quack' doctors in the cancer game," the Committee also established a careful vetting procedure for purchase requests. First requests would largely be honored, but to "weed out scoundrels" second requests would be scrutinized by the pharmaceutical houses and the FBN before receiving a final evaluation by the Committee. This process would allow the Committee to keep close tabs on Metopon, transforming a product launch into what it hoped might be a very large clinical trial. Combined with Anslinger's control over opioid imports and sales, it raised the possibility of a quasi-state monopoly over medicinal opioids.[128]

The hopes invested in Metopon did not pan out. After launch in May 1947, the drug sold reasonably well but made no serious dent in the overall market.[129] Having seen no warnings of abuse after six months, the Committee expanded the indications from end-stage cancer to other types of pain, but this had little impact on sales.[130] Sales began to slump in 1950, and the next year, concerned that restrictive licensing agreements were holding it back, the Committee relinquished the patent to the public.[131] It also worried that physicians had never heard of Metopon; Anslinger even groused that manufacturers, seeing little profit potential, had been lackluster in their marketing—hardly his usual attitude.

In the end, Metopon had been a bridge too far. Whatever the drug's medical merits, it had stood little chance of displacing well-advertised industry standards even in tightly constrained opioid markets. That the Committee and Anslinger had even made the try, however, revealed the scope of their ambitions, and suggests how thoroughly and successfully they had refashioned the commercial development of new opioids.

Biting the hand that feeds you: Oxycodone, 1949–1963

Despite all precautions, something went awry in California in the late 1950s. After the Committee supported a loosening of restrictions on Percodan—a mixture of aspirin and the semisynthetic opioid oxycodone sold by Endo Pharmaceuticals—sales began to surge unexpectedly, rising fivefold between 1955 and 1960.[132] These sales did not reflect a sudden spike in cancer patients. Instead they represented a rise in casual prescribing, encouraged by the weakened controls and by Endo's advertising, which, instead of the usual dire warning, merely stated that Percodan "may be habit forming."[133] The results were alarming. "People are eating Percodan as though it were popcorn," *California Medicine* warned in 1963, noting with worry that the problem seemed particularly acute among "persons normally not associated with the illicit drug traffic" such as pharmacists, housewives, and ministers.[134] California Attorney General Stanley Mosk predicted the emergence of "an entirely new class of drug addicts—the honest and unsuspecting citizen."[135]

California's Percodan boom sheds light on an important aspect of white market opioid regulation: the Committee's struggle to uphold rational, evidence-based policy in the face of constant pressure from an industry that provided most of its funding and with whom they were required to work closely and collegially. It would be hard to conceive of a situation more conducive to "regulatory capture," that is, the subversion of a regulatory agency so that it serves the interest of industry rather than the public. Yet the Committee was not captured. Percodan was an isolated and nearly unique slipup, and it did not last long. Despite fierce resistance from Endo, federal regulators forced changes to the drug's marketing and reestablished full controls on sales. Especially in light of what was to come a half century later—when oxycodone again made headlines as the main ingredient of Purdue Pharma's blockbuster opioid OxyContin—the Percodan episode is a valuable example of how regulators encouraged innovation while also avoiding capture.

It is important to emphasize just how fully the Committee's existence and authority depended on its ability to partner with the industry it regulated. This partnership was both financial and procedural. The Committee began soliciting pharmaceutical company donations in the late 1940s, promising in return to shoulder the expense of drug testing and to offer expert advice on research and the drug approval process.[136] Well aware of the Committee's growing power and eager for a less combative relationship, the industry was happy to agree, and quite soon individual company donations were underwriting the Committee's entire budget.[137]

While the record includes no evidence of a quid pro quo, at the same time as it began to solicit donations the Committee opened its meetings to industry; no fewer than seventeen pharmaceutical companies were listed on the roster for the fifth meeting in 1949.[138] Similar crowds attended future meetings as well, and meeting minutes make it clear they were not passive observers: they asked questions, lodged complaints, and developed close relationships with Committee members. By 1957 the cozy relationship had reached the point that Anslinger proposed formally appointing a pharmaceutical company representative to the Committee. Ironically, the idea was quashed by the company's competitors. Ultimately, the Committee concluded, members must be drawn from universities or from government so as to "keep peace among the manufacturers who are our source of support."[139]

If appointing a drug company representative was unworkable, the Committee found other ways to build relationships with its most important clients. For example, while its meetings were usually held on neutral territory (e.g., a hospital or research site), on several occasions they were hosted and presumably paid for by pharmaceutical companies. This usually happened when the Committee was investigating a drug from the hosting company. Instead of recognizing the potential conflict of interest the Committee embraced it, promising implicitly and sometimes explicitly to devote additional attention at the meeting to the company's drug. This happened with Winthrop and Demerol in 1954, and again with Smith Kline French and its drug phenazocine in 1960.[140]

Such institutional connections were held together, in part, by Nathan Eddy, America's foremost addiction pharmacologist and a central figure at the Committee for decades. His business letters reveal a personal friendliness with pharmaceutical company officers who hosted him on foreign travels, took him and his wife out for dinner and for entertainment at venues like the storied Cosmos Club in Washington, DC, and sent him gifts.[141] He clearly valued these friendships, as he later reflected in a nostalgic letter to Sterling-Winthrop's director of clinical pharmacology: "It is personally most gratifying to have such pleasant relations over the years with such nice people," he wrote, "mutually satisfying, I think, professionally, but extending so pleasantly into personal relationships."[142] He might have added that they were financially satisfying as well since Eddy regularly worked as a paid consultant for the companies he praised so warmly.[143]

Eddy's solicitousness of industry was such that it occasionally drew criticism, as when he distributed what critics called a "ballot" to pharmaceutical companies at a Committee meeting, inviting them to vote yes or no on specific requests for research funding.[144] Eddy defended what he described as a "questionnaire," arguing that the Committee needed to know "the feeling of the representatives of industry" if "the money is to continue to be forthcoming."[145] Eddy's logic appeared to win the day: a higher-up at the National Research Council praised "the fine way in which you have fostered the good will of the industry" and concluded that his only error had been attracting attention. "If there is any lesson in all this," he advised, "perhaps it is that it may be better to confer separately with our sponsors on sensitive issues than to canvass their opinion in formal session."[146]

Overall, these episodes present a damning portrait of what was almost a caricature of regulatory capture. This would have been a common occurrence in the 1950s, a decade marked by the resurgence of corporate power and influence after the lean years of the Great Depression. Therapeutic reformers focused on antibiotics, for example, despaired at the ascension of industry-friendly figures to key posts at the FDA and the US Public Health Service, where they acted more as cheerleaders for the latest would-be miracle drugs than as guardians of the public health.[147] Again, though, opioids were an exception to the rule. Even as the Committee grew ever closer to the industry it regulated, it remained remarkably resistant to their entreaties. Every year it disappointed and occasionally even enraged its friendly funders with a stream of unsparing, profit-killing assessments of new drugs.

The Committee's stance was apparent from the very first meeting after it began to accept industry funding. Endo Pharmaceuticals sent a representative to advocate for its two new opioids, one containing hydrocodone and the other oxycodone, but met with no luck. The Committee insisted that hydrocone produced "intense" euphoria and addiction and brushed off Endo's claim that no one would become addicted to the drug because it was intended for use in relatively low doses to treat coughs. Unlike the FDA, the Committee was not concerned solely with how a drug *should* be used but with how it *could* be used. No amount of instructions or warnings, it explained, would prevent a person with addiction from injecting the drug or "tak[ing] all he can get."[148]

The Committee was even harsher in its response to Endo's oxycodone product. Endo proposed to organize its marketing materials around oxycodone's chemical similarity to codeine (see fig. 3.7). The Committee rejected this approach because oxycodone was in fact more similar to morphine than codeine in its strength and addictiveness. Even warning that the drug "may be more habit-forming than codeine" was not enough because, as Nathan Eddy pointed out, once physicians saw the word "codeine" they would "pay no attention to the warning about addiction." Instead Endo should state

controls pain faster · controls
pain longer · controls pain
better than codeine plus APC

FOR PAIN

PERCODAN

Figure 3.7. Endo Pharmaceuticals compared Percodan, its brand of the powerful opioid oxycodone, to codeine, a weak opioid with relatively little addiction risk (n.d.; probably 1955). "Eukodal," FBN Papers, National Archives.

clearly and very visibly that the drug might be as habit forming as morphine. When Eddy demanded further revision of Endo's claims to superiority over existing opioids, the company jokingly (but plaintively) asked "whether it would be necessary to state that it is not as good as morphine and just as habit forming."[149]

These first shots across the bow set the tone: no matter how friendly its members, the Committee would not roll over for industry. Companies were excluded from an executive session at each meeting, and company comments were permitted only after the Committee had made its findings and communicated them to the FDA and FBN.[150] Companies angry about Committee decisions regularly tried to use their personal connections to get them changed, but they were always rejected in no uncertain terms.[151] Even hosting a meeting bought no special treatment for a company. When Sterling-Winthrop asked for special focus on its drug Demerol at the meeting it hosted in 1954, for example, the Committee agreed to do so—but then proceeded to spend the extra time emphasizing the drug's dangers and discussing an extensive report on Demerol addiction from the prison/hospital at Lexington. In a clear warning to

Sterling-Winthrop, the report concluded that physicians might not have been adequately informed about the drug's addiction risks.[152]

The Committee's stout resistance to industry influence did not mean a knee-jerk opposition to all new opioids. Quite the contrary; one of the Committee's stated goals was to encourage opioid innovation. Committee experts and industry, however, had very different ideas of what constituted an innovation. As we have seen, drug companies hyped new opioids as nonaddictive, relying on the obvious fact that a new drug, by definition, could not have produced many cases of addiction. The Committee was unbending in rejecting this as an innovation. It was perfectly willing, however, to support other more-favored opioid developments, even if doing so required pushing for real changes in US opioid regulations. For example, the Committee's research showed that opioids differed in terms of their potency, duration of action, and addictiveness, and it recognized the value of fleshing out the range of opioids available. But US policy discouraged this sort of innovation. A drug was either addictive, in which case it fell under full Harrison controls, or less addictive than codeine, in which case it avoided all narcotics regulations and was governed only by the FDA. This binary setup, the Committee argued, reduced the incentive for companies to develop sorely needed drugs in the middle of the range—those with intermediate potency and relatively low addictiveness.[153]

It was the Committee's desire to encourage midrange opioids that gave Endo enough room to inflate Percodan sales in the late 1950s. Oxycodone seemed as though it might be one of those intermediate drugs: closer to morphine than codeine, to be sure, but still possibly not as addictive as morphine. So in 1955 the FBN agreed to place oxycodone on a list of drugs that, if combined in limited proportions with nonopioid ingredients, could be ordered by phone rather than through written federal narcotics prescription pads.[154] Endo, dubiously interpreting this as evidence that authorities had deemed Percodan to have "relatively little or no addiction liability," changed its marketing materials—without asking permission from the FDA or the FBN—so that the warning read simply, "may be habit forming."[155] The mild warning and easier prescribing quickly led to a fivefold spike in oxycodone sales by 1960. Many of these sales appeared to be in California, which had loosened Percodan controls by eliminating a state requirement for written triplicate prescriptions.[156]

Faced with what appeared to be a break in the carefully maintained opioid quarantine, California authorities reacted swiftly, asking the legislature to reimpose full controls over Percodan in 1961. Endo fought back, however. As far as the company was concerned, the FBN had given Percodan the stamp of approval, and there was no evidence to contradict it. Indeed, Endo pointed out, the Bureau's own statistics identified only twenty-seven cases of Percodan addiction in the entire United States. Armed with such arguments Endo persuaded California's state medical, dental, and pharmaceutical associations, and 12,000 letter-writing physicians, to oppose Percodan controls.[157] Strikingly, the company's position was also supported by none other than Nathan Eddy. Eddy, recently retired but still working part time for the Committee, happened to be in California; he had been invited by the American Pharmaceutical Manufacturers Association to discuss the regulation of codeine. When Endo requested that he testify against the strict Percodan bill, Eddy agreed. While he believed oxycodone should face full narcotics controls, he explained, he also thought that written triplicate forms were too much of an inconvenience for physicians.

To California's attorney general, Stanley Mosk, Eddy's arguments were an absurd fig leaf to mask bought-and-paid service to Endo. Eddy had never complained about triplicate forms before, Mosk pointed out, and whatever his explanation, he was in practice opposing the only option available under California law to strengthen Percodan controls. It was precisely through such hairsplitting objections that industry lobbyists killed disfavored bills.[158] Two years later Mosk persuaded state medical associations and Eddy to switch sides, but the bill still failed in the face of fierce resistance from Endo. Federal authorities finally interceded in 1963. FDA Commissioner George Larrick opened an investigation into possible mislabeling, and Anslinger's successor at the FBN, Henry Giordano, removed Percodan from the list of drugs exempted from written prescribing.[159] The next year, national oxycodone sales immediately declined by nearly 40 percent.[160]

Overall, the Percodan saga showed the opioid control system working imperfectly but well. It had made sense to lessen regulatory constraints on the drug when evidence suggested it would be safe to do so. When Endo, given an inch, took a mile, authorities noticed a problem and, after waiting to make sure the problem was real and not just a blip, took action to reimpose tighter controls. The controls were strict but were calibrated to the situation rather than being a panicky resort to total prohibition. Percodan remained legally available; prescribers and consumers were merely provided with fuller information about risks. Sales dropped because of increased bureaucratic red tape but did not fall below their levels before the episode. All-out lobbying had bought Endo two extra years, but it had not been enough to entrench expanded markets for oxycodone. The system held.

Overshooting the mark: Methadone, 1946–1963

The Committee's dedication to science and rational drug development had its limits. It did envision a more supple and variegated system of narcotics control, but not because it opposed the black-and-white approach of totally prohibiting "nonmedical" opioid use or had any sympathy for people with addiction. It urged regulatory nuance only because it believed this solution would encourage development and use of less addictive opioids. The Committee's informed skepticism helped it guard the door against an unending parade of would-be miracle opioids. But that same skepticism, combined with its contemptuous views of people with addiction, led to one of its biggest failures: not recognizing that a new opioid, methadone, could be highly addictive yet also represent a genuine, badly needed innovation that deserved encouragement.

Methadone was first synthesized in Germany in the late 1930s.

Although it was not immediately recognized, the new drug had a unique quality: it was highly addictive, but a single dose could prevent opioid withdrawal for much longer than morphine or heroin—more than 24 hours. Methadone could thus be an important tool for treating addiction because, if supplied regularly, it could free people from the constant need to find and purchase drugs. That this potential did not register on Anslinger, who strongly opposed maintenance, is not surprising. But the Committee, too, failed to imagine the possibility—in part because it, too, opposed maintenance, but also because of its mission to prevent profit-hungry companies from inventing new uses for opioids. As a result, methadone was not widely adopted until the 1960s, when a new generation of path-breaking addiction experts recognized the drug's potential.

Methadone first came to Anslinger's attention in 1946, when Eli Lilly and other American companies received information about the drug through US government programs designed to transfer German technologies to American industry.[161] Fresh from the battle over Demerol, Anslinger quickly asked the Committee for an evaluation. A few months later, Eddy informed him that methadone produced tolerance in animals and could substitute for morphine in people with addiction, but it did not appear to produce euphoria in "normal" subjects. Withdrawal symptoms seemed "very minor," but more research needed to be done. This was a wise caution: methadone does indeed cause addiction and withdrawal, just not in the short time frame used in the Committee's initial research.[162]

Meanwhile, Eli Lilly remained optimistic and, despite Anslinger's protests, provided methadone to thirty or so clinicians for testing. They tried to mollify Anslinger by promising to discuss all research results with him before launching the drug, but Anslinger was unmoved. He asked FDA chief Paul Dunbar to delay approval and had the FBN's chief legal counsel draft a justification for the delay. He also moved to remedy a loophole in federal narcotic law: the Bureau could limit opium imports to the nation's medical need but did not have similar control over domestic manufacturing of synthetic narcotics.[163] Some industry figures were alarmed that Anslinger, who already enjoyed "absolute control," wanted to stop even initial clinical testing of a drug until his own experts had weighed in—especially when those experts were currently attempting to market their own patented opioid (Metopon).[164] Nonetheless, by January 1947 the Committee had determined that methadone was "definitely a dangerous drug" that needed full Harrison controls, and Lilly had also accepted this (although its preferred descriptor was "potent" rather than "dangerous").[165]

Lilly also, however, planned to manufacture 150,000 ounces per year and requested permission to produce an "exempt" preparation (in other words, a combination medicine with a small enough quantity of methadone that it would not trigger Harrison controls).[166] Anslinger was horrified. Such enormous production, he argued, "greatly exceeds the total quantity of morphine sold by all manufacturers for the year 1945," and given that Lilly was only one of several manufacturers interested in methadone, he feared "a race to supply and oversupply the trade" with an addictive opioid.[167] He warned Lilly that the drug would surely be added to the narcotic law and that even initial clinical investigation should proceed under its rules.[168]

Without a law to back him up, however, Anslinger's power was limited. Pharmaceutical companies ignored his warnings and placed advance orders with manufacturing companies, who began to produce the bulk drug.[169] Anslinger and others at the FBN were outraged, but they could do little; a law giving them authority over total production volume was not passed until 1948.[170] Worse, many of the companies thought to be interested in the drug had little or no experience with narcotics.[171] Capping it off, someone had already alerted the popular media about the drug; even as Anslinger was battling de Kruif over Demerol, *Time* magazine was praising methadone as "much less likely to cause addiction than morphine."[172] Anslinger quickly fed a counterattack to sympathetic reporters, who compliantly reported on the "New Dope Peril," highlighting the drug's addictiveness and Nazi origins.[173]

Rescue finally arrived in 1947 when methadone was officially declared a "narcotic" and thus subject to the Harrison Act.[174] The FBN immediately issued a circular specifying the rules for manufacture and sales, and reminding physicians to report all instances of addiction.[175] The Bureau was just as quick to put the brakes on Lilly's marketing plan, quashing a proposal to provide free samples to a selected group of 5,000 physicians (the emphatic handwritten response took up an entire half page despite consisting primarily of a single word: "No").[176]

This deep, battle-hardened skepticism of pharmaceutical narcotics added another dimension to Anslinger's and the Committee's resistance to methadone maintenance when it was eventually proposed in the early 1960s. While a new generation of addiction experts were thinking about treatments for addiction, federal regulators had long been preoccupied with a very different problem: a pharmaceutical industry eagerly pushing at every possible loophole or soft spot in regulatory restraints. From this perspective, methadone was nothing special; it was just the latest would-be miracle opioid. By the 1960s, this attitude had become well entrenched, making it difficult to accept what, in effect, represented an entirely new medical use for opioids that would significantly increase overall sales.[177]

It is important not to push this argument too far. Anslinger's opposition to methadone maintenance was part of his broader rejection of any significant changes to the punitive regime on which he had built his career. This represented more than bureaucratic self-interest. It betrayed Anslinger's deeply held contempt and disgust for people with addiction, an attitude that had only intensified as the ranks of the addicted shifted to include more African Americans and Latinos in the 1950s. Committee experts also shared these prejudices. In 1963, for example, in opposing medical maintenance despite its successful application in England, Eddy explained that most English people with addiction had a "persisting medical need." American physicians, he said, already "treat similarly [that] kind of individual." Unlike England, however, America also had a "tremendous pool" of "socio-economic problem addicts" who "could not possibly be treated" with maintenance.[178] Indeed, the Committee as a whole rejected any form of noninstitutionalized treatment for addiction at all and recommended methadone only to relieve acute withdrawal symptoms "in a hospital or other secure setting" or to maintain people waiting for an opening in an abstinence-based treatment program.[179] Addiction outside of medical contexts was a psychiatric disorder representing defects so profound that they could be treated only under circumstances of near-total control—in other words, by institutional treatment almost identical to punishment (jail). From this point of view, the absolute prohibition of nonmedical markets was the only policy that made sense.

Conclusion

The FBN is remembered as a bullying agency that ignored science in favor of racist sensationalism and that used a heavy hand against consumers, physicians, and any blasphemers who dared to criticize the punitive prohibition model that justified its existence. Yet the FBN used its powers not just to inaugurate "drug wars" against informal markets but also to develop and enforce a robust regulatory system to make white market opioids safer. Where it was weak in controlling medical practice (see chapter 2), it was strong in regulating corporate activity. Thanks to its efforts, per capita medical opioid sales stayed relatively flat for most of the twentieth century, even as a wider range of useful new opioids emerged to meet diverse needs. This was a remarkable accomplishment, especially when compared to authorities' repeated failures to constrain profitable booms (and public health busts) in addictive pharmaceuticals.

Yet this Anslinger-centered regime had significant weaknesses as well. The single-minded campaign to limit opioid use as much as possible meant relatively little exploration of the benefits of opioids or how to provide them safely. This left a knowledge gap that would become tragically significant later in the twentieth century, when drug companies finally liberated opioids from their long regulatory quarantine and authorities struggled to develop safe guidelines for their use. Even before then, however, there was a more immediate consequence. The FBN's insistence on preserving moral simplicity by enforcing the stigmatizing "junkie" paradigm led to years of delay in recognizing the addictive dangers of other, non-opioid drugs sold in medical markets for use by more socially favored populations. It is to these other drugs that we must now turn our attention.

The Second Crisis

Sedatives and Stimulants, 1920s–1970s

4

Opioids out, barbiturates in

Robust opioid controls were an unlikely achievement. They were the product of a tense and temporary coalition of therapeutic reformers and anti-vice moral crusaders, and were won only at a steep cost—the destructive prohibition inflicted on informal markets and their racialized consumers. It would not be easy, or necessarily even desirable, to replicate the conflicted political coalition that had assembled this jury-rigged and highly specific system. Yet the factors that had led to overuse of opioids in the nineteenth century only intensified in the twentieth century. Both physicians and consumers still hungered for ways to ease the "pains of existence" in an increasingly fast-paced and rapidly changing society, and an economically and politically consolidated pharmaceutical industry still profited by encouraging and channeling that hunger toward psychoactive drugs. Thanks to these two inexorable factors, white markets largely bereft of opioids and cocaine were soon flush once again with highly desirable but addictive and potentially dangerous drugs: sedatives (barbiturates, benzodiazepines, etc.) and, later, stimulants (amphetamines, etc.).

Because these new drugs were not plant-based, they were manufactured entirely by the pharmaceutical industry and were thus wholly white market products. At least initially, there were virtually no informal markets. This presented both an opportunity and a challenge. The opportunity was to imagine a new kind of drug policy, relatively free of the racist moral crusading that had characterized anti-narcotic campaigns. Therapeutic reformers and consumer advocates tried to build a new, hybrid regulatory system that would protect consumers by combining the strengths of the Food and Drug Act and the Harrison Act. Like the FDA, the goal would be to enable rather than to quash mass use; consumers would be protected rather than demonized as "dope fiends." Like the FBN, however, authorities would acknowledge the risks of addiction and overdose and would thus wield real power over pharmaceutical companies, drugstores, and the medical and pharmacy professions.

Taking advantage of this opportunity would not be easy, thanks to the stark medicine-drug divide around which American policy had been built. The moral panic surrounding narcotics had already built race and class prejudices into crucial concepts like "addiction," making it difficult to apply to consumers for white market drugs like barbiturates. Moreover, like their customers, the "ethical" drug industry—the companies that voluntarily complied with the AMA's Code of Ethics—enjoyed a presumption of good faith that hampered calls for robust regulation.

For more than half a century these challenges proved insurmountable. Try as they might, drug reformers were unable to carve out a middle way in drug policy. With almost everyone (including many reformers) unwilling to recreate a Harrison-style command economy, the best they could achieve was a relatively limited strengthening of the Food and Drug Act, implemented slowly and hesitantly beginning in the 1940s—four decades after barbiturates had been introduced. These weak regulations did nothing to slow sales, allowing white markets for barbiturates to further consolidate, become entrenched, and eventually to develop their own ancillary informal markets. Within the vexed racial politics of the medicine-drug divide, truly safe, consumer-oriented regulations proved difficult to achieve. Instead, it was either feast or famine: inadequately regulated white markets or destructively policed informal markets.

Barbiturates conquer white markets

Opioids and cocaine may have been the late nineteenth century's blockbuster psychoactive drugs, but they were not the only ones. Physicians and consumers also had access to sedatives such as chloroform, chloral hydrate, sulfonal, and trional. These older drugs were not widely used to soothe the everyday stresses, pains, and sorrows that powered the era's popular and medical markets for opioids and cocaine. Categorized variously as "soporifics," "somnifacients," or "hypnotics," they were prized for surgical anesthesia and for treating severe insomnia, but they were also highly toxic, difficult to use safely, and burdened with a range of unpleasant side effects. Even for the specific problem of insomnia some medical authorities, and surely many consumers, preferred opioids.[1] Thus the market for sedatives remained comparatively small.[2]

These circumstances changed in the early twentieth century thanks to two developments. First, physicians were reluctantly persuaded to stop prescribing opioids so freely, especially for chronic or relatively milder problems such as anxiety or insomnia, while in 1919 Prohibition clamped down on another popular relaxant, alcohol.[3] Second, a new and superior class of sedatives, the barbiturates, became available starting with Bayer's Veronal in 1903.[4] Veronal was easy to use, predictable in effect, relatively safe, and—importantly—subjectively pleasant for most consumers.

Despite this fortuitous timing, Veronal did not quickly capture opioids' white market territory. It took time for drug companies, physicians, and consumers to reorient their psychoactive drug habits around insomnia and sedatives rather than pain and opioids.

Bayer initially imagined Veronal as competing with other sedatives for what was at the time a relatively narrow market for insomnia. "Veronal fills all the indications which in past years were met with chloral," explained one of the company's advertising circulars in 1915, "but with infinitely less danger, either immediate to life or the formation of a drug habit." The pamphlet recommended using Veronal not for day-to-day suffering but for significant illness such as psychoses, epilepsy, delirium tremens, seasickness, vomiting in pregnancy, pre- and post-operative care, and so forth. The focus on capturing rather than expanding the sedative market was also evident in the pamphlet's warning that "no hypnotic should be given carelessly or in cases in which sleep can be induced without its aid. Many persons are susceptible to drug influences and easily converted into drug habitués. To such persons hypnotics should rarely be given."[5] Sterling Drug Company, which sold a number of products manufactured by Bayer, displayed the same restraint in 1920, marketing the first Veronal competitor Luminal for "mental diseases in sanatorium and asylum practice" and "severe types of epilepsy."[6] Luminal could be used for sleep, another pamphlet noted in 1923, but "only the obstinate forms of insomnia, particularly those associated with severe mental derangements."[7]

This relatively narrow advertising produced relatively low sales. Use definitely increased as medical authorities added Veronal to their lists of hypnotics and acknowledged its superiority as a treatment for insomnia, but the overall market for sleeping pills remained small. By the 1920s, per capita sales were still lower than opioids.[8]

A combination of consumer enthusiasm and competitive pressures soon brought an end to this initial restraint. Physicians and consumers, for their part, found much to love in the barbiturates and, if medical authorities' complaints are to be believed, pioneered new uses for them. Therapeutic reformers in 1913 were already bemoaning the "eagerness with which new hypnotics are taken up in practice."[9] By 1923, *JAMA* was warning that Veronal's reputation as a "practically harmless hypnotic" had reached the public, which now used it "extensively for insomnia and all other conditions to which laymen apply the term 'nervousness.'"[10] It is difficult to find evidence to support or refute such claims, but what little does exist suggests that the criticisms were on target. In 1926, for example, the federal Narcotics Division, concerned about rising barbiturate sales, investigated and found them growing because physicians were prescribing them freely for "nervous diseases" and consumers were also buying them directly from druggists for everyday purposes such as "insur[ing] a night's sleep in the sleeping cars."[11]

These enterprising consumers were not acting entirely on their own in inventing new uses for barbiturates. Drug manufacturers noticed and then sought to amplify the new uses, creating a feedback cycle that dramatically expanded white market sales. The Narcotics Division investigator, for example, reported from Philadelphia that "the manufacturers of these drugs are, to my mind, very indiscreet in their advertising." As "ethical" pharmaceutical houses, they did not advertise in popular media, but, the investigator claimed, some advertised so ubiquitously in medical media that their "chief objective seems to make their product so well known that it will be taken up by the laity and used extensively by them."[12] In-person sales representatives working on commission may have pushed the marketing envelope even further. As early as 1906, for example, when printed circulars were still circumspect, one Bayer sales representative urged physicians to use Veronal for "almost every form of sleeplessness, whether due to simple nervous causes or accompanying functional or organic diseases of the nervous system."[13]

Supply-side forces soon became even more important as companies began to compete more intensely for the growing ranks of barbiturate consumers. Barbiturates, it turned out, were easy molecules to tinker with, and markets were quickly deluged with new varieties and brands. Medical ethics had recently evolved to allow patenting of "ethical" pharmaceuticals, bringing a new level of competitive risks and rewards to what had been a relatively staid part of the drug sector.[14] By 1940 *American Druggist* reported that there were dozens of brand-name barbiturates, including at least one from almost every major "ethical" pharmaceutical company (e.g., Eli Lilly, Upjohn, Ciba, American Cyanamid, Squibb, Schering, Abbot, Parke Davis).[15]

The competitive free-for-all formalized and intensified the reorientation of white markets from pain and opioids to insomnia and sedatives. Marketers accomplished this through three overlapping strategies, each designed to amplify the already emerging behavior of physicians and consumers. First, they expanded uses for barbiturates to include milder, "everyday" versions of insomnia and related suffering—a process often labeled as "medicalization."[16] Second, they created new market niches through product differentiation. Third, in an early campaign of "selling sickness," they educated physicians to pay attention to and treat insomnia. These campaigns faced little oversight from regulators—certainly nothing like what the FBN imposed on opioids. Because they served as a template for many future marketing campaigns, it is worth taking at least a brief look at each strategy in turn.

The first and most obvious strategy, emerging as early as the mid-1920s, was to expand the kinds of insomnia that called for treatment with barbiturates. Winthrop Chemical Company (a Sterling Drug subsidiary) advertised its version of Veronal for "sleeplessness arising from any cause whatsoever," for example, and by 1939 it had gone beyond insomnia to recommend use for "nervousness and restlessness" more generally.[17] To welcome a new and presumably less desperate sort of consumer, Winthrop also released a better-tasting version of Veronal (Paranoval) in the late 1920s.[18] The company performed a similar feat with Luminal starting in 1926, recommending it not just for serious illnesses but for "various nervous conditions" including hysteria, bronchitis, hypertension, dysmenorrhea, "sexual irritability," and "nocturnal pollutions."[19]

By the 1930s Veronal and Luminal had many competitors also angling to capture new therapeutic territory. Roche, for example, launched its barbiturate Sedormid in 1930 for "all cases of insomnia regardless of the cause," a claim so broad it actually ran afoul of the AMA's Council on Pharmacy and Chemistry, which rejected the drug from *New and Nonofficial Remedies*.[20] Meanwhile, Winthrop continued to expand its own barbiturate lines and its marketing claims. Phanodorn, introduced in 1924, was "the hypnotic for every-day practice" in "sleeplessness due to Worry, Excitement and Anxiety" as well as "all conditions of excitement" and "conditions of anxiety."[21] That same year came the fast-acting Evipal, touted for "that common type of insomnia" where sleep is either "delayed" or "interrupted," and for "physicians and others engaged in occasional exacting work at night."[22]

Supplementing these expansive therapeutic claims was a second strategy: combination drugs, which cracked open new market niches by identifying insomnia as part of other medical problems. In 1924, for example, Winthrop combined Luminal with a second barbiturate, carbromal, to make "Adalin-Luminal," suitable, they claimed, for "more obstinate types of sleeplessness."[23] Two years later Winthrop added three new Luminal combination products. Theominal added the vasodilator and diuretic theobromine to treat heart diseases; Lumalgin added aspirin for "all conditions in which insomnia associated with pain or other discomfort"; and Pyraminal added the fever-reducer pyramidon for "painful conditions in general" as well as "various types of headache."[24]

Even though these marketing claims were at least partly based on uses that some physicians and patients had already embraced, sales growth also required a third strategy: advertising sleeplessness and worry as legitimate medical concerns rather than ordinary suffering. Physicians had to be encouraged to look for, or at least pay attention to, signs of such problems in their patients. Winthrop pursued this strategy when it circulated an otherwise obscure passage from a textbook on "nervous indigestion" by eminent (and drug-friendly) physician Walter Alvarez. In the passage, Alvarez expressed astonishment that many physicians remained "uninterested in insomnia," and bemoaned ignorant opposition to the use of sedatives to relieve it. "Time and time again," he wrote, "I have brought a nervous patient almost back to health and full-time work, only to see her plunged again into insomnia and despair by the angry protests of some medical friend of the family who apparently did not know that modern soporifics are not related to morphine and are not ordinarily habit-forming."[25]

All three of these strategies—medicalizing a wider range of human suffering, creating market niches through product differentiation, and selling sickness—helped to legitimize insomnia as a significant medical problem and to position barbiturates as the obvious treatment.

Barbiturate manufacturers were not the only ones making these new kinds of sales pitches in the 1920s. These were boom years for the American consumer culture more generally—an auspicious time to be selling new solutions to new problems. The advertising profession was maturing as a site of visual and emotional creativity rather than utilitarian conveyers of information about product qualities. Technological development and improvements in manufacturing and transportation brought an unprecedented array of new devices to solve a dizzying array of problems that advertisers taught Americans that they should no longer have to endure.[26] It is not coincidental that these expanding consumer markets were also robustly divided by class and especially race; housing and public accommodations were central arenas for the imposition of segregation in both the South and the North.[27] The expanded claims for barbiturates and growing white markets fit very well with the consumer culture's promises of segregated convenience and comfort.

The mystery of barbiturate addiction

Walter Alvarez's insistence on the difference between barbiturates and morphine, quoted earlier, was no small matter. White market sales could boom only if barbiturates did not suffer the social opprobrium and restrictive regulations that limited opioids. Yet barbiturates carried both of the main risks associated with opioids: fatal overdose and addiction. The first US account of Veronal poisoning made headlines just three years after the drug became available (the case was reported in *JAMA* and the *New York Times*, among other places).[28] After that, barbiturate overdose deaths became a staple in both medical and popular media, and barbiturates became a common plot device in popular fiction as a favored tool of murderers and suicides.[29] The *New York Times* alone reported six deaths in the city from 1909 to 1919, and another 30 by 1930—and these were just the ones that made it into print. The Narcotics Division investigation of

Philadelphia, meanwhile, found that local hospitals there had seen 44 overdoses between 1924 and 1926.[30]

Even as a welter of new barbiturates flooded the market in the 1920s, then, they began to develop a reputation for danger. But it was not easy to recognize addiction as one of those dangers, in part because the moral crusade against "narcotics" had narrowed the cultural and legal definition of addiction. The nineteenth-century concept of "habit" had been fluid and pluralistic, applicable to opium but also a variety of other substances and behaviors including earlier sedatives such as chloral hydrate.[31] The twentieth century's anti-narcotic crusade reframed the concept of "habit" in two significant ways, however. First, it cast the opioid and cocaine habits as uniquely destructive. The Harrison Act, for example, defined "narcotics" as opium, coca, and their derivatives; it excluded all other drugs, no matter their pharmacology or psychoactive effects. Second, as we have seen, anti-narcotic campaigns associated the concept of "addiction" with poor, racialized urban drug consumers and the informal economy in which police sought to quarantine them. By the 1920s, the "drug habit" had become "drug addiction," a narrower and more terrifying concept applying to a specific set of drugs ("narcotics") and a specific type of drug user (poor, urban, criminal).

Barbiturates met neither of these new criteria. They were almost entirely a white market product, associated not with "dope fiends" but with "patients." Informal markets for opioids and cocaine were possible, in part, because even after criminalization, opium poppies and coca remained important agricultural products in the regions where they had traditionally been grown.[32] Barbiturates were fully synthetic—not derived from plants—and thus had no preexisting, entrenched supply chains. Their manufacture monopolized by "ethical" drug companies, barbiturates were relatively expensive, brand-named, patented goods available primarily to those with access to white markets. (Informal-market consumers, of course, did not need barbiturates; prohibition had not reduced their supply of heroin or cocaine.)

As white market goods, barbiturates appear to have been primarily available to white and relatively well-off consumers. The FBN's Philadelphia investigator cited earlier, for example, described barbiturate consumers as not "underworld" characters but "the leisure class," the "wealthy," theatrical types, and professionals.[33] When barbiturate consumers appeared in popular culture, they were usually portrayed as white and, if not wealthy, at least respectable. In the first twenty years of Veronal's availability, the *New York Times* reported on the drug in the context of a schoolteacher, a clergyman, an English "nobleman," a dancer, a physician, a "prominent suffragette," a gown shop owner, the wife of a financier, a young violin prodigy, several actors and actresses, a lawyer, a movie writer, a chemist, a construction engineer, a "well-dressed young woman," a stenographer, a nurse, a "broker's wife," and others.[34] While most of these were unhappy stories of overdose deaths or suicides, taken together they still gave a clear and consistent message about the type of person presumed to be using barbiturates.

Drug manufacturers did their best to play up barbiturates' cultural association with white market consumers. Advertisements were full of glorious, full-color illustrations, most commonly of beautiful white women sleeping in peaceful, implicitly affluent settings (clean white sheets, expensive hairstyles and pajamas, exotic locales, etc.).[35] These contrasted sharply to the titillating sensationalism of images of white women dreamily asleep in "Oriental" opium dens or trapped in "white slavery" by heroin "pushers."[36] Instead, they evoked an image of the consumer: implicitly white and often female, deserving of comfort and ease (see fig. 4.1). Other barbiturate advertisements featured male discoverers, explorers, and scientists whose heroic achievements brought the miracles of modern science to these beautiful damsels in distress. One series of ads for Luminal depicted (white, male) physicians as central, almost god-like figures bearing enormous responsibility for tiny, ant-like (white) patients (see fig. 4.2).[37]

The cultural status of barbiturates and their consumers left many observers in both medicine and popular media reluctant to apply the

Figure 4.1. Marketers for barbiturates like Phanodorm emphasized their status as medicines by suggesting that affluent white women (the stereotypical "patients") were their primary consumers. Bayer/Winthrop Chemical Company, 1937. Sterling Drug, Inc. Records, Archives Center, National Museum of American History, Smithsonian Institution.

concept of "addiction" when attempting to understand or explain the bizarre behavior of some longtime barbiturate users. Instead they pointed to the drug's toxicity.[38] In 1907, for example, the *Louisville Journal of Medicine and Surgery* reported the story of a woman admitted to the hospital declaring that "all she wanted was some of those [Veronal] powders; that her father had been in the habit of prescribing them for her and they had relieved her." Twelve packages of Veronal powder were taken from her, but on the way to the infirmary she slipped into a drugstore, bought more Veronal, and promptly suffered a fatal overdose. "I really never made a diagnosis in this case," the doctor concluded, before musing that perhaps the culprit had been "hysterical mania" or "some narcotic agent" (i.e., not Veronal).[39]

Physicians were similarly confused by the case of a forty-eight-

Figure 4.2. Men in barbiturate advertisements tended to be explorers, researchers, or, as in this Luminal advertisement, physicians, bringing the miracles of science to an anxious public. Winthrop Chemical Company (n.d.; probably 1930s). Sterling Drug, Inc. Records, Archives Center, National Museum of American History, Smithsonian Institution.

year-old woman who had begun taking Veronal at night because she was "nervous" and "had some irritable, mental depressive periods," reported in the *Oklahoma Medical News Journal* in 1912. After a year she "evidently increased the dose and remained in bed a week, sleeping most of the time." One day she woke up suddenly, obsessed with the urge to cut her husband's heart out; after raging about this for a while, she took more Veronal and fell into a "sleep stupor" from which "she could not be aroused." Sent to a sanitarium, she developed a "very violent, abusive" delirium for two or more weeks before gradually recovering. In their lengthy discussion of the drug's toxicity, the authors mentioned the possibility of "habit addiction," but only to dismiss it as unlikely.[40]

Many popular observers, too, applied narratives other than addiction to explain problematic use of barbiturates. In 1921, for example, barbiturates figured prominently in a legal dispute over the estate of a wealthy New York City matriarch, Mrs. Griswold. Griswold had bequeathed her substantial possessions not to her daughters but to a working-class friend who had been her caretaker for several years. Griswold's daughters challenged the will, claiming that their mother had been driven insane by continual use of Veronal administered by the inheriting caretaker. There was much talk in court and in newspaper coverage about Veronal's capacity to poison the mind, but no one ever brought up the possibility of addiction, even though that would have been a useful line of attack for the daughters.[41]

Barbiturate manufacturers did their part to sustain the belief that their products were not addictive. Winthrop, for example, claimed in a 1925 brochure that "there is no true habituation to Veronal as in the case of morphine and other narcotics." Instead, "some nervous patients" might "get into the habit of taking it regularly" but only because they believed it was necessary for sleep.[42] Luminal, too, had "no tendency to habituation," and Winthrop's 1929 list of the drug's side effects did not include addiction.[43] Throughout the 1920s, many of Winthrop's barbiturates were specifically marketed as treatments for "narcotic habituation" and "delirium tremens."[44] They were also advertised for long-term use: Lumalgin could be "taken for long periods without disturbing the stomach or affecting the heart," and Phanodorn was recommended for "sleeplessness of daily occurrence."[45] "Continuous" use of Veronal was unwise, Winthrop allowed, but only because it would lead to "loss of efficiency with consequent increased dosage and by-effects"; an easy solution was for "chronic cases" to switch hypnotics occasionally.[46]

Unlike opioid manufacturers, barbiturate manufacturers did

not have to submit such claims for expert evaluation. Even if they had, though, the results would not necessarily have been clear. Like many other observers, addiction experts were uncertain about how to explain instances of harmful barbiturate use. The earliest studies came from psychiatrists, who found that barbiturates were not themselves addictive but could become so when abused by people with serious psychological or characterological defects. A widely cited 1923 *JAMA* study, for example, explained that barbiturate addiction occurred only in "the emotionally unstable type of constitutional psychopathic inferiority groups."[47] A 1925 follow-up in *JAMA* confirmed that barbiturate addiction "involved an unstable and inferior part of society" with a "general lack of social adaptability."[48] This was the same type of language that addiction experts used to explain the behavior of "dope fiends." It cleared barbiturates for white markets, whose respectable consumers supposedly did not suffer from such defects.

Significantly, experts also took care to distinguish cases of apparent addiction to barbiturates from addiction to narcotics. Barbiturate abuse, they argued, mostly hurt the drug consumer rather than posing a broader social threat. *JAMA*'s editors, for example, explained in 1928 that "veronalism" led to mental deterioration that "precludes complicated criminality or conspiracy." At worst, a person addicted to Veronal might commit such minor offenses as carelessness, "ethical offenses, as against decency, and minor frauds," or, perhaps, a "quasicriminal complaisance with the schemes of others."[49]

When in the 1930s the Committee on Drug Addiction finally weighed in, it provided important support for this relatively unthreatening assessment. The Committee's approach to barbiturates was a conflicted one. Its members were jaded drug industry skeptics practiced at seeing through marketing hype, but at the same time they were key architects of a paradigm that defined addiction as specific to opioids and nonmedical use. The latter initially won out. The majority of early barbiturate research by Committee members focused on efficacy and toxicity rather than addiction (which they mentioned primarily to note its apparent absence in test animals).[50]

When the Committee did finally begin to study barbiturate addiction in the 1930s, it could reach no consensus other than that it was milder than opioid addiction. Take, for example, the work of Maurice Seevers, an animal researcher who studied physically measurable withdrawal symptoms rather than subjective experiences such as euphoria and craving, and who was thus the Committee researcher most likely to recognize barbiturate addiction.[51] In a 1931 article, Seevers and a colleague acknowledged that "after long use" barbiturates did "require a continuance of the drug to maintain a certain degree of functional normality." They downplayed the finding, however, distancing it from what they called "true" addiction (to opioids) and comparing it instead to habitual use of older nineteenth-century sedatives like chloral hydrate.[52] Other Committee researchers were not willing to go even that far. Nathan Eddy, for example, summarizing the latest addiction research to a popular audience in 1934, likened barbiturate addiction to habitual coffee or tea drinking. Although such use of barbiturates might do "considerable harm" to the consumer, it was not a true addiction because it did not produce euphoria, tolerance, or withdrawal symptoms.[53] Arthur Tatum described it as "habituation or psychic dependence" rather than a "true addiction as exemplified by use of morphine or heroin."[54]

Like other observers, then, America's foremost addiction researchers were hesitant to apply the concept of addiction to barbiturates. Instead they resurrected an older, pre-Harrison concept of "habit" to describe a harmful but less socially threatening condition (similar, again, to the twenty-first-century concept of "dependence").

Pharmacology likely played at least some role in their reluctance. Studies designed to find opioid addiction might have been too short to expose addiction to barbiturates, which takes much longer to develop. Psychological craving also appears to play a smaller role.

Then too, because barbiturates were usually swallowed, not injected or snorted, they took effect much more slowly; there were no dramatic spectacles of withdrawal agonies being instantly and miraculously relieved by a single dose.

The most important distinction between "addiction" and "habituation," however, remained social rather than pharmacological. Addiction had come to be seen as a broad social threat linked to criminality and sexual transgression; "habituation" described a threat better categorized as a form of poisoning in that it harmed only a (presumably innocent, if possibly foolish) consumer. In this regard, it reinvented the nineteenth-century distinction between sympathetic morphine habitués and purposefully deviant opium smokers. Most people addicted to barbiturates, one observer wrote, "go quietly on their way without attracting attention, some of them never realizing themselves that they are drug addicts."[55] As with morphine habitués, this was a self-fulfilling prophecy: with white markets providing a legal, predictable supply, most barbiturate consumers did not face the difficult choices that enmeshed informal-market consumers ever more deeply into illegal and stigmatized behavior.

These ideas were captured perfectly by Marian King's 1931 memoir, *Recovery of Myself*, written for popular audiences but published by Yale University Press and with a preface by preeminent psychiatrist Adolf Meyer. In the memoir, King, a wealthy and well-educated young woman, recounted her experience of the barbiturate "habit." She began using barbiturates, she wrote, to handle stress while attending a private preparatory and art school, and eventually found herself in the "habit" of taking some every night. Notably, her character and behavior remained perfectly respectable ("all it ever did was to make me sleep," she later told a hospital physician who specifically asked her about sexual effects).[56] One day, though, angry at her father for a relatively minor slight, she vengefully took a handful of pills, overdosed, and woke up in a hospital.[57] The rest of the narrative tracks what she portrayed as a difficult quest for the self-knowledge that would enable her to confront life assertively, without drugs.

Although its neat, Freud-influenced trajectory was certainly an update to nineteenth-century morphine narratives, in other ways King's memoir tracked them closely. She was a young, white woman who became dependent on drugs not because of immoral pleasure seeking but because of a naïve trust in medicines. She then demonstrated her fine character by struggling to free herself of her habit. In a final, crucial, homage to bygone stories of morphine habitués, King ended her memoir by blaming insufficiently regulated drug markets and calling for "more reasonable control of drugs."[58] This last point was not lost on the *New York Times*'s reviewer, who praised the book for "informing the public" of barbiturate dangers and "rousing them to protest against the laxity of physicians with regard to its use."[59]

King's memoir thus captured both the challenge and the opportunity barbiturates posed for reformers. The challenge was to build robust regulation for these dangerous and habit-forming drugs without using the cultural infrastructure of "addiction" to win the political support of anti-vice moral crusaders. The opportunity was that, freed from the agenda of policing urban "dangerous classes," reformers might be able to imagine a new and more effective regulatory system—one that used state power not for punitive prohibition but to protect consumers by ensuring safe access to valuable drugs. This would be no easy task.

The struggle for barbiturate control

Whatever their addictive qualities, barbiturates were unambiguously dangerous, and from quite early on therapeutic reformers and their allies pushed to regulate them. It was not immediately clear what type of regulation was needed, however. As psychoactive drugs that could produce addiction in at least some susceptible populations, did they require strong government oversight like the Harrison Act? Or were their habit-forming qualities minor, suggesting less strict oversight similar to that for other useful but toxic medicines? Existing law provided little clarity. All medicines were automatically covered by the Food and Drug Act, but that law had no mechanism for adding to the ten dangerous or habit-forming drugs that must be listed on the label. No postmarketing drug monitoring system existed to identify new drug threats, and the Harrison Act did not yet have a process for adding drugs other than derivatives of opium and coca.

Reformers' first idea was a familiar one: require a physician's prescription for barbiturate sales. "As with all drugs, so with veronal," the *Therapeutic Gazette* proposed in 1913: "it should not be obtainable by every layman or laywoman on direct demand without the advice of a physician."[60] As barbiturates began their period of explosive therapeutic and commercial growth in the 1920s, *JAMA*'s editors took up the baton, complaining that overdoses were on the rise because "the drug is so easily obtained without a physician's prescription."[61]

These calls came to nothing during the 1920s, an era of vibrant consumerism and pro-business government, but began to produce results quickly when political tides shifted during the 1930s. Action began at the state and local levels, where nearly thirty states restricted barbiturates to prescription only by 1939; about half that number placed some limits on prescription refills.[62] Without input from moral crusaders (who were apparently uninterested in internal white market issues), these state laws were not mini–Harrison Acts. They assumed that all white market actors—manufacturers, physicians, druggists, and consumers—shared the goal of health as defined within professional medicine. The problem with barbiturates was one of ignorance, of insufficient guidance, not of desire to profit from or to experience drugs.

As a result of this assumption of good faith, state laws invited rather than required compliance. Some required extensive record-keeping; others did not. Only a small few included a Harrison-like "good faith" clause; a prescription was evidence enough of therapeutic intentions. No law restricted manufacturers in any way. Moreover, all laws were enforced by state pharmacy boards, which had small budgets and no policing capacity. To give a sense of how ill-equipped most boards were for the task, consider that New Jersey's board actually had to plead with Hoffmann-La Roche in 1933 to "send us a list of all of the drugs and medicines which you manufacture which come under the provisions" of their new state law.[63] Nor was prosecuting offenders easy; laws varied from state to state, requiring proof of jurisdiction every time. Even when someone was convicted, penalties were usually mild.[64]

Unsurprisingly, the laws were widely ignored. Six years after Virginia passed its prescription-only law, for example, an investigative journalist had no trouble buying pills without a prescription in even the toniest and most respectable of Richmond's drugstores. Druggists claimed they had no choice but to sell without a prescription, or else they would lose customers to less scrupled competition.[65] Nationally, the rise in barbiturate sales that had begun in the 1920s accelerated dramatically, rising by more than fivefold despite the Great Depression (see fig. A.2 in the appendix).

An opportunity to fix at least some of these problems came near the end of the decade, thanks to a seemingly unrelated political development. In 1937, S. E. Massengill Company unintentionally used a lethal solvent in its version of an anti-infective "sulfa" drug. Hundreds of Americans died, but since the drug label accurately listed the solvent as an ingredient, Massengill had broken no law. Therapeutic reformers seized on this strategy to push for a long-desired modernization of the Food and Drug Act.[66] Despite sulfa drugs' dubious reputation as a cure for sexually transmitted diseases, reformers strategically showcased the death of a young white girl—a familiar consumer figure signaling the need for protection by male professionals.[67] The result was the 1938 Food, Drug, and Cosmetic Act, a milestone in consumer protection that gave the FDA the power to reject drugs before they went on the market if the agency deemed them unsafe to use according to the instructions on the label.[68]

Initially the 1938 law offered only a small victory for barbiturate reformers: it updated the FDA's list of "dangerous drugs" so that barbiturates, like opioids and cocaine, had to bear the label "may be habit forming." The FDA's creative reading of the statute, however, soon brought a much more powerful tool to the table. Drugs like the antibacterial sulfas, the FDA argued, were so dangerous that the only safe way to use them was under medical supervision. Thus, the only honest and accurate label for such drugs would be "for use by prescription only." If a drug labeled in this way were sold without a prescription, it would be misbranded. Although the power to determine whether a drug warranted a prescription-only label was left in the hands of manufacturers, the FDA did have the authority to prosecute those who sold misbranded drugs.[69]

Reformers quickly pushed to have the new prescription-only requirement applied to barbiturates. The AMA, for example, which had officially condemned the "promiscuous use" of barbiturates in 1937, explicitly argued in 1940 that "restrictions enforced by law have become increasingly necessary" and gave such restrictions its "whole-hearted approval."[70] The AMA also reached out to the public with its prescription-only message, circulating warning stories of sleep-deprived "debutantes, business men, stenographers and housewives" who accidentally overdosed after helping themselves to barbiturates without a physician's guidance. "Because he doesn't sleep well," an article in the AMA's popular magazine *Hygeia* explained, "the victim turns to a 'harmless' pill recommended by a friend. He sticks to his 'sedative,' using larger and larger doses, until some day he is rushed off to the emergency hospital suffering from acute poisoning or even accused by his friends of temporary insanity."[71] A short 1940 film produced by the AMA told a similar tale and closed with a succinct message: "The person who prescribes for himself is taking a dangerous risk."[72]

The campaign bore fruit almost immediately. In 1940, the FDA placed barbiturates alongside sulfas in the first group of drugs that had to be sold on prescription—the only group required to bear the prescription legend by the FDA rather than being left to manufacturers' discretion.[73] Refills would require a physician's authorization, and—in a rare incursion into therapeutic decision making—the FDA officially recommended a maximum of two refills.[74]

These were significant accomplishments that addressed some of the most serious flaws in the patchwork system of state laws. Yet the new prescription-only regime was still hobbled by its presumption of good faith among all white market actors. Indeed, at the beginning, the FDA appears not to have considered that the law would even require enforcement, or at least, not federal enforcement. In early 1940, the agency scoffed at the idea that its small force of agents could police America's hundreds of thousands of druggists.[75] "It is not the intention of the administration to regulate the retail distribution of drugs in general," a memo clarified.[76] Instead, the FDA imagined a "modest program" of "informal methods" to "promote a growing realization by retailers of their responsibility."[77] As late as 1943, the FDA limited its enforcement to handing out warning letters to druggists caught selling without a prescription.[78]

This initial reluctance eventually passed, and the FDA began moving, gingerly, toward real enforcement later in 1943.[79] The new prescription-only regime was not set up with enforcement in mind, however. The FDA had only 230 agents, most of whom already had full-time responsibilities. Who would actually police the hundreds of thousands of daily barbiturate sales across a vast nation? There were larger structural problems too. Unlike the Harrison Act, the 1938 law imposed no limits on advertising or on manufacturing volume, so supply was essentially unlimited—not only in terms of total volume, but also in terms of the number of manufacturers and the number of competing chemical variants or brands.[80] This was no small matter: as late as 1959, the FDA was still stumped by a simple request for a list of all barbiturate manufacturers and distributors.[81] The 1938 law was weaker than Harrison in other ways too. It imposed no restraints on physician prescribing, for example, and did not require that records be kept of prescriptions or sales. It was also difficult to prosecute since the FDA had to establish federal jurisdiction—a cumbersome process of tracking each step in the commodity chain and proving that the particular drug in question had been sold across state lines. If by some miracle a druggist were actually convicted of improper sales despite all these obstacles, penalties were quite mild: fines, temporary suspensions or, in rare cases, revocations of pharmacy licenses.

All these weaknesses and loopholes were a feature, not a bug, of the new system. Indeed, the whole setup was the jury-rigged creation of the FDA's imaginative reading of the 1938 law, which said nothing about requiring a prescription for any drug. The moment the FDA began enforcing its new policy it was challenged in court and struck down. The FDA appealed, but the process was slow; final Supreme Court approval came only years later, in 1948.[82]

Why was the prescription-only regime so weak, especially as compared to the Harrison Act? The answer returns, again, to the political coalitions that drove it. The Harrison Act had benefited from an unusual alliance between therapeutic reformers and moral crusaders; both had been required to overcome the resistance (or self-interested assistance) of major players like the pharmaceutical industry and the medical and pharmacy professions. Therapeutic reformers alone simply did not have the political power to win all those battles—nor even the political will to fight many of them in the first place. After all, therapeutic reformers were themselves major players in white markets, and as we have seen, by the 1930s many of them had come to regret the way the Harrison Act had allowed federal bureaucrats to intrude on their professional prerogatives.

Therapeutic reformers were therefore adamant that barbiturates were not narcotics and should not be controlled in the same way. The AMA endorsed the basic principle of widespread access and mass use—as long as it was overseen by physicians. While barbiturates were not "safe for Mr. Average Man to use at his own whim," *Hygeia* explained, "there is no doubt that many of the people who are now jeopardizing their health by using hypnotic drugs 'recommended by a friend' really need hypnotics and would benefit by their effects."[83]

The social and cultural politics undergirding this decision to protect mass barbiturate use can be seen by turning to a different drug that came under new federal controls at almost exactly the same time: cannabis. While cannabis had been seen as a dangerous narcotic and included in the turn-of-the-century quest for drug controls, by the 1930s circumstances had changed.[84] Cannabis no longer had formal medical uses and earned no significant profits for pharmaceutical companies; its days as a significant white market drug were over. It continued to be used in informal markets, however, where it acquired an association with poorer and racially stigmatized consumers. Historians still debate why cannabis control came precisely when it did (in 1937), but whatever the explanation, it is clear that therapeutic reformers played little role; their interest had waned as cannabis disappeared from white markets.[85] Instead, the Marihuana Tax Act of 1937 was designed primarily by moral crusaders. As a result, the act classified cannabis an addictive narcotic and essentially prohibited its sale, possession, or use. A few voices opposed this dubious classification, but nothing like barbiturates' swell of defenders. Anslinger did not want the impossible job of policing a domestic weed, but once saddled with it he pursued the mission with characteristic vigor, launching a popular campaign blaming cannabis for insanity and violence and linking it to stigmatized racial groups and sexual immorality.[86]

Cannabis criminalization and prescription-only reforms are not usually understood to be related, but it is no accident that they occurred at nearly the same time. They belong to the same story: the development of the US government's capacity to regulate drug markets, divided into problematically weak controls over white markets and problematically harsh controls over informal markets. New Deal drug policy reinforced rather than challenged the binary path charted during the Progressive Era.

Barbiturates survive the "goof ball panic"

Problems with barbiturates did not disappear—far from it. Per capita sales continued to rise during World War II, and after jumping up 50 percent after the war ended, they eclipsed the nineteenth-century opioid peak for the first time. Poisonings and overdose deaths rose significantly as well. The US Public Health Service logged 709 fatal overdoses in 1945, more than half again their 1938 tally. Meanwhile barbiturates' share of all nonfatal poisonings nearly doubled from 12.4 percent to nearly 23 percent.[87] Overdose deaths increased at even faster rates in some states: California, Illinois, Massachusetts, and Ohio all saw death rates double immediately after the war, and in some smaller states like Georgia and Oregon the increase was even higher. Barbiturates were responsible for nearly a third of all poisonings in major cities such as Boston, Chicago, and Cleveland. New York City, too, saw barbiturate deaths jump, from thirty per year in the mid-1930s to nearly sixty per year in 1941, and the city's Public Health Department, calling for a municipal law in 1945, reported that poisonings and deaths had only continued to increase since then.[88]

Beneath the rising numbers were countless individual tales of suffering and death, some captured in anguished letters to the federal government. A New York State man, for example, pleaded with President Roosevelt in 1937: "I had my wife in a hospital two year ago for to be cured of the habit. She was ok for a year and now she got hold of this drug and worse than ever. I got to send her away agin. This drugs are ruining so many lives. Please Mr. Rosevelt try and pass a bill to control the sale of the harmful drugs there is barbtall [barbital] and vernal [Veronal]."[89] Four years later an Ohio woman wrote to Anslinger after the death of her brother from an overdose. Her brother had long struggled with alcohol, but things had gotten much worse when a druggist recommended a barbiturate to "quiete his nerves." "As bad as liquor is," she wrote, "Nembutal is so much worse . . . he started taking one a day and kept taking more till he must have been taking twelve or more a day he lost weight and strength and he aged twenty years in three." Although it was too late to help her brother, she believed "their must be many people getting in the habit" who needed to be protected by a prescription-only law.[90]

Barbiturate problems were widespread enough that even people whose families had not been directly affected were driven to ask for government action. "Something should be done about the sale of barbital and veronal down here without a doctor's prescription," a Louisiana man demanded of Anslinger in 1941. "There ten times as many barbital addicts as any other kind in the south. . . . Im counting on the Government to do their part in making this a better place to live in."[91] A West Virginia labor union officer warned in 1945 that his men were "buying what they call Yellow jackets [barbiturates]" and that the pills were "runing men and women wild . . . if every there was a town needed cleaned up for dope and Bootlegging joints it Norton, Va."[92]

The concerns of private citizens were amplified by a blizzard of frightening newspaper and magazine reports about the "goof ball" menace.[93] It was far from clear what could be done about the problem, however. The FDA had already stretched the Food, Drug, and Cosmetic Act to its limits, and its assertion of power remained under court challenge until 1948. The prospects for strengthening the 1938 law seemed poor: reforms had been difficult to achieve even during the New Deal, and were almost impossible to imagine amid a postwar period of liberal retreat.

There was one exception to the inhospitable political climate: the Harrison Act and the FBN. Even as regulation of industry took a back seat to business-friendly mass consumer policies, the FBN's moralistic campaign to defend the United States from real and imagined enemies at home and abroad represented an aspect of the government that—like the military—remained in growth mode.[94] Moreover, the FBN seemed a natural fit for the job. The Harrison Act was a prescription-only law, after all, and the FBN's powers to enforce it were well developed. Unlike the FDA, the FBN had field agents trained for police work. Moreover, the Harrison Act had already been expanded twice recently to incorporate new drugs: first marijuana in 1937, and then Demerol and other synthetic opioids in 1944. Both of the new "narcotics" could be produced within the United States, meaning that the Harrison Act had expanded beyond its original role of policing imports and exports.

Therapeutic reformers seized on this possibility and began a concerted push to add barbiturates to the Harrison Act after the end of

World War II.[95] This was an awkward move for them. They were not entirely comfortable with the cultural style of a moral crusade, which typically involved demonizing both a drug and its consumers. Nor did they agree with moral crusaders' usual goal of prohibition. Instead they wanted to do something new: wield Harrison's robust powers to make mass use safer, not prohibit it.

The central vehicle for therapeutic reformers' efforts was a bill introduced in 1946 by Massachusetts Representative Edith Nourse Rogers.[96] The bill was championed by FDA head George Larrick, who provided alarming data and frightening anecdotes about the crisis and instructed Congress on the many weaknesses and loopholes that prevented his agency from enforcing the law.[97] Nourse's bill also received support from the same network of friendly amplifiers that therapeutic reformers and the FDA had long relied on, including, for example, the Federated Women's Clubs, whose Washington, DC, branch—headed by none other than Mrs. Harvey W. Wiley—began a public push against "sleeping potions" in early 1946.[98] Their efforts were augmented by latter-day muckraking journalists who transformed what had been a disconnected spate of reports on barbiturate problems into a coherent call for government action.

A central strategy in this orchestrated moral panic was to deploy sexualized, titillating sensationalism that would expand the reform coalition by appealing to moral crusaders—to, in effect, rebuild the political coalition that had made the original Harrison Act possible. Congresswoman Rogers claimed that barbiturates were "being used by thrill-seekers in a manner hideously reminiscent of the 'reefer parties' which were so common, so degrading and so deadly, before we enacted our law against marijuana."[99] Perhaps the highest-profile media series was written by none other than Samuel Hopkins Adams, the inveterate muckraker whose famous 1906 series "The Great American Fraud" had helped pass the Food and Drug Act nearly half a century earlier. Titled "Slaves of the Devil's Capsules," Adams's articles recounted a litany of car crashes, suicides, and accidental overdoses. Peppered between tragedies were moments of sexualized sensationalism, such as Adams's claim that "barbiturates could anesthetize a girl's normal resistance to immorality," supported by the story of a "22 year old blonde" whose "boy friend had been doping her with sleeping pills so that he could force her to lead a life of shame."[100]

At a first glance, then, the anti-barbiturate campaign looked a great deal like the successful campaign to rein in opioids and cocaine three decades earlier. On closer inspection, however, there was a key difference: therapeutic reformers wanted FBN powers so that they could protect white market consumers, not reduce or even eliminate those consumers' access to barbiturates. The goal was to enable mass markets by making them safe, not to quash them.

This overall agenda left a distinctive stamp on the campaign to stir fear about barbiturates. For one thing, even the most sensationalized stories emphasized the medical value of barbiturates and made clear that widespread use was fine—even beneficial—as long as consumers followed physician guidance. A *Collier's* article, influential enough to have been reprinted in the *Congressional Record*, conveyed the typical reasoning. On the one hand, it claimed that "thousands of our citizens . . . have become victims of a vicious new form of drug addiction." But on the other hand, it reassured that "no one . . . desires to interfere with the legitimate use of this drug by physicians in the course of their practice. Only the mistaken use of it by the public and the criminal misuse of it by lawless elements should be curbed."[101] *Good Housekeeping* noted that barbiturates may be dangerous, but they were also "so helpful" that "many of us will need them sometime or other."[102]

Barbiturate media stories also tended to portray drug consumers not as evil "fiends" but as innocent victims, often middle-class women, who had been ensnared not through the pursuit of pleasure but in an honest, if misguided, effort to relieve legitimate suffering. "It all started so innocently that, when I look back, I can hardly believe it," wrote the anonymous woman author of the *American Weekly* feature "I Was A Sleeping Pill Addict" (see fig. 4.3). "That's the way almost all of us began, of course. I never heard of anyone

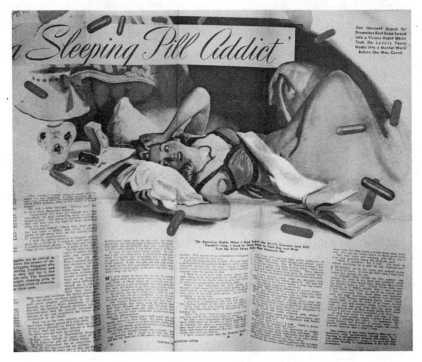

Figure 4.3. The media often portrayed people addicted to barbiturates—especially white women—as sympathetic victims; note the text box in the upper right corner: "Her Innocent Search for Dreamless Rest Soon Turned Into a Vicious Habit Which Took the Lovely Young Model Into a Mental Ward Before She Was Cured." *American Weekly*, 16 May 1948, Box 1996, Folder "Barbiturate Vol III, 1948, Jan–Dec," FDA Papers. Joe Watson Little/ American Weekly; National Archives.

deliberately getting into the sleeping pill habit except for cokies— narcotic addicts." She had no independent desire for barbiturates, in other words, and took no pleasure in them. She was just following the physician's orders. "Some nights I was too sleepy to bother," she wrote: "My mother actually used to wake up me, frequently with great difficulty, to remind me to take my pills! Neither of us knew what they were then. They were just medicine the doctor had prescribed."[103]

This focus on innocent victims, especially white women, was a standard consumer advocate strategy that had helped achieve the FDA earlier in the century. Anti-narcotics crusades, too, emphasized white women at risk: narcotic scare stories often featured thrill-seeking white women lured by foreigners or racial minorities into lives of addiction, crime, and sexual slavery. This hitched drug prohibition to the politically potent agenda of policing the sexual boundaries of race. Barbiturate stories deployed white women in a different way: to dramatize the risks innocent consumers faced in a market ruled by profit. Without regulation, warned *Everybody's Digest* in 1945, an unchecked "sales ballyhoo" would "ultimately force a goof ball down every American gullet."[104] Samuel Hopkins Adams urged regulation because otherwise, the profit motive would inevitably lead to mass overuse: "the incentive to push sales mountainously high is great, since the profit is large."[105]

Therapeutic reformers were thus trying to chart a narrow path: generate enough moral outrage to attract the interest (and support) of traditional anti-drug crusaders, while channeling that outrage not toward prohibition but regulation of legal white market institutions. It was a tough sell.

For one thing, the ultimate anti-drug crusader, Harry Anslinger, was firmly opposed. Anslinger was a cagey politician who knew a losing prospect when he saw one. His agency's ability to regulate pharmaceutical opioids rested on two things: the relative ease of controlling a medical market that physicians had already voluntarily clamped down on; and popular support for near-absolute prohibition based on simple, racist morality tales about "dope fiends," "white slaves," and international crime lords.[106] Barbiturates, on the other hand, were still wildly popular among physicians and white market consumers. Policing such an enormous and growing market would be an unprecedented logistical challenge. The FBN would have to grow significantly and request much more funding from Congress—something Anslinger had hated to do.[107] Moreover, drugs widely embraced as "medicines" by respectable white market consumers offered little cultural opportunity for the kind of brute-force demonization through which Anslinger had built his authority.

For these reasons Anslinger had always fiercely resisted the occasional call for his agency to take over control of barbiturates.[108] Instead he actively supported the passage of state laws.[109] He did waver once, during World War II, when heroin was scarce and many people with addiction turned in desperation to barbiturates.[110] Now that barbiturates were being used by easily identifiable "dope fiends," Anslinger mused that it might be "an opportune time for the Federal Government to step in and control barbiturates along with other drugs."[111] He even suggested to a friendly pharmacologist that "now is the time to develop the background for legislation similar to the work you did in connection with cannabis."[112] The effort appears to have borne at least some fruit, to judge by sensationalist articles that appeared in pulp detective magazines like *Smash Detective* and *True Detective*, claiming that "dope dealers" had switched to peddling pills.[113]

Barbiturates were low on Anslinger's busy wartime priority list, though, and he never took real action against them. When peace— and heroin commodity chains—returned, Anslinger, too, returned to his previous position. He came out strongly against the Rogers bill in private, in Congress, and to the media.[114]

Anslinger had little trouble finding allies in his fight against Rogers's plan. The pharmaceutical industry and the medical and pharmacy professions, all of whom had been brought on board the anti-narcotics bandwagon back in the 1910s, were united in opposition this time around. The drug industry would be an obvious loser if barbiturate markets shrank significantly. Pharmacists, too, fretted over "back-breaking record-keeping burdens" if barbiturates were put into the "narcotic strait-jacket," worried that refill sales would be lost to "strangling government restriction," and complained that physician dispensing would be unfairly privileged over pharmacy sales.[115] The AMA, meanwhile, had become increasingly protective of professional prerogatives and skeptical of federal interference in medicine. To them, Rogers's bill smacked of "a trend to confer more and more jurisdiction of the Federal Government over the practice of medicine."[116]

Reformist elements in all these opposing groups did believe that something ought to be done about barbiturates, if only because of the negative publicity the "barbiturate shame" was generating.[117] So the American Pharmaceutical Association convened a 1945 conference with representatives from the AMA, the pharmaceutical industry, the National Association of Boards of Pharmacy, the FDA, and the FBN (Anslinger himself).[118] The goal was to head off "drastic federal action" by developing their own alternative: a relatively lenient model state law that required a physician's prescription for retail sales (including refills), required druggists to keep records of prescriptions and sales receipts, and made possession without a prescription illegal. Manufacturers, wholesalers, and other commercial suppliers faced no new restrictions other than the requirement to retain "the usual commercial or other records" for two years.[119]

This relatively weak model state law was a clever strategy to divert reformist zeal toward shoring up the medical/nonmedical divide rather than allowing intrusive federal regulation of white markets. The barbiturate crisis was real, opponents argued, but white markets were not to blame. They were functioning properly, providing useful medicines to consumers who needed them.[120] True, there were occasional problems with dishonorable druggists or physicians, but these were extremely rare—out-and-out rogues who were best policed locally, by the professional bodies closest to the problem, rather than by distant federal bureaucrats or police. The real cause of the barbiturate crisis was criminals taking advantage of easy accessibility to divert pills to informal markets, where, without physicians' expert guidance, they caused mayhem and death.[121] To solve this problem did not require restricting white markets, but rather building stronger walls around it.[122]

Doubling down on the medicine-drug divide was a brilliant tactic that exposed a key weakness in therapeutic reformers' plan. Reformers hoped to woo traditional moral crusaders by adopting the sensationalist rhetoric of drug depravity and death. They hoped it would not matter that the targets of their sensationalism were not racialized "dope fiends" but pillars of respectable society: physicians, druggists, and the pharmaceutical industry. Opponents of Rogers's bill, meanwhile, focused squarely on criminals and deviants and promised to shut down their access to drugs. This message was much more in keeping with moral crusaders' interests and kept them from adding their considerable muscle to the anti-barbiturate campaign. On their own, therapeutic reformers did not have enough clout to overcome the breadth and depth of opposition. Rogers's bill was voted down easily in 1947 and again in 1949.

The high point of the medicine-drug divide

As the barbiturate crisis deepened, therapeutic reformers were not ready to give up. Yet obstacles intensified and their own ranks were thinning. The pro-business politics of the 1950s did not favor new efforts to regulate industry. Therapeutic reformers, too, shifted with their professions toward a deeper skepticism of government "interference." Even the most committed therapeutic reformers began to sour on the FBN's clearly failing punitive prohibition regime. Meanwhile, a surge in urban heroin markets helped moral crusaders associate addiction ever more firmly with racialized "dope fiends." The result was the high water mark of the medicine-drug divide in American history: draconian punishments for informal-market narcotics even as reformers failed almost completely in their efforts to rein in barbiturates.

The battleground for this political rout was one last, monumental effort to add barbiturates to the Harrison Act in 1951. Two developments made the time seem right for this final push. First, moral crusaders, pointing to growing heroin use in increasingly African American northern cities, sought to double down on the FBN's punitive regime with the Boggs Act, which imposed mandatory minimum prison sentences for drug infractions. Second, Committee experts such as Harris Isbell had finally produced definitive proof that, as he put it, "chronic barbiturate intoxication represents a true addiction—no matter how addiction is defined." By administering barbiturates to former narcotic addicts at the Lexington hospital for several months and then withdrawing them, Harris showed that tolerance, emotional and physical dependence, and abstinence syndrome all occurred. In fact, Isbell warned, "The manifestations of chronic barbiturate intoxication are, in most ways, much more seri-

ous than those of addiction to morphine" because mental and mo-
tor impairment were more extreme and withdrawal symptoms more
dangerous, including psychoses and grand mal seizures.[123]

Armed with Isbell's findings and seeing Congress's high-profile
anti-narcotics hearings as a perfect vehicle, Rogers once again introduced her bill while her allies sounded sensationalist warnings
about what the women's magazine *Coronet* obligingly called "Sleeping Pills: The Doorway to Doom."

Despite the seemingly auspicious moment, however, the effort
fell flat. Almost no significant interest group offered support and the
FBN continued to oppose. Anslinger (somewhat disingenuously)
argued that his agency focused on illicit sales, whereas barbiturate
commerce was largely medical; there was "no smuggling" and "very
little peddling." To focus on an enormous legal supply from "literally hundreds" of manufacturers, the Bureau would have to grow to
many times its current size. The new-look FBN would then have the
unenviable task of applying harsh police tactics against barbiturates'
largely white and middle-class consumer base. This, Anslinger
feared, would create "conditions . . . similar to Prohibition" and
make his beloved agency "a very unpopular bureau in this country."[124]

Many therapeutic reformers, meanwhile, had become even less
comfortable with a Harrison-style approach for barbiturates. The
AMA's witness, for example, told Congress that barbiturates were
indeed dangerous and should be sold only by prescription, but opposed what he described as a slippery slope of increased government
power. "If this trend is to continue," he cautioned, "we may eventually come to a situation where no drug that may be of harm to a patient if used unwisely may be prescribed by a physician without the
consent of the Federal Government."[125] Robert Fischelis, the reformist head of the American Pharmaceutical Association, noted that
barbiturate deaths were still relatively rare—similar to the number
to people jumping off the Empire State Building. "That is a problem
too," he advised sarcastically; "you could legislate on that."[126] The
National Association of Retail Druggists was, predictably, even more
dubious. Barbiturates are "sedatives and not habit-forming drugs"

produced by "all the high class manufacturers of the country," its representative insisted. True, some addiction occurred, but "any drug in the U.S. Pharmacopeia might be habit-forming to certain individuals . . . barbiturates just happen to have come to the layman's attention through the blowing up of cases in which the drug was used for suicidal purposes and made a good newspaper story."[127]

These defections hurt, but perhaps the most damaging blow came from an unlikely source: Harris Isbell. As we have seen, Isbell and his Committee colleagues had long favored a more nuanced approach to the regulation of opioids, for example, one with multiple levels of control including less stringent restrictions on weaker or mid-strength opioids. Thus for Isbell, the mere fact that a drug could be addictive did not automatically mean that it deserved the same draconian treatment Congress was debating for heroin. Barbiturates, he noted, were "one of the most important groups of drugs in medicine." Tight restrictions might "deprive a lot of people who need it sometimes." Moreover, he argued, barbiturate addiction was rare because "you have to work at it considerably harder" than opioids.[128]

Isbell's hesitance to unleash the FBN on barbiturates was augmented by what appears to have been a surprising degree of skepticism about the effectiveness of drug prohibition altogether. He described the Rogers bill as "too severe" and warned that it would just "drive the people to something else," perhaps even by buying from an "illegal operation."[129] Addiction, he explained, was a psychological problem, not a quality of drugs. "Drugs are, after all, inert substances in the sense that they can't walk up and hit a man," he explained. "There is something wrong with the people who use drugs improperly," and "merely taking away barbiturates . . . is not going to solve his problem.[130] Meanwhile, he suggested, long-term, daily drug use was not necessarily bad: if people took only "one or two capsules a day" on medical advice, it would be perfectly "legitimate."[131] Ultimately, Isbell concluded, "in spite of the fact that I am responsible, personally responsible, for showing that, with respect to physical damage to the individual and to society, barbiturate addiction is worse than morphine addiction, I am not in favor of putting barbiturates under the narcotic laws.[132]

It is notable that when confronted by a drug crisis largely involving "respectable" consumers, Isbell was willing to support what he would have seen as radical policies in the context of opioids. He opposed prohibition because it would either "drive people to something else" or encourage criminal sales, and he accepted a version of maintenance: long-term daily use under a physician's care. He (and his Committee colleagues) rejected both approaches out of hand for opioids, whose consumers they saw as psychologically or morally flawed. Only in a white market context where all players enjoyed a presumption of "good faith" was Isbell's sensible pragmatism possible.[133]

With giants like Isbell joining the FBN and the medical and pharmacy professions in opposition, the final campaign to place barbiturates in the Harrison Act died with barely a whimper. The whimper did exist: Congress passed the Humphrey-Durham Act in 1952, a face-saving law that simply ratified the prescription-only powers that the FDA had already been enforcing for years and that the Supreme Court had finally approved in 1948.[134] The push to intensify punitive "narcotics" policies, meanwhile, met with easy success. The Boggs Act of 1951 imposed harsh mandatory minimum sentences for narcotics infractions, penalties toughened even further by the 1956 Narcotic Control Act.[135]

Conclusion

The mid-1950s were the high point of the medicine-drug divide. At the same moment, the federal government stamped down brutally on informal markets for opioids while allowing white markets for barbiturates to grow with few limits. This was no accident; it both reflected and helped strengthen the underlying social logic that made the medicine-drug divide make sense. The campaign to rein in barbiturates had shown tantalizing glimpses of what a pragmatic, consumer-protection policy might be if freed from the punitive imperative of moral crusaders. That campaign's repeated failure showed the difficulty of building such a policy without challenging the medicine-drug divide. The result, as we will see in the next chapter, was a drug crisis worse than any that had come before it, in white or informal markets.

5

A new crisis and a new response

Doubling down on the medicine-drug divide in the 1950s led to public health catastrophes on both sides of the line. White markets saw a seemingly never-ending rise in relatively unregulated barbiturate sales, even as tales of addiction, tragedy, and overdose mounted. Recognizing a growth sector, the pharmaceutical industry crowded in with a host of new drugs such as amphetamine stimulants and so-called minor tranquilizers. By the mid-1960s white market consumers were awash in more addictive drugs than ever—and were also suffering their direst crisis of addiction and overdose. Meanwhile, informal markets, too, careened out of control, with sales of heroin surging in relentless waves in the late 1940s, 1950s, and 1960s. With no consumer protections in place, and punitive prohibition the only governing rule, the impact of such sales (and their policing) on already marginalized communities was devastating.

By the late 1960s both halves of the medicine-drug divide were suffering crises so serious that the whole policy structure was called into question. In particular, two new groups began calling for potentially radical reforms. The first was a reenergized consumer advocacy movement, deeply skeptical of corporate capitalism and in favor of robust protections to limit what they saw as routine and inevitable malfeasance in a wide range of industries, including pharmaceuticals. The second were medicalizers, who called for medical treatment rather than punishment for people with addiction. Both groups were influenced by civil rights and feminist activism, which were challenging the cultural hierarchies of race, class, and gender that had long served as crucial glue for the medicine-drug divide. The result was a moment of reform, capped by the 1970 Controlled Substances Act, that raised questions about, but did not ultimately overturn, some of the deepest architecture of American drug policy.

The midcentury white market drug crisis

THE CANARY IN THE COAL MINE: BARBITURATES

To understand the reforms of the late 1960s, we first need to understand the deepening white market crisis that helped provoke them. The same presumptions of good faith that had stymied policy reform also impeded enforcement, leaving manufacturers, physicians, pharmacists, and consumers relatively free to develop white markets as they wanted. It soon became clear that what they wanted was more barbiturates—for good and for ill.

A central feature of barbiturate white markets was that physicians faced virtually no limits on prescribing. White markets, after all, were defined as zones of commerce protected by physicians; it would make no sense to protect them *from* physicians. Yet as the FDA quickly realized, physicians did not always play their proper role. Therapeutic reformers had been complaining about too-free prescribing since the 1920s, and the 1951 Humphrey-Durham law gave the FDA no new tools to restrain it. Indeed, the FDA directed its agents not to search for or even ask about overprescribing doctors: they should rather be "so notoriously flagrant" that they will "inevitably come to attention in the normal course of our work."[1] Even flagrant cases were "generally not within the scope of our jurisdiction," one district office explained; "whenever it became apparent that the source of drug supply was a physician, we dropped the investigation."[2] In 1955, a district office formally admonished an agent for merely talking to a physician involved in a case: "despite our beliefs and convictions, our job is not to interfere with the practice of medicine, and regardless of motive, to do so can only invite criticism. The investigation was complete when it had been ascertained that the barbiturates obtained . . . were on legitimate prescriptions or on refill authorized by the doctor."[3]

Such restrictions meant that FDA agents could do little more than watch even "flagrant" physicians. In a single 1954 report from the Baltimore district, for example, agents complained about, but took no action on, three physicians: a Charleston county coroner literally handing out barbiturates "on the street"; a Huntington coroner who "issues prescriptions to anyone requesting them"; and a physician purchasing barbiturates "in quantities of more than 20,000 at a time."[4] In 1953, agents in Martinsville, Virginia, complained of their "inability to prevent two doctors . . . from issuing prescriptions to known addicts under fictitious names, and authorizing the sale of 50 or more capsules at a time." "The only thing that is left," they reported glumly, "is to wait for these addicts to violate some local or state law and arrest them and confiscate the drugs."[5] In Hillsville, Virginia, meanwhile, FDA agents chafed at their inability to help a local sheriff who sat impotently outside a doctor's office, arresting visibly inebriated "patients" (many from nearby Mt. Airy, North Carolina) for public intoxication as they exited.[6]

The FDA did, technically, have some authority over physicians who "dispensed," that is, who sold barbiturates directly to patients. Such physicians did not have to keep records like a pharmacist, but they were still required to abide by labeling requirements. Even in the unlikely event that the FDA did give an agent permission to investigate a dispensing physician, however, there were tight restrictions on how to do so. According to the agency's 1956 operations manual, agents conducting "sting" buys were cautioned that "it is imperative that an air of commercialism be maintained at all times." The slightest hint of medical need should be avoided: "Never display or discuss symptoms. Make it known, indirectly or directly . . . that the drugs are for nonmedical use. Purchase in as large amounts as possible and make it clear that some or all of the drugs which you are purchasing are for use by some individual other than yourself who, insofar as you know, the doctor has never seen."[7] In other words, only dispensing that did not even make a pretense of conforming to white market expectations—that was openly, even defi-antly commercial—could be subjected to scrutiny.

Physicians were virtually off-limits, but even pharmacists, over whom the FDA had unambiguous authority, often benefited from white market protections. The FDA routinely declined to prosecute cases lacking what the agency referred to as "background," "color," or "atmosphere"—in other words, behavior so outrageous that no one could defend it.[8] "We need to be able to show in all cases . . . that the store habitually violated the law and that the inspectors only gave the pharmacist an opportunity to commit violations in his customary manner," the FDA explained in rejecting a Wilmington, Delaware, agent's case in 1954.[9] Anything less than overt criminality might leave room for juries to see the transaction through its presumptive lens of good faith. For example, FDA agents attempting undercover nonprescription purchases were warned not to claim to be a medical student, to "beg drugs for an allegedly sick wife or child or relatives," or to "play upon the vendor's sympathies" in any way.[10]

Such guidelines give a sense of just how much territory was protected by the mantle of legitimate medical need. The apparent absurdity of such categorizations—that, for example, inventing a sick wife risked qualifying a transaction as medical—underscored the importance of social factors in determining white market boundaries. It was not the sick wife that made the transaction medical; it was the presumption of good faith indicated by the whiteness and respectability on both sides of the transaction. Unsurprisingly (as one FDA agent noted in 1949), many over-the-counter sales seemed to involve "quite respectable women enlisting the aid of a personal acquaintance in the profession in counter prescribing [selling without a prescription] for them."[11]

At least some pharmacists were fully aware of this dynamic and actively used it to shield themselves from oversight. In Tulsa, Oklahoma, for example, an FBN agent reported that local pharmacists had become "careful not to sell to persons who it appeared were using the drugs for other than medicinal purposes."[12] Such judgments were, of course, fundamentally shaped by the class, race, and gender presumptions built into the medicine-drug divide. Especially in small towns, they made "sting" purchases nearly impossible. Enforcement was effectively brought to a standstill in entire rural regions such as East Texas, for example, even though the FDA inspectors judged that area to be "our greatest problem" with "the indiscriminate sale of dangerous drugs, particularly sleeping tablets."[13] Resistance to federal oversight appears to have been coordinated in some cases: after the FDA investigated more than a dozen Kansas City drugstores in 1951, the state's Pharmacy Association put out a special bulletin warning druggists to beware of entrapment.[14] In any case, cagey pharmacists were enough of a problem that in 1953 the FDA advised inspectors to, in effect, become regular customers at stores before attempting to make "sting" purchases.[15]

Sometimes physicians and pharmacists worked together to protect local white markets from FDA interference. An Omaha, Nebraska, doctor who owned a drugstore, for example, left a pad of presigned prescription forms at the counter for his pharmacist employee to use whenever a customer needed one. Upon being criticized by the FDA in 1951 the doctor was unapologetic, saying that in the future he would have the druggist send customers to his office, where he would "glance at them" and write a prescription at no charge. The FDA saw no way to prosecute such behavior, although the agent did plaintively request a "text-book definition of what constitutes a prescription" (something the Harrison Act would have provided).[16] In 1955 in Bristol, Tennessee, a druggist sold thousands of pills over the counter to the secretary of the local Alcoholics Anonymous group; after his arrest, a local doctor quickly wrote up prescriptions to cover for the sales.[17]

That all of these incidents were so egregious points to another way the politics of respectability operated to protect white markets: the FDA became aware of a problem only if it was reported by trusted local authorities. The FDA had only 230 inspectors, most of whom were occupied with the agency's main mission of ensuring the safety and reliability of the nation's food and drug supply. The science-oriented agency had not been designed to police America's

50,000 drugstores and nearly 200,000 physicians.[18] It had to pick and choose who to investigate. "There will be no hit and miss visits to drugstores," agents were informed in 1948; instead, "sting" purchases should be attempted only as part of "significant" investigations developed after evidence of misbehavior.[19] As late as 1960, the FDA still proclaimed proudly that "we do not engage in random shopping of drugstores. We investigate only when we have responsible complaints—commonly from physicians, hospitals, coroners, police, or other pharmacists."[20]

Unlike the Harrison regime, in other words, there was no universal definition of a problematic drug transaction. Instead, a problematic transaction was one that caused problems for local police or physicians. Local traditions, or professional wagon circling, could thus trump consumer protection. In 1959, for example, the FDA warned agents that they should proceed in cases only where a druggist's behavior was seen as reckless and irresponsible by other druggists and physicians in the area. They cited a case against a druggist that had been dropped because sixteen area physicians had submitted affidavits stating that there was a general understanding in the town that prescriptions could be refilled without consulting the physician unless there were written instructions to the contrary.[21] A better practice, the FDA advised, was to proceed from the other direction: to begin with information from "responsible" figures such as journalists reporting on poisoning deaths or strange drug-related behavior; officials at hospitals, jails, and police stations registering overdose deaths, accidental burn cases, or suspicious druggist behavior; or concerned citizens (often pharmacists or physicians, perhaps competitors).[22]

Such constraints clearly frustrated field agents from time to time, but they served an important function: avoiding conflict with the type of respectable white market actors whose support was crucial given the FDA's weak statutory powers. The importance of this support can be seen in the fate of a seemingly reasonable plan the FDA proposed to its field offices in 1951. The idea was that, instead of hunting for problematic transactions, the FDA could go straight to the source, requiring wholesalers to provide information about all very large barbiturate sales. Agents could then visit the large-scale purchasers and make sure everything was legitimate. The FDA's field offices were completely uninterested. One office worried that the tactic would produce too many leads for them to pursue; another complained that the numbers were useless without knowing the size of the purchasing drugstore; several noted that the numbers would not provide the "background information which would lend color and weight to the case when presented in court." In the end, the FDA concluded that "this scheme is not worth the effort it takes."[23]

In theory, federal authorities should have benefited from the overlapping oversight of state medical and pharmaceutical boards, which did have much stronger regulatory power. But these boards were poorly positioned to take up the slack even when they wanted to. For one thing, state laws were variable and often weak. Some outlawed sale without a prescription but provided no penalty for transgressors. Others imposed only minor penalties such as fines.[24] Even in the strictest states, enforcement was challenging. Virtually no medical board did any investigation or disciplining of physicians for barbiturate or amphetamine practices in the 1950s.[25] Pharmacy boards, meanwhile, were ill equipped for police work and, in the vast majority of cases, were provided with no new funding. In Louisiana, for example, reformers managed to pass a barbiturate law only after funding for enforcement was stripped out.[26]

Moreover, both medical and pharmacy boards were professional advocates as well as regulatory bodies, and they were not always eager to cooperate with federal agencies. In most states, boards were appointed by the governor from a list provided by the state medical or pharmaceutical association. It is no surprise that some were zealous in protecting their professional prerogatives from federal intrusion. "Officials in a few states," an FDA researcher reported in 1953, "were frank to say that they did not approve of Federal activity in this field," and some criticized FDA enforcement methods as "approaching on 'entrapment.'"[27] New York's pharmacy board declared that it was "not charged with enforcement" of prescription-only laws; health and police officers, aware of the futility of passing along barbiturate cases, ignored them and focused solely on "narcotics violations" instead.[28] In Alaska, a Juneau pharmacy board member literally laughed when asked in 1948 whether local pharmacists kept records of sales. He pointed out that the board's total two-year budget was only $1,000, and derisively snorted that "he wasn't going out and play detective on that kind of money."[29]

Medical and pharmacy boards were thus uneven partners in enforcing prescription-only laws. In 1953, all state pharmacy boards together devoted the equivalent of twenty-three inspector years to over-the-counter investigations, approximately the same number as the FDA. They were very unevenly distributed, with over 65 percent of the inspection time coming from just four states: New York, Michigan, Florida, and California. New York alone accounted for more than 80 percent of the 564 state-level prosecutions. Meanwhile, eighteen states saw no state-level prosecutions at all, and twenty-one others saw just a handful. The FDA, meanwhile, notched only 111 convictions; these were spread relatively evenly across the fifty states, but even so, vast expanses of the country could essentially expect little to no barbiturate policing.[30]

In addition to protecting physicians and pharmacists, the white market presumption of good faith extended to consumers as well. As we have seen, the assumption that barbiturate users were health-seeking "consumers" rather than pleasure-seeking "dope fiends" or "junkies" was a truism accepted by even the most passionate reformers. Indeed, one of the most notable—and telling—differences between pharmaceutical regulations and narcotics laws in the 1950s was that possession of barbiturates without a prescription was not illegal. The FDA explicitly discouraged its agents from pursuing leads on consumers: "the time would yield more consumer protection," agents were advised, "if spent in developing cases against primary sources of supply rather than peddlers or, in this case, the user."[31]

The presumption that white market consumers did not experience pleasure from their drug use is peculiar but was so pervasive as to go essentially unmentioned. Take, for example, an unusual case from 1960, in which a pharmacist in a middle-class suburb of Milwaukee was actually disciplined for over-the-counter sales by the state pharmacy board. Despite protesting that he "carried on a reputable business" in "a nice store," he received a four-month suspension of his license.[32] His customer, however, was easily able to portray herself as an entirely passive victim just following medical advice. The board accepted without question her claim to have had no idea what she was buying: "I just—I am not familiar with anything of that sort."[33]

The presumption of innocent docility gave white market consumers privileged, unpunished access to pharmaceutical relief, but it also deprived them of sorely needed protections. Take, for example, the case of a Las Vegas woman who used aliases to garner prescriptions for twelve types of barbiturates from seven physicians in a single day. "Due to Mrs. [A]'s obviously ill condition," FDA investigators noted, "she had had no trouble in obtaining the prescriptions" despite being a heavy drinker and having accidentally set fire to five different homes in the past two years. The FDA, concluding that the sales had been legal, declined to investigate.[34] FDA records are rife with cases where agents were unable to do anything about consumers who endlessly refilled prescriptions, visited multiple physicians to bulk up on prescriptions, or engaged in other dangerous behaviors.[35] Consumers were protected not only from punishment, in other words, but also from assistance when their drug use warranted it.

Faced with such limits on its ability to regulate white market sales, the FDA shifted tactics in the 1950s. Instead of focusing on white markets, it turned its attention to the ancillary informal markets that had begun to emerge in bars, hotels, and other nonmedical locales thanks to the vast and lightly regulated flow of barbiturates.[36] Noting in 1953 that "some of the traffic at least is going underground," for example, a Florida FDA agent requested permission to develop criminal cases instead of "just hauling pharmacists in front of the Pharmacy Board."[37] The central office was listening. After Congress reduced the FDA's enforcement funds in 1954, a new memo ordered agents to stop inspecting any but the most egregious pharmacies and instead focus more on criminal cases.[38] The agency began to decline to prosecute traditional over-the-counter cases in favor of "difficult undercover investigations of critical situations."[39]

This shift to focusing on informal markets had the benefit of avoiding conflict with powerful groups such as physicians, pharmacists, and their reputable customers. Secretive sales at bars and hotels could not be portrayed as medical to sympathetic juries, nor would they be defended by professional associations. Moreover, they often involved disreputable buyers and sellers, sometimes even racial minorities, who did not enjoy a presumption of innocence. Yet, of course, the FDA's new focus on informal markets left white markets even freer than before. Even as they cracked down on truck-stop sales, for example, authorities were unable to take action against a mail-order company that supplied barbiturates to over 20,000 customers who presented a physician's certificate affirming that they suffered from epilepsy.[40]

Weak government regulation and enforcement did not mean that barbiturate white markets grew in some natural, organic way in the decade after World War II. Markets are always regulated; the question is, who regulates them and toward what end? For barbiturates, the void left by weak state oversight left the pharmaceutical industry as the primary regulator. Reflecting their priorities, white markets were not primarily oriented to maximize consumer safety or to serve the public health, but rather to encourage consumption by white, middle-class buyers, especially women.

A decade of relatively free sales was more than enough time to entrench barbiturate use in white, middle-class American life, establishing white market habits that would be very difficult to uproot. At their peak in 1954, barbiturates were estimated to be in nearly one out of every six prescriptions—quite an accomplishment in an era that saw the introduction of "wonder drugs" like antibiotics.[41] This one-in-six figure did not even include illegal over-the-counter sales, although the FDA estimated that they were as much as half of all barbiturate sales.[42]

The simple fact of widespread use does not, on its own, indicate a crisis. After all, most barbiturate use, like most drug use, was not harmful. Many consumers undoubtedly benefited from the sleep or easing of anxiety the pills offered. The problem was that barbiturate white markets were not configured to promote the beneficial kind of use and discourage the harmful kind. Instead they promoted almost any kind of use by "respectable" people and discouraged or even disallowed any kind of use by others. Few protections existed to prevent addiction, or to care for consumers if they did become addicted. It is impossible to know with certainty how many Americans were harmed by this market failure, but it is possible to make educated guesses. Sales were so massive that they could have supplied as many as 1.5 million long-term, high-dose consumers.[43] Obviously not all barbiturate sales went to such consumers, but if we apply a standard pareto distribution and assume that 20 percent of the consumers made 80 percent of the purchases, the number still remained over a million.[44] This would be an order of magnitude more than similar figures for the nineteenth century's white market crisis, and dwarfed even the direst estimates of informal-market heroin use. And for the first time, a white market crisis was also fatal. Barbiturate overdoses spiked during the sales boom, with per capita deaths rising by more than fourfold from 1933 to 1950 (see fig. A.4 in the appendix).[45]

SELLING INTO THE TEETH OF THE CRISIS: AMPHETAMINE AND TRANQUILIZERS

For a decade after World War II barbiturates were highly profitable and seemingly immune from constraining regulations. This was catnip to the pharmaceutical industry, and white markets soon saw a chaotic stampede of new psychoactive products. The two most important types were stimulants (primarily amphetamine), and sedatives (primarily "minor tranquilizers" like meprobamate and the benzodiazepines). Companies selling these drugs followed the marketing template established by barbiturates: medicalization, prod-

uct differentiation, and selling sickness. They were wildly successful. Sales quickly outpaced even the barbiturates, flooding postwar
white markets with more addictive drugs than at any other time in
the twentieth century.

The earliest new white market drug was amphetamine, discovered in 1929 and adopted as Benzedrine in 1934 by Smith, Kline &
French (SKF).[46] SKF had to work quite hard to establish the drug's
medical status. It did not initially know what it might be useful for,
so it offered free samples to physicians to try it and report on their
experiences. The company found a winner with psychiatrist Abra-
ham Myerson, who claimed good outcomes in a new condition he
had identified: "anhedonia," or mild depression. SKF recognized the
value of Myerson's coinage, which "massively broadened" a condition that had previously been thought quite rare. SKF launched a
marketing campaign to teach physicians about mild depression, built
on an infrastructure of company-funded, company-micromanaged,
and, in some cases, even company-written research. Negative studies went unpublished, and hints that amphetamine might be addictive were zealously tracked and quashed.[47] Fortunately for SKF, the
same cultural and conceptual obstacles to recognizing barbiturates'
addictiveness extended to amphetamine as well. In 1941, for example, the nation's leading pharmacology textbook declared that
"habituation to Benzedrine may occur . . . similar to the habit formation produced by caffeine and nicotine, but addiction in the strict
sense of the word is unknown."[48]

World War II interrupted the development of amphetamine as
an antidepressant, and civilian use remained relatively rare until
1945. After that, however, amphetamine sales boomed dramatically, powered by new formulations carefully tailored to address
major postwar cultural concerns. One such new formulation was
Dexedrine, marketed for obesity and "pre-obesity." Another was
the amphetamine-barbiturate combination Dexamyl, introduced
in 1950 for the treatment of "psychoneuroses," a ubiquitous, vague,
and relatively mild set of psychological problems. Dexamyl was
advertised for everyday "mental and emotional distress," and por-

trayed in advertisements as easing the anxieties, stresses, and ir-
ritabilities of middle-class housewives, businessmen, and others.[49]

SKF could make such claims because, like barbiturates, amphetamine did not face the kind of regulatory scrutiny trained on opioids. There had been no formal, premarketing assessment of amphetamine's addictiveness, and the FBN was not there to restrain
the company's dramatic expansion of amphetamine's uses. The
FDA put the drug on its prescription-only list in 1940, but even by
1953 twenty states still had no restrictions on amphetamines.[50] The
FDA thus stood largely alone in regulating amphetamine during the
crucial formative years it was on the market.

Moreover, one form of amphetamine was excluded from the prescription requirement altogether: inhalers intended to treat nasal
congestion. Ironically, these were among the most dangerous forms
of the drug since consumers could break them open to swallow the
"wick" and experience an intense version of the drug's psychoactive
effects. This type of use surfaced almost immediately in a range of
settings such as the military, the jazz scene, and avant-garde groups
such as the Beat poets. To protect the drug's reputation and to ward
off regulation, SKF added irritants to the wicks to make them unpleasant to use. This failed to deter consumers, and in 1949, with
federal prescription-only controls seemingly imminent, the company withdrew its amphetamine inhalers and replaced them with
a less psychoactive version. Because SKF had acted before federal
controls were imposed, however, inhalers remained legal for over-
the-counter sales, and other companies stepped in with their own
versions. It was not until 1959 that the FDA finally managed to declare all inhalers prescription-only.[51]

As with barbiturates, the FDA focused more on policing informal markets than regulating white markets. A large undercover investigation of truck stops received 20 percent of FDA enforcement
time in 1955.[52] For an agency designed to inspect and certify legal
markets, a police-style undertaking like this was no easy task. It
required months of specialized training and new procedures and
equipment—all paid for out of the same (shrinking) FDA budget.[53]

With regulation and enforcement so weak and advertising so intense, medical markets for amphetamine, like those for barbiturates, proliferated wildly in the years after World War II. By 1962 the FDA estimated that eight billion pills, or a remarkable forty-three per person, were being sold annually.[54] Amphetamines did not produce the kind of fatal overdoses that barbiturates did, but they could foster addiction and produce psychosis in some heavy users.[55]

As popular as it was, amphetamine was not the bestselling newcomer to postwar psychoactive white markets. This distinction belongs to the minor tranquilizers, a new generation of sedatives first introduced by Miltown (meprobamate) in 1955 and then dominated by benzodiazepines Librium and Valium starting in the early 1960s. Manufacturers for these drugs successfully transformed a white market sector oriented around insomnia into a new, far larger sector oriented around "anxiety" and "stress."

Carter Products initially made a splash with Miltown by marketing it as a scientific advance over barbiturates. Rather than dulling a person's senses, Miltown supposedly zeroed in on anxiety itself and left the consumer tranquil but alert. Carter Products—a former patent medicine company—made this claim through a full-scale blitz, beginning with a special conference for physicians at the Waldorf Astoria hotel and continuing with a constant stream of advertisements including the front-cover slot in every issue of the *American Journal of Psychiatry* for an entire decade.[56] The marketing campaign also "educated" the public about the importance of anxiety and its miraculous new treatment, using a range of techniques from cultivating friendly science journalists to stunts like commissioning famed surrealist Salvador Dali to make a sculpture, *Release from Anxiety*.[57] In all these contexts, of course, the company made sure to portray Miltown as an element of respectable, white, middle-class life and its everyday problems—necessary to prevent unwanted comparisons with the "dope" being sold outside medical markets.

Like SKF and amphetamine, Carter undertook this massive campaign to expand uses for Miltown without the kind of regulatory scrutiny or pushback that hobbled opioids. Most important, Carter was allowed to pursue a strategy repeatedly denied to opioid manufacturers: claiming that its new drug was nonaddictive based on the convenient fact that it was new and thus had not (yet) produced cases of addiction. Depicting Miltown as a nonaddictive alternative to the wildly popular but increasingly frightening barbiturates offered a hope that private enterprise could solve the white market problems that so bedeviled therapeutic reformers. Although that turned out not be the case, the market certainly rewarded Carter Products: sales nearly tripled in the year after Miltown was introduced, and at its peak Miltown was estimated to have been included in more than one out of every ten prescriptions.[58]

Roche Pharmaceuticals re-created and then surpassed Carter Product's success with the benzodiazepine tranquilizers Librium (introduced in 1961) and Valium (introduced in 1963). Powered by the marketing creativity of pioneering public relations firm William Douglas McAdams, led by psychiatrists Arthur, Raymond, and Mortimer Sackler, benzodiazepine marketing was even more intense than Miltown's had been.[59] Advertisements and "education" campaigns expanded the range of experiences that qualified as medically significant anxiety, and extended tranquilizers' reach into new areas such as cardiovascular health, stomach issues, and more. Like all other white market companies, Roche fended off fear of addictiveness by linking its products to white, middle-class consumers and their problems.[60]

By the mid-1960s white markets were awash with psychoactive pharmaceuticals and manufacturers were awash in profits. One survey estimated that a sedative or a stimulant was included in more than one out of every four prescriptions written in the United States from 1955 through 1968—and sales continued to rise through the early 1970s (see figs. A.2 and A.3 in the appendix). In 1965, 65 million prescriptions were written for barbiturates, 85 million for tranquilizers, and 26 million for amphetamine.[61] In 1967, 31 percent of all American women and 15 percent of men had used a sedative or stimulant in the past year. Use was twice as common among white as among black Americans and nearly twice as common among middle to high earners as compared to low earners. This confirmed the demographics of white markets—and suggests that the true usage rate among those white market consumers was higher than the already striking topline national numbers.[62]

Mass sales with weak consumer protection exacted a heavy toll on the public health. It is difficult to assess how many people actually suffered specifically from addiction because there was no effort to measure this statistic at the time. Then, too, the nature of white markets confounded any easy accounting because many long-term, regular consumers—people with a stable and reliable supply—were not forced by circumstance into the illegal or harmful behaviors associated with addiction. Yet as with barbiturates, available evidence does provide at least a ballpark sense of the scope. By the early 1970s, as many as 5 percent of all Americans (ten million people) reported using Valium "regularly" (daily for months or more at a time). The figure was twice that—10 percent—for women.[63] If even a small portion of these regular consumers were addicted, the numbers would be staggering. Meanwhile there may have been as many as 300,000 people addicted to amphetamine by the end of the 1960s.[64]

No matter how these numbers are sliced, one thing is clear: white market sedatives and stimulants were responsible for far more addiction and harm than informal-market drugs like heroin. This was certainly true in the 1950s, when informal markets for heroin (and cocaine) were relatively small and geographically bounded in urban centers.[65] Even as heroin markets surged in the later 1960s and early 1970s, the number of people with heroin addiction peaked at an estimated 600,000 people—a calamitous number to be sure, but nowhere near comparable figures for pharmaceuticals, which probably numbered in the millions.[66] Overdose deaths were similarly disproportionate. The per capita rates of fatalities from pharmaceutical sedatives alone were at least four times higher than from all opioids in the 1950s, and they remained atop drug fatality charts even during the resurgence of heroin use in the 1960s and 1970s (see fig. A.4 in the appendix).[67] Within their protected sphere of psycho-active commerce, white markets had nurtured a catastrophic public health crisis.

Reforming the medicine-drug divide

The white market system was enormously resilient during the post-war decades despite the growing crisis. Reform became possible only after significant social and cultural changes reconfigured the political landscape in the 1960s. Those changes came in many forms and would be impossible to capture fully here, but, for our purposes, they can be categorized into two broad (and related) developments: first, the reappearance of consumer advocacy as a significant politi-cal force; and second, the increasing political and cultural power of medicalizers who believed that addiction was an illness to be treated rather than a moral failing to be punished. Over time, as both groups were influenced by civil rights and feminist activism, at least some reformers were moved to address deeper issues of social inequality and to raise questions about the medicine-drug divide itself.

These new players changed the political calculus of drug reform. What had been a bipolar debate between two groups (therapeutic reformers and moral crusaders) became a more complex affair. The new political landscape gave rise to a series of laws that brought a limited transformation to American drug policy. For the first time in the twentieth century, reforms did not simply double down on the medicine drug divide—protecting white markets while policing informal markets. Instead, the era's signature law, the Controlled Substances Act of 1970, challenged that division and raised the possibility of a unified policy across both markets organized around regulating major commercial actors to make consumption safer. This was a hesitant and incomplete step, however. The Controlled Substances Act was also shaped by the traditional punitive agenda with its manifold racial, class, and gender disparities. Later, in the 1980s, this punitive agenda triumphed, extinguishing the moment of almost-radical change. But in a century of divided drug policy, even this relatively minor and temporary departure deserves careful attention.

THE 1965 DRUG ABUSE CONTROL AMENDMENTS

The first major development was the emergence in the late 1950s and early 1960s of a new political coalition organized around the idea of consumer advocacy. Barbiturate reformers had found few allies in their quest to tackle corporate greed in the immediate postwar years, but as time wore on this began to change.[68] Despite the introduction of miracle drugs like the antibiotics, the pharmaceutical industry found itself on the defensive by the mid-1950s as a series of scandals revealed astonishing profits, price fixing, hidden drug risks, and questionable marketing tactics.[69] Meanwhile, outside the medical world, grassroots consumer activism was stirring among groups addressing issues as diverse as racial segregation and manipulative advertising.[70] These two streams of consumer politics merged in 1959, when anti-monopolist crusader Tennessee Senator Estes Kefauver turned his attention to the pharmaceutical industry. His high-profile hearings produced a new wave of media exposés of high prices and dubious benefits.[71]

Kefauver's hearings demonstrated the political viability of consumer advocacy after years of anti-regulatory commitment to "free enterprise." It was a perfect issue for new President John F. Kennedy, who was eager for ways to deliver on his campaign promises of dynamic and muscular government. In 1962, Kennedy supported a Consumers' Bill of Rights, and prescription drugs were among the poorly regulated products named as needing new protections. "The housewife is called upon to be an amateur electrician, mechanic, chemist, toxicologist, dietitian, and mathematician," he explained, "but she is rarely furnished the information she needs to perform these tasks proficiently." The problem was only worse, he continued, with the "extensive underground traffic" in the drugs that lax regulation had allowed to spring up.[72] Kennedy's full-throated support seemed to augur a shift in the political tides. "The words 'consumer protection' are being heard . . . with greater frequency and at higher governmental levels than since Franklin D. Roosevelt's New Deal," the trade journal *Drug Topics* warned readers.[73]

Drug Topics was not wrong to be concerned: one of consumer advocates' first federal victories was scored over pharmaceuticals. The Kefauver-Harris Amendments, passed in 1962, gave the FDA authority to require proof of effectiveness before drugs could be marketed and, for the first time, authority to regulate the content of advertising to physicians.[74] This was only the beginning. In 1962, led by Missouri Representative Leonore Sullivan and Connecticut Senator Thomas Dodd, Congress once again staged hearings on the "goof ball" and "thrill pill" menace, featuring a familiar mix of sensationalist horror stories, insistence on white market consumer innocence, and calls for corporate regulation rather than arresting consumers.[75] Criticisms of the pharmaceutical industry as unethically greedy had become more common—and more blunt. "Irresponsible, profit-hungry drug manufacturers should be more strictly regulated and controlled," one witness told Congress. Another, blaming drug companies for creating "a nation of 'pill heads,'" warned that "there is no limit to the efforts they will expend to suppress information concerning the addiction liability or misuse of dangerous drugs."[76]

No bill was passed in 1962, but new developments soon increased the chances of reform. The most vociferous federal opponent of new legislation, Harry Anslinger, retired in July 1962, replaced by a loyal lieutenant, Henry Giordano, who had none of Anslinger's connections or intimidating personal authority. Two weeks later, President Kennedy's former lover, actress Marilyn Monroe, died of a barbiturate overdose. White market drugs were thus very much on the agenda when Kennedy, freed by Anslinger's retirement, convened a White House Commission on Drugs and Narcotics for a top-to-bottom reconsideration of the nation's drug policy. Among other reforms, the Commission endorsed federal control of sedatives and stimulants, and in 1964, with the support of new President Lyndon Johnson, Congress once again took up the cause.[77] Passage was all but assured in 1965, when Johnson was reelected in a landslide along with a dominating majority of liberal Democrats.

In the newly liberal Washington, moral crusaders were far less important as coalition partners, leaving consumer advocates free to focus on the pharmaceutical industry and the medical and pharmacy professions rather than "dope fiends." The result was the Drug Abuse Control Act, passed in 1965, which imposed important new consumer protections. Records had to be kept for all drug transactions so that regulators could keep track of sales and use. Prescription refills were allowed only with a physician's written permission and were limited to five refills without a new in-person consultation. The FDA could add new drugs to the law without congressional approval if the agency's experts found them to have a "potential for abuse because of its depressant or stimulant effect on the central nervous system." Companies could protest and force formal hearings on such a determination, but the final decision lay with the FDA, not with Congress.[78] The FDA quickly contracted with the latest iteration of the National Research Council's Committee (now named the Committee on the Problems of Drug Dependence) to evaluate new sedatives and stimulants just as they did opioids.[79]

Most of these new powers targeted drug manufacturers, physicians, and pharmacists—not consumers. Nonmedical sales were illegal (e.g., sales without a prescription), but buying or possessing a controlled drug was not. Requirements such as physician approval for refills were not intended to punish consumers but rather to ensure that they bought drugs only from knowledgeable people focused on their health rather than their profit potential. This was, in short, no new prohibition law; it assumed that sedatives and stimulants would (and should) continue to be used extensively, and sought primarily to make that use safer.

For all its innovations, however, the new law still operated entirely within the architecture of the medicine-drug divide, and this placed real limits on the consumer protections it provided. First, regulations remained relatively weak. The law imposed meaningful new limits on distributors and pharmacists, for example, but barely touched manufacturers or physicians, whose decisions determined the overall volume of drug supply. The FDA could add new drugs, but the process for doing so was arduous and allowed pharmaceutical companies to delay for years as markets became entrenched. For example, even though Congress had specifically named Valium as a drug that should be controlled by the new law, Roche's protests and appeals stymied FDA action until 1973—not coincidentally when the patent ran out.[80]

Second and even more important, whatever policy advances the 1965 law did achieve were entirely limited to white markets. Consumer advocates had little interest in informal markets, whose customers they did not recognize as "consumers." To the extent that they did think of informal markets at all, they shared moral crusaders' belief that nonmedical sales and use should be entirely prohibited. Indeed, one of the law's main provisions created a new agency within the FDA, the Bureau of Drug Abuse Control, which could field armed agents to investigate and shut down illicit traffic.[81]

The Drug Abuse Control Act of 1965, in short, accepted the basic division between medical and nonmedical markets. Moral crusaders may not have played a large role in its passage, but neither had their ideas been seriously challenged in the process. Indeed, consumer advocates had repeatedly emphasized the whiteness and innocence of consumers in an unspoken comparison to informal market "dope fiends." As Senator Dodd explained, he had taken care not to "make criminals out of say a housewife who might have in the house or on her person a bottle of amphetamine pills or barbiturates."[82]

CHALLENGING THE MEDICINE-DRUG DIVIDE:
THE 1970 CONTROLLED SUBSTANCES ACT

Like their white-market peers, informal-market consumers also experienced a crisis in the 1950s and 1960s. Urban heroin markets grew larger and more dangerous as corruption plagued narcotics squads who, even at their best, had rarely focused on consumer safety.[83] The evident failure of punitive prohibition gave rise to a new type of reformer: medicalizers who rejected punitive approaches in favor of medical treatment for addiction. At first medicalizers' agenda was relatively cautious. They fully accepted the medicine-drug divide and embraced the goal of total abstinence for informal-market consumers, arguing only that "treatment" (typically involuntary hospitalization) rather than "punishment" was the best way to achieve it. By the early 1960s this conservative version of medicalization had been formally endorsed by major institutions such as the American Bar Association, the American Medical Association, and the Supreme Court.[84]

As the 1960s wore on, however, at least some medicalizers raised more radical challenges to the medicine-drug divide, seeing informal-market consumers in a more sympathetic light and pushing to give at least some of them access to white market drugs such as methadone. This radical new stance stemmed from two seemingly unrelated developments. The first was civil rights activists dramatically challenging and, in some cases, dismantling the formal systems of racial segregation established in the Progressive Era. As we have seen, such systems provided the cultural logic and practical infrastructure of the medicine-drug divide. The second was a significant late-1960s increase in the number of white youths purchasing marijuana and, in smaller but still notable numbers, heroin, as they rebelliously flocked to the urban neighborhoods where informal drug markets had been allowed to flourish.[85] Combined with the white market drug crisis, these developments undermined the basic assumptions of the medicine-drug divide and radicalized at least some medicalizers.

Meanwhile, consumer advocates' campaign against the pharmaceutical industry continued to heat up as they gained new and in some cases unexpected allies in the 1960s. Some white and middle-class second-wave feminists raised the visibility of Valium addiction by using it as a graphic example of medical sexism and its consequences. Counterculture youth defended their own widely criticized drug use by turning the tables and mocking their parents' continual reliance on alcohol and pills.[86]

Thus by the late 1960s, consumer advocates were pushing to treat "medicines" more like "drugs" even as medicalizers were pushing to treat "drugs" more like "medicines." For the first time in the twentieth century, significant voices were challenging the drug-medicine divide. These new voices roiled a political landscape that had previously been dominated by therapeutic reformers and moral crusaders. New political configurations led to a series of laws and reforms, capped by the Controlled Substances Act of 1970, that temporarily brought dramatic—though incomplete—changes to American drug policy.

Historians have already explored the nature and consequences of these policy changes for informal markets. We know, for example, about the growth of therapeutic communities and methadone maintenance, and the temporary reduction in stigma for drug use that culminated in campaigns to decriminalize marijuana.[87] We do not know nearly enough, however, about the equally momentous changes in white market policies, which became more robust in regulating the pharmaceutical industry and more expansive in articulating a consumer protection approach to all potentially addictive drugs, not just medicines.

The new approach to white market governance had inauspicious origins: not in a reform campaign, but in a classic law-and-order push by President Lyndon Johnson. Seeking to play up his anti-crime bona fides as the 1968 election approached, Johnson believed he saw a winning issue in an anti-"dope" campaign. Blaming "organized, disciplined and resourceful criminals who reap huge profits at the expense of their unfortunate victims," Johnson vowed in 1968 to "serve notice to the pusher and the peddler that their criminal acts must stop."[88] Over medicalizers' protests, Congress followed the president's plan and merged the FDA's Bureau of Drug Abuse Control and the FBN in a new, tougher Bureau of Narcotics and Dangerous Drugs in the Department of Justice.[89]

The new Bureau immediately ran into both practical and political problems. At a practical level the agency's newly combined work-force had to apply different laws and procedures to different drugs; this was especially cumbersome when, as often happened, a "bust" involved both pharmaceuticals and "dope." At a political level the new emphasis on policing and punishment was out of step with expert beliefs about addiction, which increasingly favored medicalization. Few experts believed a punitive approach would pay dividends in terms of reduced drug use or crime. In short, Johnson's reorganization opened drug policy questions rather than settling them.

After Johnson decided not to run for reelection in 1968, those questions were left to be decided by the new administration of Richard Nixon. It was not immediately clear what impact Nixon's election would have on drug policy debates. Consumer advocates and medicalizers remained common in Congress and in the federal bureaucracy. Nixon himself, moreover, was somewhat hard to pin down on drug issues. On the one hand, he had staked his political fortunes on a law-and-order platform, claiming to speak for a "silent majority" angered by youth protest and racialized urban crime. A punitive approach played well with this framing since rebellious youth and urban racial minorities were widely portrayed as America's main drug users, and addiction was also widely portrayed as an important driver of crime. On the other hand, however, Nixon seems to have believed that an actual reduction in crime was important to his reelection prospects, and, aware that punitive approaches had not delivered in this respect, he invested significant new resources in treatment programs, including methadone maintenance.[90]

Nixon thus did not have a master plan to resolve the questions left by Johnson's reorganization, but his uncertainty turned out to be an unexpected opportunity for reform. In 1969 Nixon took what he likely thought of as a modest step: unifying the two laws enforced by the Bureau of Narcotics and Dangerous Drugs. His administration proposed a bill that would repeal the Harrison Act and the Drug Abuse Control Act and move their language into a new law that covered both "narcotics" and "dangerous drugs."

It may have been intended as a modest step, but owing to Nixon's conflicting impulses and the new political influence of consumer advocates and addiction medicalizers, the 1969 unification proposal unexpectedly opened a remarkable debate about drug policy. Consumer advocates and medicalizers played a strong role in this debate, but therapeutic reformers and moral crusaders had not disappeared; nor had pharmaceutical industry lobbyists. As the bill advanced through Congress these factions worked through shifting, strategic alliances on different issues, ultimately producing not a modest housekeeping measure but a signature drug policy reform that contained at least the potential to radically remake American drug markets.

The prominence of medicalizers in these debates is particularly notable. The Senate's hearings, for example, opened with Senator Dodd complaining that existing policies had done "little more than increase the penalties for drug violations," an approach that "[made] new criminals out of a large number of people whose only lawbreaking has been in connection with drug use."[91] A parade of medical experts agreed. One witness from the National Institute of Mental Health, for example, declared that "control of addiction will never be achieved by sending addicts to jail."[92]

These arguments were heartily endorsed by an unexpected ally: the pharmaceutical industry. The American Pharmaceutical Association opposed placing "undue emphasis" on "law enforcement as the major weapon," while Smith, Kline & French pointed out that supply-side restrictions just made illegal sales more profitable.[93] Roche Pharmaceuticals, too, stood up to defend drug consumers, arguing that "to punish possession for one's own use is often to punish illness, weakness, or gullibility . . . treatment and rehabilitation are more appropriate than imposing further suffering."[94]

The unlikely alliance of medicalizers and the pharmaceutical industry was enough to bring Nixon's attorney general, John Mitchell, on board. After more than half a century of ever-stricter punitive approaches, it was remarkable to hear the nation's highest-ranking police officer agree that current policy was "too severe in relation to the culpability of the user and the dangers of the drugs," and to see the law-and-order Nixon administration sign on to the goal of reducing penalties for drug consumers.[95]

Congressional debates also featured one of the strongest efforts yet to rein in the drug industry, supported by another, more familiar alliance: consumer advocates and moral crusaders. Unlike in the past, however, this time the consumer advocates were the stronger half of the pair, dictating the tone and direction of debate. Senator Dodd opened the hearings with a clear and straightforward plea for more robust regulation of industry. "It seems to me every once in a while I am reading in the paper about some drug that has been peddled to the public, and a year or two later somebody comes along and says it is a very bad thing," he recounted. "We want to control, have supervision, give it attention before it becomes a public health problem." Sedatives and stimulants were "obviously dangerous drugs," he continued; "why in the world can we allow producers to make them by the millions and peddle them wherever they want to?"[96] One representative agreed, saying "Frankly, I'm weary of watching good kids suspended from high schools—and even junior high schools—in my district, because Government cannot or will not crack down on the big drug houses."[97]

In keeping with this combative tone, proposals to regulate industry were more robust than they had been in earlier pushes for reform. Addiction specialist and medicalizer Joel Fort, for example, called for eliminating all advertising for addictive drugs.[98] Vanderbilt psychology and pharmacology professor John Griffith went even further. Noting that "the drug industry has not shown a great deal of restraint in selling addicting drugs unless required by law," he proposed an intriguing plan: making all sellers—legal and illegal—financially (not criminally) liable for damages resulting from improper sales. "You will notice," he explained, "that most private swimming pools are surrounded by a high fence. The fence is not there because the owner is goodhearted."[99] Even conservative politicians like Republican Robert Denney saw the writing on the wall. "This is the year of the consumer legislation," Denney warned a witness from Eli Lilly. "I am a great believer in private enterprise and I want to keep it that way, but public demand works its nefarious ways sometimes . . . so I suggest that you cooperate with the committee."[100]

Consumer advocates were so empowered that, for the first time since the Harrison Act, they even made an attempt to expand regulatory control over physicians. This was a difficult task, since therapeutic reformers were crucial to their political coalition and had become increasingly wary of government "interference." Earlier rounds of drug policy reform had invested heavily in physicians as white markets' best hope for consumer protection. Such confidence had been weakened, however, by the ongoing white market crisis. Meanwhile consumer advocacy had matured as a strong and diverse political force and was no longer dominated by medical and pharmacy elites.

As a result, congressional debates focused real and significant attention on ways to repair or regulate a medical profession portrayed as having lost its way. Dodd, for example, complained that state licensing boards were failing to control overprescribing doctors who diverted "millions and millions of dosage units" into informal markets. "If doctors will not control their colleagues' misuse of prescribing powers," he argued, "someone else should."[101] Multiple lawmakers supported Dodd's push for new controls over prescribing, leading a witness from the National Institute on Mental Health to worry that "unless the entire health profession regulates itself, then compulsory legislation . . . will come to pass."[102]

The pharmaceutical industry and many professional medical groups pushed back against new controls.[103] Pharmaceutical companies protested that illicit sales of medicines were not the same thing as "the organized criminal traffic in narcotics" and worried about scaring away patients already skittish about accepting a mental health diagnosis.[104] Various medical organizations were outraged at what one physician described as a government plan to "destroy the sanctity of a physician's office" and treat physicians as if they were "serving suspended sentences or on parole, so that their premises can be entered, their records rifled, their persons subpoenaed without judicial authorization."[105]

If consumer advocates had lost therapeutic reformers' support on the issue of prescription controls, however, they could still count on moral crusaders, who were relieved to find at least one place where liberals welcomed or even cheered their favored approach: the expansion of policing and punishment. However critical they were of Attorney General Mitchell's drug war mentality, consumer advocates found plenty to cheer when, sounding much like Dodd, Mitchell argued that "we are ten years too late" in "regulation of the legitimate industry," and that effective action must be taken now so that "the same is not said of us in 1980."[106] Indeed, one of the few new criminal penalties that survived the congressional gauntlet were those targeting the pharmaceutical industry. These included jail time for "willful and knowing" avoidance of recordkeeping or diversion of drugs from legitimate channels.[107]

When the dust settled and the Controlled Substances Act of 1970 had passed, it pushed American drug policy in a new and uncharted direction. The new law weakened criminal punishments for informal-market consumers, while strengthening policing of major white market commercial actors (i.e., drug companies and physicians). It also included a provision that held at least the potential for a much deeper transformation: an administrative mechanism to change the legal status of any substance without an act of Congress. This mechanism was related to the law's central reform, the creation of a Schedule of Controlled Substances that included both the drugs formerly known as "narcotics" (under the Harrison Act) and those formerly known as "dangerous drugs" (under the Drug Abuse Control Amendments). There were five schedules, ranging from the entirely prohibited Schedule I to the lightly regulated Schedule V. At least in theory, each substance would be placed in a schedule according to experts' assessment of the comparative therapeutic value and addiction risks.

A central question, of course, was who would have control over such assessments.[108] For most psychoactive drugs this determination had been made through informal processes driven by political and cultural concerns. The small oasis of scientific experts empowered to make decisions about opioids had been a notable exception. Now that a new law would codify more than half a century of seat-of-the-pants drug categorizations, would it also rationalize them by, for example, acknowledging research showing that cannabis was not an addictive "narcotic"? Would it impose new limits on drugs with clear potential for addiction and overdose such as Valium, at this point still excluded from even the 1965 Act owing to Roche's ongoing litigation?

This classification question generated intense debate and controversy during the hearings, even though, ironically, it had already been settled two years previously in President Johnson's original 1968 reorganization plan. Before 1968, all natural and synthetic "narcotics" (i.e., cocaine, opioids, and marijuana) were automatically placed under the Harrison Act, while "dangerous drugs" could be added to the Drug Abuse Control Amendments by the head of the Department of Health, Education, and Welfare after careful study. Johnson's 1968 reorganization placed both agencies in the Department of Justice and gave the final decision on classification to the attorney general.[109] Nixon's proposal simply left that structure in place. The FDA would keep the authority to decide whether a drug belonged on the schedule in the first place; its findings on "scientific and medical matters," including pharmacological potential for addiction, were binding. In making the final decision, however, the attorney general could also consider other factors such as the existence, extent, and duration of actual "abuse."[110]

The fierce debate over scheduling highlighted one radical and certainly unintentional implication of the Nixon plan: its potential to weaken the longstanding, racialized lines dividing drugs from medicines. Again, Nixon did not intend to introduce any such major changes. His administration's bill was designed to simply recreate existing law in a new unified structure. Thus, for example, traditional narcotics (opioids, cocaine, and marijuana) were placed in the strictest schedules, I and II, and were covered by Harrison-style controls. "Dangerous drugs," meanwhile, were distributed among the remaining three more lenient schedules and were covered by controls taken from the Drug Abuse Control Amendments.

Consumer advocates and medicalizers had already challenged this simple transfer of existing policies by weakening narcotics punishments and beefing up commercial regulation. They were ready to make changes to scheduling, too—changes that called for fundamentally rethinking the medicine-drug divide. "In the past, dangerous drugs were grouped arbitrarily, sometimes by historical accident rather than with regard for their differing characteristics and their specific and distinct effects," psychiatrist and head of the National Institute of Mental Health Stanley Yolles argued. He hoped the new law would provide "a more logical grouping" since "virtually every category of pharmacologic agent that has some sort of effect on mood is being misused at this time."[111] A California representative made the point more pithily:

> Mood-control substances are legally available and their use is increasing with society's approval. Mood-control substances are illegally available and their use is increasing, but condemned by society. These two statements are contradictory, but both are true. As a matter of fact, in many instances the same drugs are involved. . . . [No wonder] we are rightfully charged with hypocrisy."[112]

This kind of reasoning had surprisingly wide support during the congressional debates, probably because all factions could see it as a potential vehicle for their agenda. For medicalizers it held the promise of easing punitive controls over less harmful drugs like marijuana; for consumer advocates, increased controls over drugs like Valium; for moral crusaders, crackdowns on new informal markets for drugs like "speed" (amphetamine); and for the pharmaceutical industry, easing controls over unfairly maligned products.

While most of the congressional debate centered on the attorney general's role in making a final scheduling decision, there was unnoticed but remarkable unanimity on a much more radical issue: allowing the legal status of individual drugs to be changed administratively, without Congress having to pass a new law. As the head of the Bureau of Narcotics and Dangerous Drugs put it, the schedule was designed to be "flexible," with substances able to change categories as "public interest dictates."[113] A version of the bill that required congressional approval before moving a drug from Schedule II to a less strict category was dropped, and the final bill allowed the attorney general to transfer or even remove "any drug or other substance" after making formal findings justifying the move.[114]

The Controlled Substances Act was thus at least potentially far more significant than initially intended.[115] Obscured by Nixon's public crime-fighting rhetoric, it contained the seeds of a dramatic rethinking of American drug policy. On the one hand, it accepted widespread use of addictive drugs while robustly regulating sales to protect and fully inform consumers. On the other hand, it reduced punishments for consumers while investing significant resources in providing treatment for those who developed addiction despite the protections.[116] The radical possibility of seeing these reforms as two sides of the same coin—as a new template and rationale for drug policy—was captured most fully by the Schedule of Controlled Substances itself, which offered the potential for evening out or even rationalizing the arbitrary and sometimes absurd binary categorization of addictive substances into medicines and "narcotics."

It is important not to go too far with this interpretation of the Controlled Substances Act. Medicalizers and consumer advocates still shared moral crusaders' complete opposition to nonmedical drug use, and this consensus also marked the law. Consumer protection rhetoric and compassion for nonmedical drug users was explicitly linked to the supposedly new prevalence of drug use among America's white middle classes. Senator Dodd's outrage came, in part, because he saw drug companies bringing addiction to places it did not belong. "Hardened drug addicts" using "narcotics" in "the slums and ghettos of our large cities" was one thing, but "college students" and "young affluent professional people and other white collar workers" hooked on pills was something else altogether.[117] For Dodd and most others involved in the congressional debate, rational and compassionate drug policy was worth fighting for only in the context of white market consumers.

This underlying logic played out most clearly in two nearly unanimous compromises that effectively smuggled old policy binaries into the new law: the continued criminalization of even small-scale drug "pushers," and the continued assertion that all nonmedical use was "drug abuse."

Nixon set the anti-"pusher" tone when he introduced the bill: "However far the addict himself may fall," he told Congress, "his offenses against himself and society do not compare with the inhumanity of those who make a living exploiting the weakness and desperation of their fellow men." For them, "society has few judgments too severe, few penalties too harsh."[118] Here, unlike in other areas, Nixon met with no opposition; "pushers" had no defenders in Congress. As a result, the law's penalties were built around a simple divide between sellers and consumers. As noted earlier, consumers fared relatively well. "Simple possession" was illegal if "knowing or intentional," but penalties had been reduced from their 1950s-era peak: a maximum of one year imprisonment and a $5,000 fine for a first offense, which courts could replace with probation; youths under twenty-one could then have their records expunged. For "pushers," however, penalties were much more severe. Even a first offense could bring up to fifteen years imprisonment and a fine of $25,000.[119]

The distinction between sellers and consumers, however, made practical sense only in white markets, where sellers were easily identifiable corporations, physicians, and pharmacists. In informal markets the line was far harder to draw because people with addiction so often also sold drugs to support their habits. Moreover, a white market consumer could legitimately keep a month's supply of a drug, while possession of even a relatively small amount of illicit drugs was evidence of "intent to sell." Finally, even "simple possession" did not mean the same thing in both markets. To be illegal, "simple possession" had to be "knowing and intentional"; as we have seen, white market consumers had long been able to claim ignorance and argue that they were just following physicians' orders. Informal-market consumers could make no such claims; possession itself was evidence of a crime. In multiple ways, then, this key compromise (protecting consumers but punishing "pushers") undermined the Controlled Substance Act's challenge to the drug-medicine divide.

A second key decision, to define all nonmedical use of controlled substances as "abuse," had similar consequences. This was no minor element of the law. Indeed, the schedule was almost entirely structured around the assumed desirability of medical use and the assumed undesirability of nonmedical use. The criteria for determining where to schedule a drug included the potential for "dependence" and "abuse," but also whether the drug had "a currently accepted medical use in treatment in the United States." As some critics noted, the public health catastrophe in white markets had seriously weakened the case for such criteria. "Medical" use had not helped prevent the most significant consequence: harm to consumers and society. Leo Hollister, a leading psychopharmacologist who had played an important role in establishing the addictive potential of Valium, protested in vain: "Scheduling of dangerous drugs and substances should be based on criteria of the liability of abuse, the danger to individual and the danger . . . for society," he urged; "the criterion of medical use should be abandoned."[120]

The continued focus on prohibiting informal markets limited but did not eliminate the bite of some white market consumer protections. The Controlled Substances Act required recordkeeping for all sales and transfers, thus establishing at least a possibility for close surveillance and regulation—although the intent was to prevent diversion to informal markets rather than to police physicians, who faced no new restrictions beyond those already imposed by the 1965 law. The drug industry faced real oversight with recordkeeping requirements and the possibility of criminal penalties for intentional transgressions. New sedatives and stimulants would now be screened for addiction potential by the National Research Council's Committee.[121] Production quotas were imposed only for Schedule I and II drugs, however, meaning all the others could still be manufactured without limit. Perhaps most significant, despite near universal condemnation, no new restraints were imposed on drug marketing.

Conclusion

The Controlled Substances Act was a complex achievement that contained the tools to pursue contradictory agendas. On the one hand, some elements could be used to replace the arbitrary divide between medicines and drugs with a consumer protection regime that accepted extensive use of addictive drugs and sought to make that use safer. On the other hand, many elements did the opposite, doubling down on the medicine-drug divide and recommitting authorities to prohibiting nonmedical use and punishing nonmedical sales. Moral crusaders eventually had the last laugh, transforming the law into a renewed drug war by the 1980s. Before that, however, while the coalition of consumer advocates and medicalizers remained strong, the Controlled Substances Act gave a glimpse of a different kind of drug policy, especially for the white markets for which it was best tailored. The next chapter takes a close look at this moment because, given the long and disastrous history of American drug policy, even such temporary and limited successes deserve careful attention.

6

White markets, under control

The Controlled Substances Act inaugurated a new era for sedative and stimulant white markets, which faced stringent controls for the first time. These controls were unlike the Harrison Act in key respects. Rather than purchasing consumer protections at the cost of a near-prohibition policy, the Controlled Substances Act assumed that markets would continue to sustain extensive use. It also did not forbid long-term use of sedatives or stimulants, even for consumers who had become addicted. It did, however, impose robust new limits on manufacturers and prescribers in an effort to make addiction and related harms less likely.

Together these tactics were more effective than any other drug policy in the twentieth century in white or informal markets. The 1970s saw declines in both the overall volume of sedative and stimulant use, and the overall volume of emergency room visits and fatal overdoses linked to those drugs. The system was not perfect, of course. It could and did overshoot or undershoot the mark with particular drugs. It also had at least one unintended consequence: the emergence of "gray markets" where the pre-1970 style of white market prescribing evolved into purposefully commercial "pill mills" partly protected by their quasi-medical status. In the end, though, despite these flaws, 1970s reforms provide a tantalizing glimpse of what supply-side drug policies might look like—and how effective they might be—if they were designed for consumer safety rather than prohibition.

Regulating white markets

PRESCRIPTION SEDATIVES AND STIMULANTS AS A "DRUG" PROBLEM

The 1965 and 1970 laws had one unexpected but not surprising consequence: an explosion of research into sedative and stimulant addiction. What had been a reform movement powered by sensationalized anecdotes transformed into a governing regime powered by increasingly sophisticated epidemiological and market research.

It was no accident that the first major, reliable epidemiological studies of sedatives and stimulants appeared soon after the 1965 Drug Abuse Control Amendments. The most prominent early researchers were a collaboration begun in 1967 between George Washington University's Social Research Group, Berkeley's Institute for Research in Social Behavior, and the National Institute of Mental Health. Their findings were shocking: nearly one in four Americans had used a prescription sedative or stimulant in the past year (nearly one in three women). Nearly a third of these had used the drugs daily for six months or more in a row.[1] These attention-grabbing studies began a self-reinforcing research cycle, legitimizing sedatives and stimulants as a subject of study and building professional and financial incentives for scholarly investigation. Soon, a raft of more specialized studies provided a fine-grained, demographically precise portrait of the vast extent of sedative and stimulant use. These studies, in turn, provided journalists with new, shocking headlines and a new type of drug expert to interview. The result was very wide dissemination of the results and near-universal recognition of the problem.[2]

The federal government soon waded into epidemiology with its own national surveys, the Household Survey on Drug Abuse (1971) and the Drug Abuse Warning Network (DAWN, 1972).[3] DAWN collected and operationalized data from emergency rooms about incidents of drug-related harm or death. This was, in effect, a systematic version of what the FDA had been doing on an ad hoc basis for decades. DAWN sampled only America's largest metropolitan areas,

Figure 1
Percent Distribution Among Selected Drug and Control Categories
DAWN V Emergency Rooms
July 1976 — September 1976

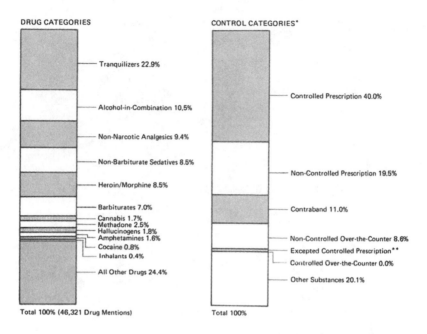

DRUG CATEGORIES

— Tranquilizers 22.9%

— Alcohol-in-Combination 10.5%

— Non-Narcotic Analgesics 9.4%

— Non-Barbiturate Sedatives 8.5%

— Heroin/Morphine 8.5%

— Barbiturates 7.0%
— Cannabis 1.7%
— Methadone 2.5%
— Hallucinogens 1.8%
— Amphetamines 1.6%
— Cocaine 0.8%
— Inhalants 0.4%

— All Other Drugs 24.4%

Total 100% (46,321 Drug Mentions)

CONTROL CATEGORIES*

— Controlled Prescription 40.0%

— Non-Controlled Prescription 19.5%

— Contraband 11.0%

— Non-Controlled Over-the-Counter 8.6%
— Excepted Controlled Prescription**
— Controlled Over-the-Counter 0.0%

— Other Substances 20.1%

Total 100%

Figure 6.1. DAWN Data, Part 1. New epidemiological data showed that "medicines," especially sedatives (tranquilizers, nonbarbiturates like Quaalude, and barbiturates), were responsible for more emergency room visits than "drugs" ("contraband"). *DAWN Quarterly Report*, July–September 1976 (GPO, August 1977), 4. US Department of Justice, Drug Enforcement Administration; US Department of Health, Education, and Welfare, National Institute on Drug Abuse.

where drug use patterns were most likely unusual because of flourishing informal markets. Even so, the results offered striking evidence of the dangers of widespread sedative and stimulant use (see figs. 6.1 and 6.2). In 1976, pharmaceutical sedatives were by far the most common drug listed as involved in an ER visit (38.4 percent), with heroin/morphine a significantly lower 8.4 percent. Pharmaceuticals accounted for nearly two-thirds of drug-related ER visits, while Schedule I drugs—that is, "contraband"—accounted for only 11 percent. The figures for drug-related fatalities were less lopsided, but data from medical examiners still showed sedatives involved in a higher proportion of deaths (32.1 percent versus 25.7 percent).[4]

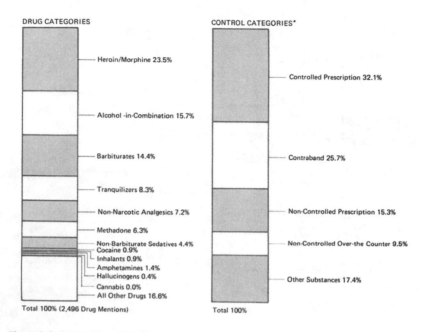

Figure 4
Percent Distribution Among Selected Drug and Control Categories
DAWN V Medical Examiners
April 1976 — June 1976

DRUG CATEGORIES

— Heroin/Morphine 23.5%

— Alcohol -in-Combination 15.7%

— Barbiturates 14.4%

— Tranquilizers 8.3%

— Non-Narcotic Analgesics 7.2%

— Methadone 6.3%

— Non-Barbiturate Sedatives 4.4%
— Cocaine 0.9%
— Inhalants 0.9%
— Amphetamines 1.4%
— Hallucinogens 0.4%
— Cannabis 0.0%
— All Other Drugs 16.6%

Total 100% (2,496 Drug Mentions)

CONTROL CATEGORIES*

— Controlled Prescription 32.1%

— Contraband 25.7%

— Non-Controlled Prescription 15.3%

— Non-Controlled Over-the Counter 9.5%

— Other Substances 17.4%

Total 100%

Figure 6.2. DAWN Data, Part 2. Rates of drug-related deaths were closer, but medicines still accounted for more. *DAWN Quarterly Report*, July–September 1976 (GPO, August 1977), 12. US Department of Justice, Drug Enforcement Administration; US Department of Health, Education, and Welfare, National Institute on Drug Abuse.

Meanwhile, a different set of researchers was expanding authorities' ability to track the supply of white market sedatives and stimulants. As we have seen, earlier efforts at white market regulation had been hampered by legal and technological limits on surveillance. The Harrison Act's recordkeeping requirements, for example, were serviceable at the wholesale level, where copies of all transactions had to be deposited with the FBN, but they were weak at the retail level, where pharmacies and physicians only had to save copies of prescriptions for two years. After literally decades of effort, a similar but weaker setup was finally imposed on pharmaceutical sedatives and stimulants in 1965. Under the law, physicians were not required to make and keep duplicates of prescriptions. Pharmacies did have to preserve prescriptions, but not separately from their other records.[5] Characteristically, the Controlled Substances Act maintained this distinction while opening the possibility of reconfiguring it. Harrison-style recordkeeping was required for drugs in Schedule II, but drugs in less strict schedules just inherited existing 1965 requirements.[6]

Rudimentary surveillance was one reason that so much pharmaceutical enforcement required shoe-leather detective work such as visiting emergency rooms and coroners' offices or responding to complaints and tips from "responsible" quarters. Only after a potential problem had come to light would a deep dive into a pharmacy's or physician's records be warranted. As noted earlier, this was in effect a system of visibility: authorities only became aware of behavior that transgressed social norms or resembled "dope fiend" stereotypes. In effect, this meant that a very large portion of white market transactions remained invisible to authorities because they took place between respectable physicians, pharmacists, and patients.

Even as the FDA relied on this uneven surveillance, however, pharmaceutical industry analysts were building much more sophisticated tools to track drug sales. In the 1950s R. A. Gosselin and Lea Associates developed the National Prescription Audit and the National Disease and Therapeutic Index, respectively. Both used IBM punch cards to tally and calculate sales figures (Audit) and prescribing decisions (Index) gathered from a voluntary sample of pharmacies and physicians. When collated with the AMA's registry of American physicians, these databases could be cross-checked to a granular level because they included individual information about each physician (e.g., medical license number).[7]

In the 1950s and 1960s, these databases were used to assist marketers and increase sales, not to regulate or limit markets. Even at their most granular, they could reveal information about only the miniscule fraction of American pharmacists and physicians selected as samples. After 1970, however, the federal government took a page from the private sector and began to use the vast troves of data produced by its recordkeeping requirements. The central innovation was a new program, ARCOS (Automation of Reports and Consolidated Order Systems). Sales records from manufacturers, distributors, pharmacies, hospitals, and dispensing physicians, including information about the purchaser and the amount purchased, were fed into computers, which then cross-referenced them to provide overall snapshots of the market.[8]

Like earlier epidemiological studies, the resulting data literally reenvisioned the story of American drug use. Take, for example, ARCOS maps of secobarbital sales in Wisconsin in 1976. The first one, reporting volume of sales by zip code, appears to support traditional prejudices about drug use: the majority of sales are concentrated around the city of Milwaukee (southeast corner)—the kind of old-line urban center long identified as the locus of heroin use. The same data could be rearranged, however, to show sales volume per capita rather than by zip code, providing a very different portrait (see fig. 6.3).

In effect, ARCOS reversed the visibility of drug problems: instead of generating data only after a transgression had been discovered or reported, the agency could now point to data as evidence of a potential problem even if no one involved had attracted disrepute. This worked on two levels. First, by tracking sales trends, ARCOS could identify potential new drug "fads" as they developed, drawing attention to a product earlier in its life cycle. Second, ARCOS identified physicians and pharmacists who purchased in unusually high volumes, allowing authorities to investigate the situation even if it had not (yet) produced visible trouble.

All this data gave new ammunition to the drug policy reformers seeking to draw parallels between medicines and drugs. Since the aftermath of the Harrison Act, addiction had been associated with use of heroin by socially marginalized racial minorities living in major cities. Thanks in part to reams of new research data, addiction came to be recognized in the 1970s as a problem of pharmaceuticals and their consumers too. Authorities began to turn away from terms like "addiction" in favor of broader terms like "substance abuse" or "polydrug abuse" that emphasized common pathways between

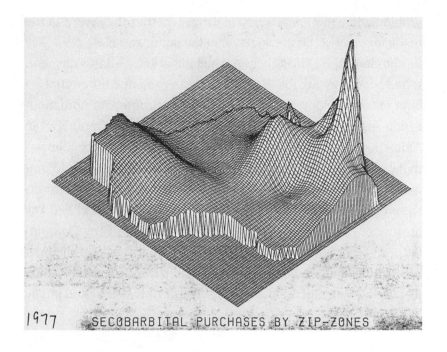

1977 SECOBARBITAL PURCHASES BY ZIP-ZONES

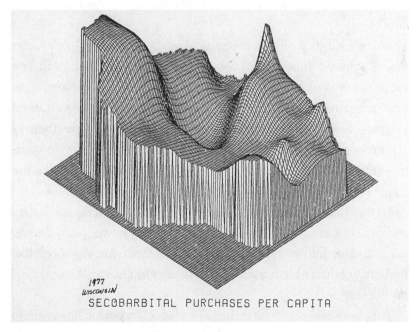

1977
WISCONSIN
SECOBARBITAL PURCHASES PER CAPITA

Figure 6.3. Secobarbital sales by zip-zone (*top*) versus per capita (*bottom*), 1977. The DEA's per capita map reveals much higher use of secobarbital in some of the whitest, nonurban areas of Wisconsin, for example Superior (northwestern corner) and Green Bay (mideastern border), rather than Milwaukee (southeastern corner). State Historical Society of Wisconsin, Box 4, Folder 40 "Controlled Substances Board, 1977–1979," PEB Correspondence, National Archives.

problematic use of psychoactive drugs whether they were in the medicine cabinet, on the street, or at the liquor store.[9]

The Controlled Substances Act had not created all this ferment. It had been brewing for years. As early as 1964 one influential arbiter of terminology, the WHO's Expert Committee on Addiction-Producing Drugs, had shifted from a binary distinction between "addiction" and "habituation" to a single term, "drug dependence," that could be specified according to the type of drug involved.[10] Immediately afterwards the National Research Council's Committee on Drug Addiction and Narcotics (whose members filled key positions in the WHO's Committee), renamed itself the Committee on Problems of Drug Dependence.[11] If federal reforms had not caused the changes, however, they did help translate arcane shifts in experts' language to much wider realms of research and public awareness.

THE FEDS CRACK DOWN—ON PHARMACEUTICAL COMPANIES

The new visibility of pharmaceutical addiction helped reformers finally achieve their goal of robust white market regulation. The 1970s marked a high point of consumer advocacy, and pharmaceutical companies like many other industries came in for sustained skepticism and investigation. A new generation of investigative reporters published a steady stream of damning reports on pharmaceutical industry malfeasance. New advocacy groups like the Ralph Nader–affiliated Health Research Group and (more specifically) the Task Force on Prescription Drugs provided research data and expert witnesses. Grassroots activist groups, especially among second-wave feminists, grabbed headlines with investigations like Barbara Seaman's birth control pill exposé *The Doctors' Case against the Pill* (1970).[12]

This work was taken up at the federal level by politicians eager to burnish their consumer-advocate bona fides. Senators Birch Bayh, Gaylord Nelson, and Edward Kennedy, for example, convened a series of congressional hearings into pharmaceutical company behav-

ior throughout the 1970s. Sedatives and stimulants featured prominently in these hearings, in part because they were one place where
liberal consumer advocates could hope for support from conservative moral crusaders. Amphetamines were on the docket in 1971
and again in 1972 and 1976; barbiturates in 1971, 1972, and 1973;
Quaalude sedatives in 1973; "psychotropics" in 1978; Valium and
Darvon in 1979. All were interspersed with a range of more targeted
congressional investigations of pharmaceutical advertising, pricing,
and other issues. The FDA was particularly effective in using the
hearings to push against the marketing of sedatives and stimulants
for "everyday or minor life stresses."[13]

Continuous congressional pressure produced a wave of new restrictions on sedatives and stimulants. The first class of drugs to
feel the pinch was stimulants. In 1970, after a National Academy of
Sciences efficacy review, the FDA announced that amphetamines
could only be properly labeled for use to treat narcolepsy, hyperkinesis ("minimal brain dysfunction"), and obesity (short term only).
In a remarkable move, the FDA also required that all amphetamines
be reevaluated as if they were new drugs, that is, using the stricter
research protocols (including randomized, placebo-controlled trials) that had become standard. "Industry has not faced its responsibility with these drugs," the FDA announced; "It is time for the
manufacturers to accept the challenge of working closely with the
FDA and the Department of Justice to stop the unnecessary production."[14] The original amphetamine, Benzedrine, did not survive this
hurdle and was withdrawn from the market.[15] The next year, 1971,
the Bureau of Narcotics and Dangerous Drugs "up-scheduled" all
amphetamines, and nonamphetamine stimulants methylphenidate (Ritalin) and phenmetrazine (Preludin), from Schedule III to
Schedule II. This was an important move because Schedule II drugs
were subject to manufacturing quotas. From 1969 to 1971, the Bureau reduced amphetamine's quota by 80 percent. After amphetamine sales stopped declining in 1973, the FDA held hearings to
consider eliminating obesity as a legitimate use, and in 1979 it actually did so.[16]

Sedatives, too, came under new federal restrictions. Following the recommendations of two presidential commissions and two congressional hearings, the Bureau of Narcotics and Dangerous Drugs moved three of the most abused barbiturates into Schedule II.[17] Methaqualone, a nonbarbiturate sedative whose brand name Quaalude had gained a passionate following and a reputation as "the love drug" among counterculture youth, was placed in Schedule II in 1973—with the full support of the American Medical Association.[18] Manufacturing quotas soon dropped for these up-scheduled sedatives, although not as quickly or dramatically as for amphetamines: by the end of the decade, they had fallen by nearly half for the three barbiturates and by 80 percent for methaqualone.[19]

During debates over the Controlled Substances Act, support for administrative flexibility in the schedule had primarily come from people hoping to down-scheduling drugs, especially cannabis. In the 1970s, however, that flexibility was far more likely to be used for up-scheduling.[20]

STATE AGENCIES JOIN THE REGULATORY TEAM

Despite the federal buildup, white market regulation continued to be primarily the responsibility of state medical and pharmacy boards. Federal authorities revoked or denied the controlled substances licenses of only fifty physicians in the 1970s.[21] In the past, state boards had often been reluctant partners, but here too the 1970s brought changes.[22] Forty-two states passed a Uniform Controlled Substances Act, which, among other things, required dedicated agencies for drug control.[23] For many states this meant their own interagency Controlled Substances Board or a Diversion Investigation Unit. Often funded by federal grants from the Law Enforcement Assistance Administration, Diversion Investigation Units were designed to consolidate what had been "scattered and uncoordinated" and "in some instances non-existent" oversight of addictive pharmaceuticals.[24] The first units were established in 1972 in Texas, Michigan, and Alabama; ten more states had followed their lead by 1977.[25]

As these developments suggest, many states began to be more serious about policing controlled pharmaceuticals, including, for the first time, physician prescribing. The examples of Wisconsin and Illinois, which kept excellent records of the process, give a good sense of how this state-level crackdown worked.

As we have seen, Wisconsin's medical board had been an unreliable partner for federal narcotic authorities, sometimes cooperating but other times balking. After 1970, however, instances of cooperation became far more common. Wisconsin passed the Uniform Controlled Substances Act in 1972 and appointed a new agency, the Controlled Substances Board (CSB), to administer it. The Board included representatives from the pharmacy and medical boards as well the Department of Justice, the Bureau of Alcohol and Other Drug Abuse, a range of other state agencies, and area DEA agents.[26]

A good example of the CSB in action came in the spring of 1976, when, after consulting with the state medical and pharmacy boards, it requested ARCOS data on purchases of Wisconsin's most popular amphetamine, Pennwalt's Biphetamine-20.[27] The result more than justified the inquiry. ARCOS statistics revealed that just 26 of the state's 9,500 licensed physicians had bought 71 percent of all Biphetamine-20 in 1975—and just 4 individual practitioners were responsible for the vast majority of that 71 percent.[28] The numbers were similar for pharmacies: less than 5 percent of the state's pharmacies bought nearly one-half of all Biphetamine.[29] When pharmacy sales were traced back to the prescribing physicians, it revealed the same pattern. In Milwaukee County, for example, just 8 physicians had prescribed 82 percent of all Biphetamine doses sold.[30]

Based on these and other data the CSB convened all relevant state agencies for a symposium on drug diversion, setting the stage for a dramatic change in policy by the state medical board. The most common use of amphetamines or other stimulants, weight loss, was banned. Prescribing was restricted to narcolepsy, hyperkinesis, drug-induced brain dysfunction, epilepsy, or (in rare cases) depression.[31] The changes were immediately followed by a dragnet operation to investigate physicians who dispensed or prescribed unusually large volumes of stimulants. Within three years the Board had opened over thirty investigations, each of which began with a form letter asking for detailed information about, and justification for, unusual orders of scheduled substances.[32]

As might be expected, many white market participants were confused or even angry about the disruption of their traditional arrangements. One small-town physician, for example, requested permission to continue providing Dexamyl (a combination amphetamine and barbiturate) to a patient so she could "fulfill her duties as a housewife" despite chronic depression.[33] A consumer raged, "What gives with you people. Do you hate all the women of Wisconsin . . . my wife has had a complete hysterectomy and the frame of mind she is in she needs some of the very drugs you want to do away with."[34] "I am angry beyond words," wrote another consumer (who signed anonymously as "an irate tax-payer"); "I have now gained 20 pounds since your stupid ban."[35]

Such protests were evidence that the new policies truly were disrupting traditional white market practices. Statistics told a similar tale: amphetamine sales fell by 97 percent in just two years (see fig. 6.4). In 1976, Wisconsin had ranked twenty-eighth in the nation for amphetamine sales; in 1977, it fell to forty-fifth.[36] Pointing to the figures as evidence that most amphetamine prescribing was not medically legitimate, Wisconsin controlled substances authorities called on the DEA to lower the overall manufacturing quota.[37] The DEA was not the only one paying attention to the Wisconsin experiment. Multiple other states requested information and advice on developing amphetamine rules and enforcement procedures, and the FDA called on Wisconsin officials to testify at its hearings on whether to restrict use of amphetamines to treat obesity.[38]

A similar story of regulatory transformation was unfolding next door in Illinois. Illinois passed its Controlled Substances Act in 1972 and created a Drug Compliance Unit in the Department of Regulation and Education (which also housed the state medical and pharmacy boards).[39] The Unit had few personnel and little funding, however, and its initial impact was limited. From 1969 to 1974, the

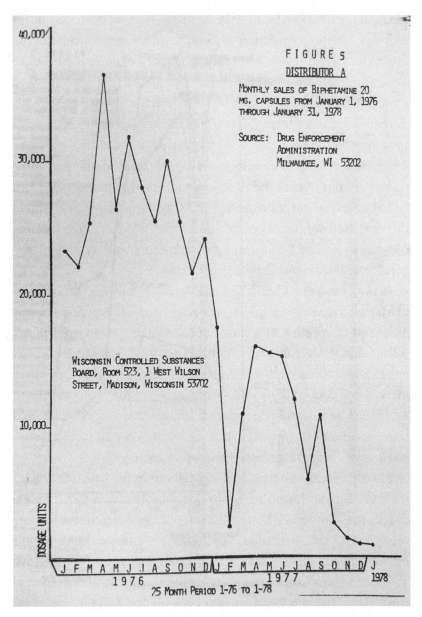

FIGURE 5

DISTRIBUTOR A

MONTHLY SALES OF BIPHETAMINE 20
MG. CAPSULES FROM JANUARY 1, 1976
THROUGH JANUARY 31, 1978

SOURCE: DRUG ENFORCEMENT
ADMINISTRATION
MILWAUKEE, WI 53202

WISCONSIN CONTROLLED SUBSTANCES
BOARD, ROOM 523, 1 WEST WILSON
STREET, MADISON, WISCONSIN 53702

40,000

30,000

20,000

10,000

DOSAGE UNITS

J F M A M J J A S O N D J F M A M J J A S O N D J
1976   1977   1978
25 MONTH PERIOD 1-76 TO 1-78

Figure 6.4. Reforms in Wisconsin led to a sharp reduction in prescriptions for the state's most popular amphetamine, Biphetamine-20. From David Joranson, "Reducing Licit Amphetamine Supply: Results in Wisconsin." State Historical Society of Wisconsin. Box 1, Folder 6 "Amphetamine Rule 1978–1983," SBME Correspondence, National Archives.

medical board disciplined only eight physicians, each one in response to a felony conviction—closing the door very much after the horses had left the barn.[40] The vast majority of complaints led to no action after "informal hearings." One of the rare actions was a physician found guilty of murder who "voluntarily suspended" his license three years later.[41] The Illinois Medical Society warned in 1973 that the state was plagued by "quasi-legitimate drug markets" for "weight control, the 'nervous housewife,' the 'insomniac' businessman," but made little headway against what it described as a "what's the use" attitude among state regulatory agencies, which, the state medical board complained, were "too busy investigating complaints against beauticians, tree trimmers, and water well diggers" to deal with problematic prescribing.[42]

In 1975, however, Illinois saw a sea-change in its approach to regulating pharmaceuticals. First, the state Medical Practice Act was amended to create a new medical coordinator, supported by six full-time investigators and adequate funding.[43] State agencies began to computerize triplicate prescription records so that they could identify and contact high-volume prescribers. In 1975 alone, this led to thirteen high-profile disciplinary actions.[44] As one official noted proudly, the state boards were no longer just "a conduit for licenses" but a true "consumer oriented regulatory agency."[45]

Illinois's push also involved strengthening the broader regulatory structure surrounding controlled substances. In 1976, for example, the Dangerous Drugs Advisory Council required triplicate prescriptions for Schedule II barbiturates.[46] The next year, Illinois established a Diversion Investigation Unit, and a special task force developed plans to generate state-level sales data to assist enforcement.[47] In 1979, the Department of Regulation and Education required that all investigations be presented to the medical board for formal determination; "under no circumstances" could a case be dropped after only "informal hearings."[48]

Wisconsin's and Illinois's reforms were obviously unique to those states, but many other states were taking similar steps. Utah's state medical board acted against amphetamine in 1970, Maryland ended amphetamine use for obesity in 1972, and ten other states joined them by the end of the decade.[49] Many medical boards began to comply for the first time with AMA requests for information about disciplinary actions.[50] In 1970, thirty-five state pharmacy boards had formal arrangements to share information with federal drug surveillance networks.[51] California, long among the most cooperative of states when it came to drug enforcement, set up its own Diversion Investigation Teams and computerized prescription and sales surveillance in 1971.[52] New Jersey formed a Diversion Investigation Unit in 1974 and sharply increased its oversight of physician prescribing.[53] "Doctors are recognizing that the board is not here to protect them," *Medical Economics* reported; "its responsibility is to protect the consumers, and it is showing that it takes that responsibility seriously."[54] Virginia was proud enough of its own stepped-up enforcement actions that it began to circulate a newsletter, *Board Briefs*, which devoted most of its front page to disciplinary actions and investigations.[55] Many other states had no newsletter but did circulate notices of their recent actions, as did the Federation of State Medical Boards in its monthly "Board action report."[56]

WHITE MARKETS GOT SMALLER AND SAFER

Stepped-up federal restrictions and state enforcement led to real changes in white markets for sedatives and stimulants. For the first time since the late nineteenth century, the overall volume of white market sedative and stimulant sales declined. Amphetamine plummeted by a factor of ten, from 4 billion pills in 1969 to 400 million in 1972, and then fell even further when new restrictions were imposed later in the decade (see fig. A.3 in the appendix).[57] Sedative sales dropped by half in the decade after 1973 (see fig. A.2 in the appendix).[58] Notably, this white market contraction was accompanied by a decline in fatal overdoses and other drug-related harms (see fig. A.4 in the appendix). In the decade after 1976, for example, emergency room visits involving sedatives fell by a remarkable two-thirds. Stimulant-related ER visits, already low by 1976, dropped an additional 20 percent. Even pharmaceutical opioids were affected, with ER visits dropping by half or in some cases two-thirds.[59]

The rise of "dope docs" and "scrip mills"

One indication that stricter enforcement was changing white markets was an unintended consequence: the expansion and consolidation of a distinct "gray market" sector of physicians and pharmacists who refused to comply with the newly restrictive regime. Instead, they continued their traditional practice of providing drugs freely to white market consumers. Thanks to increased surveillance, policing, and media exposés, these providers became publicly visible and medically marginalized. In many cases they were coerced into changing their behavior. In other cases, however, they responded to pressure by digging in their heels and adopting an openly rebellious attitude. Some insisted on their professional right to practice medicine in the way they believed was best for their patients. Others abandoned all but the pretense of providing therapy and sold prescriptions under the cloak of medical respectability. All came to be known derisively as "scrip doctors," and their practices as "scrip mills" or "pill mills."

These resistant physicians were not making their decisions in a vacuum. Instead, they operated in a dynamic relationship with their patients. White market consumers also had choices to make as the lines between therapy and abuse were redrawn. Casual or occasional consumers often complied with the new rules and reduced or ended their use of sedatives and stimulants. Some consumers, however, would not or could not do so, especially if they had developed an addiction. Obtaining sedatives or stimulants, once so easy for these white market consumers, now meant navigating new obstacles. For at least some consumers, it required disreputable or even illegal behavior that consolidated a stigmatized identity as "drug seeking" rather than "health seeking."

These gray markets were not entirely new. As we have seen, high-volume prescribers, sellers, and consumers had been com-

mon throughout the twentieth century. Such behavior had not traditionally been excluded from white markets, however; rather, it
sat at one end of a spectrum of accepted—if not always praised—
medical behavior. For example, in 1956 the FDA had discovered that
a pharmacy in Gary, Indiana, was selling an unusually large volume
of amphetamine prescribed by three local diet physicians, one of
whom was a part-owner of the drugstore. Because all sales were on
prescription, the FDA concluded that "no further investigation appears warranted," and there is no record of state authorities picking
up the matter.[60] This made sense; however distasteful their practice
may have been, these physicians remained firmly within the bounds
of white market legitimacy. In the 1970s, however, this diet clinic
setup would have been flagged by ARCOS or another surveillance
program as a clear violation. Gray markets themselves were nothing
new; what had changed was their visibility, and their transformation
into a distinct sector of the pharmaceutical economy, recognized by
providers, consumers, and authorities alike.

Broadly speaking, two types of physicians were active in gray
markets. The first were long-practicing physicians who simply refused to adapt to the new regime and instead continued to prescribe
in the traditional white market manner. The second were physicians
who did not see themselves as providing therapy and instead were
motivated by profit or other openly nontherapeutic considerations.
It is worth taking a close look at both types because they provide a
valuable lens into what had, and had not, changed in the era's white
markets.

The first type of physician—the stubborn traditionalist—typically
practiced in small towns and was practically (sometimes explicitly)
committed to the racial, class, and gender logic of white markets.
More than a quarter of physicians flagged for heavy prescribing
during Wisconsin's mid-1970s crackdown fit this profile, and Illinois regulators also claimed that "generally these [overprescribing]
doctors were older men in their late 60s through early 80s."[61] These
physicians could be quite fiery in defending themselves against
what they considered to be unwarranted, indeed offensive, regula-

tory intrusion. Take the case of Dr. B, a long-practicing physician in the small town of Kenosha, Wisconsin.[62] Summoned to explain his loose prescribing to the state medical board in 1976, he explained that "I prescribe controlled substances only for patients I know well and who I feel will not abuse the drug," and pointed out that, for example, he refused to prescribe amphetamines to "those on welfare." For those patients, he joked, "I recommend cutting their welfare benefits to force them to reduce weight."[63] The board was initially sympathetic, describing Dr. B as "a naïve, easy touch for experienced drug users" who "has a difficult time saying no," but as Dr. B persisted, the board finally revoked his controlled substances license in 1982.[64]

Another long-practicing Wisconsin physician, from the tiny town of Kiel, was even less cooperative when summoned before the board in 1977. Claiming to have "ladies who need these pills for pep," Dr. T fumed that "I'll go underground or you'll see a big jump in the narcolepsy cases around here." If the board decided to investigate his practice, he blustered, "there will be a fire in my office" destroying all records.[65] At his formal disciplinary hearing, Dr. T was proud of his unorthodox prescribing, defiantly explaining that he gave patients amphetamines to help them maintain normal weight rather than to diet; to "make them feel a little peppier" when they "happen to be a little depressed or slightly tired in the morning"; to help working housewives "keep up with the housework"; and, sometimes, simply because they "are paying for an office call [and] want relief—they don't want you to say go home and take two aspirins." He gave many patients near-automatic prescription refills after only a brief examination by an untrained office "nurse." Despite all this, Dr. T—the town's single largest purveyor of psychoactive drugs— assured authorities that Kiel had no "black market" for pills, at least, "nothing like the city."[66] In 1983, the board revoked Dr. T's license to prescribe Schedule II stimulants.[67]

Throughout the long investigation and disciplinary proceedings, both physicians seemed mystified and affronted at the questions raised about their professional judgment after decades of respectable practice. They had a point: for most of their careers, dispensing drugs freely to known and trusted patients had been a perfectly legal and appropriate part of medical practice.

Because of the relatively thin archival record, we are able to pick up the stories of Dr. B and Dr. T only near the end—after they had already become committed gray market prescribers. To get a fuller sense of the pathways, practices, and subjective perspectives of both types of physicians (stubborn traditionalists and commercially driven), it is necessary to find more in-depth cases that left a bigger paper trail. For these cases, there is no better drug than the nonbarbiturate sedative methaqualone, better known by its brand name Quaalude, which became one of the most notorious gray market drugs of the 1970s.

Methaqualone was first synthesized in 1951 and developed commercially in Europe and Japan by the early 1960s.[68] William H. Rorer Company introduced Quaalude in America in 1965. This was propitious timing: reformers had just finally won restraints on barbiturates, the main competitor sedative. Quaalude, as a new drug, was not included in the law. Despite worrying evidence from Germany and Japan, Rorer had not undertaken any tests for addiction potential, nor had the FDA requested any.[69] The best federal regulators could do was to require a label that stated, "no cases of addiction have been reported; however, addiction potential has not been established."[70]

Rorer made the most of the situation, advertising its sleeping pill as a nonaddictive alternative to barbiturates. A 1971 ad, for example, took pains to point out that Quaalude was "chemically unrelated to barbiturates" and produced no "hangover" or "'drugged' aftereffects in the morning."[71] One physician later recalled that he had received boxes of free Quaalude samples in the mail, with instructions suggesting they be "disperse[ed] to your patients as nonbarbiturate, nonaddictive, sleeping pills."[72] Rorer and a small number of competitor companies reaped decent, though perhaps not spectacular, rewards: $7 million with over 100 million doses prescribed in 1972.[73]

Not all of this use was legitimate. In fact, by all accounts, Quaalude quickly became popular with counterculture youth, among whom, reports indicated, it was called "the love drug" for its ability to ease social inhibitions and prolong sex. Such reports soon landed Quaalude in the parade of pharmaceuticals facing increased scrutiny in the 1970s. The *New England Journal of Medicine* and *JAMA*, but also popular media like the *Washington Post* and *Rolling Stone*, reported on a "silent but pervasive" Quaalude "epidemic" that was "all over the place and getting even bigger."[74] By 1973, Quaalude hearings were under way in the Senate, where, in language characteristic of the era's pharmaceutical reformers, one witness accused drug companies of being "as much a pusher as the man on the corner who is selling a few bags of heroin."[75]

Hoping to stave off federal regulation, methaqualone manufacturers instituted some voluntary reforms. Parke, Davis (which sold the competing brand Sopor) stopped sending free samples; Rorer eliminated "unsolicited" samples; and both heightened security at their manufacturing plants.[76] It was to no avail, however. After relentless prodding from congressional anti-drug crusaders and their allies, methaqualone was placed in Schedule II in 1973 and its manufacturing quota was lowered aggressively.[77]

Despite shrinking sales and guidelines that discouraged long-term use, however, no hard limits were imposed on how physicians could prescribe Quaalude. And even as many physicians abandoned the drug due to its souring reputation and the bureaucratic hassle of prescribing a Schedule II substance, it was still prized by many white market consumers. These were perfect conditions for the emergence of gray markets and for "scrip doctor" prescribers of both the traditionalist and the commercial variety.

The best documented case of a traditionalist is that of Dr. C, a Madison, Wisconsin, physician who became the state's top Quaalude prescriber and a highly controversial public figure in the 1970s. It is a tricky case to interpret historically. On the one hand, based on comparisons with other (less well-documented) cases, Dr. C's story was fairly typical and reveals in valuable detail many of the dynamics that produced gray market prescribers. On the other hand, there was one way in which Dr. C was extremely unusual in the gray market context: unlike any other "scrip doctor" I have encountered in the archives, he was African American. There can be little doubt that racism played a role in all parts of Dr. C's story, intensifying a feedback loop between his appeal to white youths and heightened scrutiny from state authorities. It is possible to use his case to glean insight about broader phenomena, but we must do so carefully.

Dr. C was born in 1907, earned a PhD in organic chemistry in 1933, and an MD in 1943. He was a professional powerhouse, publishing over sixty papers in chemistry and medicine and holding important positions at several universities, hospitals, and professional societies. He was also politically active, taking leadership roles in the Urban League and the NAACP.[78]

By the late 1960s, Dr. C had settled into private practice in downtown Madison near the University of Wisconsin.[79] There he appears to have been a fairly traditional white market prescriber, which, because of his proximity to a large state university, meant that he prescribed a large volume of sedatives and stimulants to the university's overwhelmingly white students. This had been, and still was, an unremarkable way to practice medicine.

As regulatory tightening began to reconfigure white markets, however, Dr. C did not shift with the times. Instead he continued his "traditional" prescribing practices. By 1974, these practices had attracted the attention of the state medical board.[80] Dr. C defended his ready recourse to the prescription pad, insisting that physicians should not "cross examine patients" and arguing in a series of speeches and editorials that "tense and restless" students genuinely needed Quaalude.[81] Such public defiance endeared him to at least some university students—white market consumers who did not want to give up their privileged access to sedatives and stimulants. "Let's leave the man alone," pleaded one undergraduate in a student newspaper, praising Dr. C's willingness to treat students even as "most other doctors will not prescribe sedatives to young people, sleeping problems irregardless."[82] Many of Dr. C's patients refused to cooperate with the medical board. "You can expect no co-operation from me in your attack on Dr. C.," one wrote in response to a request for permission to use her medical records in the case; "In my opinion he has given me extremely good, and 'proper,' medical care."[83]

While Dr. C's defenders drew on traditions of white market entitlement to make their case, they also showed an awareness that his type of practice had become rare. This awareness was part of a developing recursive loop that was changing Dr. C's practice. As he became more visible as a Quaalude prescriber, he began to see more patients who were specifically drawn to him for that reason. Dr. C continued to see relatively privileged, white patients, but they were increasingly the type of "drug-seeking" consumers that physicians were being told to avoid: people with addiction, people with criminal records, and people who were young and clearly part of the "counterculture."[84]

Over time, as Dr. C's patient population shifted, so too did his practice. Most important, it came to be ever more oriented around prescribing psychoactive drugs. His Quaalude prescriptions, for example, doubled from 1975 to 1976—right after his public spat with the state board.[85] According to ARCOS, in 1976 Madison had by far the highest sales of Quaalude, with a total volume at least a quarter higher than the much larger city of Milwaukee (see fig. 6.5).[86] Moreover, the vast majority of Quaalude purchases in Madison took place in just three of the city's nearly forty pharmacies. At those pharmacies, Dr. C had written over 98 percent of the Quaalude prescriptions filled.[87]

Dr. C's practice changed in other ways, too. He continued to examine new patients and never prescribed more than a month's supply of any given drug, but as his patient population became ever more focused on securing prescriptions, he began to spend less time on therapeutic niceties. As one of his patients later told investigators, students in the waiting room would openly joke about seeing each other later "stumbling around," and everyone knew that telling Dr. C "I can't sleep" would result in Quaaludes after a perfunctory

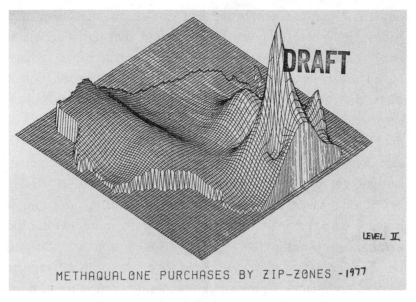

Figure 6.5. Methaqualone sales per capita, 1977. Dr. C's dominance of Wisconsin methaqualone prescribing only intensified in 1977, as this per capita ARCOS map shows (south-central peak is in Madison). State Historical Society of Wisconsin. Box 9, Folder 35 "C.—Drug Research," SBME Investigations, National Archives.

ten-minute examination devoid of any of the usual cautions (e.g., not to use if pregnant).[88] Patients could also get around the thirty-day limit on supply by asking for more than one type of sedative or stimulant (or both).[89] Dr. C persisted in these practices even as clear evidence emerged that at least some of the patients with whom he spent so little time were deeply troubled and were being seriously harmed by their drug use.[90]

To put this another way, Dr. C had slowly evolved so that he was no longer a traditional white market prescriber. Instead, his practice had come to resemble that of a classic "pill mill." This was a remarkable state to have arrived at given his illustrious career before the white market crackdown. Dr. C never showed any indication of crass commercial motives; he was consistent in his critique of the new regulatory regime and in his defense of older ways of practicing medicine. And yet he still ended up squarely in the gray market, as the authorities, his patients, the media, and even he clearly recognized. Some observers (but not Dr. C) charged that he had been targeted for enforcement because of his race, and this is certainly believable, especially given his continued civil rights activism. Dr. C's connections to Madison's counterculture do appear to have fueled his rebellious attitude and accelerated the transformation of his practice. Yet he was only one of dozens of Wisconsin physicians accosted by state authorities for lax prescribing in the 1970s, and, as noted earlier, he was hardly the only older physician who refused to abandon what he considered to be perfectly good therapeutic practices just because professional authorities demanded it.

One final aspect of Dr. C's story is worth noting: how long it lasted. He first came under investigation in 1974, but neither the medical board nor the state attorney general took action.[91] Despite Dr. C's open defiance, it was only in 1977, when ARCOS reports showed his Quaalude prescribing increasing even as most of his peers in the state had stopped using the drug altogether, that the board reopened the case.[92] Dr. C faced multiple investigations and the potential loss of his license but was still practicing when he finally agreed in 1979 to retire, at age seventy-two, in return for the state board closing the books on his case.[93]

Dr. C's longevity highlights an important aspect of pharmaceutical gray markets. They were disreputable and did not meet professional standards of care, but because of the difficulty of drawing clear and fast boundaries around therapeutics, they still enjoyed many of the protections of the medical enterprise. As long as prescribers had a current license, stayed near the letter of the law, and maintained a clientele that did not diverge too much from traditional white market consumers, it was not difficult to stay one step ahead of the inspector—for a while, at least.

Gray markets' semi-protected status is shown clearly by a look at the second category of prescriber: commercially minded physicians who sold prescriptions with only the minimum necessary therapeutic cover. Such physicians tended to be younger, to practice in cities, and to have links to the era's drug-suffused counterculture. In the early 1970s, they favored amphetamine sales through diet clinics, but as the decade wore on they increasingly turned to Quaalude in stress clinics.

One unusually large chain of half a dozen stress clinics in New York and Chicago was investigated and ultimately shut down by federal authorities in the late 1970s, leaving an enormous paper trail.[94] The chain had begun as a single diet clinic but, as amphetamine regulations tightened, shifted to a Quaalude stress clinic model. It offers a unique opportunity to explore detailed information about the clinic's operations and medical employees—and about how it managed to remain in business for several years despite such notoriety that a television news exposé featured one of its physicians as the "King of 'Ludes.'"[95]

The clinics were run by a small-time New York mobster, but their day-to-day operations were handled by a succession of three managing physicians. The first, Dr. S, had the most straightforward trajectory. Soon after attaining his medical degree in 1959, Dr. S had begun to supply himself with prescription drugs, and by the time he agreed to help found a diet clinic in 1976, he was addicted and already on the margins of the profession.[96] At that time, he was perfectly comfortable with the mercenary motive that he later admitted to a jury: "To make money."[97]

The second physician, Dr. G, received his degree in 1973 and initially worked for a mobile crisis intervention unit and in foreign disaster relief with the Red Cross. He was looking for work in 1977 after these positions ended when Dr. S, who he had met during his internship, offered him a place to stay and a temporary job at the diet clinic.[98] Like many of his generation, Dr. G smoked marijuana, but unlike Dr. S he was not addicted and, moreover, he was still somewhat of an idealist. He joined the clinic reluctantly, at first refusing to write prescriptions and then insisting on new policies such as rejecting "very, very thin people" as patients.[99] But his employers resisted these moves and, as Dr. G began to develop his own addiction to Quaalude and cocaine, he gave in, signing hundreds of prescriptions.[100]

The third physician, Dr. A, earned his medical degree in 1957 and had worked in the Swiss pharmaceutical industry before moving to Manhattan to serve as an associate medical director for Pfizer in 1974.[101] Seemingly liberated by the city, Dr. A joined one of Manhattan's countless drug subcultures, often prescribing amphetamine for friends. He soon quit his job at Pfizer and began working at a series of lower-status positions including a brief stint treating obesity with protein shakes before joining the stress clinic in 1976. Like Dr. G, he was hesitant at first and tried to introduce a variety of treatments for stress at the clinic such as biofeedback, meditation training, and the like. As his own addiction deepened, however, these efforts fell away.[102]

Each of the three physicians had taken a different path to the clinic, but their stories shared certain similarities. None were traditional white market holdovers. All were affiliated in one way or another with the city's youthful drug cultures, and all had accepted a position during a moment of change or crisis in their careers. Only one of the three had begun with clear, purposeful intent to make money; the other two convinced themselves, at least initially, that they were serving a therapeutic purpose.

The clinics were a large enough business that they required far more than just those three managing physicians. Just one clinic, the flagship Manhattan Center, employed more than forty part-time physicians during its eighteen months of operation. These physicians, too, arrived at the clinic for a variety of reasons. About a quarter of them seem to have recognized the commercial nature of the job and were perfectly comfortable with it. Others, often just beginning their careers, had applied more or less randomly as part of a routine job search. They appeared to have been unaware of the clinic's nature, and many quit when they discovered it: one-third of the part-time physicians quit in less than ten days.[103] Almost half of them may have been squeamish but willing to work for up to eight weeks while looking for another position.[104]

The physicians who worked at the Manhattan Center showed that there was still extensive overlap between white market and gray market medicine; many of them moved between the two worlds. But the line dividing them was hardening. Whatever path they had taken to employment at the clinic, prescribers ultimately found themselves faced with a choice: get with the program, or quit.

One reason prescribers faced such a stark choice were the rigid operational requirements the clinic owners imposed to mimic a medical enterprise as closely as they could under the circumstances. This involved hewing to the letter of the law as much as possible—indeed, probably more carefully than ordinary physicians. Some of this was standard fare. When clients arrived, they reported their medical problems in writing and undressed for a physical exam; they were weighed, measured, and examined; and every three months, they were given an order for a range of blood tests and an EKG. Upon payment, they signed two additional forms acknowledging that they were receiving "potent" drugs and promising to follow the doctor's instructions carefully.[105]

Other clinic requirements were more unusual, however. For example, 97 percent of visits ended with exactly the same prescription for Quaalude, the maximum amount allowed by the *Physicians' Desk Reference*.[106] All patients were provided with two refills—again, the maximum allowed—after which they were required to return to the clinic for an evaluation and a new prescription (such long-term use was definitely frowned on but was not illegal). Since many reputable drug stores no longer stocked Quaalude or dispensed it with great caution,[107] all patients were directed toward one or two cooperating pharmacies.[108] One such pharmacy went from filling a paltry thirty-five Quaalude prescriptions to filling more than one thousand, over 90 percent of which came from the clinic. By 1980, the pharmacy had become the single largest purveyor of Quaalude in New York State, dispensing nearly 10,000 prescriptions.[109]

In addition to micromanaging physician prescribing, the clinics went far beyond the norm in insisting that patients fit the stereotypical profile of white market consumers. To avoid association with the youthful drug counterculture, for example, no one under twenty years old was permitted as a patient. Also excluded was anyone who *looked* as though he or she had drug problems (a charge that carried clear class and race overtones), and, more specifically, anyone who directly requested drugs.[110] The clients who made it through this vetting procedure were largely white-collar, middle-class professionals who were able to maintain appearances and who could believably claim to be suffering from anxiety, insomnia, "nerves," or other stereotypically white-collar ailments.[111]

The purpose of all these careful policies became clear when the clinics' managers finally ended up in court being prosecuted for illegal drug sales. "We have here," a clinic lawyer summed up sarcastically, "the terrible problem of licensed physicians prescribing approved medications via licensed pharmacies by approved and licensed pharmacists. . . . That is their crime."[112] Similar arguments had protected white market prescribers in the past, but by the late 1970s they no longer worked as well. Prosecutors dispatched them easily in the Manhattan Clinic case, and in a series of other high-profile state and federal prosecutions in the 1970s and early 1980s.[113]

The consolidation of "scrip mill" prescribers signaled real changes in American white markets. Prescribing practices that had been acceptable, if frowned on, had been decisively rejected by medical authorities and faced new legal consequences. Therapeutic autonomy still made it difficult to shut down transgressing prescribers, but far less so than in the past. Ironically, these shifts heightened the visibility of rogue physicians and pharmacists, giving the 1970s a lasting reputation as a decade awash in Quaalude and other addictive pharmaceuticals. The reality was quite the opposite: a dramatic curtailment of white markets that had been large and growing for half a century.

Not a new drug war

The consolidation of pharmaceutical gray markets sheds light on a central mystery of the 1970s: why did the crackdown work so well, given the long and almost entirely discouraging history of such "supply-side" strategies? When legal supplies are cut off, people who want to use drugs, especially people with addiction, turn to more dangerous illegal (unregulated) supplies. Why did this not happen when authorities moved to cut off white market supplies in the 1970s?

The answer is that not all supply-side policies are created equal. The best known supply-side policy is punitive prohibition: the criminalization of a substance, its sellers, and its consumers. This is the ineffective approach that gave supply-side policies their bad name. White markets in the 1970s, however, mostly featured a different sort of supply-side policy, one based at least partly on principles of consumer protection that were quite different from prohibition.

The first and most important feature of the consumer protection approach was that it did not prohibit sales and use. Instead, the goal was to reduce unsafe sales and use. This meant robustly regulating, but certainly not shutting down, major market actors such as pharmaceutical companies, prescribers, and pharmacists. As drug reformer (and future federal drug czar) Peter G. Bourne wrote in 1974, because they "serve useful medical needs . . . there will continue to be a high level of use of psychoactive drugs by the American public."[114]

Accordingly, sedatives and, for a while, stimulants remained medically available to a much greater extent than, say, morphine had in the aftermath of the Harrison Act. Gray markets were part of this continued availability, providing consumers with quality-assured, brand-name products (if few other consumer protections). But gray markets were a last resort that most white market consumers found unnecessary. All sedatives, for example, remained medically available in the 1970s, and despite new regulatory pressures, there was no legal limit on how long a physician could prescribe for a patient. Unlike under Harrison, maintaining a person addicted to sedatives was not illegal. Supply-side controls did not target this type of prescribing.

Instead, 1970s reforms made sedative white markets safer in two other ways. First, new red tape and new professional norms helped reduce casual prescribing that unnecessarily exposed patients to the risk of addiction. Refill limits, for example, meant that deliberate decisions had to be made before allowing long-term use (they did not make such use illegal). Second, federal and state controls shifted markets toward the safest sedatives by imposing stricter controls over more dangerous drugs. Thus, for example, short-acting barbiturates and Quaalude were placed in Schedule II in the early 1970s, helping to shift markets toward safer benzodiazepines such as Valium that remained in Schedule IV. Valium was not free of risk, of course, and as it came to dominate sedative markets it had its turn atop lists of ER visits and fatal overdose. Nonetheless, benzodiazepines were the safest of the sedatives, and their dominance could be considered a real, if imperfect, public health success.

One reason this approach worked was that sedatives were all "cross-tolerant" with each other: a person with addiction might prefer their chosen sedative, but they could stave off withdrawal symptoms with any of them. When Quaalude was moved to Schedule I (i.e., entirely outlawed) in 1983, this was not the same thing as a general prohibition policy; instead, it was a strong incentive for consumers to shift to a different legal sedative.

Valium's story offers one other interesting piece of evidence that sheds light on this era's drug policy successes. Despite the very public and influential campaign to expose the dangers of Valium and America's crisis of Valium addiction in the 1970s, no new legal restrictions were imposed. Even so, prescriptions and sales dropped sharply in the second half of the decade. It is impossible to know with certainty, but this decrease in Valium use appears to have been driven by consumers themselves, in part as a result of feminists' successful use of the drug as a symbol of medical sexism. There is, at minimum, evidence that some patients began to reject Valium prescriptions over the objections of their physicians, who, on the whole, remained skeptical of what they considered to be a hysterical overreaction to the drug's addictive potential.[115] In other words, Valium's decline was not fully a supply-side affair but appears to have been powered, at least in part, by a reduction in demand.

Intriguing, but speculative, evidence that drug availability was an important part of policy successes in the 1970s can be found in the counterexample of amphetamine. At first, amphetamine's story was similar to that of sedatives: new controls that restricted but did not prohibit sales and use. By the mid-1970s, however, when authorities became dissatisfied with the rate of decline in prescribing and concerned about growing informal use among counterculture youth, stricter federal and state controls were imposed that came much closer to outright prohibition.

As noted earlier, at least some physicians and patients protested vigorously against the new restrictions. Some of this was encouraged or even orchestrated by pharmaceutical companies, but the mixture of medical concern and political passion were clearly genuine.[116] Notably, at least some of these protests were not simply outrage at being denied a traditional privilege. Rather, they were thoughtful objections to a policy that would suddenly deprive people of a drug they had used continuously for long periods of time.

Examples from Wisconsin after that state's early and draconian amphetamine restrictions give a good sense of these objections. "The law is appropriate in that it is designed to prevent abuse in the future," a Sheboygan, Wisconsin, physician wrote to the state medical board, but "there has to be an allowance for dealing with the end result of that abuse in the past years." Should an eighty-year-old patient who had been taking amphetamines for twenty-five years be forcibly withdrawn "just so the law could be met," he asked?[117] A desperate consumer wrote the medical board to "declare myself an addict of amphetamines in the form of Dexamyl" because her doctor would prescribe for her only if he was authorized to "treat me as an addict." Her physician (who mailed the letter for her) confirmed that "with the use of Dexamyl, she was able to overcome alcoholism and return to a productive life."[118]

There is no indication of what happened to these consumers left marooned when white market boundaries were redrawn to exclude their use. Most likely, the elderly ones mentioned in these letters had little choice but to stop using amphetamine, with unpredictable consequences for their health.

For other former white market consumers, an alternative possibility may have presented itself. As it happens, the 1970s also witnessed the return of a fully criminalized drug that had long been mostly absent in America: cocaine. According to the federal government's National Household Survey on Drug Abuse, cocaine had reappeared at precisely the moment that authorities clamped down on amphetamines. The first large jump in first-time use came in 1974, and the next eight years—the period of increasing amphetamine restrictions—saw significant increases. Granted, first-time cocaine users tended to be fairly young (average age in the early twenties), but otherwise their demographics matched those of pharmaceutical white markets.[119]

It is very important not to overstate this link. The return of transnational cocaine commodity chains to US informal markets occurred for many reasons and can be more than adequately explained without reference to amphetamine restrictions.[120] Nonetheless, given the relatively upscale social status of early cocaine consumers in the 1970s, it is not unreasonable to suspect that some of them may have found their way to informal markets after being locked out of amphetamine white markets.

Finally, in evaluating the success of 1970s reforms, it is important not to forget one central aspect of the era's broader drug policy: a massive investment in addiction treatment that dramatically expanded its availability. Thanks to addiction medicalizers, in the late 1960s and early 1970s the federal government and many states shifted emphasis (and funding) from punishing drug consumers to addiction treatment programs.[121] True, treatment during these years was problematic in any number of ways, from the predominance of ineffective abstinence-only approaches to unequal accessibility along lines of class and race.[122] Even so, it is significant that the absolute scale of increased treatment capacity—especially for relatively privileged white market consumers—was probably larger than the total contraction of white market drug availability. And, as we will see in the next chapter, in at least one way the treatment surge actually *expanded* white markets, and in an unprecedented and radical way: methadone maintenance opened white markets to poorer, nonwhite, and addicted consumers who had never had access to them before.

Conclusion

The history of American drug policy offers precious few success stories. For this reason alone, it is important to learn as much as possible about even partial and flawed successes such as those in the 1970s. In this case, the lesson seems clear: supply-side controls can be effective if designed to achieve consumer safety rather than prohibition.

Yet to learn from the 1970s, we must also be keenly conscious of their limits and flaws. The most important of these was depressingly familiar. With the significant exception of methadone maintenance (which had its own problematic aspects, as we will see), these successful policies were reserved almost exclusively for white markets. For those familiar with 1970s history, it may have been something of a surprise to read about this particular decade as a drug policy success story. After all, these were the years when President Richard Nixon officially declared a "war on drugs," and the moment of public investment in addiction treatment turned out to be brief and quickly overshadowed by skyrocketing investments in criminal enforcement.

The rebirth of informal-market prohibition even as relatively effective policies were ending a white market crisis was no coincidence. Rather, it was a clear sign that the medicine-drug divide had survived its first real challenge. The 1970s reforms had redrawn the divide, making white markets smaller and safer, but they had also reinforced the existence of the divide itself. As a result, the decade's remarkable successes did not last or become the model they should have been for future policy. Instead, as the next chapter will show, they disappeared and were forgotten or misremembered, paving the way for another crisis, the worst yet, in both white and informal markets.

The Third Crisis

Opioids, Sedatives, and
Stimulants, 1990s–2010s

7

White market apocalypse

As reformers reined in white market sedatives and stimulants in the 1970s, white market opioids continued their highly constrained existence in what was nearly a command economy. Companies introduced new drugs they claimed were less or even nonaddictive, but the system largely succeeded in preventing new opioid booms. This was remarkable because, in the 1960s and 1970s, opioid white markets were confronted with the most dramatic innovations since the appearance of Demerol in the 1940s: methadone as a maintenance treatment for people with addiction, and pentazocine (Talwin), a new type of opioid initially believed to be nonaddictive even by the skeptical experts at the National Research Council's Committee. Despite these potentially transformative developments, opioid white markets remained stable and, with the advent of methadone maintenance, became less socially discriminatory. By the 1970s, it was possible to say that white market drug policy worked—far from perfectly, but it worked.

This relatively functional setup rested on what turned out to be a precarious basis, however. The coinciding political strengths of consumer advocates, addiction medicalizers, and civil rights and feminist activists had made it possible to implement changes that blunted some of the worst consequences of the medicine-drug policy divide. Their moment of strength turned out to be brief, however. In 1980, Ronald Reagan was elected on the back of a new conservative political coalition defined by its opposition to each of the constituencies that had powered 1970s reforms. Anti-regulatory reformers vowed to repeal bureaucratic red tape, revitalized moral crusaders competed to pass the most punitive informal-market drug prohibitions, and white backlash politicians sought to reinstate America's traditional social hierarchies of race and gender.

In this new political context, the tenuously achieved successes of the 1970s were quickly abandoned. Informal markets worsened first, as waves of affordable cocaine and heroin hit economically devastated central cities, leading to harmful addiction crises made worse by punitive crackdowns and racialized mass incarceration. White markets soon spiraled out of control as well. Freed of "burdensome" regulations, the pharmaceutical industry rebounded with a new generation of blockbuster psychoactive drugs in the 1980s and 1990s. Pharmacologically these were quite similar or even identical to previous white market products. The renewed drug war, however, had rebuilt the traditional association of addiction with marginalized, urban informal-market consumers. This made it easier for pharmaceutical companies to resurrect white market logic and portray their minor innovations as revolutionary triumphs. They did so not just with sedatives and stimulants but, for the first time, also with opioids. Led by Purdue Pharma's OxyContin, white market opioids finally slipped free in the 1990s after nearly seventy years of carefully monitored stability, igniting an unprecedented sales boom that surpassed even the late nineteenth century in it scale and public health consequences.

As authorities became aware of the emerging white market crisis in the early 2000s, their responses showed that the lessons of the 1970s had been poorly learned. In fact, new policies were nearly the opposite of the successful 1970s model. They cracked down on white market supply, but focused less on reducing casual prescribing than on cutting off access to people with addiction. For many years, in fact, such "abusers" were blamed for the crisis, delaying efforts to regulate major market actors like pharmaceutical companies. Meanwhile, new investments in treatment were slow to come and did not match the scale of need. Together these responses transformed what had been an addiction crisis into an overdose crisis, as white market consumers turned in desperation to informal markets, where they purchased riskier drugs of uncertain quality.

In the early twenty-first century, then, the United States faced the worst of both worlds: morgues filling up with fatal drug over-doses even as prisons continued to fill with drug offenders. It was the most terrible manifestation yet of the basic structural flaws that had dogged American drug policy for a century. This last chapter tells the story of how it came to that pass. It begins by picking up the opioid story where we left it off, in the 1960s.

Opioids in the reform era

RADICAL INNOVATION: METHADONE MAINTENANCE

White market regulations did more than prevent pharmaceutical companies from inflating harmful opioid sales booms. They also handled a much more complex task: incorporating genuine inno-vations without compromising consumer protections. They did not do this perfectly. Yet in a century of marketing-driven boom-bust cycles, they are worth examining as a relatively successful effort to manage pharmaceutical innovation.

The most radical change, without doubt, was the introduction of methadone maintenance as a treatment option for people with opioid addiction. We have encountered methadone before, in the late 1940s, when Anslinger and the Committee stopped Eli Lilly from launching it as a miracle opioid. The emergence of methadone maintenance nearly twenty years later has been recognized as a dra-matic turnabout in American ideas about addiction treatment, but it was also transformative in other ways. It was, for example, the first new use for opioids approved in a half century. It was also the first time since the short-lived early twentieth-century narcotics clinics that white markets had been expanded to poorer, racialized, and (in this case) addicted consumers, who had long been relegated to informal markets. Like more privileged Americans, those consum-ers could now buy legitimately manufactured, quality-controlled, and tightly regulated drugs, provided by people trained to care for their health. This was a radical challenge to the basic architecture of white markets. This challenge was blunted, however, by a combination of continued prejudice against people with addiction and consumer advocates' wariness about loosening their chokehold over opioid manufacturers.

The methadone maintenance story began in 1964, when physicians Vincent Dole and Marie Nyswander provided the drug experimentally to twenty-two people with heroin addiction and published positive results in *JAMA*.[1] In 1967, the pair reported more definitive results after treating 750 "criminal addicts": 88 percent had avoided arrest, and 59 percent held down jobs and had become "productive members of society." According to Dole and Nyswander, these results reversed decades of conventional wisdom about opioids. Many of the health and legal problems with addiction, they theorized, were the result of being forced to procure drugs in illicit markets, rather than signaling personality defects or the nature of addiction itself. People with addiction suffered from a permanent metabolic illness that made them need drugs, much as a diabetic needs insulin.[2] Provided with cheap and long-lasting methadone, people with addiction were freed from those needs and able to pursue more socially acceptable life goals.

This was sorely needed good news for American cities, which had been experiencing waves of heroin addiction. Urban informal markets had rebounded vigorously along with global commerce more generally after World War II. The central-city neighborhoods with informal-market infrastructure had been changing as the Great Migration and residential segregation filled them with young African American and Latinx families. This exposed new generations of socially and economically marginalized young people to unregulated opioids. These were perfect conditions for an addiction crisis, and from the end of World War II through the 1960s, that was exactly what happened—repeatedly. Initial responses to these crises were to double down on informal market prohibition. Laws were tightened and penalties increased. Predictably, these did little to stop the heroin "plague."[3]

This disastrous policy failure gave an opening for addiction medicalizers, who were very interested in Dole and Nyswander's methadone research.[4] Jerome Jaffe, a psychiatrist who had worked at the federal narcotics facility in Lexington, Kentucky, integrated methadone maintenance into his new "multimodal" addiction treatment program in Illinois beginning in 1968. In 1969, the first methadone clinics opened in New York City and, under Peter G. Bourne, in Atlanta. The next year psychiatrist Robert DuPont, working for the city's Department of Corrections, opened a very large treatment network in Washington, DC. When Washington's crime rates dropped, DuPont's reforms got the attention of an unlikely drug reformer: President Nixon.[5]

Nixon was eager to fulfill his law-and-order campaign promises and believed that addiction was a major driver of crime; he was also fearful that addicted soldiers returning from Vietnam would pose a major social threat. So he hired Jaffe to head up a new agency, the Special Action Office of Drug Abuse Prevention, which received over $100 million to build an addiction treatment infrastructure. By late 1973, more than 70,000 people across the United States had enrolled in methadone maintenance programs, many of them federally funded.[6]

This expansion took place despite the opposition of the nation's leading addiction experts at the National Research Council's Committee, who shared Anslinger's opposition to maintenance and restrictive view of methadone.[7] From the Committee's perspective, methadone was a highly addictive narcotic, and in addition to opposing ambulatory treatment, their years of experience fending off industry-hyped "innovations" left them wary of allowing an expansion of uses for any opioid.[8] In the early 1970s, however, with states and the federal government increasingly permitting, encouraging, and funding methadone programs, the Committee finally relented and worked with the AMA to develop the first official practice guidelines for methadone treatment in 1971. These guidelines were very restrictive. They required stand-alone clinics rather than regular office practices, routine urine testing of patients, monitoring of patient arrest records, and exclusion of patients who could not prove addiction of at least two year's duration.[9] These restrictions were written into federal policy in the early 1970s.[10]

The restrictions highlight two different and somewhat contradictory elements of methadone maintenance. On the one hand, methadone policies differed in important ways from other 1970s drug reforms. Most important, they targeted clients as criminals or potential criminals rather than consumers in need of protection and care. Requiring urine testing and evaluating therapeutic success by monitoring arrest records had little value as consumer protections. Instead such policies enlisted clinics into surveilling, policing, and if necessary, punishing consumers.[11] Methadone regulations, in other words, were shaped not only by caution about a new type of legal opioid sales, but by fear of expanding white markets to a stigmatized and mistrusted population. While methadone maintenance was an unquestionable advance in addiction treatment, and an important step in making white markets fairer and more equitable, it also revealed real and meaningful limits in how far authorities were willing to go in these directions.

On the other hand, however, methadone restrictions were quite in line with the overall thrust of white market reforms in the 1970s. This was the first significant new approved use for opioids in the twentieth century. To skeptical authorities, it made sense to keep one foot on the brakes to make sure that it did not become yet another marketing-driven sales boom. Requiring stand-alone clinics, for example, limited how fast methadone sales could grow while making markets easier to track and, if necessary, discipline. By at least one measure, these cautions appeared to have been successful: after becoming widely available to people with addiction by the mid-1970s, methadone sales did not continue to boom but stayed relatively flat and even declined somewhat at the end of the decade as the heroin crisis receded. To put it mildly, this was not the usual trajectory for a radical new psychoactive drug therapy.

SCIENTIFIC INNOVATION: THE CASE OF TALWIN

With methadone, the opioid regulatory system managed a radical therapeutic innovation. With another drug, pentazocine, the system faced a different sort of challenge: the discovery of what appeared to be a nonaddictive painkiller—a potentially revolutionary pharmacological innovation. Here, too, regulators did a capable job, loosening restrictions when it seemed warranted but remaining wary and ready to act even in the face of industry opposition.

The pentazocine story began in the early 1960s, after researchers made a surprising discovery: opioid antagonists—drugs that reverse the effects of an opioid—could have painkilling properties much like opioids themselves.[12] Unfortunately the strong antagonists (e.g., nalorphine) could produce very unpleasant side effects such as hallucinations. But to Sterling-Winthrop, manufacturers of Demerol and one of the bigger players in the opioid industry, this was a genuine lead. They quickly set their researchers to tinkering with molecules to find weaker antagonists that had painkilling properties but that produced neither addiction nor hallucinations. Their search soon narrowed to a chemical family known as benzomorphans, the most promising of which they forwarded to Committee researchers for testing.[13]

One of these drugs, WN 20,228, performed particularly well.[14] Its painkilling strength was similar to morphine's, but it produced no hallucinations and did not prevent withdrawal symptoms in opioid-dependent monkeys.[15] This was enough to convince the Committee to approve tests in people with a history of opioid addiction. Single doses were administered to people not currently using opioids to test for subjective euphoric effects; the drug was substituted for morphine among people with current opioid dependence to see whether it would prevent withdrawal; and it was administered chronically, in increasing doses, to people without current addiction for seven days and then abruptly withdrawn to test whether it could produce physical dependence.[16]

After the drug passed all these tests, the Committee made a recommendation it had long dreamed of: unlike every narcotic before it, Eddy reported in early 1963, WN 20,228 "need not be subject to narcotics control."[17] Late in 1965 the FBN formally agreed, and after navigating the FDA's new drug application process, Sterling-Winthrop introduced the compound as Talwin in 1967.[18]

Like other manufacturers of would-be miracle opioids, Sterling-Winthrop made sure that the popular media got wind of Talwin long before it was available. This time there was a difference, however: instead of being swatted back by experts from the Committee or the FBN, media reports cited experts' research or even quoted them directly. The *New York Times* did not sound rosier than the Committee when it reported in 1963 that pentazocine was "as potent as morphine" but could "eliminate" the "fear of addiction in chronic pain."[19] Nor was the *Herald Tribune* being too dramatic in describing how Sterling-Winthrop's chemists, "building on knowledge painfully acquired over 30 years of almost fruitless effort, seem to have come to the goal."[20] When Talwin was finally introduced, both medical and popular media sang the same song: at last, scientists had discovered the holy grail of narcotic research, a nonaddictive drug as strong as morphine and perfect for treating chronic pain.[21] And this time, Nathan Eddy, who had dashed so many opioid hopes for so long, was singing with the choir. Talwin, he wrote, "represents essentially complete dissociation of analgesia and physical dependence."[22]

Sterling-Winthrop complemented its public relations push with a full-spectrum advertising blitz to physicians. One lushly illustrated pamphlet series titled "What Makes It Great?" featured commentary on the nature of greatness by notable figures such as literary critic Lionel Trilling.[23] All advertisements shared a central "hook": Talwin was not a narcotic but "an alternative to the narcotics." In some sense, this was true. Since 1937, when marijuana was added to the Harrison Act, "narcotic" had been a legal term more than a

Figure 7.1. Winthrop-Stearns's early Talwin advertisements emphasized their freedom from Harrison Act narcotic controls and suggested a vastly expanded population of consumers (n.d.; 1960s–1970s). Sterling Drug, Inc. Records, Archives Center, National Museum of American History, Smithsonian Institution.

pharmacological one, and, as Sterling-Winthrop pointed out in all its material, Talwin "is not classified as a narcotic and is not subject to narcotic controls."[24] The company also continually highlighted the fact that addiction experts had certified the drug as "non habit-forming," and that it also did not produce tolerance (i.e., the need to increase the dose over time to maintain the same pain relief).[25] As a result, they claimed, Talwin was particularly useful in treating chronic disorders because it could be administered "for as long as pain persists."[26]

Within a year of Talwin's introduction, caveats had been attached to such claims. In late 1968, the AMA's Council on Drugs reported that thirty cases of Talwin addiction had been identified.[27] The addiction was difficult to produce, in part because large doses of Talwin produced unpleasant hallucinations. Physical dependence appeared to be relatively mild. And most of the cases involved circumstances almost designed to produce addiction: after receiving injections under medical supervision, patients were given free rein to self-administer. Anecdotal reports of Talwin addiction did appear in the medical literature, but they were overshadowed by larger studies showing that such cases were extremely rare and that people with opioid addiction almost universally disliked the drug.[28]

Given this mixed record, the FDA and the AMA, like most other national and international authorities, urged caution in using Talwin but opposed placing it under narcotics controls.[29] Sterling-Winthrop did have to change its labeling and package inserts to acknowledge the possibility of Talwin addiction, although this language was permitted to be much milder than other opioids. "Patients with a history of drug abuse should be under close supervision," the fine print warned in one advertisement, because "there have been instances of psychological and physical dependence on Talwin in patients with such a history and, rarely, in patients without such a history."[30] A handful of states, more cautious than national and international authorities, placed Talwin on their controlled substances lists, despite Sterling-Winthrop's vigorous (and in some cases successful) opposition.[31]

When the other shoe finally dropped for Talwin, it came from an unexpected direction. It turned out that if Talwin was mixed with a widely available antihistamine (trippelennamine) and injected, it produced a "high"—and an addiction—very much like heroin. Stories vary on how "T's and Blues" (tripelennamine pills were blue) became popular among heroin users in the late 1970s. One observer traced the story to a sympathetic Chicago physician who prescribed Talwin to people with addiction during a late 1970s heroin drought.[32] Another theorized that a reservoir of popular knowledge remained from a 1950s drug boomlet, "Blue Velvet," in which tripelennamine had been combined with paregoric.[33]

However it happened, informal-market consumers embraced T's and Blues enthusiastically in a few midwestern cities in the late 1970s, particularly in Chicago. The first signs of the surge came from two sources: drug addiction treatment programs, which suddenly found themselves grappling with hundreds of Talwin users—more than a fourth of all their clients—and the state's Medicaid program, which saw a sharp and unexpected rise in payments for Talwin prescriptions.[34] A Chicago police officer, describing a facility selling so much Talwin that lines formed out the door, reported that "you have to see it to believe it. They are giving it up like it was candy."[35] The T's and Blues boom soon began to register in the city's emergency rooms, too, with Talwin-related visits shooting up from less than 50 in 1974 to nearly 140 in just the first three months of 1978.[36]

The sudden spike in addictive and dangerous use of Talwin galvanized the state's already active and well-developed regulatory infrastructure, which responded rapidly before the sales boom could become entrenched. In August 1978, the Dangerous Drug Commission placed Talwin on Schedule II of the state controlled substances list.[37] The state's Medicaid program also asked for and received the power to expel mis-prescribing physicians from the program, and convened a standing committee of eleven physicians to evaluate the offenders and, if appropriate, refer them to legal authorities.[38] The result was immediate and dramatic: sales of Talwin dropped to half of their peak, and the number of people with T's and Blues addiction registering in Cook County's addiction treatment programs fell by two-thirds.[39]

After Illinois clamped down on Talwin prescribing, the traffic shifted to Wisconsin, which had been among the first states to control the drug but only in the relatively lax Schedule III. As had happened in Illinois, addiction treatment programs suddenly faced a sharp spike in Talwin-using patients (in Milwaukee, they accounted for more than a third of all clients).[40] The Controlled Substances Board pushed to up-schedule the drug, but it was stymied by a "full blown effort . . . on the part of the manufacturer to stop it."[41] Wisconsin's Controlled Substances Board turned for advice to Illinois's Dangerous Drugs Commission, which had succeeded in up-scheduling Talwin despite Sterling-Winthrop's five court challenges and last-minute lobbying push at the state legislature (similar strategies had foiled Ohio's up-scheduling effort).[42] Wisconsin ultimately succeeded in 1982; Talwin use and addiction plummeted.[43]

It is easy to recognize the racial dimensions of this story: authorities cracked down on Talwin when it escaped from medical markets and became popular among poor and racialized informal-market consumers. But the crackdown was also shaped, in part, by the distinctive configuration of 1970s drug policy reforms. For example, authorities did not spend much time or resources cracking down on Talwin consumers, even though they were largely poor and non-white; instead, they were guided to addiction treatment, including methadone maintenance. Disciplinary firepower was trained on the pharmaceutical industry (and secondarily, gray market prescribers), and even here the goal was not prohibition but a heavily regulated availability.

The centrality of consumer protection in the Talwin campaign was on clear display when Congress held hearings in 1978. In the US Senate it seemed almost beyond debate that the problem was not Talwin's users, or even Talwin's gray market providers, but Sterling-Winthrop: "The manufacturer is the one that you have to really regulate more than anyone else," Illinois Senator Richard Daley argued.[44] When Sterling-Winthrop executives reminded legislators of the initial excitement about Talwin as a drug whose "potential was immense," it provoked this cynical response:

> Q: When you say immense can you define that in numbers?
> A: It was a very exciting development in those days.
> Q: It was a $20-million exciting development to your company. Proceed, then.[45]

Ultimately, one senator concluded, the Talwin affair indicated "a serious breakdown somewhere within the system of controls that we are supposed to have over the flow of licit drugs."[46]

The hearings accomplished their goal: after languishing since 1971, a petition to put Talwin on the Schedule of Controlled Substances was finally adopted in 1979, although it was placed in the lenient Schedule IV rather than the originally requested Schedule III.[47] Sterling-Winthrop responded by reformulating Talwin so that it included the full antagonist naloxone; naloxone was inert when swallowed but would bring on withdrawal symptoms if injected. Even then, some states remained skeptical. Wisconsin, for example, which had moved Talwin to Schedule II, decided to wait until there was real-world evidence that consumers could not "wash" the reformulated Talwin to get rid of the naloxone.[48]

Talwin's saga, like methadone's, showed both the accomplishments and limits of white market opioid governance. On the one hand, it revealed a robust but also flexible system of controls marked by a default (but not knee-jerk) skepticism of the pharmaceutical industry and, to a lesser extent, of professional medicine and pharmacy. However wary they might be to do so, state and federal authorities could distinguish genuine innovations from marketing puffery and were willing to loosen regulations to accommodate them. On the other hand, the Talwin crackdown showed a continued commitment to shut down all nonmedical use as a matter of principle. T's and Blues caused real problems where they became a phenomenon, but their informal-market availability could also be seen as providing quality-controlled, brand-name opioids to people who were already addicted. Such partial, unequal, and only loosely regulated availability is hardly the gold standard for addiction treatment. The clamor for Talwin, however, might have exposed gaps in methadone availability or resistance to methadone among some people with addiction. By reflexively classifying it as simple "abuse" rather than seeing it as a flawed but still potentially positive step by people with addiction, authorities showed the cost of strong pharmaceutical controls.

The end of the reform coalition

DRUG WARS REBORN

Even before the 1970s were over, there were signs that the flawed accomplishments of the era's drug reforms would not be long-lived. The reforms had been built by a series of shifting political alliances anchored in a coalition of consumer advocates and addiction medicalizers. It was this anchoring coalition that consistently drew parallels between white markets and informal markets, and nudged both sides of American drug policy toward a more unified approach. Starting early in the 1970s, however, addiction medicalizers began to fade and moral crusaders returned to political power.

The first step in this process was not subtle. New York's Republican governor, Nelson Rockefeller, had styled himself a moderate and had helped build an addiction treatment system that included methadone maintenance. The political costs of this approach were high, however. Treatment facilities were never sufficient for New York City's large addicted population, and opening new facilities required a constant battle against neighborhood groups opposed to having one placed in their communities. Heroin use and crime rates, meanwhile, continued to increase, especially in New York City's poorer areas. New treatment programs had no power to affect fundamental drivers such as deindustrialization, racial segregation, unemployment, and a giant new population of youths as the baby boomers came of age.[49]

Rockefeller decided that drug war liberalism was a political loser and, recognizing that the Republican Party had shifted away from moderates like himself, decided to stake his future on a political rebranding. In late 1972, he declared that after an honest attempt the treatment model had shown itself a failure, and he proposed a new, "tougher" approach: life in prison, without parole, for anyone caught selling illegal drugs. To promote his new strategy, Rockefeller resurrected old stereotypes of "dope fiends" and their suppliers as merciless nonwhite criminals who were only encouraged by liberal coddling. "Whole neighborhoods have been effectively destroyed by addicts as by an invading army," he told legislators, who responded by passing a slightly softened version of his bill.[50]

Although it had no beneficial impact on New York's drug problems, Rockefeller's law was an enormous political success. The governor's national reputation rose sharply—something that politicians across the United States watched carefully.[51] Persuaded by his reasoning or just afraid to seem "soft" during an era of rising crime rates, both Democrats and Republicans were soon competing to pass the harshest drug laws. On the national stage President Nixon, too, retreated from drug treatment, withdrawing support from medicalizer Jerome Jaffe (who resigned) and reversing the balance of federal spending so that funding for police enforcement surpassed funding for treatment by mid-decade.[52] The new political recalibration was encouraged by the emergence in the late 1970s of grassroots anti-drug activism, most prominently in the form of a white, suburban, middle-class "parent movement" outraged by the push to decriminalize marijuana.[53]

The resurgent drug war reached a new pitch during the "crack" cocaine crisis of the 1980s. Long a minor part of the American drug scene, cocaine had begun to return in the 1970s, at first as an exotic drug available primarily to the well-off. In the early 1980s, however, innovators developed a very cheap version of cocaine: smokeable "crack," available in small doses for just a few dollars. Crack was perfectly suited for the poor, racially marginalized urban neighborhoods that had long been home to America's largest informal drug markets.[54] With the addition of crack, the conditions were right for a new crisis. Central-city economies had collapsed, marooning a generation of urban youth without obvious employment opportunities—a reserve army of employees and consumers in the informal economy. The dominance of Rockefeller-style drug warriors meant that informal-market consumers received not protection but racist invective and criminal enforcement from authorities. And finally, the nation's shrinking addiction treatment system focused primarily on opioids.[55]

Central city neighborhoods, already struggling from strategic disinvestment and discriminatory policing, were hit hard at multiple levels. Cocaine addiction and its associated harms skyrocketed. Violence rose, too, as sellers competed for territory in informal (and thus unregulated) markets. Whole communities bore the brunt of increased punitive policing and entanglement with the criminal justice system, especially after harsh new drug laws were passed in 1984 and 1986 with draconian provisions for crack-related offenses.[56]

The crack sales boom and the policing it provoked did incalculable damage to some of America's most vulnerable communities. They also undermined the political alliances and cultural logic that had sustained 1970s reforms. Drug treatment remained available, especially to white and middle-class drug users, but addiction medicalizers had suffered a mortal political blow.[57] This left the public stage to moral crusaders, who resurrected hoary stereotypes of people with addiction as animalistic black and brown criminals rather than people suffering from an illness.[58] In public discourse, "addicts" were no longer people who needed protection, but people the public needed to be protected from.

THE DECLINE OF CONSUMER ADVOCACY

Consumer advocates also lost influence in the 1980s, as conservatives mounted a challenge to what they called burdensome federal regulations. The FDA was a common target of such challenges. Even during the 1970s, when reformers were more likely to accuse the agency of being too soft rather than too strong in its stance toward the drug industry, influential voices could be heard complaining that FDA requirements were stifling innovation. As early as 1968, future president Ronald Reagan described the FDA as part of the "regulatory nightmare unfolding in Washington."[59] At the heart of these critiques was the so-called drug lag, or the slower pace at which new drugs were being introduced.[60] Some drug lag critics were ideological warriors like the American Enterprise Institute, which sponsored a series of books expanding on the topic and hosted speakers like Reagan.[61] But the notion that burdensome regulations caused serious problems also gained ground among Democrats in President Jimmy Carter's administration. For example, the US General Accounting Office issued a report in 1980 entitled *FDA Drug Approval—A Lengthy Process That Delays the Availability of Important New Drugs.*[62]

These anti-regulatory stirrings became a much stronger force in 1981, when Reagan and a host of new Republican senators and representatives arrived in Washington. Within a few days of taking office, Reagan ordered a sixty-day freeze on all pending regulations and issued an executive order requiring cost-benefit analyses of all new regulations. He also established a task force to invite regulatory horror stories and suggestions from businesses, private-sector groups, and state officials.[63] Secretary of Health and Human Services Robert Schweiker considered a range of ideas to eliminate "unnecessary delays" in drug approval, including closer cooperation with industry and production goals.[64] Editors at the conservative *Wall Street Journal* supported these moves from afar, blaming bureaucratic delay for over 100,000 unnecessary deaths and questioning "whether we should even have an FDA."[65]

Skeptical views of the FDA were not limited to conservative politicians. Rather, conservative politicians were elected, in part, because such skepticism had become widespread. "Alternative" medicine devotees and HIV/AIDS activists, for example, also protested what they saw as unnecessarily tight control over drug markets. In the 1970s, advocates of alternative medicine touted the value of

Laetrile, a derivative of apricot kernels, as a treatment for cancer. The FDA opposed sale of Laetrile because it had not gone through premarket testing—a laborious and expensive process. The FDA's decision generated powerful grassroots opposition from some cancer sufferers and their loved ones. Then, in the 1980s, HIV/AIDS activists used a variety of passionate and creative strategies to portray the FDA as literally killing people through what they decried as its unwillingness to act quickly on new drugs. The FDA responded in a variety of ways, including offering expedited review of urgently needed drugs.[66]

Encouraged by these new anti-regulatory attitudes, the Reagan and Bush administrations froze FDA budgets and began to explore a range of reforms to speed up drug review, including the possibility of outsourcing to the private sector.[67] A compromise was soon struck. In 1992, the Prescription Drug User Fee Act levied a special tax on pharmaceutical companies to help defray costs of drug review; in return, the FDA promised to accelerate its reviews.[68] Critics charged that this encouraged unhealthy ties between industry and regulator, and placed pressure on the FDA to avoid offending pharmaceutical companies. They pointed to drugs that had made it through the new pipeline with insufficient vetting such as the anti-acne drug Accutane, which had been approved on an expedited basis and then improperly prescribed to pregnant women, resulting in thousands of birth defects.[69] Such criticisms were muted, however, in an era marked by optimistic faith in private-sector innovation and mistrust of the government bureaucracy that supposedly slowed it down.

Anti-regulatory reformers secured one other important coup in the 1980s and 1990s: FDA approval of direct-to-consumer marketing. "Ethical" pharmaceuticals had been defined, in part, by the promise not to advertise to the public, and manufacturers of prescription-only drugs had formally followed suit (although, as we have seen, both types of drugs were vigorously promoted to the public through various other marketing strategies). Starting in 1985, however, the FDA allowed prescription-only drugs to be formally advertised to the public as long as the mandated informational language was included. Spending on direct-to-consumer advertising skyrocketed from $12 million in 1989, to $340 million in 1995, to $1.1 billion in 1998, and then to $2.24 billion in 1999.[70]

The return of white market sedatives and stimulants

White markets were powerfully affected by the increasing strength of both moral crusaders and anti-regulatory reformers. The two were closely linked: moral crusaders' ideological quarantining of addiction as separate from "the public" made it more difficult for consumer advocates to convey the urgency of protecting consumers from potentially addictive pharmaceuticals.

Even when they had been implemented, the 1970s restrictions on sedatives and stimulants had been deeply unpopular with at least some white market consumers. Tellingly, these consumers had often expressed their dissatisfaction through the logic of political conservatism and the racialized drug war. "I suppose I could be considered one of the silent majority," an Arizona man wrote to his congressman. "One by one they are disappearing—our freedoms—down the bureaucratic drain."[71] Others relied on racial code words in an effort to rebuilt white market logic. A physician from Osceola, Wisconsin, for example, complained that "the purpose of the law [amphetamine restriction] is to discourage the weight clinics in the Milwaukee and other areas. For those of us in the bordering communities, this problem does not come up."[72]

Meanwhile, as anti-regulatory conservatives gained power in the 1980s, at least some therapeutic reformers looked back with dismay on what they identified as anti-drug hysterias that had ruined perfectly good medicines in the 1970s. Valium, the most recent subject of popular criticism, was the most important example of such revisionist analysis. "Where are all the tranquilizer junkies?" asked an article in *JAMA*, one of many similar retrospectives.[73] Asking about "tranquilizer junkies" deployed a classic stereotype of addiction to highlight the supposed absurdity of a medicine like Valium ever being a real source of addiction. There was a logic to this, although not the intended one. People who developed dependence on or addiction to Valium were unlikely to have "acted like junkies" because with their safe and assured white market supply, they had no need to. Their drug use may have caused them problems—serious and sometimes fatal—but those problems looked different than consumers navigating unpredictable, risky, and illegal markets.

As these criticisms and misgivings show, 1970s reforms had not eliminated consumers', prescribers', and (of course) manufacturers' desire for robust white markets. All the necessary ingredients remained; the only thing missing was a new set of medical rationales and a new generation of drugs to replace the ones that had been discredited in the 1970s. That missing ingredient soon appeared, thanks to a revolution in American psychiatry.

The revolution was launched in 1980 when the American Psychiatric Association, seeking greater scientific legitimacy (and a surer basis for insurance reimbursements), published a new diagnostic handbook, the *DSM-III*. Traditional, Freudian-influenced psychiatry had classified mental illnesses based on what had caused them, but this approach had produced endless debate and little hard evidence. So the new *DSM-III* defined illnesses not by causes but by the presence, frequency, and intensity of a checklist of symptoms. If a person suffered from enough items on the checklist, he or she could be diagnosed as having the illness. This avoided conflict over etiology and made it easier to produce statistical evidence of effectiveness through double-blind, placebo-controlled trials favored by the FDA and insurance companies.[74]

The checklist approach vastly expanded the number of mental illnesses. Because causes did not matter, any coherent combination of symptoms had the potential to be a distinct illness. As one critic observed, "Chronic dissatisfaction with life could be renamed 'dysthymia'; the distress arising from problems with spouses or lovers could be called 'major depression'; the disturbances of troublesome children could be renamed as conduct, personality, or attention deficit disorders."[75] The *DSM-III* listed 265 distinct, discrete mental illnesses; its 1987 update had 292; and the 1994 *DSM-IV* had nearly 400.[76]

The proliferation of new mental illnesses was a boon to pharmaceutical companies selling psychoactive medications. Each new illness created the possibility of a new, patentable drug treatment. Drug companies were often involved in developing and defining new diagnoses, thus increasing the chances that their medicines would be a good match. Each new diagnosis also created an opportunity to "sell sickness" through educational campaigns and "astroturf" (industry-funded grassroots) political advocacy by sufferers.[77]

The shift to the *DSM-III* created new medical justifications, backed by double-blind placebo-controlled trials, to expand white market access to sedatives and stimulants. The shift also provided pharmaceutical companies an ideal way to produce and certify a new generation of supposedly innovative sedatives and stimulants to fill the increased need.

The first of these products, the antidepressant Prozac, was perfect for the task. It was nonaddictive and, because it was linked to the cutting edge (and eventually disproven) theory that depression was caused by a deficiency of the neurotransmitter serotonin, its manufacturer, Eli Lilly, portrayed it as a technological breakthrough—a scientifically sculpted "clean" drug that could cure a specific illness with minimal side effects. Such arguments were bolstered by thoughtful boosterism from influential psychiatrists like Peter Kramer, whose book *Listening to Prozac* climbed the bestseller lists along with the blockbuster drug it explored.[78]

With Prozac as the proof-of-concept, pharmaceutical companies quickly introduced a host of sedatives and stimulants following the same template. Xanax, for example, was just another benzodiazepine when it was introduced in 1981; it was actually slightly more addictive than some of its chemical cousins because it was relatively fast-acting. Pfizer eventually differentiated it from existing sedatives by casting it as a magic bullet for "panic disorder." Sales of Xanax and other new sedatives such as the sleeping pill Ambien (introduced in 1992) shot up, recovering to their pre-1970s levels and then continuing on, seemingly without limit, as sedatives once again became some of America's most widely prescribed medicines (see fig A.2 in the appendix).

It turned out that the same process could also be used to rescue old drugs. Ritalin (methylphenidate), an amphetamine-like stimulant sold since the 1950s, got a new life in the 1980s and 1990s as a treatment for the *DSM-III* condition of attention deficit disorder in children. Amphetamine itself returned in 1994 with Adderall, advertised for the same condition (now renamed attention deficit and hyperactivity disorder). Diagnoses and prescriptions soared; like sedatives, stimulant sales easily recaptured their pre-1970s territory and then continued to grow with no end in sight (see fig. A.3 in the appendix).

These campaigns would not have passed muster in the 1970s. Claims of miraculous specificity with few side effects and no addiction would have been met with great skepticism by regulators, medical experts, journalists, and even many consumers. It was only in the 1980s and 1990s, after the triumph of moral crusaders and antiregulatory advocates, that such magical marketing claims could be persuasive. Addiction was again associated with poor and racialized informal-market consumers, and the pharmaceutical industry was again praised as a force for innovative problem solving. In such circumstances it was possible to buy the unlikely argument that miraculous new sedatives and stimulants could be sold without risk or restraint to white market consumers.

The white market opioid boom

FINDING A DIAGNOSTIC VEHICLE: THE PAIN REFORM MOVEMENT

The return of white market sedatives and stimulants offered a template for a more radical development: the rehabilitation of white market opioids. For sedatives and stimulants, rehabilitation had come from new diagnoses that justified wider prescribing and provided a new narrative to replace existing stories of addiction. For opioids, the new diagnosis was pain. Pain was a very old problem, of course, but it had gained new prominence in the decades since World War II as pain reformers worked to establish it as a subject of medical research and treatment. Most of these reformers remained wary of opioids and some even identified opioid use as an example of America's problematic approach to pain care—as a reason for reform, not a potential solution. A radical minority of reformers, however, disagreed and called for opioids to be used much more widely to treat more types of pain.

The pain reform movement began during World War II when physicians treating injured soldiers confronted pain and suffering on a massive scale. After the war, the large number of injured veterans made pain a visible and pressing social problem. Some experts warned that taking pain seriously might reward "malingerers" or foster dependence (or "learned helplessness"), but others explored political and medical strategies to ease suffering. In politics, reformers added chronic pain as one of the disabilities covered by the Social Security Act. In medicine, specialists developed new multimodal treatments that mixed psychiatric, anesthetic, surgical, and pharmacological approaches.[79] Many were not designed to eradicate pain but to help patients control and manage it in a manner best suited to their particular life circumstances. Helping to organize and circulate research were new professional societies such as the International Association for the Study of Pain (1973), the American Pain Society (1977), and the American Academy of Pain Medicine (1983), as well as a host of specialist medical journals such as the Pain Society's *Pain* (1975).[80]

One subset of pain reformers did call for more use of opioids: those focused on advanced cancer and other terminal illnesses. They argued that physicians were too reluctant to ease end-of-life suffering with opioids—that at its fringes, extreme manifestations of opioid conservatism could actually be harmful. This was not an absurd claim. One 1956 cancer textbook, for example, advised physicians to use opioids only as a very last resort, typically when a patient's life "can be measured in weeks."[81] A 1973 study of a Bronx,

New York, hospital revealed that nurses and house staff provided only 25 to 50 percent of prescribed opioids for pain, even though many patients complained of pain.[82]

Soon, a raft of studies showed that opioids were being withheld unequally: elderly and very young cancer patients received few opioids; women were given fewer than men; and working-class and racial minority patients received even less.[83] Racial disparities were particularly acute because they were compounded by multiple forms of prejudice. Most physicians were taught that African Americans experienced pain less intensely than whites, for example, and most probably also shared popular prejudices associating racial minorities with addiction. Both made treatment of any sort, but especially opioid prescriptions, less likely—and that was on top of the difficulty racial minorities faced in gaining access to healthcare in the first place. In the late 1960s and early 1970s, civil rights activists drew attention to such racial disparities as they advocated for increased treatment of sickle cell anemia, a chronically painful illness whose disproportionately African American sufferers had long been ignored or rejected for medical care.[84]

The problem of cancer pain, meanwhile, worsened as treatments improved and even terminally ill patients lived longer. So in the 1970s, physician reformers at St. Christopher's Hospice in London and the Memorial Sloan-Kettering Cancer Center in New York pushed back against the most extreme manifestations of opioid conservatism. Studies at both hospitals found that advanced cancer patients did not in fact become easily addicted, and that when used carefully and tailored to the individual, opioids could contribute to increased well-being at the end of life.[85] In 1982, the World Health Organization invited many of the most prominent pain treatment specialists to develop official guidelines for treating cancer pain. The guidelines suggested a "ladder" of treatment, starting with non-opioid painkillers, then moving to weak opiates like codeine, and finally to stronger opiates like morphine.[86]

The campaign to reform cancer pain treatment was quite visible and successful, but it was far from enough to have instigated a wholesale reconsideration of the place of opioids in medical practice. Cancer pain specialists were just one part of the broader movement to reform pain care, and most reformers, even cancer specialists, still shared traditional wariness of opioids and actively discouraged their use for most types of chronic pain.[87]

A few, more radical reformers took a very different approach, however. One of the earliest and most visible of these was Kathleen Folcy, a physician at the Memorial Sloan-Kettering Cancer Center. Like other cancer specialists, Foley critiqued physicians' reluctance to use opioids for that condition.[88] But she was ready to go further and argue that opioids might also be useful in chronic noncancer pain. "Although fear of addiction limits narcotic use by both physicians and patients," she wrote in 1981, "there are no published long-term data to support the thesis that chronic use of narcotic analgesics causes addiction." She described but then rejected classic studies warning of addiction risks, pointing instead to what she described as a "more recent prospective study" by Jane Porter and Hershel Jick that showed only four cases of addiction in nearly 12,000 hospitalized patients given opioids at least once. This data, combined with her own small study at Sloan-Kettering, she concluded, "suggests that medical use of narcotics is rarely, if ever, associated with the development of addiction."[89]

This was an aggressive claim to make on the basis of one study. Especially since that huge "prospective study" turned out to be no study at all but a five-sentence letter to the editor of the *New England Journal of Medicine* offering an interesting side observation about opioids from a long-running program that tracked adverse side effects of medications administered in selected Boston hospitals.[90] The overall program had not been designed to assess the addiction risk of opioids in chronic pain: all opioid use had taken place in the hospital, so no conclusions could be drawn about use for nonhospitalized patients; the figure of 12,000 study subjects included patients who had died, who had been given only short-term opioids, or who had been hospitalized for surgery rather than pain; patients with a history of addiction had been excluded from the tally; and assessments of "addiction" were informal and highly problematic.[91] Even more remarkable, Foley reported that in her own small study, "2 of 17 patients with chronic non-malignant pain abused their drugs, continually took more than prescribed amounts, and over-dosed on the drugs prescribed." Although those two patients had had prior histories of "drug abuse behavior," this was still more than 10 percent of study participants—not exactly "rarely, if ever."[92]

Foley's was initially a lone voice in the pain reform movement, but during the 1980s she was joined by a few other pain specialists. One of the most important was Foley's colleague, pain specialist Russell Portenoy. Foley and Portenoy authored one of the most widely cited calls for rethinking opioids and chronic pain treatment in 1986 in the journal *Pain*. The article did not abandon all opioid cautions; for example, it advised using opioids only after "all reasonable attempts at pain control have failed." But such precautions were perfunctory and brief, and far outweighed by the paper's most dramatic claim: that long-term opioid treatment for chronic pain virtually never caused addiction and was "more humane" and less risky than other approaches. To support this claim, Foley and Portenoy described their own modest thirty-eight-person retrospective study of opioid-treated pain patients, and introduced Porter and Jick's letter to the editor—described inaccurately as a major, careful, relevant study—to a mass medical audience.[93]

The article's mixture of token cautions and boosterish enthusiasm echoed an important earlier work in the white market renaissance, Peter Kramer's *Listening to Prozac*, which also included thoughtful cautions that were overshadowed by attention-grabbing promises of medical miracles. The use of faint damns to make high praise more believable is well captured by Foley and Portenoy's recommendation to warn patients of the possibility of addiction because "the current data cannot refute [it] absolutely."[94]

Actually, Foley and Portenoy did not counsel physicians to warn patients about the risk of *addiction*. Instead they used the term "psychological dependence." This usage highlights another important strategy in their article: redefining addiction. Tolerance and physical dependence, Foley and Portenoy argued, were normal, expected side effects of opioid treatment and should not be thought of as elements of addiction. Instead addiction should be understood as "a set of aberrant behaviors marked by drug craving, efforts to secure its supply, interference with physical health or psychosocial function, and recidivism after detoxification."[95] This was a complex and costly redefinition. On the one hand, it promised to reduce the stigma associated with pain patients' opioid use by normalizing their experiences of dependence. On the other hand, it reinforced the stigma of nonmedical consumers, whose pursuit of opioids in unpredictable and illegal informal markets often required "aberrant behaviors." As had happened repeatedly throughout the twentieth century, protections for white market consumers were built, in part, at the cost of contrasting them with other, more socially marginalized drug consumers.

Another important effort to redefine addiction along these lines came in 1989 from another pair of radical pain reformers, J. David Haddox and David Weissman. Haddox and Weissman theorized that even when pain patients appeared to exhibit addiction, they were actually experiencing "pseudoaddiction": addiction-like symptoms caused by insufficient pain relief.[96] The appropriate medical response under these circumstances was more opioids. Here again, an effort to destigmatize and medicalize pain patients' opioid use depended on an implicit contrast with nonmedical use. Under the pseudoaddiction theory, almost no behavior by pain patients would qualify as true addiction, no matter how closely it mimicked the behaviors of informal-market consumers. In effect, this boiled "addiction" down to its most essential social components: addiction described the behavior of informal-market drug consumers, while white market consumers could experience only pseudoaddiction.

Claims that opioids were not addictive when used by pain patients and theories like pseudoaddiction created new tools to accomplish an old task: defining white market drug consumption as fundamentally different than informal-market drug consumption. Whatever its medical pedigree, the new conceptual infrastructure relied on (and reinforced) longstanding cultural ideas about white markets: the presumption of good faith by all parties, the supposed lack of desire for drug-induced pleasure or drug-borne profits, the implicit (and sometimes explicit) contrast with racialized criminal "dope fiends." This carved out a zone of respectable drug sales at the cost of doubling down on the stigmatization and criminalization of informal-market drug consumers. As the implicit contrasting case, informal market consumers were not included in newly sympathetic ideas of opioid use; their stigma remained intact. As Americans were about to learn, this was an unstable and dangerous setup—even for the white market consumers who were supposed to benefit from it.

WHITE MARKET OPIOID BREAKTHROUGH

Among those paying close attention to radical pain reformers was the pharmaceutical industry. The arguments put forward by Foley, Portenoy, and Haddox were quite similar to claims that opioid manufacturers had been trying to make for decades. One company was particularly intrigued: Purdue Pharma, owned by the Sackler brothers, the physician-advertisers whose marketing genius had powered the Valium juggernaut in the 1960s and 1970s. Purdue was preparing to launch a new slow-release brand of oxycodone, OxyContin, that was designed for use by chronic pain patients. For most of the twentieth century, pure, strong opioids such as oxycodone were strongly discouraged or even disallowed for chronic pain. If Foley, Portenoy, and others won the day, however, OxyContin's commercial potential would be limitless. So Purdue, and soon other opioid manufacturers as well, lavished radical pain reformers with funding and other forms of support, helping to raise the professional status and authority of what had been minority voices.[97] Portenoy served as president of the American Pain Society (APS) and the American Pain Foundation (APF), for example, and Haddox—who later took an executive position at Purdue—got the chief post at the American Academy of Pain Medicine (AAPM).[98] All these and other pain organizations, along individual physicians associated with them, received millions of dollars from opioid manufacturers—as much as 90 percent of their budget in the case of APF.[99]

As we saw in chapter 3, this was not the first time that industry-supported medical voices, even prominent ones, had raised challenges to restrictive opioid controls. The historical context for such challenges had changed in at least three ways, however. First, the success and institutionalization of the pain reform movement established new formal networks and institutions (pain societies, pain journals, etc.). Pro-opioid voices speaking from these new positions of authority—"key opinion leaders" in drug industry parlance—carried much more weight than individual physicians, no matter how eminent, speaking solely for themselves in earlier decades. Second, formulations like pseudoaddiction were far likelier to gain acceptance on the heels of the crack cocaine crisis, when addiction was once again associated with impoverished, inner-city racial minorities. Third, political zeal to unleash markets by cutting down on government red tape raised new doubts about the robust anti-opioid regulatory regime, already an odd "big government" holdout in a conservative era. This was no mere philosophical issue. Political battles over pain had reached a fever pitch in the 1980s, as the Reagan administration sought to cut large numbers of people with chronic pain from the Social Security Disability rolls while liberals indicted the move as immoral. In this context, opioid manufacturers' promise of high-tech, private-sector solutions to the political stalemate were more particularly appealing.[100]

Purdue was the first opioid manufacturer to grasp the commercial potential of the new opioid landscape. The company faced a tough marketing challenge: oxycodone, the main ingredient of its new product OxyContin, was not a new drug, and its history in the United States was a checkered one. As we saw in chapter 3, the NRC Committee had prevented Endo Pharmaceuticals from marketing oxycodone as a less addictive opioid in the late 1940s, and the drug was also the key ingredient in Percodan, which had caused such problems in California in the early 1960s. Despite these precedents, in 1995 Purdue succeeded in getting OxyContin through the regulatory and professional gauntlets that had kept a lid on pharmaceutical opioids for so long.

The first step was to get FDA approval to market OxyContin—a pure, strong opioid—as appropriate for long-term use in moderate, chronic, noncancer pain. To do so they used an entirely new strategy that relied on radical pain reformers' new medical theories about opioids and addiction. Purdue made no studies of OxyContin's addictiveness; instead, the company stipulated from the beginning that oxycodone had "an abuse liability similar to morphine" and agreed that it should be treated as cautiously as morphine. In the past, this would have spelled doom for a would-be miracle opioid because it would have triggered the full weight of the restrictive opioid control system. Now, however, Purdue could point to influential medical figures like Foley and Portenoy to argue that being as addictive as morphine was not, in fact, a big problem, at least not for chronic pain patients. The company's proposed label for OxyContin, approved by the FDA, admitted addictiveness similar to morphine but then went on to make three softening claims. First, that "iatrogenic 'addiction' to opioids legitimately used in the treatment of pain is very rare." Second, that physical dependence, tolerance, and "preoccupation with achieving adequate pain relief" were all normal, expected aspects of legitimate therapy for some patients and were not the same thing as addiction. Third, that OxyContin was actually less addictive than other opioids because it released the medication slowly, which, the company claimed (based on no research or evidence), "is believed to reduce the abuse liability of a drug."[101] Acceptance of these radical new claims was smoothed by increasingly cozy relations between the drug industry and its regulators; two years after approving Purdue's language, for example, the FDA medical officer overseeing the OxyContin application, Curtis Wright, accepted a position as the company's executive director of medical affairs.[102]

Purdue was not the only one to seize the favorable turn-of-the-century moment. Indeed, much as had happened in the long-ago barbiturate boom, many competitors quickly joined in. Among many others, for example, Johnson and Johnson's subsidiary Janssen began marketing its fentanyl patch Duragesic in the mid-1990s; Cephalon (later Teva) marketed Actiq, a fentanyl lollipop, in 2000; and Endo Pharmaceuticals released a pure oxymorphone drug Opana in 2006.

Once the new-generation opioids had been approved for chronic pain, the next job was to advertise them. For the first time in living memory, there would be relatively little oversight of this process. The result was a nearly overwhelming ocean of marketing that transformed minority, radical views about opioids into universally recognized common sense. These campaigns would certainly not have been allowed in earlier years. Federal regulators had grown less hawkish, less well funded, and less capable in the anti-regulatory era, however, and opioid manufacturers had coopted many of the professional organizations that had previously served as bulwarks of opioid control, transforming them into enthusiastic opioid boosters.

Purdue's OxyContin provides a good example of how the new opioid marketing campaigns worked. One central challenge was changing physicians' long-ingrained reluctance to prescribe opioids for moderate pain.[103] Toward this end Purdue tripled its promotional spending and directed its in-person sales representatives to assure physicians that fears of addiction were overblown.[104] It advocated OxyContin for a range of chronic uses long disallowed for opioids including back pain, osteoarthritis, neuropathic pain, postoperative pain, rheumatology, dentistry, sports/rehabilitation, and, in 2002, "primary care."[105] Addiction appeared in these marketing materials primarily in the context of claims that old fears of addiction were "unwarranted" and had contributed to the undertreatment of pain.[106] Sales representatives were encouraged to focus on physicians who prescribed unusually high volumes of opioids—a reversal of previous eras when such high-prescribing physicians might have been investigated as potential problems, not potential sources of profit.[107]

As powerful as it is, however, advertising can only go so far. To combat physicians' deeply entrenched concern about opioid addiction, Purdue had to do more than advertise. Fortunately for Purdue, by investing in pro-opioid medical voices, it had already taken a large step toward a complementary strategy: coopting the professional and state regulatory bodies that governed medical standards, transforming them from agents of opioid restriction into agents that encouraged or even required more opioid use.

Thanks in part to their sizable industry funding, these organizations dominated professional discussion of pain and opioids and powerfully influenced medical guidelines and regulations. In 1997, the American Association of Pain Management joined with the American Pain Society to publish a consensus statement on opioids and chronic pain treatment. This statement, written by a committee chaired by David Haddox (co-inventor of the psuedoaddiction concept), and with Russell Portenoy as its sole consultant, boldly challenged the restrictive opioid consensus in a manner that closely followed the industry line. For example, after identifying pain as a growing health issue that is "often managed inadequately despite the ready availability of safe and effective treatments," the statement identified only one of those treatments by name: opioids. It then devoted itself to debunking longstanding opioid fears. Addiction, for example, was extremely rare, and the risk of fatal overdose had been overblown: "it is now accepted," the statement said, that respiratory depression was "short-lived," reversed by pain, and, in any case, occurred only in opioid-naïve patients.[108]

The vice chair of the consensus committee, David Joranson, was especially committed to the goal of reforming state laws, regulations, and medical board policies.[109] Toward this goal, he helped to found and run an organization within the University of Wisconsin–Madison called the Pain & Policy Studies Group (PPSG). Purdue and many other opioid manufacturers poured millions of dollars into PPSG.[110]

Opioid manufacturers were amply rewarded for their generosity by an influential campaign to reform state opioid policies. Joranson and a rotating mix of other industry-supported opioid advocates argued that "physicians' fears of being investigated for prescribing opioids" were responsible for America's "inadequate management of pain." They urged state medical boards to fix the situation by "adopt[ing] policies that encourage adequate pain management and dispel physicians' fears of being disciplined." Doing so, they argued, required an extensive campaign: not just new policies but new enforcement guidelines, new medical education programs, and joint professional-public awareness campaigns. They concluded with a warning: if such efforts did not produce change, "frustration with physicians who do not provide adequate pain management will mount and may lead to policies that penalize *inadequate* pain management." Such moves, the authors noted, were already being considered by the prestigious Institute of Medicine and several state boards. "If pain management is to be an expected part of quality medical practice," they insisted, "then substandard pain management practice must be subject to review and corrective action as in any other area of medical practice."[111]

This was a breathtaking position: not only should states loosen their oversight so as to allow opioid prescribing without fear, but states should actually reverse their traditional practices and discipline physicians who failed to prescribe liberally enough.

The PPSG pursued its agenda by lobbying state medical boards and issuing annual "report cards" evaluating states' opioid policies. Their efforts, combined with other campaigns by opioid manufacturers, appear to have been quite successful. In 1998, for example, the Federation of State Medical Boards, which received $2 million from opioid manufacturers starting in 1997, issued model guidelines for state boards to follow. The guidelines were developed with the help of the American Association for Pain Management, the American Pain Society, and PPSG, among others.[112]

The Federation's guidelines closely echoed Joranson in arguing that myths about addiction and fear of being disciplined prevented American physicians from providing adequate pain relief. After a brief mention of "non-pharmacologic modalities," the guidelines focused exclusively on the benefits of opioids, which, they explained, were safe and superior and carried little risk of addiction (especially when cases of pseudoaddiction were excluded). They explicitly reassured physicians not to "fear disciplinary action from the Board or other state regulatory or enforcement agency." Indeed, according to the model guidelines, state boards would not even punish physicians who failed to follow the new loose rules as long as "good cause is shown for such deviation." Opioid use would not be evaluated based on "quantity and chronicity of prescribing" but on the individual needs of the patient.[113]

The Federation's guidelines were widely distributed and endorsed, and over twenty state boards had adopted some version of them by 2004. But industry-supported opioid advocates argued that physician behavior was not changing fast enough, and the Federation issued new and even more aggressive guidelines in 2004. These guidelines continued to focus exclusively on opioids but added a threat of punishment for underprescribing physicians: "inappropriate treatment, including the undertreatment of pain" would be considered a "departure from an acceptable standard of practice."[114]

State medical boards were not the only regulatory body to implement opioid manufacturers' preferred new approach. Another key organization, the Joint Commission on the Accreditation of Healthcare Organizations, collaborated with PPSG to produce hospital accreditation standards for pain and opioids—required, not recommended, practices.[115] Issued in 2001, the new standards described pain as the "Fifth Vital Sign," required that all patients be asked to rate their pain on a numeric scale of 1 to 10, and required caregivers to reduce pain to the low end of the scale.[116] This was a bonanza for opioid manufacturers. Purdue won an exclusive agreement to help the Commission develop materials to educate hospitals and the public about the new standards—campaigns that, the company noted, provided its sales force with "many door-opening opportunities."[117] Internal Purdue documents described the "Fifth Vital Sign" campaign as "an important promotional initiative."[118]

By the late 1990s and early 2000s, then, industry-funded opioid advocates had been given bigger and more prestigious individual platforms to circulate their views, and these views had also been institutionalized among the (also industry-funded) professional and regulatory bodies that determined and enforced medical standards of care.

Purdue and its competitors also marketed the new gospel of opioids to the general public. They invested heavily in "selling sickness," using websites, films, books, pamphlets, and other materials to educate Americans about the importance of pain as a medical problem, and to inform patients of their right to receive opioid treatment. Industry-funded "thought leaders" like Portenoy filled the lecture and media circuit with the same message.[119] These company-specific campaigns were supplemented by new popular magazines (e.g., *Pain Community News* and *Pain Monitor*) and pamphlets (e.g., *Treatment Options: A Guide for People Living with Pain*) published by industry-sponsored professional groups such as the American Pain Foundation.

Popular education materials could be quite explicit, even aggressive, in urging readers to demand opioid treatment. The *Treatment Options* pamphlet, for example, warned that "despite the great benefits of opioids," many physicians still believed "myths and misunderstandings" and might be "afraid to give them." Patients should therefore inform themselves about treatment options; be unafraid to speak up and challenge the myths; and, if necessary, "bring a relative or friend to your appointments to provide any support you might need."[120]

Central to all these marketing campaigns was a visual vocabulary that portrayed patients as stereotypical white market consumers: white, respectable, and health seeking. This visual vocabulary served as a linchpin, situating OxyContin and other new opioids firmly in the white market tradition where they could benefit from a century of cultural work that helped make marketing claims believable. Purdue and other companies seemed to be well aware of this, to judge not just from their advertising imagery but from the geographic patterns of their marketing campaigns, which initially focused on demographically white regions such as northern New

England, Kentucky, and West Virginia. The best way to protect a drug's reputation remained near-exclusive use by traditional white market consumers.[121]

The end product of all this maneuvering was that sales of pharmaceutical opioids, like sales of sedatives and stimulants, increased to unprecedented levels (see fig. A.1 in the appendix). A public health catastrophe was not long in following. Opioid addiction surged to levels not seen since the 1960s, then to levels not seen since the nineteenth century, and then finally to levels that had never been seen before. Drug-related harm rose too. In 2001, five years after OxyContin's launch, fatal oxycodone overdoses had increased by 400 percent and emergency room visits by 1,000 percent.[122] In a tragic white market synergy, nearly half of those overdoses also involved a pharmaceutical sedative; it was not entirely clear which drug should be blamed for those deaths.[123] From there, the numbers just continued to get worse (see fig. A.4 in the appendix). After a century of problems and risk, the white market apocalypse had finally arrived.

It is important not to draw too simplistic a line between the new gospel of opioids and the ensuing health crisis. The connection was complicated in two ways. First, like many successful marketing campaigns the gospel was built on kernels of truth. The great majority of people addicted during the crisis did have a previous history of nonmedical drug use, and most were friends and families of pain patients rather than pain patients themselves.[124] This was in line with opioid reformers' claims that addiction risks were low for pain patients with no prior drug problems.

This is far from a simple or easily applied finding, however. The lifetime prevalence of problematic alcohol or drug use in America was quite high (as much as 20 percent), meaning that large numbers of pain patients belonged to the at-risk group (and that figure does not include "behavioral" addictions such as gambling).[125] Moreover, it is not easy for physicians to know in advance where an individual patient fell on the risk spectrum. Social prejudices often took the place of actual knowledge: physicians were comfortable prescribing to white patients, for example, but reluctant to prescribe to racial minorities.

Safely expanding opioid treatment of pain would thus have required a significant investment of time, energy, and resources to identify and protect at-risk consumers (both pain patients and their friends/families). Doing so without discriminating against racial minorities, the poor, and other stigmatized groups would have required even more care. The gold-rush mentality of the opioid boom left no room for such nuanced and expensive precautions. Quite the opposite: manufacturers, distributors, and retail pharmacy rejected precautions as vestiges of old anti-opioid myths, and happily sold ever-greater volumes even as problems mounted.

A second factor complicating simple links between opioid marketing and the opioid crisis has to do with immediate versus root causes. Opioid addiction and overdose were not the only "deaths of despair" to rise in the early twenty-first century; for example, suicide and alcohol-related liver disease also shot up. Some observers have thus argued that the true cause of the opioid crisis was not opioids per se but a one-two punch of political injustices: first, social and economic dislocation that left downwardly mobile communities traumatized and vulnerable to addiction; and second, drug criminalization that targeted people with addiction for punishment rather than treatment.[126]

This interpretation is sometimes taken to be in conflict with a focus on white market opioid boosterism. It is more accurate to say that they address different steps on the causal chain. Social injustices may have prepared the groundwork for a health crisis by creating widespread trauma, but we still need to know why that crisis took the form of opioid addiction and overdose. Why did the opioid crisis initially strike whites rather than racial minorities who faced even more social and economic marginalization? Then, too, the United States has always been home to stark poverty and social inequality. Why were there no opioid crises for most of the nation's history, including calamitous moments such as the Great Depression? To understand the addiction crisis, we need to understand root causes such as social injustice, but also immediate causes such as opioid manufacturers' all-out sales frenzy.

Allowing pharmaceutical companies free rein is one form of inadequate market regulation. Punitive prohibition is another. They are, as we have repeatedly seen, two sides of the same coin, delivering the same result: insufficient protection for consumers.

From addiction crisis to overdose crisis

The twenty-first-century white market boom showed that many of the hard-learned lessons of the 1970s had been forgotten or purposefully abandoned. Authorities' responses to the opioid crisis confirmed this. The first round of policies, implemented in 2001 after problems of addiction and overdose had become national news, were the exact opposite of what had been successful in the past. Instead of imposing strict new commercial regulations, authorities initially chose to build stronger walls around white markets to protect them from the criminal drug "abusers" they blamed for problems of addiction. This strategy was strongly encouraged by Purdue and other opioid manufacturers. "We have to hammer on the abusers in every possible way," Purdue's Richard Sackler urged colleagues in 2001. "They are the culprits and the problem. They are reckless criminals."[127] Company executives faithfully carried the message to Congress, telling lawmakers that "virtually all" cases of addiction "involve people who are abusing the medication, not patients with legitimate medical needs under the treatment of a healthcare professional." The real victims were legitimate pain patients who would suffer from any restrictions imposed on opioid availability.[128]

Federal authorities mostly accepted this interpretation, and 2001 reforms were designed to prevent diversion rather than to alter white market practices. The FDA required Purdue to strengthen the warning labels on OxyContin, but did little to restrain medical marketing and imposed no new limits on prescribing.[129] Federal officials, meanwhile, began working with local law enforcement agencies and, in some cases, opioid manufacturers, to develop and implement Prescription Drug Monitoring Programs and Risk Management Plans designed—again—to deter nonmedical sales and use.[130]

These responses protected the core (white) markets for pharmaceutical opioids, allowing companies to continue expanding sales there for another ten years. They also did a different kind of damage. Strategies like Prescription Drug Monitoring Programs were designed to identify people with addiction—and then deny them access to white market opioids. Since people with addiction, by definition, cannot easily stop using opioids, many addicted consumers shifted to informal markets, where they had little experience navigating risks—biological or legal. Moreover, informal markets were themselves in one of their periodic transitions to more powerful (and thus more easily smuggled) substances, in this case the super-potent opioid fentanyl. This made them increasingly dangerous even for experienced consumers. Doubling down on the medicine-drug divide not only allowed white market opioid sales to keep growing, but also transformed what had been a crisis of addiction into a crisis of fatal overdose.[131]

Also contributing to the overdose crisis was a failure to expand treatment, especially opioid maintenance, at anything like the needed scale. This failure came despite a sudden and dramatic revival of popular sympathy for people with addiction, especially as the 2000s wore on and it became clear that the hated "criminal abusers" were in fact mostly the white children of economically declining suburban and rural areas. In the classic white market tradition, people with addiction were portrayed as innocent victims. Public attention focused almost exclusively on people with no problematic drug history whose addiction stemmed from medical treatment for a painful injury or illness, despite evidence that such cases were not representative.[132]

This assertion of innocent victimhood led to a rapid revival of medicalizers' belief that addiction was not a vice or a crime but an

illness—a "chronic, relapsing brain disease" according to the influential new model championed by the National Institute of Drug
Abuse. As they considered available treatments for this brain disease, authorities suddenly noticed how stigmatizing and demean-
ing methadone clinics had been designed to be, and declared them
a "poor fit for the suburban spread of narcotic addiction." Soon a
new form of opioid maintenance emerged based on a different long-
acting opioid, the partial agonist buprenorphine. New regulations
allowed buprenorphine to be prescribed in physician's offices like
other medicines, rather than being quarantined into stand-alone
clinics at the white market periphery.[133]

There were multiple problems with this approach. For one thing,
it was achieved only by doubling down on divisions between white
market and informal market addiction. To maximize political support, advocates of private-practice buprenorphine maintenance
portrayed it as specifically tailored for sympathetic white people.
The resulting regulations were shaped by this assumption about
the clientele. For example, to prescribe buprenorphine a physician
had to attend a day-long training and get a special certification. This
was an expensive hurdle that favored affluent practices, especially
since physicians were initially restricted to a maximum of thirty
buprenorphine patients (it was expanded to one hundred in 2007).
Moreover, not all states covered buprenorphine in their Medicaid
programs. Unsurprisingly, private-practice buprenorphine treatment was provided overwhelmingly to white and upper-income
patients.[134]

This carefully constructed social exclusivity also limited how
quickly buprenorphine maintenance could be expanded even for
the socially privileged people for whom it was intended—a significant problem given the scale of the opioid crisis. Authorities' first
priority continued to be cutting off white market access to people
with addiction, rather than ensuring white market maintenance as
a treatment option. Private-practice buprenorphine prescribing was
an important innovation, but there were too many barriers to getting

access to it, and, in any case, it was nowhere near ambitious enough in scale to meet the need.

Conclusion

By the 2000s, both white and informal drug markets were experiencing the most devastating episode yet in a century of drug crises. Anti-regulatory fever, renewed racialization of addiction, the reconfiguration of psychiatry, and the drug industry placing its thumb on the scale of the pain reform movement had all help rescue white markets from the regulatory doldrums of the 1970s. Sales careened out of control, with addiction and overdose not far behind. Meanwhile, renewed race and class stigma brought similar devastation to informal markets, where consumers continued to face the double catastrophe of completely unregulated risks and mass incarceration. After briefly flirting with an effective consumer protection approach in the 1970s, both halves of American drug policy had now reached a new nadir, failing worse than they had even in a century of failures.

Conclusion
Learning from the past

From a certain perspective, the history chronicled in this book can seem remarkably, depressingly static. Chapter 7 ended very much where chapter 1 began: with a racialized divide between medicines and drugs wreaking public health havoc on both sides. Despite occasional efforts at reform, the cultural and legal architecture sustaining the distinction between white and informal markets proved durable. This is hardly a surprise; racial, class, and gender hierarchies have been a defining and obdurate feature of American society more generally. Nonetheless such social inequalities had an unusually strong hold on drug policy. Even movements for drug reform have tended to traffic in, and reinforce, race and class stereotypes rather than challenging them directly. Indeed, one way to read this book would be to say that the only "progress" in the twentieth century was a relentless, profit-driven increase in the potency and availability of addictive pharmaceuticals.

There is plenty of evidence for such a reading, but it is not the only one possible. The long twentieth century has also provided occasional (and partial) glimpses of what a different drug policy might look like—one that charts a narrow path between the Scylla of prohibition and the Charybdis of the "free market." These glimpses have almost always been carefully limited to pharmaceutical white markets. They could be found, for example, in post–Harrison Act white market opioid policy, which combined robust regulatory controls on the pharmaceutical industry with extensive, though unequal and clandestine, provision of morphine to some people with addiction. Glimpses could also be found amid the consumer protection innovations of the 1970s, which maintained widespread access but made drug use safer through strong industry and professional regulation. In both of these outlier examples, drug controls were designed not to punish consumers into abstaining from drug use but to limit the way the pursuit of profit magnified the harms of already dangerous drugs.

Cloaked by their status as medical, these policies have been considered irrelevant for drug policy, or their successes have been attributed to the good qualities of white market consumers. This book has explored them as evidence that effective drug policies are possible and as templates—however flawed—for future reform.

A second hopeful takeaway from this white market history is that the heart of America's never-ending drug crises—the racialized divide between medicines and drugs—is written in culture and politics, not in stone. It can be, and has been, changed, sometimes for the better, by purposeful and collective political action. The period of reform in the early 1970s stand as the best (perhaps the only) example of this. As we have seen, those reforms were limited and flawed, and they eventually became vehicles for reinstating the traditional binary between punitively prohibited drugs and weakly regulated pharmaceuticals. Those reforms also notched impressive accomplishments, however. On the one hand, real commercial regulation led to significant reductions of unnecessary and unnecessarily harmful sales and use. On the other hand, they also helped usher in methadone maintenance, which—for the first time in US history—expanded white market access to the poorer, urban racial minorities who had always been relegated to informal markets. Despite the stigma and criminal justice governance, methadone maintenance marked a dramatic step toward reconfiguring drug markets so that they protected the safety of all consumers, not just white market "patients."

As noted in chapter 7, the political coalition that made methadone maintenance (and other 1970s drug reforms) possible receded with the return of anti-drug moral crusaders and political conservatives in the 1980s and 1990s. The coalition did not entirely disappear, however. Instead, something remarkable happened. During its years in the wilderness, its most passionate wing evolved into a new political force that, when it reemerged again in the twenty-first century, had far greater potential to transform American drug policy for the better. The primary context for this political evolution was the HIV/AIDS epidemic of the 1980s. Among the many forms of activism inspired by the epidemic was a campaign to provide sterile needles to intravenous drug users to prevent disease transmission through shared equipment. This was a radical move in the context of informal drug markets: it affirmed the human dignity of informal-market drug consumers even when they chose to continue using drugs. Activists accepted that drug use might continue, but still sought to minimize the risks and harms associated with that use and to eliminate barriers to healthcare.[1]

The history of white markets provides a variety of near-precedents for this approach since, as we have seen, white markets assumed that consumers would use drugs, often for long periods of time or even permanently. While the record can be charitably described as mixed, regulation of such markets was at least nominally designed to make them as safe as possible. What early needle exchange activists did was similar to, but one step more radical than, what methadone maintenance programs did: expand some white market assumptions, infrastructure, and protections to consumers in informal markets.

The crucible of HIV/AIDS activism helped ensure that when drug policy reform reemerged as an issue in the early twenty-first century, its foremost proponents were not addiction medicalizers but a new, more politically radical coalition dedicated to "harm reduction." There was a big difference between the two. Medicalizers had genuine sympathy for people with addiction and were sincere in wanting to help rather than punish them. Even so, however, they endorsed many of the traditional goals of American drug policy: they believed that all nonmedical use was bad and should be eliminated, and at least some of the treatments they championed were quite punitive or disturbingly similar to incarceration. Harm reduction advocates, on the other hand, rejected these premises. Instead of ending informal-market drug use, their goal was to reduce the risks and harms related to that drug use. They were quite capacious in conceptualizing "harms," including not just individual health problems but the collective and political consequences of punitive drug policies. Some harm reductionists explicitly committed themselves to civil rights activism with the goal of undoing and, if possible, repairing the damage done by racialized prohibition policies.[2]

Harm reduction has made a mark on policy responses to the opioid crisis. The overdose-reversing drug naloxone, for example, has been widely distributed to police departments, emergency medical teams, and ordinary Americans. There has been an increased effort both locally and nationally to lower barriers to buprenorphine and other medication-assisted treatments for addiction, in settings less stigmatizing and policed than methadone maintenance. Real progress has been made in reducing the draconian criminal punishments instituted during the latest round of punitive prohibition—including the 2009 repeal of the era's signature legislation, New York's Rockefeller drug laws.

In various ways and to different extents, each of these harm reduction reforms seeks to expand the best practices of white markets to include all consumers—to reorient drug policy so that it is structured around safe and unsafe use rather than medical and nonmedical use. They are, in effect, an effort to dismantle the medicine-drug divide. In its place would come something closer to the regulatory structures that govern other markets for potentially dangerous but desirable consumer goods such as automobiles. These products also pose serious risks to consumers' (and environmental) health. Americans have decided that their benefits outweigh their risks, however, and accept that they will (or even should be) widely used. Robust regulations minimize risks, even though it is understood that no system can be perfect. Thus, for example, cars must have seat belts and air bags, and highways must have rumble strips. A harm reduction approach suggests that policy and regulations might be capable of managing drug markets similarly: accepting continued use, but doing everything possible to minimize harms even when that cuts into profits.

Actually, white market history suggests that such reforms may not be enough. It may be necessary not just to reduce but to *end* the profits that have been such a malefic force in the history of addictive drugs. As this book has shown, one of the most important factors encouraging unsafe white market drug use has been pharmaceutical companies determined to promote their products as benign despite evidence to the contrary. Barbiturate manufacturers built the template in the 1920s and 1930s, consciously reconstructing the lost nineteenth-century market for drugs to ease the "pains of existence." This was not necessarily a bad thing; physicians and patients, too, clearly wanted drugs for this purpose. In a profitable and competitive market, however, barbiturate manufacturers overpromoted their wares while fighting tooth and nail against regulatory limits that might have prevented sedatives from reigniting the nineteenth century's addiction crisis. The medicine-drug divide was an important tool in these efforts, allowing the industry to argue that sedatives were not addictive because, unlike "narcotics," they were medicines used by respectable white patients to treat legitimate illnesses. This approach was doubly harmful in that it prevented sensible regulation of sedative white markets while also reinforcing stigma and punitive approaches to informal markets.

The barbiturate template was so successful, and so profitable, that it inspired a gold rush after World War II by manufacturers of other addictive drugs. By the 1950s and 1960s, amphetamine stimulants and so-called minor tranquilizers had joined barbiturates to produce the twentieth century's largest white markets—and its largest drug-related public health crisis. Opioids, notably, were not a part of this psychoactive bonanza, but only because of continual vigilance by the FBN and its allied experts.

It was not until the late 1960s and 1970s that a new round of reforms expanded this type of oversight to sedatives and stimulants. With real regulation imposing strong discipline on the pharmaceutical industry and reducing potential profits, white market sales shrank dramatically over the decade. Those limits proved short-lived, however, and by the 1990s, the pharmaceutical industry had once again found ways to circumvent regulatory limits. By the early twenty-first century, white market sales reached their highest levels ever. To support this profitable enterprise, the drug industry made an enormous financial and cultural investment in the racialized medicine-drug divide, implicitly (and sometimes explicitly) supporting a renewed punitive "war" against informal drug markets. Once again, the lure of profits had encouraged the industry to overshoot the mark—to inflate white markets by encouraging unsafe use, at the cost of reinforcing negative attitudes and punitive approaches to informal markets.

From this perspective, then, the history of addictive pharmaceuticals is fairly unambiguous in its pessimism: little evidence supports profit as a safe organizing principle for the circulation of addictive drugs. If Americans choose to have large and vibrant white markets supplying consumers with addictive drugs—and for well over a century, this has indeed been a clear and consistent choice—those markets are likely to be much safer if they are not a source of significant profit. Profit-driven drug markets follow a predictable damaging cycle. Companies hype new medicines as safe and beneficial and sell with insufficient regard to consumer safety; a health crisis ensues as consumers are left ill equipped to make informed decisions; authorities respond with consumer protections and destructive drug wars; the pharmaceutical industry devises strategies to circumvent the new restrictions and start the cycle over again. After umpteen repetitions of this cat-and-mouse game, it may be time to acknowledge the impossibility of establishing a safe, for-profit market for addictive drugs. Alternatives exist: state monopolies, for example, or public utility models.[3] We need to consider these and other creative ideas for dramatically minimizing or even eliminating profit from psychoactive capitalism.

Despite new sales limits and more than 1,600 lawsuits against opioid manufacturers, twenty-first-century reformers have thus far

shown little inclination to consider such underlying structural issues, instead reading the opioid crisis as a singular event resulting
from the criminality of specific companies and their collaborators.
The Sacklers and their company, Purdue, have come in for special
and well-deserved criticism. While it is necessary to hold people and
companies accountable for their actions, however, it is also necessary to think seriously about the structural factors that allowed them
to engage in such dangerous behavior for so long. Otherwise, we are
certain to face another crisis, with another set of seemingly unique
criminal actors—over and over.

Pharmaceutical company profits are not the only factor that
makes the early twenty-first century's moment of hope also a moment of peril. Other dangers lurk too. Even as many harm reductionists directly challenge the racism of American drug wars, for
example, their political successes have often come, at least in part,
because of a newfound popular sympathy for the suburban white
people who served as the public face of the opioid crisis. In this
way, even the most radical twenty-first-century challenges to the
medicine-drug divide still smuggle in the divide's century-old racial
logic. Will it be possible to apply harm reduction principles to future
drug crises among less privileged populations? History suggests a
real risk that policies based on harm reduction principles, like past
examples of effective policies, will end up quarantined to white markets and privileged drug consumers.

There are already indications that this problematic quarantining may be taking place in the twenty-first century. As in the 1970s,
harm reduction reforms have been accompanied by other policies
that continue or even strengthen more punitive drug policy traditions. Arrests and incarceration for minor drug charges have hardly
been eliminated, nor have those who champion such punitive approaches disappeared. In many jurisdictions, new laws allow or even
encourage murder charges against anyone who provided drugs to
someone who subsequently suffered a fatal overdose. Since many
people with addiction in informal market settings make small sales

to support their own habits, these laws substantively contradict or undermine efforts to ease punishments for addiction.

Taken together, these perils show why it has been so difficult to develop and implement sensible drug policies. Reformers must put together a political coalition strong enough to rein in the pharmaceutical industry, and they must do so without relying on either of the two most obvious tactics: playing on sympathy for white drug consumers, or making an alliance with anti-drug moral crusaders. To build such a coalition, drug policy debates must be weaned from familiar categories that seem obvious and natural but were in fact built within the problematic racial politics of the Progressive Era. Whatever the merits of that era's reformers, few of their cultural constructions have survived as unscathed as the medicine-drug divide. It is long past time to rethink a set of concepts designed for a segregated era that have served as a vehicle for segregative policies in the century since—and that have helped nourish a never-ending cycle of profit-driven drug crises.

Appendix

White market sales and overdose rates, 1870–2015

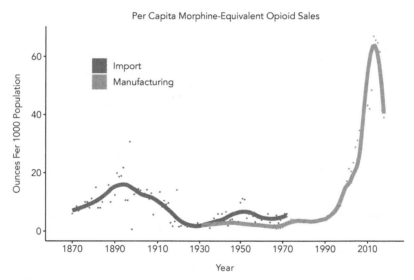

Per Capita Morphine-Equivalent Opioid Sales

Figure A.1. Opioids (converted to their equivalent weight in ounces of morphine) per 1,000 Americans. The two lines represent different sources of data (one that measured imports, the other that measured manufacturing). Buprenorphine, an important addiction treatment drug, was not included because I was not able to find sales figures. *Sources:* David Courtwright, *Dark Paradise: A History of Opiate Addiction in America*, enlarged ed. (Cambridge, MA: Harvard University Press, 2001); US Department of Commerce and Labor, Bureau of Statistics, *Foreign Commerce and Navigation of the United States* (Washington, DC: Government Printing Office, annually); Bureau of Narcotics, US Treasury Department, *Traffic in Opium and Other Dangerous Drugs* (Washington, DC: Government Printing Office, annually); United Nations Permanent Central Narcotics Board, *Statistics on Narcotic Drugs*; United Nations International Narcotic Control Board, *Demand and Supply of Opiates for Medical and Scientific Needs*; DEA aggregate production quotas, *Federal Register*; *Narcotics Legislation, Pursuant to S. Res 48, S. 1895, S. 2590, S. 2637: Hearings Before the Subcomm. to Investigate Juvenile Delinquency of the S. Comm. on the Judiciary*, 91st Cong. (1969).

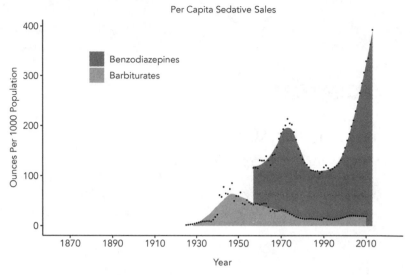

Figure A.2. Ounces of barbiturates and nonbarbiturate sedatives such as methaqualone and benzodiazepine tranquilizers per 1,000 Americans. The lines are additive. Data are approximate because they were pulled from many different sources that used different metrics and in many cases conflicted with each other. The graph should thus be used for trends rather than specific figures. *Sources:* David Herzberg, *Happy Pills in America: From Miltown to Prozac* (Baltimore: Johns Hopkins University Press, 2009); Mickey Smith, *Small Comfort: A History of Minor Tranquilizers* (New York: Praeger, 1985); Department of Commerce, Bureau of the Census, *Biennial Census of Manufactures*; US Tariff Commission, Tariff Information Series, *Census of Dyes and Coal-Tar Chemicals*; US Tariff Commission, Tariff Information Series, *Census of Dyes and Other Synthetic Organic Chemicals*; US Congress, House of Representatives, Committee on Ways and Means, *Control of Narcotics, Marihuana, and Barbiturates*, 82d Cong., 1951; US Congress, House of Representatives, Committee on Ways and Means, *Traffic in, and Control of, Narcotics, Barbiturates, and Amphetamines*, 84th Cong., 1955–1956; *American Druggist* fortnightly prescription surveys; Mitchell Balter and Jerome Levine, "The Nature and Extent of Psychotropic Drug Usage in the United States," *Psychopharmacology Bulletin*, October 1969; Institute of Medicine, *Sleeping Pills, Insomnia, and Medical Practice: Report of a Study* (Washington, DC: National Academy of Sciences, 1979); Hugh Parry, "Use of Psychotropic Drugs by U.S. Adults," *Public Health Report* 83, no. 10 (1968): 799–811; US Congress, Senate, Subcommittee to Investigate Juvenile Delinquency, Committee on the Judiciary, *Barbiturate Abuse, 1971–72*, 92d Cong., 1971–1972; US Congress, Senate, Subcommittee on Health and Scientific Research, Committee on Labor and Human Resources, *Examination on the Use and Misuse of Valium, Librium, and Other Minor Tranquilizers*, 96th Congress, 1979; Jane Prather, "Prescription Practices of Psychotropic Drugs Leading to Possible Misuse and Abuse," in US Congress, House of Representatives, Select Committee on Narcotics Abuse and Control, *Abuse of Dangerous Licit and Illicit Drugs—Psychotropics, Phencyclidine (PCP), and Talwin*, 95th Cong., 1978; DEA aggregate production quotas, *Federal Register*.

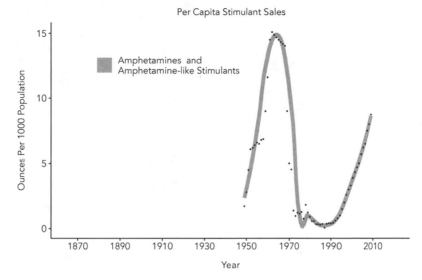

Figure A.3. Ounces of amphetamine and amphetamine-like stimulants per 1,000 Americans. Figures are approximate, but trends are reliable. *Sources:* Nicolas Rasmussen, *On Speed: The Many Lives of Amphetamine* (New York: New York University Press, 2008); Nicolas Rasmussen, "America's First Amphetamine Epidemic 1929–1971," *American Journal of Public Health* 98, no. 6 (June 2008): 974–85; DEA aggregate production quotas, *Federal Register*.

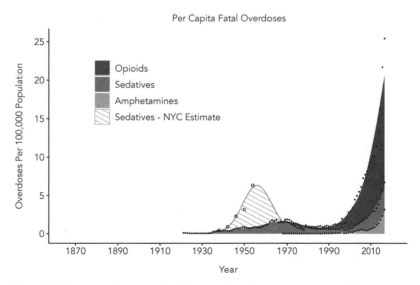

Figure A.4. Fatal overdoses per 100,000 population. Annual overdoses are almost certainly undercounted. Note, for example, the estimated national rate of barbiturate-related fatal overdoses extrapolated from confirmed New York City cases in the 1950s. Accuracy probably improved in the early twenty-first century with increased attention to opioid-related fatalities. *Source: Vital Statistics of the United States*.

Acknowledgments

It took a decade to research and write this book. This was possible, first and foremost, because I am lucky enough to enjoy something that has become increasingly rare in these days of academic precarity: a tenured, unionized position in the History Department at the University at Buffalo (SUNY), a public research university. This position gave me the time, support, and resources I needed, and I am grateful for it. I am alarmed by the disappearance of such secure, living wage positions in the humanities. We must find ways to renew the promise of academic freedom—and security—for the next generation of scholars. We need them.

I have also benefited from a range of grants and fellowships that funded research and provided time for writing. Most important was a three-year grant from the National Institutes of Health administered by the National Library of Medicine under the G13 program for "Scholarly Works in Biomedicine and Health." (Research reported in this book was supported under award number 5G13LM012050.) This program is a crucial source of public support for projects in the medical humanities; it was certainly crucial for this project. The American Institute for the History of Pharmacy in Madison, Wisconsin, also assisted with travel grants to visit its extensive archives and the excellent collections at Wisconsin's State Historical Society. Other support came from the University at Buffalo. The Baldy Center for Law and Social Policy provided funding for research trips, funding and venues for symposia and other events, and an important intellectual venue for interdisciplinary conversations. The Humanities Institute provided "seed money" and time off from teaching at the beginning of the project; this early support was invaluable in starting research and securing later funding.

Thanks are also due to the many friends and colleagues who helped me find my way through the daunting intellectual and political complexities associated with this topic. Amazingly, there were a few who read the entire manuscript, some more than once! Susan Cahn and Mike Rembis read from beginning to end and uncomplainingly let me turn many of our Spot Coffee get-togethers into white-market-drug-a-thons. Nan Enstad provided her unique mix of inspiring confidence and mind-reordering suggestions (and not just on scholarly topics). David Courtwright was a generous and exacting reader from the beginning; I can't say that I have satisfied all his hopes for this book, but it is better for his forceful enthusiasm and friendly skepticism. Erin Hatton bravely read execrable "zero" drafts of every chapter, offering level-headed views of the forest when I was most lost in the trees. I also learned a great deal from many others who discussed and debated drugs and drug policy over the years, among them Caroline Jean Acker, Nancy Campbell, Isaac Campos, Emily Dufton, Erika Dyck, Joseph Gabriel, Paul Gootenberg, Jeremy Greene, Helena Hansen, Greg Higby, Marie Jauffret-Roustide, Nils Kessel, Kenneth Leonard, Yan Liu, Donna Murch, Jules Netherland, Matthew Pembleton, Scott Podolsky, Nicolas Rasmussen, Lucas Richert, Samuel K. Roberts, Nancy Tomes, Keith Wailoo, and Ingrid Walker.

Many parts of the book were first developed for symposia and other events that helped me understand how my research fit into broader intellectual and scholarly projects. These included the History of Medicine Seminar Series at the University of Saskatchewan; the Colloquium in the History of Science, Medicine, and Technology at Johns Hopkins University; the two "Challenging Punishment" events (a symposium at Rutgers University, and a conference at Columbia University and the Schomburg Center for Research in Black Culture); the Psychiatry and Culture in Historical Perspective

Working Group at Yale University; "Addictions Old and New" at the University of Richmond; the Colloquium in the History of Science and Medicine at Yale University; the Science Studies Working Group at New York University; the History of Science, Technology, and Medicine colloquium at the University of Minnesota; the Consortium for the History of Science, Technology, and Medicine at the College of Physicians of Philadelphia; and the UCLA Center for Social Medicine and the Humanities. I am also grateful for valuable conversations with participants at three symposia I co-organized: "Gender and the Drug War" at UB's Baldy Center for Law and Social Policy (with Nancy Campbell); "Addiction as a Chronic Illness?" at the Baldy Center (with Nils Kessel); and "Narratives of Progress, Risk, and Decline in Medicine" at the Université de Strasbourg (with Nils Kessel and Joseph Gabriel).

Like most historians I am in deep debt to many archivists and librarians, especially MaryKay Schmidt at NARA, Cathy Keen at the Smithsonian, and Janice Goldblum at the National Academy of Sciences. I also owe thanks to Osiris Gomez, Maria Daxenbichler, Richard Deverell, Elisabeth George, Justin Masucci, and Derek Taylor for research assistance, and to Wes Bernegger for data visualization. Karen Merikangas Darling at the University of Chicago Press helped keep me going with warm encouragement and never-ending patience.

Thanks, finally, to family and friends for crucial ingredients of love and joy, without which I would not have made it (much less have written a book). My parents Don and Vickie; my sister Jill; Nan; and above all Erin, Rex, Leo, and Felix: whatever is beyond thanks, that goes both above and below and all around it: that.

Notes

Archive Abbreviations

AMA Papers. Historical Health Fraud and Alternative Medicine Collection. Department of Investigations Records. American Medical Association Archives, Chicago.

- Box 221, AMA, Dept. of Investigation, Records, Drugless Healing, Ryan, Edmund Joseph—Drugs, Corr, 1951
  - · Folder 7 "Drugs, Special Data, 1899-1966"
  - Folder 8 "Drugs, Special Data, 1967-1974"
- Box 222, AMA, Dept. of Investigation, Records, Drugs, Correspondence, 1952—Drugs, Non-Prescribed, Patent Medicines, Correspondence, 1947
  - Folder 4 "Drugs, Illegal Prescribing and Selling, Correspondence"
- Box 321, AMA Dept. Investigations Records, Harrell, J. Randolph—Harrison Anti-Narcotic Law, Correspondence, 1951
  - Folder 6 "Harrison Anti-Narcotic Law—Special Data 1916-1944"
  - Folder 9 "Harrison Anti-Narcotic Law—Correspondence, 1919-1931"
  - Folder 10 "Harrison Anti-Narcotic Law—Correspondence, 1932-1936"
  - Folder 11 "Harrison Anti-Narcotic Law—Correspondence, 1937-1939"
  - Folder 13 "Harrison Anti-Narcotic Law—Correspondence, 1950-51"
- Box 322, AMA Dept. Investigations Records, Harrison Anti-Narcotic Law, Correspondence, 1952-1974
  - Folder 7 "Harrison Anti-Narcotic Law—Correspondence, 1957-58"

CA MEB Drugs. Department of Consumer Affairs—Medical Examiners Board Records. 10. Subject Files. F3760:381-583. California State Archives, Office of the Secretary of State, Sacramento.

CA MEB Investigations. Department of Consumer Affairs—Medical Examiners Board Records. 20. Physician and Clinic Investigative Files, 1921-1964. F3760:827-885. California State Archives, Office of the Secretary of State, Sacramento.

- Box 21, "Investigation—Investigations of physicians clinics and others"

CABPR. Dept. of Consumer Affairs, Board of Pharmacy Records. Investigation and Violation Log Book. F3888:110. California State Archives, Office of the Secretary of State, Sacramento.

Case Histories, KP. Lawrence Kolb Papers. 1912–1972. Located in Modern Manuscripts Collection, History of Medicine Division, National Library of Medicine, Bethesda, MD.; MS C 279

• Box 7, Folder "Narcotics Case Histories 1924–1928"

DASA Admin. Department of Alcoholism and Substance Abuse, "Prevention
and Education Division Administrative Files," Record Series 223.006, Illinois
State Archives, Springfield.

DASA Minutes. Department of Alcoholism and Substance Abuse, "Commission
Meeting Minutes," Record Series 223.004, Illinois State Archives, Springfield.

DPR Admin. Department of Professional Regulation, "Administrative Files,"
Record Series 208.045, Illinois State Archives, Springfield.

FBN Papers. Subject Files of the Bureau of Narcotics and Dangerous Drugs, 1916–
1970, Record Group 170, National Archives II, College Park, MD.

• Box 41, Miscellaneous subject files arranged numerically re: Addiction, Clinics, Associations 1930–1966, Folder "Addiction: Dr. Addict, Thru December
1959"

FDA Papers. Records of the Food and Drug Administration, Record Group 88,
National Archives II, College Park, MD.

Fischelis Papers. Robert P. Fischelis Papers, 1821–1981. Mss 619 MAD 3M/78/
Kg-N5. Wisconsin Historical Society, Division of Library, Archives, and Museum Collections, Madison.

KP. Lawrence Kolb Papers. 1912–1972. Located in Modern Manuscripts Collection,
History of Medicine Division, National Library of Medicine, Bethesda, MD.;
MS C 279.

LA NDDC. Correctional Agencies Records. Dept. of Corrections Records. Director's Office Records. Director's Subject Files. Los Angeles County Narcotics
and Dangerous Drugs Commission Files. F3717:322, F3717:1558-59. California State Archives, Office of the Secretary of State, Sacramento.

NAS-NRC Papers. Records of the Committees on Drug Addiction, Drug Addiction (Advisory), and Drug Addiction and Narcotics, 1928–1965, National
Academy of Sciences, Washington, DC.

PEB Complaint and Revocation Files. Wisconsin. Pharmacy Examining Board.
Complaint and Revocation Files, 1952–1979, 1993. Series 2673 MAD 3/14/
C6, Wisconsin Historical Society, Division of Library, Archives, and Museum
Collections, Madison.

PEB Correspondence. Wisconsin. Pharmacy Examining Board. Correspondence
and subject files, 1927–1988. Series 2638 MAD 3/16/F5-7, Wisconsin Historical Society, Division of Library, Archives, and Museum Collections, Madison.

Permit File, FBN Papers. Subject Files of the Bureau of Narcotics and Dangerous Drugs, 1916–1970, Record Group 170, National Archives II, College
Park, MD.

• Box 41, File 0120-6 "Addiction: Permits for Drugs 1932–1944"

SBME Correspondence. Wisconsin. Medical Examining Board. Correspondence
and subject files, 1938–1989. Series 1610 MAD 3/41/C2-5, Wisconsin Historical Society, Division of Library, Archives, and Museum Collections, Madison.

SCP. Stanley Cobb Papers, Box 29, fd.608, Subject Files "Committee on Drug Addiction: Report on Personality, neurological, and Psychotic Studies on Drug
Addicts [in the Philadelphia General Hospital], by R. B. Richardson, Dec 1,

1927, in Francis A. Countway Library of Medicine Center for the History of Medicine, Boston.

Sterling Drug Papers. Sterling Drug, Inc. Records, Archives Center, National Museum of American History, Series 3: Sales and Marketing, Catalogs and Price Lists, Price Lists, Smithsonian, Washington, DC.

Warren Papers. Earl Warren Papers. Governor's Office Administrative Files. 288: Medical Examiners, State Board of. F3640:3206-13. California State Archives, Office of the Secretary of State, Sacramento.

WI SBME Investigations. Wisconsin. Medical Examining Board. Investigations, 1929–2005; Series 1616, MAD 2m/9/G3-H3, K6-7; additional accessions, Wisconsin Historical Society, Division of Library, Archives, and Museum Collections, Madison.

Witt. *U.S. v Witt*; Case File 82 Cr. 33-CSH; General Case Files; United States District Court for the Southern District of New York; Records of District Courts of the United States, Record Group 021; National Archives and Records Administration—Central Plains Region (Lee Summit, MO).

Introduction

1   See, e.g., Barry Meier, *Pain Killer: An Empire of Deceit and the Origin of America's Opioid Epidemic* (New York: Random House, 2018 [2003]); Anna Lembke, *Drug Dealer, MD* (Baltimore: Johns Hopkins University Press, 2016); Beth Macy, *Dopesick: Dealers, Doctors, and the Drug Company That Addicted America* (New York: Little, Brown, 2018).

2   See, e.g., Michelle Alexander, *The New Jim Crow: Mass Incarceration in the Age of Colorblindness* (New York: New Press, 2012).

3   "New breed" quotes from online front-page "teasers" (no longer online; screen captures available on request) for Henry L. Davish, Dan Hereck, Lou Michel, and Susan Schulman, "Rx for Danger," *Buffalo News*, March 20, 2011, https://buffalonews.com/2011/03/20/rx-for-danger-all-too-often-doctors-and-dealers-converge-in-the-illegal-prescription-drug-marketplace-nationally-and-in-western-new-york/. See also, e.g., David Amsden, "The New Face of Heroin," *Rolling Stone*, April 3, 2014, https://www.rollingstone.com/culture/culture-news/the-new-face-of-heroin-107942/.

4   See, e.g., Paul Starr, *The Social Transformation of American Medicine: The Rise of a Sovereign Profession and the Making of a Vast Industry* (New York: Basic, 2017 [1982]); Harry Marks, *The Progress of Experiment: Science and Therapeutic Reform in the United States, 1900–1990* (Cambridge: Cambridge University Press, 1997); Joseph Gabriel, *Medical Monopoly: Intellectual Property Rights and the Origins of the Modern Pharmaceutical Industry* (Chicago: University of Chicago Press, 2014); Nancy Tomes, *Remaking the American Patient: How Madison Avenue and Modern Medicine Turned Patients into Consumers* (Chapel Hill: University of North Carolina Press, 2016).

5   See, e.g., Lizabeth Cohen, *A Consumers' Republic: The Politics of Mass Consumption* (New York: Vintage, 2008); Lawrence Glickman, *Buying Power: A History of Consumer Activism in America* (Chicago: University of Chicago Press, 2009).

6   See, e.g., David Musto, *American Disease: Origins of Narcotics Control*, rev. ed. (1973; repr., New York: Oxford University Press, 1999); Caroline Jean Acker,

Creating the American Junkie: Addiction Research in the Classic Era of Narcotic Control (Baltimore: Johns Hopkins University Press, 2002); Lisa McGirr, *The War on Alcohol: Prohibition and the Rise of the American State* (New York: W. W. Norton, 2016).

7   See, e.g., Charles O. Jackson, *Food and Drug Legislation in the New Deal* (Princeton, NJ: Princeton University Press, 1970); James Harvey Young, *Pure Food: Securing the Federal Food and Drugs Act of 1906* (Princeton, NJ: Princeton University Press, 1989); Philip J. Hilts, *Protecting America's Health: The FDA, Business, and One Hundred Years of Regulation* (Chapel Hill: University of North Carolina Press, 2003); Daniel Carpenter, *Reputation and Power: Organizational Image and Pharmaceutical Regulation at the FDA* (Princeton, NJ: Princeton University Press, 2010); Lucas Richert, *Conservatism, Consumer Choice, and the Food and Drug Administration during the Reagan Era: A Prescription for Scandal* (Lanham, MD: Lexington, 2014).

8   See, e.g., Nancy Campbell, *Using Women: Gender, Drug Policy, and Social Justice* (New York: Routledge, 2000); Eric Schneider, *Smack: Heroin and the American City* (Philadelphia: University of Pennsylvania Press, 2011). For exceptions who examine FBN as pharmaceutical regulator, see Kathleen Frydl, *The Drug Wars in America, 1940–1973* (New York: Cambridge University Press, 2013), and Suzanna Reiss, *We Sell Drugs: The Alchemy of U.S. Empire* (Berkeley: University of California Press, 2014).

9   David Herzberg, "Pills," in *Rethinking Therapeutic Culture*, ed. Timothy Aubry and Trysh Travis (Chicago: University of Chicago Press, 2015).

10   See, e.g., National Institute on Drug Abuse, "Is There a Difference between Physical Dependence and Addiction?" in *Principles of Drug Addiction Treatment: A Research-Based Guide*, 3rd ed. (Washington, DC: NIDA, 2018), https://www.drugabuse.gov/publications/principles-drug-addiction-treatment-research-based-guide-third-edition/frequently-asked-questions/there-difference-between-physical-dependence.

11   For example, I have relied on the following works extensively: Nicolas Rasmussen, *On Speed: The Many Lives of Amphetamine* (New York: New York University Press, 2008); Andrea Tone, *The Age of Anxiety: A History of America's Turbulent Affair with Tranquilizers* (New York: Basic, 2008); David Herzberg, *Happy Pills in America: From Miltown to Prozac* (Baltimore: Johns Hopkins University Press, 2009); Frydl, *Drug Wars in America*. Other synthetic works have bridged the divide in different ways; see, e.g., David Courtwright, *Forces of Habit: Drugs and the Making of the Modern World* (Cambridge, MA: Harvard University Press, 2002), and *The Age of Addiction: How Bad Habits Became Big Business* (Cambridge, MA: Belknap Press of Harvard University Press, 2019); Lucas Richert, *Strange Trips: Science, Culture, and the Regulation of Drugs* (Montreal: McGill-Queen's University Press, 2019).

12   David Herzberg, "Entitled to Addiction? Pharmaceuticals and Race in America's First Drug War," *Bulletin of the History of Medicine*, September 2017, 586–623.

Chapter One

1   David Courtwright, *Dark Paradise: A History of Opiate Addiction in America*, enlarged ed. (Cambridge, MA: Harvard University Press, 2001; first published

1982); Joseph Spillane, *Cocaine: From Medical Marvel to Modern Menace in the United States, 1884–1920* (Baltimore: Johns Hopkins University Press, 2000).

2   Jean-Paul Gaudillière and Volker Hess, eds., *Ways of Regulating Drugs in the 19th and 20th Centuries* (Basingstoke, UK: Palgrave Macmillan, 2013).

3   Courtwright, *Dark Paradise*, 46–51.

4   George Wood and Franklin Bache, *The Dispensatory of the United States of America*, 11th ed. (Philadelphia: J. B. Lippincott, 1858), 568–69, 1148.

5   Courtwright, *Dark Paradise*, 48.

6   Clifford Albutt, "On the Abuse of Hypodermic Injections of Morphia," *Practitioner: A Monthly Journal of Therapeutics* 5 (July–December 1870).

7   Spillane, *Cocaine*, chap. 1.

8   Courtwright, *Dark Paradise*, chap. 2.

9   Spillane, *Cocaine*.

10   Courtwright, *Dark Paradise*, chap. 3; Spillane, *Cocaine*, chap. 5.

11   Tomes, *Remaking the American Patient*, 24–28.

12   Joseph Gabriel, "Restricting the Sale of Deadly Poisons: Pharmacists, Drug Regulation, and Narratives of Suffering in the Gilded Age," *Journal of the Gilded Age and Progressive Era* 3 (July 2010): 313–36.

13   Caroline Jean Acker, "Portrait of an Addicted Family: Dynamics of Opiate Addiction in the Early Twentieth Century," in *Altering American Consciousness: The History of Alcohol and Drug Use in the United States, 1800–2000*, ed. Caroline Jean Acker and Sarah Tracy (Amherst: University of Massachusetts Press, 2004).

14   Timothy Hickman, *The Secret Leprosy of Modern Days: Narcotic Addiction and Cultural Crisis in the United States, 1870–1920* (Amherst: University of Massachusetts Press, 2007); Diana L. Ahmad, *The Opium Debate and Chinese Exclusion Laws in the Nineteenth-Century American West* (Reno: University of Nevada Press, 2014).

15   "Opium Eating," *Daily Union and American*, March 4, 1866, 4 [byline listed as the *Cincinnati Commercial*].

16   Susan Zieger, *Inventing the Addict: Drugs, Race and Sexuality in Nineteenth-Century British and American Literature* (Amherst: University of Massachusetts Press, 2008); Hickman, *Secret Leprosy*.

17   Nayan Shah, *Contagious Divides: Epidemics and Race in San Francisco's Chinatown* (Berkeley: University of California Press, 2001).

18   See Ahmad, *Opium Debate*, 27.

19   Editorials, "The United States Opium Commission," *JAMA* 51, no. 8: 678–79.

20   "The Sorcery of Madjoon," *Scribner's Monthly*, July 1880, 416–22.

21   Campbell, *Using Women*.

22   See, e.g., "Pretty but Depraved: Sixteen Years of Age and a Confirmed Opium Smoker," *New York Times*, November 12, 1884.

23   Jacob Riis, "Chinatown," chap. 9 in *How the Other Half Lives* (New York: Charles Scribner's Sons, 1890). See also, e.g., "The Opium Death," *Arthur's Illustrated Home Magazine*, February 1873; Allen Samuel Williams, *The Demon of the Orient, and His Satellite Fiends of the Joints: Our Opium Smokers as They Are in Tartar Hells and American Paradises* (New York, 1883), cited in Gabriel, "Deadly Poisons," 331; "The Opium Habit in San Francisco," *Medical and Surgical Reporter*, December 10, 1887, cited in Courtwright, *Dark Paradise*, 77.

24   Jim Baumohl, "Dope Fiend's Paradise Revisited: Notes from Research in Progress on Drug Law Enforcement in San Francisco, 1875-1915," *Drinking and Drug Practices Surveyor* 24 (June 1992); Ahmad, *Opium Debate.*

25   See Municipal Code of Chicago 1620 (Chicago: Beach, Barnard, 1881), 378, https://babel.hathitrust.org/cgi/pt?id=uc2.ark:/13960/t1sf3060h&view=1up &seq=390. See also New York City's similar ban, "An Act in Relation to the Sale and Use of Opium," chap. 165, *Laws of the State of New York Passed at the One Hundred and Fifth Session of the Legislature*, vol. 1 (Albany: Parsons, 1882).

26   See, e.g., "An Act to Amend an Act Entitled 'An Act Defining Nuisance and Securing Remedies' Approved November 12, 1875," *Laws of the Territory of Washington Enacted by the Legislative Assembly, in the Year 1877* (Olympia, WA: C. B. Bagley, 1877), which listed "opium dens" along with "houses of ill fame" including "squaw dance houses," "squaw brothels," saloons, gambling houses, etc. (305). See also Baumohl, "Dope Fiend's Paradise"; Spillane, *Cocaine*; Courtwright, *Dark Paradise.*

27   Courtwright, *Dark Paradise*; Ahmad, *Opium Debate*; Baumohl, "Dope Fiend's Paradise."

28   US citizens were also forbidden from importing opium into China. *Supplemental Treaty between the United States and China, Concerning Intercourse and Judicial Procedure*, proclaimed October 5, 1881; 22 Stat. (1864-1883), 828.

29   South Dakota was the only state that forbade smoking opium no matter where it took place. See Martin Wilbert and Murray Galt Motter, *Digest of and Regulations in Force in the United States Relating the Possession, Use, Sale, and Manufacture of Poisons and Habit-Forming Drugs*, Public Health Bulletin 56, November 1912.

30   "The Opium Habit's Power," *New York Times*, December 30, 1877.

31   Harry Hubbell Kane, *Drugs That Enslave: The Opium, Morphine, Chloral, and Hashisch Habits* (Philadelphia: Presley Blakiston, 1881), 24-25. See also, e.g., "The Opium Habit," *Catholic World*, September 1881.

32   W. Xavier Sudduth, "The Psychology of Narcotism," *JAMA* 27, no. 16 (1896).

33   See Hickman, *Secret Leprosy.*

34   George Beard, *American Nervousness: Its Causes and Consequences* (New York: G. P. Putnam's Sons, 1881).

35   Kane, *Drugs That Enslave*, 17. See also Hickman, *Secret Leprosy*, 33-46.

36   See Hickman, *Secret Leprosy*, who analyzes this as a distinction between *juridical* and *volitional* addiction (67, 128-50).

37   Fitzhugh Ludlow, "What Shall They Do to Be Saved?," *Harper's New Monthly Magazine* 207 (August 1867), 377.

38   "Opium Habit's Power," *New York Times*, 1877. See also, e.g., H. H. Kane, *The Hypodermic Injection of Morphia: Its History, Advantages, and Dangers* (New York: Chas. I. Bermingham, 1880), 269; Kane, *Drugs That Enslave*, 33.

39   "Opium Habit's Power," *New York Times*, 1877.

40   Sudduth, "Psychology of Narcotism."

41   "Women Using Narcotics," *New York Times*, January 10, 1897.

42   "Death in a Needle's Point," *New York Times*, November 19, 1882.

43   "Opium Death," *Arthur's Illustrated*, 1873.

44   "Lavish" from "Opium Habit's Power," *New York Times*, 1877; "careless" from Kane, *Hypodermic Injection*, 268, 306-7, and "Opium Habit," *Catholic World*,

1881; "weak" from Kane, *Drugs That Enslave*, 18; "almost criminal" from "Women Victims of Morphine," *New York Times*, October 25, 1895. See also, e.g., N. J. Phenix, "The Morphine Habit," *Southwestern Medical Record*, 1896, 206-14; Courtwright, *Dark Paradise*; Musto, *American Disease*.

45   T. L. Corwin, "Has the Pharmacist the Moral Right to Sell Opiates Indiscriminately Even If He Complies with any Existing Laws as to Its Registration?" *Pharmaceutical Record*, July 1885, 204, cited in Gabriel, "Deadly Poisons," 330.

46   Spillane, *Cocaine*, chap. 1, and 32-42.

47   Courtwright, *Dark Paradise*, 51-52, Spillane, *Cocaine*, 32-42.

48   J. C. Wilson, "The Causes and Prevention of the Opium Habit and Kindred Affections," *JAMA* 11, no. 11 (1888): 817.

49   "Editorial," *American Journal of Pharmacy*, January 1880, 58, cited in Gabriel, "Deadly Poisons," 331. See also, e.g., Harry Nickerson, "The Relation of the Physician to the Drug Habit," *Journal of Medicine and Science*, 1900, 50-51.

50   Marks, *Progress of Experiment*; Gabriel, *Medical Monopoly*.

51   Categorization from Tomes, *Remaking the American Patient*; Gabriel, "Deadly Poisons," 323; Marks, *Progress of Experiment*; James Mohr, *Licensed to Practice: The Supreme Court Defines the American Medical Profession* (Baltimore: Johns Hopkins University Press, 2013); David Johnson and Humayun Chaudhry, *Medical Licensing and Discipline in America: A History of the Federation of State Medical Boards* (Lanham, MD: Lexington, 2012).

52   See Ruth Horowitz, *In the Public Interest: Medical Licensing and the Disciplinary Process* (New Brunswick, NJ: Rutgers University Press, 2013); Tomes, *Remaking the American Patient*, 20.

53   P. C. Remondino, "The Hypodermic Syringe and Our Morphine," *Medical Sentinel* 4 (1896).

54   Regina Morantz-Sanchez, *Sympathy and Science: Women Physicians in American Medicine* (New York: Oxford University Press, 1985).

55   James Harvey Young, *Pure Food: Securing the Federal Food and Drugs Act of 1906* (Princeton, NJ: Princeton University Press, 1989), 6-12.

56   Deborah Blum, *The Poisoner's Handbook: Murder and the Birth of Forensic Medicine in Jazz Age New York* (New York: Penguin Press, 2010), 1-3, cited in Marian Moser Jones and Isrubi Daniel Benrubi, "Poison Politics: A Contentious History of Consumer Protection Against Dangerous Household Chemicals in the United States," *American Journal of Public Health* 103, no. 5 (May 2013): 801-12; Edward Kremers and George Urdang, *History of Pharmacy: A Guide and a Survey* (Philadelphia: Lippincott, 1963), 216.

57   Tomes, *Remaking the American Patient*.

58   Generally, they did not have patents despite their common name; see Joseph M. Gabriel, "A Thing Patented is a Thing Divulged: Francis E. Stewart, George S. Davis, and the Legitimization of Intellectual Property Rights in Pharmaceutical Manufacturing, 1879-1911," *Journal of the History of Medicine & Allied Sciences* 64, no. 2 (April 2009): 135-72; Gabriel, *Medical Monopoly*.

59   See James Harvey Young, *Toadstool Millionaires* (Princeton, NJ: Princeton University Press, 2016); T. J. Jackson Lears, *Fables of Abundance: A Cultural History of Advertising in America* (New York: Basic, 1994).

60   Gabriel, *Medical Monopoly*; Tomes, *Remaking the American Patient*; Young,

Toadstool Millionaires; Jonathan Liebenau, *Medical Science and Medical Industry: the Formation of the American Pharmaceutical Industry* (Basingstoke, UK: Palgrave Macmillan, 1987).

61 For pharmacy laws, see Kremers and Urdang, *History of Pharmacy*, 215; chronological list in app. 3. For medical licensing laws, see Paul Starr, *The Social Transformation of American Medicine* (New York: Basic,1982); Ronald Hamowy, "The Early Development of Medical Licensing Laws in the United States," *Journal of Libertarian Studies* 3, no. 1 (1979); Samuel Baker, "Physician Licensure Laws in the United States," *Journal of the History of Medicine & Allied Sciences* 39, no. 2 (April 1984): 173-97; Johnson and Chaudhry, *Medical Licensing*, chap. 1; Horowitz, *In the Public Interest*, chap. 2.

62 Musto, *American Disease*, 8-10. For an example of a Dover's Powder exemption, see, e.g., Act of Aug. 26, 1909, No. 207, S. 87, § 13, 1909 Ala. Laws 214, 222-23; for exemptions of "patent medicines" with small amounts, see, e.g., Ohio's 1886 law, Act of Apr. 8, 1886, H.B. No. 66, 1886 Ohio Laws 69, 69-70.

63 See Wilbert and Motter, *Digest of and Regulations in Force*; Musto, *American Disease*, 8-10.

64 Wilbert and Motter, *Digest of and Regulations in Force*.

65 California's pharmacy board, for example, mostly occupied itself with sanctioning opium dens as unlicensed pharmacies. California Board of Pharmacy, *Investigation and Violation Log Book*, CABPR.

66 "San Francisco Opium Den," *New York Times*, December 23, 1876, 7.

67 Young, *Pure Food*, 152-71.

68 Courtwright, *Dark Paradise*; Spillane, *Cocaine*.

69 Young, *Toadstool Millionaires*.

70 Young, *Toadstool Millionaires*, 17-18.

71 Samuel Hopkins Adams, *The Great American Fraud: Articles on the Nostrum Evil and Quacks, Reprinted from Collier's Weekly*, 4th ed. (Chicago: JAMA, 1907), 3-11, "subtle poisons," 32-39.

72 Adams, *Great American Fraud*, 34, 40, 43. See also, e.g., "Women Victims of Morphine," *New York Times*, 1895.

73 Glickman, *Buying Power*; Cohen, *Consumers' Republic*.

74 Adams, *Great American Fraud*, 11, 54.

75 See, e.g., North Carolina Representative E. Y. Webb's long list of patent medicine evils in *Hearing on H.R. 13086 Before H. Comm. on Interstate and Foreign Commerce*, 59th Cong. 9-11 (1906).

76 Richard Lewis, President of the National Conference of State and Provincial Boards of Health, and a Vice President of the Public Health Association, in *Hearing on H.R. 13086*, 16-17.

77 Gabriel, "Restricting the Sale of Deadly Poisons."

78 Representative Mann, speaking on S. 88, in 40 Cong. Rec. 8892 (1906); see James Harvey Young, *Pure Food: Securing the Federal Food and Drugs Act of 1906* (Princeton, NJ: Princeton University Press, 1989), 257.

79 Harvey C. Wiley speaking to the National Pure Food and Drug Congress in 1898, quoted in Oscar Anderson, *The Health of a Nation: Harvey W. Wiley and the Fight for Pure Food* (Chicago: University of Chicago Press, 1958), 124-25.

80 An Act for Preventing the Manufacture, Sale, or Transportation of Adulter-

ated or Misbranded or Poisonous or Deleterious Foods, Drugs, Medicines, and Liquors . . . , Pub. L. No. 59-384, 34 Stat. 768 (1906).

81 Musto, *American Disease*, 30-36.

82 William McAllister, *Drug Diplomacy in the Twentieth Century: An International History* (London: Routledge, 2000), 27-30.

83 An Act to Prohibit the Importation and Use of Opium for Other Than Medicinal Purposes, Pub. L. No. 221, ch. 100, 35 Stat. 614 (1909). For resistance to the law, see, e.g., Senator Bailey, speaking on S. 8021, on January 26, 1909, 43 Cong. Rec. 1396-97 (1909).

84 This weakness mollified industry opponents; see, e.g., E. G. Swift (of Parke, Davis) to Representative Mann, *To Prohibit the Importation of Opium for Other than Medicinal Purposes: Report (to Accompany H.R. 24863)*, H. Rep No. 60-1878, at 2-3 (1909).

85 Courtwright, *Dark Paradise*.

86 Spillane, *Cocaine*.

87 Matthew Frye Jacobson, *Whiteness of a Different Color: Europe Immigrants and the Alchemy of Race* (Cambridge, MA: Harvard University Press, 1999); David Roediger, *Working towards Whiteness: How America's Immigrants became White* (New York: Basic, 2006).

88 Spillane, *Cocaine*; Acker, *Creating the American Junkie*.

89 An Act to Provide for the Registration of . . . Persons Who Produce, Import, Manufacture, . . . Opium or Coca Leaves, Their Salts, Derivatives, or Preparations . . . , Pub. L. No. 223, ch. 1, 38 Stat. 785 (1914). See Musto, *American Disease*, for analysis of congressional debates.

90 *Importation and Use of Opium: Hearings Before the H. Comm. on Ways and Means*, 61st Cong. 146-47 (1910 1911).

91 *JAMA*, March 1915, 835.

92 Wilbert and Motter "Digest of Laws and Regulations in Force."

93 Musto, *American Disease*, 69-90, 100-115.

94 US Treasury Department, *Regulations No. 35 Relating to the importation, manufacture, production, compounding, sale, dispensing, and giving away of opium or coca leaves, their salts, derivatives, or preparations thereof, revised November, 1919* (Washington, DC: Government Printing Office, 1919), art. 117, 51, https://archive.org/stream/regulationsno35roounit/regulationsno35roounit _djvu.txt.

95 Kurt Hohenstein, "Just What the Doctor Ordered: The Harrison Anti-Narcotic Act, the Supreme Court, and the Federal Regulation of Medical Practice, 1915-1919," *Journal of Supreme Court History* 26, no. 3 (2001): 231-56.

96 United States v. Friedman, 224 Fed. Rep. 276 (1915). See Musto, *American Disease*, 124-31.

97 United States v. Jin Fuey Moy, 241 U.S. 394 (1916). See Hohenstein, "Just What the Doctor Ordered," for the argument that *Moy* did not address prescribing question.

98 "States Rights and Harrison Law," *JAMA*, July 1916, 37-38.

99 McGirr, *War on Alcohol*; Margot Canaday, *The Straight State: Sexuality and Citizenship in Twentieth-Century America* (Princeton, NJ: Princeton University Press, 2011).

100 S. D. Hubbard's survey, "New York City Narcotic Clinic and Differing Points

of View on Narcotic Addiction," *Monthly Bulletin Department Health of New York City* 10 (1920): 46–47, cited in Musto, *American Disease*, 158, for example, found that more than one-third of the clinic's patients were foreign born. Many others must have been the children of immigrants, as suggested by New York data from ten years later, which found a great majority of people committed to a public hospital for addiction were born in America (86 percent) but that only one-third had parents born in America (34 percent); over 80 percent were either Catholic or Jewish; see Richardson, "Neurological and Psychotic Studies on Drug Addicts in Philadelphia General Hospital," 1927, in SCP; Alexander Lambert et al., "Report of the Mayor's Committee on Drug Addiction," *American Journal of Psychiatry* 87 (1930): 468. National figures from 1930 showed that slightly under half of those arrested under the Harrison Act were either foreign born or of "foreign parentage," and another 15 percent were American-born "blacks"; see W. L. Treadway, "Further Observations on the Epidemiology of Narcotic Drug Addiction," *Public Health Reports* 45, no. 11 (March 14, 1930): 545–46.

101 McGirr, *War on Alcohol.*
102 Musto, *American Disease*, 184.
103 Webb v. United States, 249 U.S. 96, 97–99 (1919); United States v. Doremus, 249 U.S. 86 (1919).
104 See, e.g., "Problem of the Narcotic Addict," *JAMA* 27, no. 15 (1921): 1199.
105 Musto, *American Disease*, 151–72.
106 Musto, 158, 164–66.
107 Courtwright, *Dark Paradise*, 123–37; Acker, *Creating the American Junkie.*
108 Acker, *Creating the American Junkie.*
109 Musto, 148, 186.
110 US Treasury Department, *Regulations No. 35, as Amended 1921 and 1925*, in Los Angeles County Medical Association, *A Digest and an Editorial Article of the Federal Narcotic Laws as They Apply to Doctors of Medicine* (Los Angeles: LA County Medical Association, November 1925), KP.
111 Musto, *American Disease*, 185.
112 See, e.g., A Bill to Strengthen the Harrison Narcotic Act, S. 4085, 69th Cong. (1926); H.R. 11612, 69th Cong. (1926).
113 William Woodward, "Physicians as Narcotic Addicts and Panders: Federal Legislation vs. State Laws," *AMA Bulletin*, in KP.
114 Linder v. United States, 268 U.S. 5 (1925).
115 Lambert et al., "Report of the Mayor's Committee," 534. See also Musto, *American Disease*, 85.
116 This argument drawn from Gabriel, "Restricting the Sale of Deadly Poisons."
117 Eric Schneider, *Smack: Heroin and the Postwar City* (Philadelphia: University of Pennsylvania Press, 2013).
118 Acker, "Portrait of an Addicted Family."

Chapter Two

1 Lawrence Kolb to Dr. B. R. Rhees, Narcotic Agent in Charge, 7 March 1925, Case Histories, KP.
2 Kolb to Rhees, 7 March 1925.

3   Kolb to Rhees, 7 March 1925.
4   Levi C. Nutt to Lawrence Kolb, 10 September 1925, Case Histories, KP.
5   Acker, *Creating the American Junkie*; Campbell, *Using Women*; Curtis Marez, *Drug Wars: The Political Economy of Narcotics* (Minneapolis: University of Minnesota Press, 2004); Eric Schneider *Smack: Heroin and the American City* (Philadelphia: University of Pennsylvania Press, 2011).
6   David Courtwright, "Preventing and Treating Narcotic Addiction—A Century of Federal Drug Control," *New England Journal of Medicine* 373 (November 26, 2015): 2095–97.
7   Acker, *Creating the American Junkie*.
8   Courtwright, *Dark Paradise*, chap. 5.
9   Lawrence Kolb, "Drug Addiction: A Study of Some Medical Cases," *Archives of Neurology and Psychiatry* 20, no. 1 (1928): 182. See also Acker, *Creating the American Junkie*, 52.
10 See Elizabeth Lunbeck, *The Psychiatric Persuasion: Knowledge, Gender, and Power in Modern America* (Princeton, NJ: Princeton University Press, 1994).
11 Acker, *Creating the American Junkie*, esp. 141.
12 Acker, *Creating the American Junkie*; Courtwright, *Dark Paradise*; Schneider, *Smack*.
13 Schneider, *Smack*.
14 See, e.g., the influential 1930s *JAMA* series on the "indispensable uses of narcotics": Morris Fishbein, "The Indispensable Uses of Narcotics: Introduction," *JAMA* 96, no. 11 (1931): 856; Horatio C. Wood Jr., "The Indispensable Uses of Narcotics: The Therapeutic Uses of Narcotic Drugs," *JAMA* 96, no. 14 (1931): 1142; Frederick Tice, "The Indispensable Uses of Narcotics: In the Practice of Medicine," *JAMA* 96, no. 12 (1931): 944–46; Robert Hatcher, "The Indispensable Uses of Narcotics: In the Treatment of Coughing," *JAMA* 96, no. 17 (1931): 1383–86; Robert Hatcher, "The Indispensable Uses of Narcotics: In the Treatment of Diseases of the Gastro-intestinal Tract," *JAMA* 96, no. 18 (1931): 1475–77.
15 See Courtwright, *Dark Paradise*, and E. N. Gathercoal, *The Prescription Ingredient Survey* (Washington, DC: American Pharmaceutical Association, 1933), for early figures; and US Department of Commerce and Labor, Bureau of Statistics, *The Foreign Commerce and Navigation of the United States* (Washington, DC: Government Printing Office, annually), and US Treasury Department, *Traffic in Opium and Other Dangerous Drugs* (Washington, DC: Government Printing Office, annually), for later figures.
16 Gathercoal, *Prescription Ingredient Survey*.
17 For the idea of using a pareto distribution, I am grateful to David Courtwright; this does not mean that he has endorsed these figures.
18 For the FBN's estimate, see *Illicit Traffic in Narcotics, Barbiturates and Amphetamines in the United States: Hearings Before a Subcomm. of the H. Comm. on Ways and Means*, 84th Cong. 9 (1956).
19 W. A. Bloedorn, "Studies of Drug Addicts," *U.S. Naval Medical Bulletin* 11 (1917): 305–18; Thomas Joyce, "Treatment of Drug Addiction," *New York Medical Journal* 112 (1920): 220–22; Carleton Simon, "Survey of the Narcotic Problem," *JAMA*, March 1, 1924, 675–79; Adolphus Knopf, "The One Million Drug Addicts in the United States," *Medical Journal and Record* 119 (1924): 135–39;

Lambert et al., "Report of the Mayor's Committee"; Treadway, "Further Observations," 545-46; Michael Pescor, "Statistical Analysis of Clinical Records of Hospitalized Drug Addicts," *Public Health Reports*, Supp. 143 (1938): 1-23.

20   Francis Dercum, "Relative Infrequency of the Drug Habit Among the Middle and Upper Classes," *Pennsylvania Medical Journal* 20 (1917): 362-64; Charles Sceleth and Sydney Kuh, "Drug Addiction," *JAMA* 82, no. 9 (1924): 679-82; Lawrence Kolb and A. G. Du Mez, "The Prevalence and Trend of Drug Addiction in the U.S. and Factors Influencing It," *Public Health Reports* 39 (1924): 1179-1204.

21   Figures from Thomas Blair, "Is Opium the 'Sheet Anchor of Treatment?'" *American Journal of Clinical Medicine* 26 (1919): 829-34. See also Thomas S. Blair, "Narcotic Drug Addiction as Regulated by a State Department of Health," *JAMA* 72, no. 20 (1919): 1141-45; Thomas S. Blair, "Some Statistics on Drug Addicts under the Care of Physicians in Pennsylvania," *JAMA* 76 (1921): 608; Thomas S. Blair, "The Doctors, the Law and the Drug Addict," *American Medicine*, November 1921, 581-88.

22   Blair, "Is Opium the 'Sheet Anchor of Treatment?'"

23   Charles Terry, Mildred Pellens, and J. W. Cox, *Report on the Legal Use of Narcotics in Detroit, Michigan, and Environs for the Period July 1, 1925 to June 30, 1926, to the Committee on Drug Addictions* (New York: Bureau of Social Hygiene, 1931), 20. Even using these self-reported (and thus, likely low) numbers, the authors calculated that if this rate were nationally uniform, there would be approximately 36,500 people with addiction purchasing in white markets in the United States. Underreporting may have been less of an issue because Charles Terry was sympathetic to people with addiction and favored medical maintenance—but he was still strongly opposed to casual prescribing, which he blamed for addiction. See Acker, *Creating American Junkie*; David Courtwright, "Charles Terry, the Opium Problem, and American Narcotic Policy," *Journal of Drug Issues* 16 (July 1986): 421-34.

24   Terry et al., *Report on Legal Use of Narcotics in Detroit*, 11-12.

25   See Box 0321, Folder 13, AMA Papers; mimeographed version Box 0322, Folder 07, AMA Papers.

26   Virginia Dwyer, Directory-Biographical Department, to Homer Pearson, MD, Secretary, Florida State Board of Medical Examiners, 25 January 1957, Box 0322, Folder 07, AMA Papers. This folder also contains multiple other examples.

27   "Information on Loss of Narcotics Stamps," AMA House of Delegates resolution 41, 15 June 1963, Box 104, 105, Folder "MED: Committee on Drug Addiction & Narcotics: Cameron-Eddy Correspondence, 1961-1965," NRC Papers.

28   *Report on Narcotic Addiction to Attorney General by the Citizens Advisory Committee to the Attorney General on Crime Prevention* (Sacramento: California State Printing Office, March 26, 1954), 17.

29   Irwin Greenfield to Walter Morris, 23 May 1957, Box 41, Folder "Addiction: Dr. Addict, Thru December 1959," FBN Papers.

30   John A. O'Donnell, *Narcotic Addicts in Kentucky* (Washington, DC: Department of Health, Education and Welfare, 1969), 5. The researchers did note that after a crackdown in 1935, the rate of new cases of addiction decreased.

31   Thanks to David Courtwright for suggesting this possibility.

32   See, e.g., Acker, *Creating the American Junkie*, 51.
33   Internal Revenue Regulations No. 35, Law and Regulations Relating to the Production, Importation, Manufacture, Compounding, Sale, Dispensing, or Giving Away of Opium or Coca Leaves, Their Salts, Derivatives, or Preparations," *Code of Federal Regulations*, May 1916, 16.
34   "Internal Revenue Regulations No. 35, *Code of Federal Regulations*, November 1919, art. 117.
35   "New Narcotic Drug Instructions," *JAMA* 77, no. 18 (1921): 1427; see also "New Regulations for Narcotic Drugs," *JAMA* 77, no. 18 (1921): 1431.
36   Linder v. United States, 268 U.S. 5, 8, 20 (1925).
37   "Internal Revenue Regulations No. 5, Relating to the Importation, Manufacture, Production, Compounding, Sale, Dispensing, and Giving Away of Opium or Coca Leaves, Their Salts, Derivatives, or Preparations," *Code of Federal Regulations*, 1927: 58-59. Rules affirmed in 1934 in *Treatment of Narcotic Drug Addiction Permissible under the Harrison Narcotic Law*, Narcotic Pamphlet N-No. 56 (Washington, DC: Treasury Department, Bureau of Narcotics, 1934).
38   State Board of Medical Examiners v. Friedman, 263 S.W. 75 (Tenn. 1934).
39   "The Doctor as Narcotic Purveyor," *Northwest Medicine* 33, no. 11 (November 1934): 396.
40   *Amendments to the Harrison Narcotic Act: Hearings Before a Subcomm. of the H. Comm. on Ways and Means*, 69th Cong. (1926); "A federal narcotics dictator," *JAMA*, 8 February 1930, 412; *Bureau of Narcotics: Hearings Before the H. Comm. on Ways and Means*, 71st Cong. (1930).
41   William C. Woodward, "Physicians as Narcotic Addicts and Panders: Federal Legislation versus State Laws," *American Medical Association Bulletin* [n.d.; 1926 or 1927], 171-78, Box 7, Folder "Harrison Law—Legislation + Documents," KP.
42   C. A. Dawson, MD, Secretary of Wisconsin Board of Medical Examiners, to Harry J. Anslinger, 7 November 1947, Box 1, Folder 42 "HAZ-HOFF," WI SBME Investigations; John W. Davison to Dr. Dawson, 3 March 1949, Box 1, Folder 13 "CH-CO," WI SBME Investigations.
43   For 1935 data, see Anslinger, "Narcotic Problem in its Relation to Physicians and Surgeons," *American Journal of Surgery* 28 (1935): 157-59; for 1946 data, see H. J. Anslinger, "The Physician and the Federal Narcotic Law," *American Journal of Psychiatry* 102 (March 1946): 609-18.
44   Musto, *American Disease*, 184.
45   Musto, 58-59.
46   The other three: a physician who prescribed narcotics before officially receiving his medical license; an addicted physician prescribing for himself; and an addicted nurse who forged prescriptions for her own use. Register of convictions for violating the Medical Practice Act, Box 1, Volume 1. Register of Convictions for Violating the Medical Practice Act, 1920-1932. CA2.01/series 251X. Massachusetts Archives. Boston.
47   Registers of complaints and charges made against registered physicians. Box 1, Volumes 1 and 2. MEDICINE Hearings: Records of physicians appearing for hearings beginning July, 1925. CA2.01/series 1349X. Massachusetts Archives. Boston.

48   Ibid. Two physicians did lose their license in 1936, but for abortion, not narcotics.

49   Tallied from Boxes 1-4, WI SBME Investigations.

50   Cases were: Glenn F. Treadwell, Box 3, Folder 9 "TO-TY"; Loraine Karl Everson, Box 1, Folder 28 "E"; L. A. Kliese, Box 2, Folder 7 "KA-KR"; H. W. Kleinschmit, Box 2, Folder 7 "KA-KR"; George H. Lawyer, Box 2, Folder 10 "LA-LEWIS"; all WI SBME Investigations. It was Lawyer who could not explain his narcotics prescription.

51   Case of Boyd T. Williams, Box 4, Folder 3 "Williams, Boyd T.," WI SBME Investigations.

52   Case of Robert C. Thackeray, Box 3, Folder 8 "TA-TI," WI SBME Investigations.

53   Case of Philip G. Welton, Box 4, Folder 1 "WA-WEN," WI SBME Investigations.

54   Wisconsin: Cases of King David Cammack, Box 1, Folder 15 "Cammack, King D." and James Carter, Box 1 Folder 12 "CA-CE," both WI SBME Investigations. California: Case of Arrington Weaver, Box 21, Folder "Weaver, Arrington—reports, misc. court cases, memoranda, photos 1938-1960," CA MEB Investigations.

55   US Treasury Department, US Public Health Service, *Proceedings of the Conference of Representatives of Medical, Dental, Pharmaceutical, and Veterinary Associations and Other Scientific Associations and Agencies with the Surgeon General of the USPHS*, Washington, DC, August 12, 1930, Supp. No. 96 to *Public Health Reports* (Washington, DC: Government Printing Office, 1931), 71-73, Box 0321, Folder 09, AMA Papers.

56   "Dope and Doctors," *New York American*, January 23, 1935. See also "Makers of Addicts," *Washington Herald*, January 25, 1935. Both in Box 41, Miscellaneous subject files arranged numerically re: Addiction, Clinics, Associations 1930-1966, Folder "Addiction: Dr. Addict, Thru December 1959," in FBN Papers.

57   For the FBN survey finding that 1 percent of physicians were addicted (far more than the general public), see Stephen Gibbons, Assistant Secretary, to Dr. Edward E. Cravener, March 29, 1935; for the "prevalence" quote, see "Makers of Addicts," *Washington Herald*; both in Box 41, Folder "Addiction: Dr. Addict, Thru December 1959," in FBN Papers.

58   William S. Woodward to Mr. H. J. Anslinger, n.d. (ca. 1935), Box 41, Folder "Addiction: Dr. Addict, Thru December 1959," in FBN Papers.

59   William S. Woodward, Director AMA, to The Presidents, Constituent State Medical Associations, December 19, 1934, Box 11, Folder "State Board of Medical Examiners, Central File Records, General Subjects, Narcotics #1, Correspondence Memoranda, 1934-1971," CA MEB Drugs.

60   See Box 0321, Folders 09 through 12, AMA Papers.

61   Arthur J. Cramp, AMA Bureau of Investigation & Propaganda Department, to B. D. Harison, Secretary, Michigan Board of Registration in Medicine, June 24, 1924; B. D. Harison to A. J. Cramp, July 22, 1924; both in Box 0321, Folder 09, AMA Papers.

62   "Narcotic Case Report, Case File No. Wis.507, Clarence L. Treadwell, MD; Box 3, Folder 10 "Treadwell, C. L.," WI SBME Investigations.

63   Kenneth S. White, Attorney for the Board, to Clive J. Strang, District Attorney, July 9, 1945; Box 3, Folder 10 "Treadwell, C. L.," WI SBME Investigations.

64   Kenneth S. White to Will S. Wood, Deputy Commissioner of Narcotics, May 2, 1945; Kenneth White to R. G. Arverson, March 17, 1945; both in Box 3, Folder 10 "Treadwell, C. L.," WI SBME Investigations.

65   "In the District Court of the United States of America for the Western District of Wisconsin," December 1943, Box 3, Folder 10 "Treadwell, C. L.," WI SBME Investigations.

66   Kenneth S. White to Fulton Collipp, District Attorney, August 28, 1946; Fulton Collipp to Kenneth S. White, August 16, 1946; both in Box 3, Folder 10 "Treadwell, C. L.," WI SBME Investigations.

67   Fulton Collipp to Kenneth S. White, October 22, 1946, Box 3, Folder 10 "Treadwell, C. L.," WI SBME Investigations. See also the case of Lyder O. Gulbrandsen. Gulbrandsen was brother to the county district attorney; the state board secretary advised that he was a "pretty decent chap and I would dislike seeing the doctor's license revoked, providing he would straighten up"; see Robert E. Flynn, MD, Secretary to Attorney General James E. Finnegan, July 6, 1935, Box 1, Folder 38 "GR-GY" WI SBME Investigations.

68   Oscar W. Lewis, Narcotic Agent to Kenneth S. White, 6 November 1946; Oscar Lewis to George White, District Supervisor, 6 November 1946; both in Box 3, Folder 10 "Treadwell, C. L.," WI SBME Investigations.

69   See "In the Matter of the Practices of Dr. Robert James Hudson," 8 June 1944, page 10, Box 1, Folder 43 "HOFL-HY," WI SBME Investigations.

70   Holman Taylor, Secretary to William C. Woodward, January 21, 1928, Box 0321, Folder 09, AMA Papers.

71   William C. Woodward to Holman Taylor, January 27, 1928; Box 0321, Folder 09, AMA Papers.

72   A. J. Cramp to Dr. West, August 9, 1933; [unstated] to Dr. E. A. Meyerding, August 10, 1933; both in Box 0321, Folder 09, AMA Papers.

73   H. T. Nugent, Confidential memorandum for Mr. Anslinger in re: Demerol, May 2, 1944; Folder "Drugs: Demerol (Dolantin): Isonipecaine, 1940–1943," FBN Papers.

74   Case of John L. Dach, Box 1, Folder 22 "DA-DU," WI SBME Investigations.

75   For California's strictness, see "Narcotics Warning!" in *The Bulletin of the LA County Medical Association*, August 16, 1934, 623–24, Box 11, Folder "State Board of Medical Examiners, Central File Records, General Subjects, Narcotics #1, Correspondence Memoranda, 1934–1971, CA MEB Drugs. That folder also includes other examples of Board actions reported directly to Anslinger. In 1942, California investigated eight physicians for narcotics violations; four had their licenses revoked, three got several years of probation, and one was dismissed; the number declined to six in 1943, went back up to ten in 1944, and then to eight in 1945. The state board investigated an average of fifteen accusations against physicians each year from 1949 to 1951, out of the more than 20,000 physicians licensed in the state. The great majority of those cases were for doctors who had become addicted (see "Hearings on Charges of Unprofessional Conduct," Folder "Earl Warren Papers—Administrative Files, P&V Standards-Medical Examiners Bd., 1943–1945," Warren Papers; and "The Sale of Illegal Narcotics—A Profitable Business," in *The Narcotics Problem in California: A Survey-Report*, January 25, 1952, Box 8, Folder "State Board of Medical Examiners, Central File Records, General Subjects, Narcot-

ics #3, Misc. Newspaper Articles, Memoranda, Reports, 1952–1963," CA MEB Papers. See also Jim Baumohl, "Maintaining Orthodoxy: The Depression-Era Struggle over Morphine Maintenance in California," in *Altering American Consciousness: The History of Alcohol and Drug Use in the United States, 1800–2000*, ed. Sarah Tracy and Caroline Jean Acker (Amherst: University of Massachusetts Press, 2004).

76   "More Physicians on Probation," *California Medical News*, 31 July 1926, 331; Box 0321, Folder 06, AMA Papers.

77   C. B. Pinkham to Dr. Warnschuis, CA Medical Association, 31 December 1934, Box 11, Folder "State Board of Medical Examiners, Central File Records, General Subjects, Narcotics #1, Correspondence Memoranda, 1934–1971," CA MEB Drugs.

78   See H. J. Anslinger to Dr. Walter L. Treadway, Assistant Surgeon General, 3 August 1938, Box 41, Folder "Addiction: Dr. Addict, Thru December 1959," FBN Papers.

79   See Box 0321, Folder 11, AMA Papers.

80   John R. Ronan, Acting Special Agent, to Charles B. Pinkham, Secretary-Treasurer, Board of Medical Examiners, 11 September 1937, Box 0321, Folder 11, AMA Papers.

81   C. B. Pinkham to Bureau of Narcotics, 3 November 1934; Pinkham to State Department of Health, 3 November 1934; Pinkham to US District Court, 3 November 1934; Albert Carter, Special Agent, to Charles B. Pinkham, 3 November 1934 (two letters on that date); Carter to Pinkham, 10 January 1935; all Box 0321, Folder 11, AMA Papers.

82   James A. Arnerich to James Welsh, 13 February 1948; Earle Montague to Earl Warren, 11 February 1948; Helen MacGregor to James Walsh, 9 February 1948; all in Folder "Earl Warren Papers—Administrative Files, P&V Standards-Medical Examiners Bd.," 1943–1945, Warren Papers.

83   C. B. Pinkham to US Bureau of Narcotics, 5 November 1934; H. J. Anslinger to Charles B. Pinkham, 10 October 1934; both in Box 0321, Folder 10, AMA Papers.

84   Conrad Lee Klein, Deputy Attorney General, to Robert O. Merritt, District Supervisor, Division of Investigation, 23 December 1964, Box 11, Folder "State Board of Medical Examiners, Central File Records, General Subjects, Narcotics #1, Correspondence Memoranda, 1934–1971," CA MEB Drugs.

85   Conrad Lee Klein to Robert Merritt, 19 March 1965, Box 11, Folder "State Board of Medical Examiners, Central File Records, General Subjects, Narcotics #1, Correspondence Memoranda, 1934–1971," CA MEB Drugs.

86   Bureau of Narcotics, US Treasury Department, *Traffic in Opium and Other Dangerous Drugs* (Washington, DC: Government Printing Office, 1936), 58.

87   *Traffic in Opium*, 55.

88   Memorandum, "from 1920 to November 12, 1935," Box 41, Folder "Addiction: Dr. Addict, Thru December 1959," FBN Papers.

89   See Joseph Spillane, "Building a Drug Control Regime, 1919–1930," in *Federal Drug Control: The Evolution of Policy and Practice*, ed. Jonathon Erlen and Joseph Spillane (New York: Pharmaceutical Products Press, 2004), 47–48.

90   "Biographical Note," Lawrence Kolb Paper 1912–1972, KP.

91   Acker, *Creating the American Junkie*.

92 Acker, *Creating the American Junkie*, first revealed this aspect of Kolb's work.
93 See, e.g., L. M. Graves, Narcotic Inspector, to Dr. B. R. Rhees, Narcotic Agent in Charge, Washington, DC, 9 December 1924; Lawrence Kolb to Colonel L. G. Nutt, 30 January 1925; both in Case Histories, KP.
94 Lawrence Kolb to B. R. Rhees, 7 March 1925, re: H. D., Case Histories, KP.
95 Lawrence Kolb to Colonel L. G. Nutt, December 1925, re: I. R., Case Histories, KP.
96 Kolb to Rhees, 11 May 1926, re: W. McI., Case Histories, KP.
97 Kolb to Rhees, 6 January 1926, re: A. Q., Case Histories, KP.
98 Kolb to Rhees, 18 September 1926, re: K. L., Case Histories, KP. Acker discusses this case in *Creating the American Junkie*, 146 (Mrs. L).
99 Kolb to Nutt, 23 February 1926, re: L. B., Case Histories, KP.
100 Kolb, Examination of Mr. B, 26 January 1925, Case Histories, KP.
101 Kolb to Nutt, 2 July 1925, re: C. I., Case Histories, KP.
102 See Examination forms in Case Histories, KP.
103 Kolb, n.d., "C. B." and "M. B.," Box 41, Folder "Medical addicts," FBN Papers.
104 Kolb to Nutt, 5 January 1926, re: F. P., Case Histories, KP.
105 Kolb to Doctor J. F. Wine, 7 September 1926, re: W. B., Case Histories, KP. Acker, *Creating the American Junkie*, 150, describes W. B. as having been rejected for maintenance by Kolb.
106 Kolb to Nutt, 9 November 1925, re: B. H., Case Histories, KP.
107 Alice McI. to Lawrence Kolb, 7 May 1926; W. P. McI. to Lawrence Kolb, 9 June 1926; Kolb's examination of W. P. McI.; all in Case Histories, KP.
108 Kolb to Nutt, 10 November 1924, re: S. McC., Case Histories, KP.
109 Kolb to Nutt, 26 February 1926, re: L. B., Case Histories, KP.
110 Kolb to Rhees, 18 February 1926, re: C. G. vB., Case Histories, KP.
111 Kolb's examination of W. P. McI., Case Histories, KP.
112 Kolb to Rhees, 26 January 1925, re: A. F. B. and Kolb's examination of same, in Case Histories, KP.
113 Kolb to Nutt, 8 June 1927, re: C. P., Case Histories, KP.
114 Kolb to Nutt, 9 November 1925, re: H. H., Case Histories, KP.
115 Kolb to Rhees, 15 February 1926, re: C. G. vB., Case Histories, KP.
116 Kolb to Nutt, 25 June 1928, re: T. M. G., Case Histories, KP. Acker, *Creating the American Junkie*, discusses Mr. G on page 152.
117 Kolb's examination of I. R., 25 December 1925, Case Histories, KP.
118 Kolb to Rhees, 26 January 1926, re: N. S. F., Case Histories, KP. Later, Kolb advised forgoing withdrawal for N. S. F. altogether because of continued drug taking including cocaine; it is "unlikely that he will ever be permanently well of his addiction."
119 Kolb examination of C. C. A., 22 June 1926, Case Histories, KP.
120 Kolb to Rhees, 4 August 1926, re: L. J. W., Case Histories, KP.
121 Kolb examination of W. C. B., 4 September 1926, Case Histories, KP.
122 Kolb to Narcotic Agent in Charge, 21 June 1928, re: G. A. B., Case Histories, KP.
123 Lawrence Kolb Sr., Surgeon General of US, to Colonel R. G. Nutt, Chief, Narcotics Division, 13 March 1926, Folder "Medical addicts," Box 41, FBN Papers.
124 B. R. Rhees, Narcotics Agent in Charge, Washington, DC, to Colonel R. G.

Nutt, Narcotics Division, 4 November 1926; W. E. Turner, Narcotic Agent, to B. R. Rhees, 5 November 1926. Both in Box 41, Folder "Medical addicts," FBN Papers.

125 Dr. E. D. Rollins to B. R. Rhees, 16 October 1926, Box 41, Folder "Medical addicts," FBN Papers.

126 Ibid.

127 Mrs. Jenny Cooper to B. R. Rhees, 23 November 1926, Box 41, Folder "Medical addicts," FBN Papers.

128 G. W. Cunningham, Narcotic Agent in Charge, Nashville Division, to Levi Nutt, Head, Narcotic Division, 6 December 1926, Box 41, Folder "Medical addicts," FBN Papers.

129 John W. Martin, MD, to Commissioner of Narcotics, 10 April 1937, Permit File, FBN Papers.

130 Theodore L. Sharpe, D. O. to Mr. H. L. Aslinger [sic], 15 October 1955, Permit File, FBN Papers.

131 Dr. Leo T. Heguer [probably] to Hon. James Hughes, Washington, DC, 20 May 1933; [unreadable physician name], Sr. to Hon. John N. Sandlin, US House of Representatives, 27 October 1932; both in Permit File, FBN Papers.

132 Chilton Swank of Swank & Swank, Lawyers to Congressman Tom Steed, 16 January 1954, Permit File, FBN Papers.

133 [page with name not included] to Chief Narcotic Officer, Washington, DC, 27 October 1932, Permit File, FBN Papers. See also B. O. McDaniel, MD, to Hon. J. B. Greeson, 7 March 1933, Permit File, FBN Papers.

134 Mrs. M. L. to Commission Anslinger, 17 February 1956, Permit File, FBN Papers. See also J. R. to Mr. J. M. Doram, Washington, DC, 26 December 1933, Permit File, FBN Papers.

135 Senator James Eastland to Honorable H. J. Anslinger, 12 May 1959, Permit File, FBN Papers.

136 Acker, *Creating the American Junkie*, 145, refers to this as a "crisis of availability."

137 E. W. to Mr. Harry J. Ansligner, 19 August 1933, Permit File, FBN Papers.

138 Mrs. M. E. T. to US Treasury Department, Bureau of Narcotics, 11 January 1940, Permit File, FBN Papers.

139 Narcotic Agent John A. Sheehan, "Narcotic Case Report," 9 March 1951, Permit File, FBN Papers. FBN chief Harry Anslinger was infuriated and denounced the letter as "dangerous and detrimental" because it might "fall into the hands of a narcotic peddler who would thereby be furnished with an almost unlimited supply of narcotic drugs." H. J. Anslinger to Administrator, Veterans Administration, 15 March 1951, Permit File, FBN Papers.

140 J. D. C. to H. J. Anslinger, 27 March 1936, Permit File, FBN Papers.

141 Lucien E. Coleman, Lawyer to US Department of Narcotics, 14 October, 1933, Permit File, FBN Papers.

142 A. J. S. [probably; handwriting difficult to read] to Hon. Mr. Anslinger, 10 March [1930 or 1938], Permit File, FBN Papers.

143 L. H. S. [probably; handwriting difficult to read] to Mr. H. J. Anslinger, 10 December 1934, Permit File, FBN Papers.

144 Mrs. B. C. to "Sir," 21 February 1933, Permit File, FBN Papers.

145 J. W. Slate, MD, to Narcotic Commissioner, 16 December 1932, Permit File, FBN Papers.

146 F. B. to "Dear Sir," 14 December 1942; A. G. D. to Hon. Kenneth McKellar, 15 December 1932; see also D. B. to Anslinger, 6 November 1955; all in Permit File, FBN Papers.

147 W. L. J. to Mr. Anslinger, 12 April 1949 and 29 March 1951; both in Permit File, FBN Papers.

148 J. J. M. to Mr. H. J. Anslinger, 16 April 1936, Permit File, FBN Papers.

149 J. M. Gose, MD, to "To Whom It May Concern," 11 March 1936, Permit File, FBN Papers.

150 W. S. P. to Hon. J. E. Rankin, 13 June 1944, Permit File, FBN Papers.

151 J. H. B. to Mr. H. J. Anslinger, 18 March 1936, Permit File, FBN Papers.

152 Mrs. J. B. A. to "the head of the Dept of Justice," 15 April 1934 [possibly 1954], Permit File, FBN Papers. She recommended "providing for the older ones and letting them die off."

153 L. J. Ulmer, District Supervisor to Harold V. Smith, Chief, Bureau of Narcotic Drug Control, 17 July 1933, Permit File, FBN Papers.

154 J. L. to "The Head of Internal Revenue Dept," 1933, Permit File, FBN Papers.

155 Nancy Campbell, *Discovering Addiction: The Science and Politics of Substance Abuse Research* (Ann Arbor: University of Michigan Press, 2007); Musto, *American Disease.*

156 Musto, *American Disease.*

Chapter Three

1 Dominique A. Tobbell, *Pills, Power, and Policy: The Struggle for Drug Reform in Cold War America and Its Consequences* (Berkeley: University of California Press, 2011); Carpenter, *Reputation and Power*; Scott Podolsky, *The Antibiotic Era: Reform, Resistance, and the Pursuit of a Rational Therapeutics* (Baltimore: Johns Hopkins University Press, 2015); Elizabeth Seigel Watkins, *The Estrogen Elixir: A History of Hormone Replacement Therapy in America* (Baltimore: Johns Hopkins University Press, 2007) and *On the Pill: A Social History of Oral Contraceptives, 1950-1970* (Baltimore: Johns Hopkins University Press, 2001); Rasmussen, *On Speed*; Herzberg, *Happy Pills in America*; Tone, *Age of Anxiety*; Jeremy Greene, *Prescribing by Numbers: Drugs and the Definition of Disease* (Baltimore: Johns Hopkins University Press, 2007).

2 Stephen Snelders, Charles Kaplan, and Toine Pieters, "On Cannabis, Chloral Hydrate, and Career Cycles of Psychotropic Drugs in Medicine," *Bulletin of the History of Medicine* 80, no. 1 (2006): 95-114.

3 "Heroin Hydrochloride," *JAMA* 47 (1906): 1303.

4 Morris Manges, "The Treatment of Coughs with Heroin," *New York Medical Journal* 68 (1898): 768-70; F. C. Floeckinger, "Clinical Observations on Heroin and Heroin Hydrochloride," *New Orleans Medical and Surgical Journal* 52 (1900): 636-46; Max Einhorn, "A Few Remarks on the Therapeutic Efficacy of Heroin," *Philadelphia Medical Journal*, October 29, 1899, 829; James Daly, "A Clinical Study of Heroin," *Boston Medical and Surgical Journal*, February 22, 1900, 190-92; Samuel Horton Brown and Erle Duncan Tompkins, "Heroin as an Analgesic," *Therapeutic Gazette*, 1900, 75; A. Nusch, " A Study of Heroin in over Two Hundred Cases," *New Albany Medical Herald*, 1901, 939.

5 Marks, *Progress of Experiment*, 74-75.

6   Jeremy Greene and David Herzberg, "Hidden in Plain Sight: Marketing Prescription Drugs to Consumers in the Twentieth Century," *American Journal of Public Health* 100, no. 5 (2010): 793-803.

7   Nancy Tomes, *Remaking the American Patient: How Madison Avenue and Modern Medicine Turned Patients into Consumers* (Chapel Hill: University of North Carolina Press, 2016).

8   Marks, *Progress of Experiment*.

9   Advertisement, *Interior Journal*, May 8, 1906, 1. I am grateful to Joseph P. Gabriel for information about the legal and commercial status of Heroin during this period.

10   Schneider, *Smack*.

11   Courtwright, *Dark Paradise*.

12   An Act Prohibiting the Importation of Crude Opium for the Purpose of Manufacturing Heroin, Pub. L. No. 274, chs. 351-53, 43 Stat. 657 (1924).

13   Will S. Wood to Bilhuber-Knoll Corporation, 8 November 1932; Bilbhuber-Knoll Corporation to Mr. Will S. Wood, 11 November 1932; "Copy of Pamphlet: Dihydromorphinone Hydrochloride (Dilaudid, Bilhuber-Knoll): A Powerful Analgesic with Some Advantages over Morphine; Reprinted from the *Proceedings of the Staff Meetings of the Mayo Clinic* 7: 480-83 (Aug. 17) 1932"; all in "Dilaudid," FBN Papers.

14   "Copy of Pamphlet: Dihydromorphinone Hydrochloride"; "Dilaudid," FBN Papers.

15   For Scripps Service articles, see "Dilaudid," *JAMA* 100, no. 13 (1933): 1031-35, reprinted in National Research Council, *Report of Committee on Drug Addiction, 1929-1941 and Collected Reprints 1930-1941* (Washington, DC: NRC, 1941), 1124-37.

16   "Dilaudid, a Morphine Derivative," Bilhuber-Knoll, June 1932. For the 5,000 figure, see H. J. Anslinger to Dr. Howard A. Kelly, July 20, 1933, "Dilaudid," FBN Papers.

17   "Five Times Stronger Than Morphine: Dilaudid," Bilhuber-Knoll, June [nd but probably 1933]; "Dilaudid," FBN Papers.

18   Nicolas Rasmussen, "The Drug Industry and Clinical Research in Interwar America: Three Types of Physician Collaborator," *Bulletin of the History of Medicine* 79, no. 1 (2005): 50-80; Greene and Herzberg, "Hidden in Plain Sight."

19   Gautham Rao, *National Duties: Custom Houses and the Making of the American State* (Chicago: University of Chicago Press, 2016); Reiss, *We Sell Drugs*.

20   Narcotic Drugs Import and Export Act, Pub. L. No. 227, ch. 202, 42 Stat. 596 (1922).

21   Department Publishes Act Approved May 26, 1922, with Emergency Regulations Approved by the Federal Narcotics Control Board and Instructions to Customs Officers in Accordance Therewith (T.D. 39154), 41 Treas. Dec. Int. Rev. 391-92 (1922).

22   Regulations of the Federal Narcotics Control Board for the Information and Guidance of Customs Officers and Others Concerned (T.D. 39308), 42 Treas. Dec. Int. Rev. 183-85 (1922).

23   *Hearings on H.R. 10561, A Bill to Create in the Treasury Department a Bureau of Narcotics, Before the H. Comm. on Ways and Means*, 71st Cong. (1930).

24   "Subpart A—Imports, Part 202—Regulations under the Narcotic Drugs Import and Export Act," *Code of Federal Regulations* (1938): 1065-66.

25   Acker, *Creating the American Junkie*; Campbell, *Discovering Addiction*.

26   Will S. Wood to Bilhuber-Knoll Corporation, 8 November 1932; H. J. Anslinger to Dr. William Charles White, 29 November 1932; Wm. Charles White to Mr. H. J. Anslinger, 8 December 1932; all in "Dilaudid," FBN Papers.

27   Nathan B. Eddy, "Dilaudid," FBN Papers; also published in *JAMA* 100, no. 13 (1933): 1031-35.

28   Howard A. Kelly to Mr. H. J. Anslinger, 14 July 1933, "Dilaudid," FBN Papers.

29   H. J. Anslinger to Dr. Howard A. Kelly, 20 July 1933, "Dilaudid," FBN Papers.

30   Dr. E. A. Bilhuber to Dr. [*sic*] Anslinger, 8 August 1933; H. J. Anslinger to Hon. Hugh S. Cumming Attn: Dr. Treadway, 11 August 1933, "Dilaudid"; H. S. Cummings, Surgeon General, to H. J. Anslinger, August 17, 1933, "Dilaudid," FBN Papers.

31   E. A. Bilhuber to H. J. Anslinger, 11 September 1933, "Dilaudid," FBN Papers.

32   Dr. Treadway to H. J. Anslinger, 3 October 1933; H. J. Anslinger to Bilhuber-Knoll Corporation, 11 October 1933; both in "Dilaudid," FBN Papers.

33   E. A. Bilhuber to H. J. Anslinger, 4 October 1933, "Dilaudid," FBN Papers.

34   H. J. Anslinger to Bilhuber-Knoll, 11 October 1933, "Dilaudid," FBN Papers.

35   Bilhuber-Knoll Corporation to Dr. [*sic*] H. J. Anslinger, 14 October 1933, "Dilaudid," FBN Papers.

36   "Dilaudid: In Place of Morphine," Bilhuber-Knoll Corporation, 5 December 1933; Louis Ruppel, Acting Commissioner, to Bilhuber-Knoll Corporation, 17 May 1934; H. J. Anslinger to Leonard A. Seltzer Company, 5 July 1934; Leonard J. Seltzer to Bureau of Narcotics, 14 July 1934; all in "Dilaudid," FBN Papers.

37   W. E. Turner, Narcotic Agent, to B. M. Martin, Acting District Supervisor, "In re: Purchases of Dilaudid," 21 April 1934; B. M. Martin to Commissioner of Narcotics, 26 April 1934; Louis Ruppel, Acting Commissioner to Mr. B. M. Martin, Acting District Supervisor, Baltimore, "In re: Purchases of Dilaudide," 21 July 1934. For surveillance order, see Division Memorandum No. 122(a), 29 March 1935, "Dilaudid," FBN Papers.

38   The Hoffman-La Roche Chemical Works to "Dear Doctor," November 1928; "From the Juice of the Poppy," Roche, n.d. [probably 1927 or 1928], both in Box 134, File 0480-64, "Drugs: Pantopon, 1927-1959," FBN Papers (hereafter cited as "Pantopon," FBN Papers).

39   Mallinckrodt Chemical Works to Colonel L. G. Nutt, 19 November 1928, "Pantopon," FBN Papers.

40   L. G. Nutt to Mr. Maxwell M. Hamilton, Division of Far Eastern Affairs, Department of State, 19 January 1929, "Pantopon," FBN Papers.

41   "Reports of the Council on Pharmacy and Chemistry: Pantopon-Roche Omitted from N.N.R.," *JAMA* 97, no. 14 (1931): 1001, "Pantopon," FBN Papers.

42   [unreadable name of Merck representative] to Mr. H. J. Anslinger, 5 November 1931; Elmer H. Bobst, Executive Director Hoffmann-La Roche, Inc., to "Dear Doctor," September 1931; see also similar letter from September 1930 and November 1931; all in "Pantopon," FBN Papers.

43   Evaluation: W. L. Treadway to Hon. H. J. Anslinger, November 23, 1931; "Pantopon," FBN Papers. Collecting cases: Will S. Wood to District Supervi-

sor, District No. 4, 5 March 1932; T. E. Middlebrooks, District Supervisor, to Commissioner of Narcotics, 7 January 1935; and W. E. Turner, Narcotic Agent to Mr. B. M. Martin, District Supervisor, 24 June 1935; all in "Pantopon," FBN Papers.

44 Technically, "exempt" preparations could include only one of several opiate alkaloids; Pantopon, containing several of them, did not qualify. Hoffmann-La Roche, Inc. to Treasury Department, January 15, 1932; S. Lowman, Assistant Secretary of the Treasury, to Hon. Robert J. Mawhinney, Solicitor of the Treasury, 22 March 1932; Woodward to H. J. Anslinger, 25 January 1933; all in "Pantopon," FBN Papers.

45 See "Opium, Torn to Shreds," Pantopon circular, and "Directions for Filling Out Federal Narcotic Blank," 15 February 1938, "Pantopon," FBN Papers.

46 H. J. Anslinger to Hoffmann-La Roche, Inc., 7 April 1938, "Pantopon," FBN Papers.

47 Roche's defense, E. H. Bobst to Mr. H. J. Anslinger, 12 April 1938, "Pantopon," FBN Papers; Anslinger's threat, H. J. Anslinger to Hoffmann-La Roche, Inc., Attention: Mr. E. H. Robst, President, 23 April 1938, "Pantopon," FBN Papers.

48 E. H. Bobst to Mr. H. J. Ansligner, 4 May 1938, "Pantopon," FBN Papers.

49 *Registrants Mimeograph 92*, 27 January 1949, Folder "Bureau of Narcotics, General, 1961–1965," NAS-NRC Papers.

50 *Registrants Mimeograph 108*, 8 February 1952, cited in *Registrants Mimeograph 136*, 12 July 1960, in Folder "Bureau of Narcotics, General, 1961–1965," NAS-NRC Papers.

51 H. J. Anslinger to Hoffman-LaRoche, Inc., 18 January 1951, "Pantopon," FBN Papers.

52 H. J. Anslinger to Mr. N. F. Peterson, Executive VP Hoffmann-LaRoche, Inc., 26 January 1951, "Pantopon," FBN Papers.

53 N. F. Peterson to Honorable H. J. Anslinger, 7 February 1951, "Pantopon," FBN Papers.

54 Actually, it was initially two pharmaceutical companies, Winthrop and Alba Pharmaceuticals, but Sterling purchased Alba and folded it into Winthrop.

55 "T. G. Klumpp, 91; Was Drug Company and F.D.A. Official," *New York Times*, October 12, 1997, http://www.nytimes.com/1997/10/12/us/t-g-klumpp-94 -was-drug-company-and-fda-official.html.

56 Theodore Klumpp to Mr. H. J. Anslinger, 24 February 1944, Folder "Isonipecaine: Jan-March 1944," File 480–91, "Drugs: Demerol (Dolantin)" (hereafter cited as "Demerol," FBN Papers).

57 "Memorandum: Re: Substitute for Morphine," Harry J. Anslinger, 23 October 1940, "Demerol," FBN Papers; C. K. Himmelsbach, "Studies of the Addiction Liability of 'Demerol' (D-140)," *Journal of Pharmacology and Experimental Therapeutics* 75 (May 1942): 64–68. For Himmelsbach's conclusion and contact with NRC, see Memorandum of Conversation between Dr. William Charles White, National Health Institute, and Mr. H. J. Anslinger, 15 April 1942, "Demerol," FBN Papers. It is important to note that these tests involved re-addicting institutionalized patient "volunteers" who were compensated with the drug of their choice. Later, critics would point to Lexington as a classic example of unethical research. Campbell at least partly disagrees with

such criticism; the best source on the research and on the ethical controversies is her *Discovering Addiction*.

58   C. K. Himmelsbach to the Surgeon General, 9 February 1942, Folder "MED: Com on Drug Addiction, Advisory: Requests for Advice & Drugs, Demerol, 1942–1944," NAS-NRC Papers.

59   "Memorandum of conversation, Demerol, Dr. Hiebert and a colleague of the Alba Pharmaceutical Company and H. J. Anslinger," 11 May 1942, "Demerol," FBN Papers.

60   Robert C. Batterman, "Clinical Effectiveness and Safety of a New Synthetic Analgesic Drug, Demerol," *Archives of Internal Medicine* 71, no. 3 (1943): 355–56; Robert C. Batterman and C. K. Himmelsbach, "Demerol—A New Synthetic Analgesic," *JAMA* 122, no. 4 (1943): 222–26.

61   Lawrence Kolb to H. J. Anslinger, 15 October 1942, "Demerol," FBN Papers. See also "Memorandum RE: Demerol," 15 October 1942, Folder "MED: Com on Drug Addiction, Advisory: Requests for Advice & Drugs, Demerol, 1942–1944," NAS-NRC Papers.

62   J. Mark Hiebert, MD, to H. J. Anslinger, 28 May 1942, "Demerol," FBN Papers; "Memorandum of conversation, Demerol, Dr. Hiebert and a colleague of the Alba Pharmaceutical Company and H. J. Anslinger," 11 May 1942, "Demerol," FBN Papers.

63   Rasmussen, "Drug Industry and Clinical Research."

64   James J. Biggins to H. J. Anslinger, 12 December 1944, "Demerol," FBN Papers.

65   Robert Hoffman, MD, "Demerol, a New Departure in Anesthesia: An Evaluation of Present Day Therapeutic Claims," *Anesthesia and Analgesia*, November-December 1943, 336–40; "Demerol," FBN Papers.

66   Robert Hoffman, MD, "A Report of Experience with Demerol—A New Departure in Analgesia," *Journal of the Indiana State Medical Association* 36, no. 2 (1943): 135–36; "Demerol," FBN Papers.

67   Robert Hoffman to Will Wood, Narcotic Commissioner, August 7, 1944, "Demerol," FBN Papers.

68   Robert Hoffman to The Honorable Leon Sharken, House of Representatives, Frankfort, Kentucky, 25 March 1944, "Demerol," FBN Papers.

69   James J. Biggins to H. J. Anslinger, 12 December 1944; Robert Hoffman to Commissioner Harry J. Anslinger, 23 October 1946; Robert Hoffman to Commissioner Harry J. Anslinger, 6 November 1946; all in "Demerol," FBN Papers.

70   Greene and Herzberg, "Hidden in Plain Sight."

71   Gobind Behari Lai, "Stop Look Listen When the Prescription Says 'DOPE'," *American Weekly*, January 16, 1944, 18; "Demerol," FBN Papers.

72   Robert D. Potter, "No Longer Any Excuse for Becoming a Dope Slave," *American Weekly*, April 1944; "Demerol," FBN Papers.

73   Science Service, "Morphine Substitute Now Generally Available," *Washington News*, September 3, 1943; "Drug Without Addicts," *Newsweek*, September 13, 1943; "Painkiller," *Time*, April 13, 1942; "Science Again! Non-Habit-Forming Morphine Substitute," *Minneapolis Star Journal*, April 1, 1942; "Non-Habit Forming Substitute for Morphine Proved in Tests," *New York Herald Tribune*, April 1, 1942; "Demerol," FBN Papers.

74   H. J. Anslinger to Dr. Morris Fishbein, Editor, 12 May 1942, "Demerol," FBN Papers.

75   C. K. Himmelsbach, "Further Studies of the Addiction Liability of Demerol," *Journal of Pharmacology and Experimental Therapeutics* 79, no. 1 (1943): 5–9. See also "Excerpt from pamphlet entitled 'Further Studies of the Addiction Liability of Demerol,' By C. K. Himmelsbach," "Demerol," FBN Papers.

76   For examples of Anslinger peddling the article, see H. J. Anslinger to Mr. Bertil A. Renborg, Secretary, Drug Supervisory Body [League of Nations], 21 May 1942; Paul Dunbar, Assistant Commissioner FDA to Hon. H. J. Anslinger, 9 June 1942; all in "Demerol," FBN Papers.

77   L. B. McSorley, Chief Chemist, to Dr. H. J. Wollner, 24 August 1942; Mr. Anslinger to Mr. Tennyson, Re: Demerol (Dolantin), 2 October 1942; Joseph Levine, Chemist, Memorandum to Mr. H. J. Wollner Re: Dolantin, 9 October 1942; Mr. Tennyson to Mr. Anslinger, 10 October 1942; all in "Demerol," FBN Papers.

78   Mr. Tennyson to Mr. Anslinger, Subject: Demerol, 28 September 1942, "Demerol," FBN Papers.

79   See Basil[?] Renborg, Drug Supervisory Body, to Harry J. Anslinger, 9 July 1942; [Basil] Renborg to Harry J. Anslinger, 9 December 1942; Order No. 148 "Relating to the inclusion of dolantin [Demerol] in tables 'A' and 'B' of the general instructions concerning the use of and trade in narcotic drugs," 28 April 1944; all in "Demerol," FBN Papers.

80   H. J. Anslinger to Mr. Lynch, Assistant General Counsel, 11 October 1943, "Demerol," FBN Papers.

81   "Demerol," n.d. (probably 1943 or 1944), "Demerol," folder "April 1944–," FBN Papers.

82   Memorandum of Conversation, Subject DEMEROL, between Dr. J. Mark Hiebert, Theodore Klumpp, and H. J. Anslinger, 11 February 1944, "Demerol," FBN Papers.

83   Memorandum for Mr. Anslinger Re: Demerol, 21 March 1944, "Demerol," FBN Papers.

84   See "'Demerol' Bill Sent to White House," *Brokmeyer Bulletin*, 29 June 1944, 1, "Demerol," FBN Papers.

85   See, e.g., "Memorandum for the Commissioner," 3 December 1934; "Tentative Itinerary" for Mrs. Bass [n.d.]; Anslinger to Mrs. Elizabeth Bass, District Supervisor, 7 December 1943; "Current Legislative Sessions," 24 January 1944 [plus weekly updates through at least February 1944]; all in "Demerol," FBN Papers. For strategic advice, see T. E. Middlebrooks, District Supervisor to Mr. H. Gerard Scholtens, Narcotic Inspector, 29 January 1944; "Demerol," FBN Papers.

86   "Demerol (Isonipecaine)," undated memo but in March-December 1946 folder, "Demerol," FBN Papers.

87   *Registrants Mimeographs 64*, 3 July 1944, and *65*, 14 July 1944; Bureau of Narcotics General Circular No. 144, 14 July 1944; J. W. Holloway Jr., AMA, to Mr. H. J. Anslinger, 26 July 1944, promised that "the Current Comment followed very closely the phraseology of your letter of July 14 and was prepared and is published in the Journal at your request"; all in "Demerol," FBN Papers.

88 R. W. Artis, District Supervisor, to Mr. H. J. Anslinger, 19 July 1944, "Demerol," FBN Papers.

89 H. J. Anslinger to Mr. Robert W. Artis, District Supervisor, 5 July 1944; dozens of reports of Demerol addiction can be found in "Demerol," FBN Papers.

90 H. J. Anslinger to Winthrop Chemical Co., Inc., 16 April 1945; H. J. Anslinger to Winthrop Chemical Company Inc., 2 October 1945; for "boost your sales" ad, see Demerol ad, *Drug Topics*, 16 April 1945, 32; "Conference in Mr. Anslinger's office relative to demerol advertising," 7 October 1946; Theodore G. Klumpp, President, Winthrop Chemical, to Mr. H. J. Anslinger, 11 May 1945; all in "Demerol," FBN Papers.

91 Anslinger to Federal Trade Commission, 18 June 1946, "Demerol," FBN Papers.

92 Winthrop Chemical Company, "Demerol Hydrochloride" [pamphlet], n.d. (probably late 1944/early 1945); "Demerol," FBN Papers.

93 Demerol ad, *Modern Medicine* 13(9), September 1934; "Demerol," FBN Papers.

94 See, e.g., Anslinger to Dr. R. H. Felix, 14 May 1946; C. K. Himmelsbach to R. H. Felix, 24 May 1946; Dale C. Cameron (Mental Hygiene Division) to Mr. H. J. Anslinger, 5 June 5 1946; all in "Demerol," FBN Papers.

95 H. J. Anslinger to Winthrop Products, Inc., 30 August 1946, "Demerol," FBN Papers.

96 Greene and Herzberg, "Hidden in Plain Sight" Herzberg, *Happy Pills*.

97 "Thousands achieve 'comfortable delivery' with new drug for childbirth," Winthrop Chemical Company, Inc. and Frederick Stearns & Co. Divisions Sterling Drug Inc., 19 June 1946, "Demcrol: Paul de Kruif," FBN Papers.

98 J. Willicombe to Hon. H. J. Anslinger, 5 November 1943, "Demerol: 1940–1943," FBN Papers; Memo, Mr. Anslinger to Mrs. Bessie M. Cummings, 18 January 1944, "Demerol: Jan-March 1944," FBN Papers.

99 "Nazi's Ersatz Morphine Sold American Addicts," *Chicago Sun*, May 14, 1944; "Demerol: April 1944–," FBN Papers.

100 "Synthetic Drug Reaching Addicts," *Omaha World-Herald*, May 15, 1944; "Morphine-Like Dopes Freely Sold in U.S.," *Washington* (DC) *Times-Herald*, May 21, 1944; "Addicts Buy Ersatz Drug," *Detroit News*, May 15, 1944; "Demerol: April 1944–," FBN Papers.

101 Paul de Kruif, "God's Own Medicine—1946," *Reader's Digest*, June 1946, 15–18; "Demerol: Paul de Kruif," FBN Papers.

102 H. J. Anslinger to Mrs. Joseph Lindon Smith [cc: Mrs. Harvey W. Wiley], n.d. (1946?); "Demerol: Paul de Kruif," FBN Papers.

103 *JAMA*: H. J. Anslinger to Dr. Morris Fishbein, 3 June 1946; Morris Fishbein to Dr. [sic] H. J. Anslinger, 18 June 1946; R. H. Felix to Mr. H. J. Anslinger, 8 July 1946; and H. J. Anslinger, "Addiction to Demerol and the Reader's Digest," *JAMA* 131, no. 11 (1946): 937; all in "Demerol: Paul de Kruif," FBN Papers. Others: James J. Biggins to Mr. H. J. Anslinger, 10 June 1946; "Strong Warning against Demerol Issued by Federal Narcotics Commissioner," Science Service, 11 July 1946; Watson Davis, Director, to Mr. H. J. Anslinger, 9 July 1946; see also "God's Own Narcotic," *Time*, July 29, 1946; "Strong Warning Issued against Use of Demerol," *Science News Letter*, July 20, 1046; "Cites Danger of Addiction," *Boston Post*, July 21, 1946; "Demerol, New Pain Killer, Termed Habit Forming," *Buffalo News*, July 10, 1946; Peter Stone, "'Digest' Dopes

the Public Literally," *Daily Worker*, August 12, 1946; all in "Demerol: Paul de Kruif," FBN Papers.

104 Morris Fishbein to Dr. [*sic*] H. J. Anslinger, 29 July 1946; they included a copy of de Kruif's letter to the editor; "Demerol: Paul de Kruif," FBN Papers. Paul de Kruif, C. K. Himmelsbach, and H. J. Anslinger, "Demerol," *JAMA* 132, no. 1 (1946): 43-44. *JAMA* editors wrote a brief "Current Comment" supporting Anslinger's criticisms in the same issue.

105 Max Samter, "Experiences with Demerol in Europe," *JAMA*; A. B. Crisler, District Supervisor, to Mr. H. J. Anslinger, 14 October 1946; unsigned letter to Dr. Chauncey Leake, Dean UT School of Medicine, requesting that Leake "develop" the article under his own more influential name, 23 October 1946; all in "Demerol: Paul de Kruif," FBN Papers. For examples of successfully placed articles, see Leake, "Demerol and Drug Addiction," n.d., *Journal of the Texas Medical Association*; Ralph A. Johnson, MD, "The Exploitation of Medical Literature," *Detroit Medical News*, n.d., 8; "The Demon Demoral in Sheeps Clothing ala Paul de Kruif," *Journal of the Oklahoma State Medical Association*, November 1946, 461; "Demerol IS Habit-Forming," *Texas Hospitals*, n.d., 14; "Experience with Demerol in Europe," *Arkansas Druggist*, December 1946. All in "Demerol: Paul de Kruif," FBN Papers.

106 Roland H. Berg to Commissioner H. J. Anslinger, 14 August 1946; Garland E. Williams, District Supervisor, to Mr. H. J. Anslinger, 22 August 1946; both in "Demerol: Paul de Kruif," FBN Papers.

107 Dewitt Wallace to Hon. H. J. Anslinger, Commissioner, 14 August 1946; "Questions submitted to H. J. Anslinger, accompanying letter of Sept. 5, 1946"; Albert Q. Maisel, "Fighter for the Right to Live," *Reader's Digest*, December 1946, 91+, and January 1947, 43-49; Anslinger to Mr. DeWitt Wallace, 27 December 1946; M. L. Harney, "Memorandum for the files," 18 May 1948, all in "Demerol: Paul de Kruif," FBN Papers.

108 Memorandum for the files, 7 October 1946 (between Anslinger, Klumpp, and other Winthrop representatives), "Demerol: Paul de Kruif," FBN Papers.

109 "Federal Control of Demerol," 3 May 1947, "Demerol: 1947," FBN Papers.

110 H. J. Anslinger to Mr. Charles Wesley Dunn, 22 May 1947, "Demerol: 1947," FBN Papers.

111 Ray Richards, "U.S. Battles Killing Grip of New Narcotic," *Herald-American*, May 12, 1947; "Demerol: 1947," FBN Papers. FBN Papers includes dozens of clippings of this and similar articles, see "Demerol: 1947," FBN Papers.

112 Mr. Anslinger to Mr. Springern, 10 February 1947, "Demerol: 1947," FBN Papers. Anslinger also asked whether the FTC might assert its authority over advertising to physicians, which the FDA did not yet police.

113 Acker, *Creating the American Junkie*, 90-91.

114 Marks, *Progress of Experiment*; Podolsky, *Antibiotics*; Tobbell, *Pills*; Alan Brinkley, *The End of Reform: New Deal Liberalism in Recession and War* (New York: Vintage, 1996).

115 H. J. Anslinger to Dr. Lewis E. Weed, Chairman, Div. of Med. Sciences, NRC, 27 November 1941; Albert L. Barrows, Exec. Sec'y, "Office Memorandum No. 1138," 14 November 1941; both in Folder "MED: Com on Drug Addiction, Advisory: Beginnings of Program, 1941," NAS-NRC.

116 For Anslinger's support, see Wm Charles White to Dr. Lewis Weed, 20 June

1945, Folder "MED: Com on Drug Addiction, Advisory: Appointments, Members, 1941-1945," NAS-NRC; Dr. William C. White to Dr. Weed, 19 April 1946, Folder "MED: Com on Drug Addiction, Advisory: General, 1941-1946," NAS-NRC. For reconstitution of Committee see Nathan B. Eddy, *Role of the National Research Council in the Opiate Problem* (Washington, DC: National Academy of Sciences, 1973), 48-53.

117 National Research Council, Committee on Drug Addiction and Narcotics [hereafter CDAN], "Minutes of Meeting—2 October 1947," Folder "Meetings: 1st: Minutes, 1947 October," NAS-NRC.

118 CDAN, "Minutes of Meeting—2 October 1947," Folder "Meetings: 2nd: Minutes, 1948 Jan," NAS-NRC. For an example of a drug rejected for testing because it had not been proven superior, see Everette L. May [CDAN committee member] to Dr. Nathan Eddy, 3 October 1963, Folder "MED: Committee on Drug Addiction & Narcotics: Membership: May E L, 1961-1966," NAS-NRC.

119 The goal was practical: to "eliminate some drugs and thus reduce the burden on Lexington." See "Memorandum," 31 January 1957, Folder "MED: CDAN, 1955-1959," NAS-NRC. Also CDAN, "Eighteenth Meeting—21-23 January, 1957; APPENDIX P: Screening for Addiction Liability," Folder "meetings: 18th: Minutes, 1957 Jan," NAS-NRC. They had begun to explore this possibility as early as 1948, but at that point Seevers's lab did not yet have the capacity—nor the necessary protocols—to serve in this function (1948, 3rd meeting).

120 Isaac Starr, MD, to Nathan B. Eddy, MD, Secretary, 18 November 1958, Folder "Med: CDAN, 1955-1959," NAS-NRC.

121 R. Keith Cannan to Mr. George P. Larrick, 12 February 1959, Folder "MED: Committee on Drug Addiction & Narcotics: General, 1950-1960," NAS-NRC.

122 "Minutes of Twentieth Meeting—10 and 11 January, 1959 [Executive session]," Folder "Com on Drug Addiction and Narcotics; Meetings: 20th: Minutes; 1959 Jan," NAS-NRC; Dr. R. Keith Cannan and Herbert N. Gardner, "Role of the Committee on Drug Addiction and Narcotics," 23 December 1958, Folder "Med: Committee on Drug Addiction & Narcotics, 1955-1959," NAS-NRC; R. Keith Cannan, "Review of Drug Addiction Committee with Lawyer and Dr. Eddy," 5 January 1959; Folder "MED: Committee on Drug Addiction & Narcotics: General, 1950-1960," NAS-NRC.

123 Acker, *Creating the American Junkie*.

124 Methyldihidromorphinone; see Acker, *Creating the American Junkie*, 90-91.

125 Albert L. Barrows, Exec. Sec'y, "Office Memorandum No. 1138," 14 November 1941, Folder "MED: Com on Drug Addiction, Advisory: Beginnings of Program, 1941," NAS-NRC.

126 The manufacturers were Merck, Mallinckrodt, and New York Quinine. "Memorandum of conference in the office of the Commissioner of Narcotics to discuss production of metapon [*sic*], 10:00 A.M., May 3, 1946, Folder "MED: Com on Drug Addiction, Advisory: Projects; Production & Distribution of Metapon[sic], 1940-1946," NAS-NRC. For the statement see "METOPON," n.d. [probably May 1946], Folder "MED: Com on Drug Addiction, Advisory: Projects; Production & Distribution of Metapon [*sic*], 1940-1946," NAS-NRC. It is not clear that they ever actually issued the statement; see "Memorandum of meeting held in the office of the Commissioner

of Narcotics, January 15, 1951 at 10:30 A.M. on the question of a revised procedure for the distribution of Metopon," Folder "Bureau of Narcotics: General, 1961–1965," NAS-NRC.

127 No title, no date, although a handwritten note attached to one copy of it says "Mss. by Sam Isbell, Room 655, Earle Bldg, Washington D.C., 1940?" Based on facts presented in the manuscript, however, it is more likely to have been written closer to 1945; Folder: "MED: Com on Drug Addiction, Advisory: Projects; Production & Distribution of Metapon [*sic*], 1940–1946," NAS-NRC.

128 "Conference on Metopon, June 6, 1946, 1:30 P.M.," Folder "MED: Com on Drug Addiction, Advisory: Projects; Production & Distribution of Metapon [*sic*], 1940–1946," NAS-NRC.

129 National Research Council, "Observations on the Metopon Study, October 1947," Folder "MED: Com on Drug Addiction & Narcotics, 1947–1949," NAS-NRC; CDAN, "Minutes of Meeting—2 October 1947" and "Minutes of Second Meeting—17 January 1948," both in Folder "Com on Drug Addiction & Narcotics, Meetings: 1st: Minutes, 1947 Oct," NAS-NRC.

130 Eddy, Metopon Hydrochloride: An Experiment in Clinical Evaluation," *Public Health Reports* 64 (1949): 93; and Eddy, *JAMA* 137, no. 4 (1948): 365–67.

131 Nathan B. Eddy, Secretary to Honorable Oscar Ewing, Administrator, Federal Security Agency, 6 February 1951, Folder "MED: Com on Drug Addiction & Narcotics, 1950–1953," NAS-NRC; CDAN, "Minutes of Seventh Meeting—15 January 1951," Folder "Com on Drug Addiction & Narcotics, Meetings: 7th: Minutes, 1951 Jan," NAS-NRC.

132 These national figures were believed to be primarily in California; see *Traffic in Opium and Other Dangerous Drugs*, 1962, 81–82.

133 "Review of Cooperation on Drug Policies among the Food and Drug Administration, National Institutes of Health, Veterans' Administration, and Other Agencies," in *Interagency Coordination in Drug Research and Regulation, Part 4: Hearings Before the Subcomm. on Reorganization and International Organizations of the S. Comm. on Government Operations*, 88th Cong. 1479–81 (1963).

134 Edward Bloomquist, "The Addiction Potential of Oxycodone (Percodan)," *California Medicine* 99, no. 2 (1963): 127.

135 "Housewives," in *Illegal Narcotics Traffic and Its Effect on Juvenile and Young Adult Criminality, Part 11: Hearings Before the Subcomm. to Investigate Juvenile Delinquency of S. Comm. on the Judiciary*, 87th Cong. 2698 (1962); "entirely new class," *Interagency Coordination*, 1484.

136 CDAN, "Minutes of Fifth Meeting—5 November 1949."

137 CDAN, "Minutes of Seventh Meeting"; see also "Appendix G: Research Fund," Folder "Com on Drug Addiction & Narcotics, Meetings: 12th: Minutes, 1953 Nov," NAS-NRC.

138 CDAN, "Minutes of Fifth Meeting."

139 Isaac Starr, MD, Chairman, to R. Keith Cannan, Chairman, 3 September 1957, Folder "MED: Committee on Drug Addiction & Narcotics: General, 1950–1960," NAS-NRC.

140 Dr. Cannan, Dr. Cole, "Meeting of the Committee on Drug Addiction and Narcotics," 8 October 1954; CDAN, Minutes of 14th Meeting, both Folder

"MED: Committee on Drug Addiction & Narcotics: Meetings: General, 1954–1965," NAS-NRC; CDAN, Minutes of 21st Meeting (SKF). For SKF request for special focus on phenazocine, see Nathan B. Eddy, MD, to Dr. Mancel T. Mitchell [of SKF], 25 November 1959, Folder "MED: Committee on Drug Addiction & Narcotics: General, 1950-1960," NAS-NRC. The thirteenth meeting, also in 1954, took place in three locations, the NYAM but also Merck Institute for Therapeutic Research and Hoffmann-LaRoche Laboratories. See "Minutes of Thirteenth Meeting." Eli Lilly invited the Committee in 1968, see Kenneth G. Kohlstaedt, MD, to Dale C. Cameron, MD, 24 May 1967, Folder "Lilly Research Laboratories, 1960-1969," NAS-NRC.

141 F. J. Bolton [of J. F. MacFarland & Co.] to Dr. N. B. Eddy, 18 September 1963, Folder "J F Macfarlan & Co Ltd, 1961-1963," NAS-NRC; Earl H. Dearborn, PhD, MD, Director, Experimental Therapeutics Research, Lederle Laboratories to Dr. Nathan B. Eddy, Executive Secretary, 11 March 1965, Folder "Lederle Laboratories 1961-1967," NAS-NRC; Nathan B. Eddy, MD, to Dr. Joseph G. Bird, Director of Clinical Pharmacology, Sterling-Winthrop Research Institute, 2 January 1964, Folder "Sterling-Winthrop Research Inst 1961-1964," NAS-NRC.

142 Nathan B. Eddy, MD, to Dr. Joseph G. Bird, 15 February 1966, Folder "Sterling-Winthrop Research Inst 1965-1966," NAS-NRC.

143 See Eddy's defense of the practice in Nathan B. Eddy, MD, to Hon. Hubert H. Humphrey [Senator from Minnesota], 14 June 1963, Folder "MED: Committee on Drug Addiction & Narcotics: General, 1961-1965," NAS-NRC.

144 Louis Lasagna, MD, to Dr. R. Keith Cannan, 2 February 1956, Folder "MED: Committee on Drug Addiction & Narcotics, 1955-1959," NAS-NRC.

145 Nathan B. Eddy to Dr. Keith Cannan [NRC], 10 February 1956, Folder "MED: Committee on Drug Addiction & Narcotics, 1955-1959," NAS-NRC. For some in the industry, this was apparently not enough; they opposed keeping Eddy on as secretary in 1960 out of annoyance at his strong push for Metopon a decade earlier. See Jonathan O. Cole, MD, to Dr. R. Keith Cannan, 14 July 1960, Folder "MED: Committee on Drug Addiction & Narcotics: Membership, 1960-1964," NAS-NRC.

146 R. Keith Cannan, Chairman NRC to Dr. Nathan B. Eddy, 14 February 1956, Folder "MED: Committee on Drug Addiction & Narcotics, 1955-1959," NAS-NRC.

147 Podolsky, *Antibiotic Era*, chap. 1. See also Tobbell, *Pills, Power, and Politics*.

148 CDAN, "Minutes of Fifth Meeting—5 November 1949."

149 CDAN, "Minutes of Fifth Meeting—5 November 1949."

150 Isaac Starr, MD, to Nathan B. Eddy, MD, Secretary, 18 November 1958; Dr. R. Keith Cannan and Herbert N. Gardner, "Role of Committee on Drug Addiction and Narcotics," 23 December 1958; both in Folder "MED: Committee on Drug Addiction & Narcotics, 1955-1959," NAS-NRC.

151 See, e.g., Endo Products Inc. to Honorable H. J. Anslinger, 1 September 1954; T. G. Klumpp to Dr. R. Keith Cannan, Chairman, Division of Medical Sciences, NRC, 26 January 1960; Isaac Star, MD, to R. Keith Cannan, MD, Chairman, 8 February 1960; all in Folder "MED: Committee on Drug Addiction & Narcotics: General, 1950-1960," NAS-NRC.

152   CDAN, "Minutes of Fourteenth Meeting—1 and 2 October 1954"; Dr. Can-
      nan, Dr. Cole, "Meeting of the Committee on Drug Addiction and Narcotics,"
      8 October 1954; CDAN, "Minutes of 14th Meeting"; both in Folder "MED:
      Committee on Drug Addiction & Narcotics: Meetings: General, 1954-1965,"
      NAS-NRC.

153   CDAN, Sixteenth Meeting, 30 September and 1 October 1955, Folder "Com
      on Drug Addiction & Narcotics, Meetings: 16th: Minutes: Sep-Oct, 1955,"
      NAS-NRC; CDAN, Minutes of the Seventeenth Meeting—20 and 31 January
      1956, Folder "Com on Drug Addiction & Narcotics, Meetings: 16th: Min-
      utes, 1956 Jan," NAS-NRC; R. Keith Cannan, Chairman of Division, to Mr.
      George P. Larrick, 12 February 1959, Folder "MED: Committee on Drug Ad-
      diction & Narcotics: General, 1950-1960," NAS-NRC.

154   The other drugs were codeine and hydrocodone; nalorphine and nalline
      could be prescribed orally even without other ingredients; "Subchapter D—
      Miscellaneous Excise Taxes, Part 151—Regulations under the Harrison Nar-
      cotic Law, as Amended," *Code of Federal Regulations* (1955): 228-29.

155   *Interagency Coordination*, 1479-81, 1489.

156   *Interagency Coordination*, 1482-84.

157   *Interagency Coordination*, 1467-81. For FBN data, see *Traffic in Opium and
      Other Dangerous Drugs*, 1962, 59.

158   "California Seeks Inquiry on Pain-Relieving Drug," *New York Times*, June 2,
      1963; Stanley Mosk, Attorney General, to Hon. Hubert H. Humphrey, 9 July
      1963; R. Keith Cannan to Dr. Nathan B. Eddy, 6 June 1963; Nathan B. Eddy,
      MD, to Hon. Hubert H. Humphrey, 14 June 1963; all in Folder "MED: Com-
      mittee on Drug Addiction & Narcotics: General, 1961-1965," NAS-NRC.

159   *Interagency Coordination*, 1465-96; also Department of Treasury, "Deletion
      from Oral Prescription Procedure of Dihydrohydroxycodeinone (Oxycodone,
      Eucodal) Compounds," 29 Fed. Reg. 48 (Jan. 3, 1964), https://cdn.loc.gov
      /service/ll/fedreg/fr029/fr029002/fr029002.pdf.

160   *Traffic in Opium and Other Dangerous Drugs*, 1967, 41.

161   "Look for Big News on Synthetic Narcotics," *F-D-C Reports* 8, no. 42 (1946);
      Will S. Wood to Mr. Garland H. Williams, 25 March 1947; Lyndon F. Small,
      Head Chemist, to Mr. H. J. Anslinger, 10 May 1946; both Box XX, File 0480-
      203A, "Amidone Invest," hereafter "Amidone," FBN.

162   Nathan B. Eddy, Principal Pharmacologist, to Hon. H. J. Anslinger, 9 July
      1946; Lyndon F. Small and Nathan B. Eddy, "Memorandum re Narcotic Drug
      known as 10820 (German name—Amidone)" [n.d.; probably July 1946];
      Nathan B. Eddy, "10820 (Amidone), a preliminary statement," 24 September
      1946; all in "Amidone," FBN.

163   A. H. Fiske, Vice President, Eli Lilly, to Mr. H. J. Anslinger, 16 October 1946;
      H. J. Anslinger, "Memorandum for Mr. Tennyson [FBN legal counsel]," 18
      November 1945; H. J. Anslinger to Mr. Paul B. Dunbar, 19 November 1946;
      "Amidone," FBN.

164   "Synthetic Narcotics," *F-D-C Reports* 8, no. 49 (1946).

165   Narcotic Inspector Lovelace [of Lexington, KY] to Mr. Cunningham, 20 Jan-
      uary 1947; G. W. Cunningham to Mr. H. J. Anslinger, 23 January 1947; A. H.
      Brown, Director of Purchases, Eli Lilly, to Honorable H. J. Anslinger, 24 Janu-

ary 1947; "Amidone," FBN. See also "Tolerance and addiction liability of 4,4
-diphenyl-6-dimethylamino-heptanone-3," n.d. (probably early April 1947),
and "Summary of a meeting of the Committee on Drug Addiction," 15 April
1947; "Amidone," FBN. Also see "Report of Committee on Drug Addiction
to the National Research Council, on Amidone," 22 April 1947, Folder "MED:
Committee on Drug Addiction & Narcotics, 1947-1949," NAS-NRC.

166 A. H. Brown, Director of Purchases, Eli Lilly, to Honorable H. J. Anslinger, 24
January 1947, "Amidone," FBN.

167 H. J. Anslinger, untitled memorandum, 29 January 1947, "Amidone," FBN.

168 H. J. Anslinger to Eli Lilly & Company, 5 February 1947, "Amidone," FBN.

169 "Memorandum for Mr. Anslinger," 8 July 1947, "Amidone," FBN.

170 "Summary of a conference of the Committee on Drug Addiction of the National Research Council, and others, relating to Amidone and Metopon," 22
April 1947, "Amidone," FBN.

171 "Summary of a conference of the Committee on Drug Addiction of the National Research Council, and others, relating to Amidone and Metopon," 22
April 1947; Lewis H. Weed, MD, to the Honorable John W. Snyder, 24 April
1947; "Amidone," FBN.

172 "Morphine Substitute," *Time*, April 28, 1947, 51.

173 Ray Richards, "Synthetic Drugs New Dope Peril," *New York Journal-American*,
May 14, 1947; "Farben Drug Deared as Narcotic," *Binghampton Press*, May 21,
1947; "Control Urged for Amidone, German Drug," *New Haven Register*,
May 21, 1947; "Doctors Divide on Dangers of Germans' Drug," *Chicago Tribune*, May 22, 1947; "Amidone," FBN. Anslinger also apparently quashed a
glowingly positive review of amidone under consideration for publication by
the USPHS through its Office of Health Information(!), which Robert H. Felix
submitted to him for preclearance; see Marion Robinson, Clearance Officer,
Office of Health Information, USPHS, to Commissioner H. J. Anslinger,
"10820, by David W. Maurer, Ph.D. and Victor H. Vogel, M.D.," 2 June 1947,
"Amidone," FBN.

174 "Drug Amidone an Opiate: By the President of the United States of America:
A Proclamation," July 31, 1947, "Amidone," FBN. Anslinger had officially requested this action on 9 June 1947, see H. J. Anslinger, untitled memo, 9 June
1947, "Amidone," FBN.

175 Will S. Wood, "General Circular No. 181," 7 August 1947, "Amidone," FBN.

176 I. H. Small, Manager, Shipping Department, Eli Lilly, to Mr. Will S. Wood,
9 September 1947; Will S. Wood to Eli Lilly & Company, Attention: Mr. I. H.
Small, 15 September 1947, "Amidone," FBN.

177 For this interpretation/argument, and for providing copies of the RG170
methadon records, I am grateful to David Courtwright.

178 Minutes of Twenty-fifth Meeting—15, 16, and 17 February, 1963, Folder "Com
on Drug Addiction & Narcotics, Meetings: 25th: Minutes: Volume I, 1963
Feb," NAS-NRC.

179 Nathan B. Eddy, MD, to Dr. R. Keith Cannan, 26 May 1960, Folder "MED:
Committee on Drug Addiction & Narcotics: Resolution: Applicability of
Civil Commitment to Treatment of Addicts, 1960," NAS-NRC; "The Use of
Narcotic Drugs in Medical Practice and the Medical Management of Nar-

cotic Addicts, A Statement of the AMA's Council on Mental Health and the NAS-NRC," June 1963, Folder "MED: Committee on Drug Addiction & Narcotics: General, 1961–1965," NAS-NRC.

Chapter Four

1   George B. Wood and Franklin Bache, *The Dispensatory of the United States of America*, 11th ed. (Philadelphia: J. B. Lippincott, 1858), 884–93; Wood and Bache, *Dispensatory*, 12th ed. (1870), 1576; Wood and Bache, *Dispensatory*, 14th ed. (1881), 268–71; Wood and Bache, *Dispensatory*, 15th ed. (1883), 406–10; Wood and Bache, *Dispensatory* (1907), 1200–1201; Edmund Charles Wendt, "Sulfonal, A New Hypnotic," *Medical Record* 33, no. 22 (1888): 597–98; Charles E. Sajous, "Trional," *Annual of the Universal Medical Sciences and Analytical Index*, vol. 5 (Philadelphia: F. A. Davis, 1896), A-157–60; "A New and Valuable Hypnotic," *New York Medical Journal and Philadelphia Medical Journal*, September 19, 1903, 562–63; A. A. Stevens, *A Manual of Therapeutics* (Philadelphia: W. B. Saunders, 1894), 206. See also James Inciardi, "The Changing Life of Mickey Finn: Some Notes on Chloral Hydrate Down Through the Ages," *Journal of Popular Culture*, Winter 1977, 591–96.

2   See, e.g., US Department of Commerce and Labor, Bureau of Statistics, *Annual Report from the Director of Statistics on the Commerce and Navigation of the United States for the Year Ending June 30, 1866* (Washington, DC: Government Printing Office, 1866), 167; 1868 *Report*, 277; 1870 *Report*, 623; 1875 *Report*, 638, 721; *American Druggist and Pharmaceutical Record* 52–53 (1908), 66.

3   Frederick Tice, "The Indispensable Uses of Narcotics: In the Practice of Medicine," *JAMA* 96, no. 12 (1931): 944–46.

4   Walter Sneader, *Drug Discovery: A History* (New York: Wiley and Sons, 2005), 365–66; Francisco Lopez-Munoz, Ronaldo Ucha-Udabe, and Cecilio Alamo, "The History of Barbiturates a Century after Their Clinical Introduction," *Neuropsychiatric Disease Treatment* 1, no. 4 (2005): 329–43.

5   The Bayer Company (New York), *Veronal, Veronal Sodium, Hypnotics and Sedatives* (n.d.; probably 1915 or 1916), 9–15, Box 168, Folder 33 "Veronal, 1920s–1930s," Sterling Drug Papers.

6   Winthrop Chemical Company, *Luminal, Luminal-Sodium: Powerful Hypnotics and Sedatives* (1920), Sterling, Luminal, Box 51, Folder 15–16 "Luminal, 1920s–1940s," Sterling Drug Papers.

7   Winthrop Chemical Company, *Luminal: Answers to Questions* (1923) Box 41, Folder 15–16, "Luminal, 1920s–1940s," Sterling Drug Papers.

8   For medical acceptance, see, e.g., A. A. Stevens, *A Manual of Therapeutics* (Philadelphia: W. B. Saunders, 1909); Wood and Bache, *Dispensatory* (1907), 1691; Wood and Bache, *Dispensatory* (1916), 45. For early market size, see Gathercoal, *Prescription Ingredient Survey*; *Foreign Commerce and Navigation of the United States*, vol. 2 (1925), 79; US Tariff Commission, *Diethylbarbituric Acid and Derivatives* (Washington, DC: Government Printing Office, 1925), 3–4; US Tariff Commission, *Tariff Information Series—No. 32, Census of Dyes and other Synthetic Organic Chemicals, 1923* (Washington, DC: Government Printing Office, 1924), 116; *Synthetic Organic Chemicals, 1925*, 145.

9   See, e.g., "Luminal, Its Toxic Effects: With the Report of Two Cases," *JAMA* 61, no. 3 (1913): 192.

10   William Cole, "Acute Barbital (Veronal) Poisoning: Report of Case with Fatal Outcome," *JAMA* 80, no. 6 (1923): 373–74.

11   John Day, Narcotic Inspector to Colonel L. G. Nutt, 18 October, 1926, Box 138, Folder "Barbituric / Barbiturate, 1934–1939," FBN Papers.

12   Day to Nutt, 18 October 1926.

13   Continental Color and Chemical Co., *Chemical—Pharmacological NOTES*, n.d. (probably 1906), Series 3, Box 200, Folder 8 "1013: Catalogs/Price Lists 1930s," Sterling Drug Papers.

14   Joseph Gabriel, "Pharmaceutical Patenting and the Transformation of American Medical Ethics," *British Journal of the History of Science* 49, no. 4 (2016): 577–600.

15   Irving Rubin, "Compilation of the Proprietary Barbiturates," *American Druggist*, March 1940 [reprint], in Series 3, Box 207, Folder 8 "Handbooks 1940," Sterling Drug Papers.

16   See, e.g., Peter Conrad, *The Medicalization of Society: On the Transformation of Human Conditions into Treatable Disorders* (Baltimore: Johns Hopkins University Press, 2007).

17   Winthrop Chemical Company, *'Veronal' and 'Veronal'-Sodium*, n.d. (probably mid-1920s), Series 3, Box 168, Folder 33 "Product Files U-Z, 1920s," Sterling Drug Papers; Winthrop Chemical Company, *Veronal: Elixir of Veronal, Veronal Sodium* (1939), Series 3, Box 168, Folder 34 "Product Files U-Z, 1930s," Sterling Drug Papers.

18   "Paranoval: Non-bitter Readily Soluble Veronal," n.d. (probably late 1920s or early 1930s), Series 3, Box 113, Folder 13 "Product Files O-P, C, 1930s," Sterling Drug Papers.

19   Winthrop Chemical Company, *Luminal and Its Combinations*, 1926, Series 3, Box 51, Folder 15–16 "Product Files I-L, 1920," Sterling Drug Papers; "nocturnal pollutions" in *Luminal, Luminal-Sodium Sedatives and Hypnotics* (1939), Series 3, Box 51, Folder 15–16 "Product Files I-L, 1920," Sterling Drug Papers.

20   AMA Council on Pharmacy and Chemistry, "Sedormid Not Acceptable for N.N.R.," *JAMA* 110, no. 10 (1938).

21   Winthrop Chemical Company, *Phanodorn* (n.d.; 1933–1936), Series 3, Box 117, Folder 16, 19 "Product Files O-P 1927," Sterling Drug Papers; Bayer-Meister Lucius, *Phanodorn*, n.d. (probably late 1926), Series 3, Box 117, Folder 16, 19 "Product Files O-P 1927," Sterling Drug Papers.

22   "Quickly carries patient over threshold of sleep . . . *then withdraws, allowing nature to complete the task*," 1935, Series 3, Box 181, Folder 30 "Product Files O-P 1927," Sterling Drug Papers.

23   Winthrop Chemical Company, *Luminal and Its Combinations*, 1926; Adalin-Luminal first advertised in Winthrop Chemical Company, Inc., *Luminal, Luminal-Sodium: Hypnotics and Sedatives* (1924); both in Box 51, Folder 15–16 "Product Files I-L, 1920," Sterling Drug Papers.

24   Winthrop Chemical Company, *Universal Analgesic Sedative* (1927); Winthrop Chemical Company, *New Luminal Products* (1926); Winthrop Chemical Company, *Luminal and Its Combinations* (1926); H. A. Metz Laboratories, "Since

1898" (1928); all in Box 51, Folder 11 "Product Files I-L, 1920," Sterling Drug Papers; Winthrop Chemical Company, *Luminal, Luminal-Sodium, Hypnotics and Sedatives* (1924); Winthrop, *Pyraminal: Non-Depressing Analgesic Sedative* (1928); Winthrop, *Pyraminal: Nondepressing Analgesic Sedative* (1935); H. A. Metz Laboratories, *Pyraminal* (1930); Box 135, Folder 16 "Product Files O-P, 1920s," Sterling Drug Papers.

25   "Nervous Indigestion," *Clinical Excerpts* 6, no. 1 (1931): 12–13, Box 214, Folder 10 "Clinical Excerpts," Sterling Drug Papers. For original, see Walter C. Alvarez, *Nervous Indigestion*, 7th Impression (London: William Heinemann, 1939), 178–79.

26   Roland Marchand, *Advertising the American Dream: Making Way for Modernity, 1920–1940* (Berkeley: University of California Press, 1985); T. J. Jackson Lears, *Fables of Abundance: A Cultural History of Advertising in America* (New York: Basic, 1995).

27   Grace Elizabeth Hale, *Making Whiteness: The Culture of Segregation in the South, 1890–1945* (New York: Vintage, 1999); Victoria Wolcott, *Race Riots and Roller Coasters: The Struggle over Segregated Recreation in America* (Philadelphia: University of Pennsylvania Press, 2012); Brian Purnell, Jeanne Theoharis, Komozi Woodard, eds., *The Strange Careers of the Jim Crow North: Segregation and Struggle Outside of the South* (New York: New York University Press, 2019).

28   John Germann, "A Case of Poisoning from Veronal," *JAMA* 46, no. 26 (1906): 1999; "Killed by Sleep Tablets," *New York Times*, January 19, 1906, 1.

29   See, for e.g., "Dying from an Overdose," *New York Tribune*, September 6, 1910, 14; "Divorcee Found Dead," *Chicago Daily Tribune*, June 12, 1917, 2; "Tries to End Life," *Los Angeles Times*, November 7, 1921, II, 15. For serialized potboilers, see, e.g., Kohn Prothero, "Apples of Gold, Chapter XI," *Boston Daily Globe*, June 16, 1909, 12; June 28, 1909, 12; July 1, 1909, 12.

30   Day to Nutt, 18 October 1926, FBN Papers.

31   Kane, *Drugs That Enslave*. The flexibility of "habits" can be seen in an 1896 article in the *New York Times*, which referred both to "patients who have been in the habit of using the drug" and "physicians who have been in the habit of freely prescribing it." "Use and Abuse of Sulphonal," *New York Times*, April 6, 1896, 6.

32   See, e.g., McAllister, *Drug Diplomacy in the Twentieth Century*; Paul Gootenberg, *Andean Cocaine: The Making of a Global Drug* (Chapel Hill: University of North Carolina Press, 2008).

33   Day to Nutt, 18 October 1926, FBN Papers.

34   See George Germann, "Edward Germann's Death: Veronal Prescribed by a Physician Who Had Never Heard of It," *New York Times*, January 22, 1906, 6; "Clergyman Dies at Baths," *New York Times*, December 14, 1911, 13; "Poison Killed Earl's Relative," *New York Times*, February 2, 1913, C1; "Dancer Pens Death Note, Takes Drug," *New York Times*, March 29, 1914, 1; "Suffragette Found Dead," *New York Times*, June 9, 1914, 3; "Death from Poison Starts Inquiry," *New York Times*, December 27, 1919, 15; "Dies of Veronal Overdose," *New York Times*, June 19, 1920, 13; "Girl Prodigy Takes Poison," *New York Times*, November 28, 1920, 32; "Girl Suicide Proves Olive Thomas' Chum," *New York Times*, September 22, 1920, 24; "Actor Dies of Overdose of Veronal,"

New York Times, July 16, 1920, 11; "Failing as Actress, Girl Takes Veronal," *New York Times*, September 6, 1922, 14; "C. D. Pinkney's Death Is Laid to Veronal," *New York Times*, January 21, 1921, 14; "Inquire into Death of Movie Writer," *New York Times*, September 21, 1921, 4; "Dies of Veronal Overdose," *New York Times*, October 26, 1922, 9; "Drug Kills New Yorker," *New York Times*, September 11, 1922, 6; "Girl Stricken in Street," *New York Times*, November 21, 1922, 40; "Tries a Second Time to Die," *New York Times*, June 4, 1922, 21; "Woman Takes Neronal [*sic*]," *New York Times*, March 22, 1922, 32; "Broker's Wife Ends Life at Long Beach Home," *New York Times*, August 21, 1925, 1.

35 See, e.g., Bayer, *Phanodorn: The Well-Known Hypnotic* (1926); Winthrop Chemical Company, *Tranquility* (1926); Bayer, *Therapy of Sleep Disturbances*; all in Box 117 Folder 16 "Product Files O-P 1926," Sterling Drug Papers; and *EVIPAL* (1934), Box 181, Folder 30, Sterling Drug Papers.

36 Campbell, *Using Women*.

37 Luminal ads, Box 51, Folder 13 "Product Files I-L 1950s," Sterling Drug Papers (P1020463-4).

38 See, e.g., James Burnet, "Veronal: A Resume of the Results Obtained from its Administration," *Medical Times and Hospital Gazette*, November 26, 1904, 753; J. C. Larkin, "Veronal, or Diethylbarbituric Acid," *Columbus Medical Journal* 29, no. 8 (1905): 365–67.

39 Thomas Hunt Stucky, "Veronal Poisoning—Report of a Case," *Louisville Monthly Journal of Medicine and Surgery* 14 (1907): 244.

40 "Veronal Poisoning," *Oklahoma Medical News-Journal* 20 (1912): 77–78.

41 "Big Gifts Figure in Griswold Case," "Alienists Testify in Griswold Case," and "Griswold Case Argued," *New York Times*, October 11, 1921, 18; October 22, 1921, 10; November 16, 1921, 14. Even when they did discuss chronic use, they tended to describe people as "being in the habit of taking veronal" or being "a habitual user," in an informal rather than an addictive sense; see "Inez Bennett Dead," *New York Times*, April 5, 1911, 8; "Poison Killed Earl's Relative," *New York Times*, February 2, 1913, C1; "Inquire into Death of Movie Writer," *New York Times*, September 21, 1921, 4.

42 Winthrop Chemical Company, *Veronal: Answers to Questions* (1925); see also Winthrop, *Above the Clouds*; both in Box 168, Folder 33 "Product Files U-Z 1920s," Sterling Drug Papers.

43 Winthrop Chemical Company, *Luminal, Luminal Sodium: Sedatives and Hypnotics* (1924; "no tendency") and (1929; "by effects"); both in Box 51, Folder 15-16 "Product Files I-L, 1920," Sterling Drug Papers. Winthrop did raise the issue of "tolerance" to Luminal, but used the term only in the sense of how well a patient tolerated the drug's effects—a clear sign of the conceptual distance between barbiturates and the vocabulary of addiction; see Winthrop Chemical Company, *Luminal, Luminal Sodium: Sedatives and Hypnotics* (n.d.).

44 See, e.g., Winthrop, *Veronal: Answers to Questions*; Winthrop Chemical Company, *Veronal, Veronal-Sodium: Hypnotics and Sedatives* (n.d.); Bayer, *Veronal and Veronal-Sodium* (n.d.); all in Box 168, Folder 33 "Product Files U-Z 1920s," Sterling Drug Papers; Winthrop, *Luminal* (n.d.); Winthrop, *Luminal and Its Combinations* (1926); Winthrop Chemical Company, *Luminal and Luminal-Sodium: Powerful Hypnotics and Sedatives* (1921); Bayer Company, *Luminal and Luminal-Sodium: The Powerful Hypnotics* (n.d.); Winthrop, *Luminal,*

Luminal-Sodium: Sedatives and Hypnotics (1929); all in Box 51, Folder 15–16 "Product Files I-L 1920," Sterling Drug Papers.

45 Winthrop Chemical Company, *Lumalgin: The Potentiated Analgesic* (1935), Box 51, Folder 15–16 "Product Files I-L 1920"; Bayer, *Phanodorn* (n.d.), Box 117, Folder 16 "Product Files O-P 1926."

46 Winthrop, *Veronal: Answers to Questions*; see also Winthrop, *Above the Clouds*, and Bayer, *Phanodorm* (1926), Box 117, Folder 16 "Product Files O-P 1926," Sterling Drug Papers.

47 Irving Sands, "Barbital (Veronal) Intoxication," *JAMA* 81, no. 18 (1923): 1519–21.

48 William Leake and Richmond Ware, "Barbital (Veronal) Poisoning," *JAMA* 84, no. 6 (1925): 434–36.

49 Irvin Page, "Barbital and Related Hypnotics," *JAMA* 91, no. 6 (1928): 398–99.

50 See, e.g., Nathan B. Eddy, "Studies on Hypnotics of the Barbituric Acid Series," *Journal of Pharmacology and Experimental Therapeutics* 33, no. 1 (1928); Nathan B. Eddy, "The Effect of the Repeated Administration of Diethyl Barbituric Acid and of Cyclohexenyl-Ethyl Barbituric Acid," *Journal of Pharmacology and Experimental Therapeutics* 37, no. 3 (1929): 261–71.

51 Nicolas Rasmussen, "Maurice Seevers, the Stimulants, and the Political Economy of Addiction in American Biomedicine," *BioSocieties* 5, no. 1 (2010); Campbell, *Discovering Addiction*, 36.

52 Maurice Seevers and Arthur Tatum, "Chronic Experimental Barbital Poisoning," *Journal of Pharmacology and Experimental Therapeutics* 41 (1931): 220, 217. Earlier studies, they noted, had not given test subjects long enough to develop physical dependence on barbiturates, which took far longer than with opioids.

53 Charles Edmunds and Nathan Eddy, "Some Studies on the Drug Addiction Problem," *Quarterly Review of the Michigan Alumnus*, October 1934, 250–51.

54 Arthur Tatum, "The Present Status of the Barbiturate Problem," *Physiological Reviews* 19 (1939): 491.

55 E. McC. Connely, "Chronic Barbital Poisoning," *New Orleans Medical and Surgical Journal* 80 (1927): 253–39.

56 Marian King, *The Recovery of Myself: A Patient's Experience in a Hospital for Mental Illness* (New Haven, CT: Yale University Press, 1931), 121.

57 King, 133.

58 King, 148.

59 "Adventures with Veronal," *New York Times*, April 5, 1931, 62.

60 "Veronal Poisoning," *Therapeutic Gazette* 29 (1913): 630–31.

61 Cole, "Acute Barbital (Veronal) Poisoning."

62 Robert Fischelis, "Present Status," *Journal of the American Pharmaceutical Association* 35, no. 7 (1946): 193–204; "Drugs covered in the laws regulating the sale and distribution of barbiturates, arranged according to similarity of requirements of the various states," Box 138, Folder "Barbituric 1945—Jan. thru December," FBN Papers.

63 Robert P. Fischelis to Hoffmann-La Roche, Inc., 22 July 1933, Box 27, Folder 3 "Court cases (various), 1931–1939," Fischelis Papers.

64 Fischelis, "Present Status."

65 *Richmond News Leader*, "'Dry Drunk' Pills on Sale Here," 14 October 1936; *Richmond News Leader*, "'Sleeping pill held often lead to 'dope' habit," 15 October 1936; both from Box 138, File 0480-110-0480-119, Folder "Barbituric 1930s," FBN Papers.

66 Carpenter, *Reputation and Power*, 80-85.

67 Carpenter, *Reputation and Power*, 98-99.

68 An Act to Prohibit the Movement in Interstate Commerce of Adulterated and Misbranded Food, Drugs, Devices, and Cosmetics, and for Other Purposes, Pub. L. No. 75-717, 52 Stat. 1040 (1906).

69 Carpenter, *Reputation and Power*; Marks, "Revisiting the Origins."

70 Hambourger, "A Study of the Promiscuous Use of the Barbiturates"; "Barbital and Its Derivatives," *JAMA* 114, no. 20 (1940): 2020-21.

71 Lois Mattox Miller, "Dangerous Lullabyes," *Hygeia* 16 (July 1938): 584.

72 "Medicine in the News" [advertisement from American Medical Association run on NBC radio news 15 May 1940]; clipping in Box 138, Folder "Barbituric 1940-1945," FBN Papers.

73 FDA, "FD&C Act Trade Correspondence 56," 12 February 1940, Box 248, Folder "500.671-500.692, 1940," FDA Papers; FDA, "FD&C Act Trade Correspondence 350," 9 January 1941; "Drugs which, in the opinion of the Food and Drug Administration, may be sold only on a prescription . . ."; both in Box 402, Folder "500.671-500.692," 1941," FDA Papers.

74 District of Columbia Pharmaceutical Association, "Warning: Post that all may see," 12 April 1940, Box 138, Folder Barbituric 1940—1944, FBN Papers.

75 "Memorandum of Interview," 28 March 1940, Box 253, 1940," Folder 511.07-.10—511.09-.67, FDA Papers.

76 W. G. Campbell to Chief, Central District, 22 October 1940, Box 253, Folder 511.10—511.10-.67, FDA Papers.

77 W. G. Campbell to Chiefs of Districts, 23 December 1941, Box 402, Folder 500.671-500.692, 1941, FDA Papers.

78 W. G. Campbell to Mr. Rowland Jones Jr., NARD, 24 February 1943; R. S. Pruitt, Chief, Cincinnati Station to Wuir's Drug Store, 2 November 1942; both in Box 627, Folder 500.671—500.692, FDA Papers.

79 See, e.g., W. A. Queen, Chief, Division of State Cooperation to Mr. N. C. McAllister, North Carolina Board of Pharmacy, 8 May 1944, Box 707, Folder 500.66—500.69, FDA Papers; G. P. Larrick to Western District Administration, 11 May 1945, Box 794, Folder 500.67, FDA Papers.

80 W. G. Campbell to J. H. Stoddart Company, 9 July 1942, Box 522, Folder 511.08-511.10-.23, FDA Papers.

81 Herbert W. Ayres, Inspector to Chief, Chicago District, 21 December 1955, Box 2692, Folder 500.66-500.671 Sept + Dec, FDA Papers.

82 United States v. Sullivan, 332 U.S. 689 (1948); Marks, "Revisiting the Origins"; Nicolas Rasmussen, "Goofball Panic: Barbiturates, 'Dangerous' and Addictive Drugs, and the Regulation of Medicine in Postwar America," in *Prescribed: Writing, Filling, Using, and Abusing the Prescription in Modern America*, ed. Jeremy A. Greene and Elizabeth Siegel Watkins (Baltimore: Johns Hopkins University Press, 2012), 23-45.

83 Miller, "Dangerous Lullabyes," 584.

84   Adam Rathge, "Cannabis Cures: American Medicine, Mexican Marijuana, and the Origins of the War on Weed, 1840–1937" (diss., Boston College, 2017).

85   Rathge, "Cannabis Cures"; Richard J. Bonnie and Charles H. Whitebread, *The Marijuana Conviction: A History of Marijuana Prohibition in the United States* (Charlottesville: University Press of Virginia, 1974); William B. McAllister, "Harry Anslinger Saves the World: National Security Imperatives and the 1937 Marihuana Tax Act," *Social History of Alcohol and Drugs* 33, no. 1 (2019): 37–62.

86   See, e.g., Campbell, *Using Women.*

87   This represented a rise in the portion of all hospital admissions from 3 out of 10,000 to 5 out of 10,000. Samuel Goldstein, "Barbiturates: A Blessing and a Menace," *Journal of the American Pharmaceutical Association, Scientific Edition* 36, no. 1 (1947), reprinted in *Miscellaneous Bills,* H. Comm. on Ways and Means, 80th Cong. 92–100 (1947).

88   Goldstein, "Barbiturates"; Garland B. Williams, FBN New York District Supervisor, to Harry Anslinger, 9 October 1945; "Proposals for Changes in the Sanitary Code of the City of New York to Restrict Sale of Barbiturates," 8 October 1945; Ernest Stebbins to Dr. E. M. L. Corwin, Exec. Secretary of Committee on Public Health Relations, NYAM, 25 September 1945; all in Box 138, Folder "Barbituric 1945—Jan. thru December," FBN Papers. See also New York Academy of Medicine, "Report on Barbiturates: The New York Academy of Medicine," *Public Health Reports* 81, no. 11 (1956): 1144–58, showing deaths continued to rise through the 1950s.

89   Mr. M. A. Strickland to "Dear Sir" ["Mr. Roosevelt"], 26 May 1937; Roosevelt's office forwarded the letter to the FBN, who advised him to contact his representative (Will S. Wood to Mr. M. A. Strickland, 25 June 1937). Both in Box 138, Folder "Barbituric 1934–1939," FBN Papers.

90   Miss Sarah Travers to "Dear Sir," 22 June 1941; H. J. Anslinger to Miss Sarah Travers, 5 July 1941; both in Box 138, Folder "Barbituric 1940–1945," FBN Papers.

91   Mrs. W. J. Drew to H. J. Anslinger, 23 March 1941, Box 138, Folder "Barbituric 1940–1945," FBN Papers.

92   J. M. Houchins to Mr. Anslinger, 17 November 1945, Box 138, Folder "Barbituric 1940–1945," FBN Papers.

93   "Drug Menace to be Bared: Samuel H. Adams Tells of 'Devil's Capsules,'" *New York Journal and American,* 17 November 1945, in FBN clipping file that also includes many other similar stories, located in Box 138, Folder "Barbituric 1945—Jan. thru December," FBN Papers.

94   See, e.g., Matthew Pembleton, *Containing Addiction: The Federal Bureau of Narcotics and the Origins of America's Global Drug War* (Amherst: University of Massachusetts Press, 2017); McGirr, *War on Alcohol.*

95   Rasmussen, "Goofball Panic."

96   "Rogers Confident on Her Barbiturate Bill," *Drug Topics,* 8 July 1946. She had insisted that Anslinger provide the bill's language, which he did under protest; see Mr. Speck to Commissioner Anslinger, 17 April 1946. Both in Box 138, Folder "Barbituric 1946," FBN Papers. Bill (H.R. 588) and Rogers's introduction of it in Box 138, Folder "Barbituric 1947," FBN Papers.

97 George Larrick to Hon. Edith Nourse Rogers, May 16, 1947, reprinted in *Miscellaneous Bills*, H. Comm. on Ways and Means, 80th Cong. 72-74 (1947).

98 See, e.g., "Drive Against Narcotics Pushed by Federation: Dangers of 'Sleeping Potions' Stressed by Woman's Club Leader," *Washington* (DC) *Times Herald*, 26 February 1946; Mrs. Harvey W. Wiley to "Member of the House of Representatives," 4 June 1946; Mrs. Gertrude Parks, President, DC Federation of Women's Clubs, to "Member of the House of Representatives," 19 June 1946; all in Box 138, Folder Barbituric 1946, FBN Papers.

99 "Control for the Devil's Capsules," *American Weekly*, 20 July 1947, Box 138, Folder "Barbituric 1947," FBN Papers.

100 Samuel Hopkins Adams, "Slaves to the Devil's Pills," Box 138, Folder "Barbituric 1945—Jan. thru December," FBN Papers.

101 Vera Connolly, "Lethal Lullaby," *Collier's*, 19 October 1946, 86, 95-97. See also, e.g., Rita Halle Kleeman, "Sleeping Pills Aren't Candy," *Saturday Evening Post*, 24 February 1945, Box 138, Folder "Barbituric 1945—Jan. thru December," FBN Papers; J. D. Ratcliff, "The Truth about Sleeping Pills," *Women's Home Companion* 73 (April 1946): 31, 69; "Sleep-Pill Problem," *Business Week*, 24 March 1945; Albert Deutsch, "The Truth about Sleeping Pills," *Science Digest* 17, no. 4 (1945): 1, 4. Even the fire-breathing Adams acknowledged that "properly employed under expert supervision, it is a valuable agent in the practice of medicine"; Adams, "Slaves of the Devil's Capsules."

102 Maxine Davis, "Sleeping Pills," *Good Housekeeping*, June 1947, 26-27, 240-43.

103 "I Was a Sleeping Pill Addict" pts. 1 and 2, 1948, *American Weekly*, 16 and 23 May 1948, Box 1996, Folder "Barbiturate Vol III, 1948, Jan—Dec," FDA Papers. See also, e.g., Deutsch, "Truth about Sleeping Pills"; Kleeman, "Sleeping Pills Aren't Candy", Stewart Robertson, "America's New Dope Peril," *Saturday Home Magazine*, 20 October 1945, Box 138, Folder "Barbituric 1945—Jan. thru December," FBN Papers; "Robbery for the Devil's Capsules," *American Weekly, Times-Herald*, 1 September 1946, Box 138, Folder "Barbituric 1946," FBN Papers; Norman and Madelyn Carlisle, "Thrill Pills Can Ruin You," *Collier's*, 23 April 1949, 59-61; R. Judson, "Our Bootleg Druggists!" *Smash Detective* 4 (n.d.): 7, 62, Box 138, Folder "Barbituric 1940-1945," FBN Papers.

104 John Roeburt, "Beware the Sleeping-Pill Racket," *Everybody's Digest*, May 1945, 45-47, Box 138, Folder "Barbituric 1945—Jan. thru December," FBN Papers.

105 Adams, "Slaves of the Devil's Capsules."

106 Campbell, *Using Women*; Jill Jonnes, *Hep-Cats, Narcs, and Pipe Dreams: A History of America's Romance with Illegal Drugs* (Baltimore: Johns Hopkins University Press, 1999); Matthew R. Pembleton, "The Voice of the Bureau: How Frederic Sondern and the Bureau of Narcotics Crafted a Drug War and Shaped Popular Understanding of Drugs, Addiction, and Organized Crime in the 1950s," *Journal of American Culture* 38, no. 2 (2015): 113-29.

107 See H. J. Anslinger to Mrs. Rogers, 15 February 1946, Box 138, Folder "Barbituric 1946," FBN Papers; and E. H. Foley Jr., Acting Secretary of the Treasury, to Mr. Chairman, 12 May 1947, Box 138, Folder "Barbituric 1947," FBN Papers.

108   See, e.g., D. Roush, Narcotic Inspector to H. J. Anslinger, 14 January 1938; H. J. Anslinger to Dr. William C. Woodward, 3 February 3, 1938; both in Box 138, Folder "Barbituric 1934-1939," FBN Papers. See also Musto, *American Disease*, and Rasmussen, "Goofball Panic."

109   See, e.g., Anslinger providing Maryland's law ("Barbital and Other Hypnotic Drugs Act") as a model to follow; Box 138, Folder "Barbituric 1934-1939," FBN Papers.

110   See, e.g., Matthew Crouch, Narcotic Agent to A. B. Crisler, Acting District Supervisor, 15 January 1940, Box 138, File 0480-110-0480-119, Folder "Barbituric 1940-1945," FBN Papers.

111   H. J. Anslinger to Herbert Gaston, Assistant Secretary of the Treasury, 16 April 1941, Box 138, Folder "Barbituric 1940-1945," FBN Papers.

112   H. J. Anslinger to Dr. James Munch, 4 September 1940; James C. Munch to Mr. Harry J. Anslinger, 28 October 1940; both in Box 138, Folder "Barbituric 1940-1945," FBN Papers.

113   "Our Bootleg Druggists!" *Smash Detective*; Edward Radin, "Ersatz Narcotics," *True Detective*, November 1944, 67; both in Box 138, Folder "Barbituric 1940-1945," FBN Papers.

114   H. J. Anslinger to Mrs. Rogers, 15 February 1946; "Narcotics Chief Serves Notice Bureau 'Unalterably Opposes' Federal 'Straight Jacket' for Barbiturates," *F-D-C Reports*, 28 September 1946, 11; "Narcotics Unit Balks at Asking Federal Curbs on Barbiturates," *Drug Trade News*, 20 May 1946; all in Box 138, Folder "Barbituric 1946," FBN Papers; H. J. Anslinger to Mr. Spingern, 21 January 1947, in Box 138, Folder "Barbituric 1947," FBN Papers.

115   "Back breaking": Dr. Rober L. Swain, "'Sleeping Pill' issue," *Drug Topics*, 20 August 1945, Box 138, Folder "Barbituric 1945—Jan. thru December," FBN Papers; see also Robert P. Fischelis to Members of the House of Representatives, 00 [*sic*] May 1946, Box 63, Folder 17 "APhA Barbiturates- Prog. To curb misuse 1946," Fischelis Papers. "Strait jacket": Paul Green, "The Barbiturate Time Bomb!" *American Druggist*, September 1945, Box 138, Folder "Barbituric 1945—Jan. thru December," FBN Papers; dispensing vs. pharmacy sales: F. H. Taft to C. E. Nickell, 5 December 1944, Box 138, Folder "Barbituric 1940-1945," FBN Papers.

116   Robert Geiger, "US Wolfs Sleeping Pills by the Hundred Tons," *Washington Post*, January 26, 1947, B6, quoted in Rasmussen, "Goofball Panic," 36.

117   "Narcotics and Hypnotics," *Apothecary*, June or July 1945, Box 138, Folder "Barbituric 1945—Jan. thru December," FBN Papers.

118   Robert P. Fischelis to Honorable H. J. Anslinger, 21 September 1945; American Pharmaceutical Association, "APhA inaugurates program to curb misuse of barbiturates; Holds conference on health," n.d. Both in Box 138, Folder "Barbituric 1945—Jan. thru December," FBN Papers.

119   Committee on Legislation, National Association of Boards of Pharmacy, "The Regulation of the Distribution of Barbiturates, Part III," in *1946 Proceedings of the National Association of Boards of Pharmacy, Forty-second Annual Convention Held at Pittsburgh, Pennsylvania, August 26-27, 1946*, 155-58 (quote 157-58), Box 138, Folder "Barbituric 1946," FBN Papers; "Proposed Uniform State Barbiturate Act," by the American Pharmaceutical Association, Box 138, File 0480-110-0480-119, Folder "Barbituric 1947," FBN Papers.

120 See, e.g., Willard J. Stone, "1,250,000,000 Doses a Year," *Hygiea* (n.d.), Box 138, Folder "Barbituric 1945—Jan. thru December," FBN Papers.

121 See, e.g., Wallace Werble, "Waco Was a Barbiturate Hot Spot," *Hygiea* 23 (June 1945): 432-33.

122 Goldstein, "Barbiturates," 36.

123 Harris Isbell, Sol Altschul, C. H. Kornetsky et al., "Chronic Barbiturate Intoxication: An Experimental Study," *Archives of Neurology and Psychiatry* 64, no. 1 (1950): 26; see also Harris Isbell, "Addiction to Barbiturates and the Barbiturate Abstinence Syndrome," *Annals of Internal Medicine*, July 1, 1950; Rasmussen, "Goofball Panic."

124 *Control of Narcotics, Marihuana, and Barbiturates: Hearings Before the H. Comm. on Ways and Means*, 82d Cong. 73 (1951), 204.

125 George F. Lull to Hon Robert L. Doughton, 12 April 1951, in *Control of Narcotics, Marihuana, and Barbiturates*, 211.

126 *Barbiturate Control: Hearing Before the H. Comm. on Ways and Means*, 82d Cong. 69 (1952).

127 *Barbiturate Control*, 113, 116, 117.

128 *Barbiturate Control*, 127.

129 *Control of Narcotics, Marihuana, and Barbiturates*, 200.

130 *Traffic in, and Control of, Narcotics, Barbiturates, and Amphetamines: Hearing Before a Subcomm. of the H. Comm. of Ways and Means*, 84th Cong. 412, 414 (1955 & 1956). Seevers gave similar testimony, blaming drug users who could develop a habit to anything and worrying about producing "bootlegging."

131 *Traffic in, and Control of, Narcotics, Barbiturates, and Amphetamines*, 127, 200-201.

132 *Traffic in, and Control of, Narcotics, Barbiturates, and Amphetamines*, 412, 414.

133 It is worth noting that other, more politically pioneering groups like the New York Academy of Medicine were prepared to accept the implications of such views: the Academy agreed with Isbell about barbiturates, but also supported medically prescribed opioids for people with opioid addiction. Subcommittee on Barbiturates, Committee on Public Health, New York Academy of Medicine, "Report on Barbiturates," *Bulletin of the New York Academy of Medicine* 32, no. 6 (1956).

134 Food, Drug, and Cosmetics Act Amendments, Pub. L. No. 82-215, 65 Stat. 648 (1951). See also Marks, "Revisiting the 'Origins,'"; Rasmussen, "Goofball Panic."

135 Musto, *American Disease*.

Chapter Five

1 FDA, "Regulatory Program," 1 June 1956, Box 2161, Folder 500.67 March–Dec 1956, FDA Papers.

2 Baltimore District to Administration, 3 November 1953, Boxes 1856–57, Folder 500.621 1954, FDA Papers.

3 F. D. Clerk, Chief, Minneapolis District, "Confidential—Administrative," 6 October 1955, Box 1995, Folder 500.67 Dec-Aug 1955, FDA Papers.

4 F. J. Aull, Inspector, Charleston Inspection Station, to Balt District, Subject: O-T-C, February 4, 1954, Box 1858, Folder 500.67 1954, FDA Papers.

5   George Barksdale, Inspector, Baltimore District to Baltimore District, 13 April 1953, Box 1728, Folder 500.67 1953, FDA Papers.
6   W. N. Swain, Inspector, Charlotte to Chief, Atlanta District, 17 February 1956, Box 1995, Folder 500.67 Dec–Aug 1955, FDA Papers.
7   FDA, "Regulatory Program," 1 June 1956.
8   Winton B. Rankin, Inspector to Chief, Baltimore Station, "Indiscriminate sale of dangerous drugs," 10 March 1945, Box 794, Folder 500.67, FDA Papers. Frydl, *Drug Wars*, provides an excellent, in-depth look at FDA policing and its limits.
9   John L. Harvey to Administration, 9 April 1954, Box 1860, Folder 511.07–511.09–.66, 1954, FDA Papers.
10 "Regulatory Program," FDA, June 1, 1956; M. R. Stephens to Denver District, 2 March 1959, Box 2692, Folder 500.66–500.671 Sept + Dec, FDA Papers.
11 Inspector Joseph J. Milunas to Chief Inspector, Balt. District, 19 January 1949, Box 1183 400.43–500.67, 1949, Folder 500.67, FDA Papers.
12 Harold E. Whiteley, Narcotic Inspector, to Mr. Joseph Bell, District Supervisor, Kansas City, Missouri, 17 December 1940, Box 138, Folder "Barbituric 1940–1945," FBN Papers. FDA barbiturate files (500.671) include many similar examples in the 1950s.
13 Bryan L. Eggerton, New Orleans Station to Administration, 15 November 1948, Box 1183, 1949, Folder 500.67, FDA Papers.
14 Oklahoma Pharmaceutical Association, "Urgent Warning to All Druggists!" 19 November 1951; Samuel Alfend to Administration, 19 November 1951; both in Box 1449, Folder 500.33–.67, 1951, FDA Papers.
15 A. E. Rayfield to Chiefs of Districts, 3 April 1953, Box 1728, Folder 500.67 1953, FDA Papers.
16 John L. Harvey to FDA General Counsel, 31 January 1951, Box 1449, Folder 500.33–.67, 1951, FDA Papers.
17 Sidney Weissenberg to Cincinnati District, 29 December 1953, Box 1995, Folder 500.67 Dec–Aug 1955, FDA Papers.
18 George Larrick to Senator Lister Hill, 21 October 1948, Box 1996, Folder "Barbiturate Vol III, 1948, Jan—Dec," FDA Papers. See also John Swann, "The FDA and the Practice of Pharmacy: Prescription Drug Regulation Before 1968," in *Federal Drug Control: The Evolution of Policy and Practice*, ed. Jonathon Erlen and Joseph Spillane (New York: Pharmaceutical Products Press, 2004), 145–74.
19 Chief, Philadelphia Station to Chief Inspector, Philadelphia Station, 1 September 1948, Box 1183, 1949, Folder 500.67, FDA Papers.
20 FDA, "General information for physicians who are asked to cooperate in prescription refilling investigations," n.d. (ca. 1960), Box 2884, Folder 500.67, FDA Papers.
21 M. R. Stephens to Chiefs of Districts, 6 February 1959, Box 2692, Folder 500.66—500.671 Sept + Dec, FDA Papers.
22 Wendell Vincent, Chief, Denver Station to Inspector Ryan, 22 January 1948, Box 1996 "511.07.13—511.10.67," Folder "Barbiturate Vol III, 1948, Jan—Dec," FDA Papers; P. B. Dunbar to Chiefs of Stations, 25 August 1948 and Harvey to Station Western District, 15 February 1946, both Box 1996 "511.07.13—511.10.67," Folder 511.10.31—511.10.67, 1948, FDA Papers; and Baltimore Sta-

tion to Inspectors, Baltimore Station, 18 November 1948, Box 1183 400.43—500.67, 1949, Folder 500.67, FDA Papers.

23   Atlanta District to Division of Field Operations, 16 November 1951; Seattle District to Division of Field Operations, 17 March 1952; D. Franklin Fisher to Chief Inspector, 7 February 1952; Philadelphia District to Division of Field Operations, 29 January 1952; New Orleans District to Division of Field Operations, 11 December 1951; Denver District to Division of Field Operations, 23 November 1951; St. Louis District to Administration, 16 November 1951; Chicago District to Division of Field Operations, 15 November 1951; John H. Guill to Chief, Baltimore District, 13 November 1951; Boston District to Division of Field Operations, 14 November 1951. All in Box 1577-78, Folder 500.67 1952, FDA Papers.

24   Alfred Barnard to Mr. George P. Larrick, 23 November 1953, enclosing Barnard, "Enforcement Operations on Improper Sale of Prescription Legend Drugs by State and Local Regulatory Agencies," Boxes 1856-57, Folder 500.621 1954, FDA Papers.

25   For example, Wisconsin did not even investigate, much less convict, any physician for barbiturate prescribing before 1968; California records do include investigations of two barbiturate/amphetamine sellers.

26   Barnard, "Enforcement Operations on Improper Sales."

27   Barnard.

28   Barnard.

29   Douglas C. Hansen, Inspector to Chief, Seattle Station, 10 September 1948, Box 1996, Folder "Barbiturate Vol III, 1948, Jan—Dec," FDA Papers.

30   Barnard, "Enforcement Operations on Improper Sales."

31   W. B. Rankin and E. A. R., "Referrals and Recommendations," 17 April 1953; W. B. Rankin to Chief, Baltimore and St. Louis Districts, 27 April 1953; both in Box 1728, Folder 500.67 1953, FDA Papers.

32   State Wisconsin Board of Pharmacy, "In the matter of the revocation or suspension of the registration to practice pharmacy of Erwin E. Semon, Respondent," 30 June 1960, 10-13, Box 2, Folder 26, PEB Complaint and Revocation Files.

33   Wisconsin Board of Pharmacy, "In the matter of . . . Semon," 6-7.

34   John J. Cox, Inspector, to Chief, Los Angeles District, 26 May 1956, Box 2161, Folder 500.67 March-Dec 1956, FDA Papers.

35   E. C. Boudreaux, New Orleans District to Administration, 18 November 1955, Box 2160, Folder 500.67 "Illegal Dispensing of Prescription Legend Drugs—Illicit Sales of Barbiturates and Amphetamines, 1955-1956," FDA Papers.

36   Frydl, *Drug Wars in America*, identifies and provides important analysis of this shift.

37   William J. Barbour, Miami, Florida, to Atlanta District, 10 March 1953, Box 1728, Folder 500.67 1953, FDA Papers.

38   Administration to Chiefs of Districts, 3 August 1954, Box 1858, Folder 500.67 1954, FDA Papers.

39   San Francisco District, Division of Field Operations, 30 August 1954, Box 1858, Folder 500.67 1954, FDA Papers.

40   *Barbiturate Control*, 46, 53.

41   *American Druggist* fortnightly survey.

42 Rasmussen, "Goofball Panic."

43 *Traffic in, and Control of, Narcotics, Barbiturates, and Amphetamines*, 413.

44 There is some evidentiary basis for applying the pareto here: a later survey found that one-fifth of sedative users had been using daily for over a year. See Glen Mellinger and Mitchell Balter, "Prevalence and Patterns of Use of Psychotherapeutic Drugs: Results from a 1979 National Survey of American Adults," in *Epidemiological Impact of Psychotropic Drugs*, ed. C. Tognoni, C. Bellantuono, and M. Lader (New York: Elsevier/North-Holland Biomedical Press, 1981), 117–35.

45 "Deaths from Acute Accidental Poisoning by Barbituric Acid and Derivatives and Number of Suicides," in George P. Larrick, Commissioner of Food and Drugs, Statement Before a Subcommittee on Improvements in the Federal Criminal Code of the Senate Committee of the Judiciary, Folder 500.67 Dec.–Aug., Box 1995, FDA Papers.

46 Rasmussen, *On Speed*, 15–19. The following six paragraphs are drawn largely from Rasmussen's book.

47 Rasmussen, *On Speed*, 27–50.

48 Goodman and Gilman, *Pharmacological Basis of Therapeutics* (1941 ed.), 445, quoted in Rasmussen, *On Speed*, 50. See also Rasmussen, "Maurice Seevers."

49 Rasmussen, *On Speed*, 116–36.

50 Barnard, "Enforcement Operations on Improper Sale."

51 Rasmussen, *On Speed*, 99–105.

52 Administration to Chiefs of Districts, 3 August 1954, Box 1858, Folder 500.67 1954, FDA Papers.

53 Frydl, *Drug Wars in America*.

54 Rasmussen, *On Speed*, 112, 199, 297n, 177.

55 Rasmussen, *On Speed*, 137–43.

56 Herzberg, *Happy Pills*, 25–29; the next five paragraphs are drawn largely from *Happy Pills*.

57 "Tranquil Pills Stir Up Doctors," *Business Week*, June 28, 1958, 28–30. See also Tone, *Age of Anxiety*.

58 Herzberg, *Happy Pills*.

59 For Sacklers and William Douglas McAdams, see William Castagnoli, *Medicine Avenue: The Story of Medical Advertising in America* (Huntington, NY: Medical Advertising Hall of Fame, 1999); Patrick Radden Keefe, "The Family That Built an Empire of Pain," *New Yorker*, October 20, 2017.

60 Herzberg, *Happy Pills*.

61 Herzberg, *Happy Pills*, app. B.

62 Hugh Parry, "Use of Psychotropic Drugs by U.S. Adults," *Public Health Reports*, October 1968, 802, 808.

63 Herzberg, *Happy Pills*, 138.

64 Nicolas Rasmussen, "America's First Amphetamine Epidemic 1929–1971: A Quantitative and Qualitative Retrospect with Implications for the Present," *American Journal of Public Health* 98, no. 6 (2008): 974–85.

65 Schneider, *Smack*.

66 Courtwright, *Dark Paradise*, 169–70.

67 David Hewitt and Jean Milner, "Drug-Related Deaths in the United States: First Decade of an Epidemic," *Health Services Reports* 89, no. 3 (1974): 213.

68 For an important and fascinating analysis of the legislative struggle to strengthen FDA consumer protection powers, see Matthew June, "Protecting Some and Policing Others: Federal Pharmaceutical Regulation and the Foundations of the War on Drugs" (diss., Northwestern University, June 2018).

69 Tomes, *Remaking the American Patient*, 231-42; Podolsky, *Antibiotic Era*; Tobbell, *Pills, Power, and Policy*; Herzberg, *Happy Pills*; Tone, *Age of Anxiety*.

70 Cohen, *Consumers' Republic*.

71 Podolsky, *Antibiotic Era*.

72 John F. Kennedy, "Special Message to Congress on Protecting Consumer Interest," 15 March 1962, John F. Kennedy Presidential Library, Digital Identifier JFKPOF-037-028-p0002, at 2, 6, https://www.jfklibrary.org/asset-viewer /archives/JFKPOF/037/JFKPOF-037-028. June, "Protecting Some and Policing Others," provides an excellent, detailed analysis of the legislative maneuvering behind the 1965 Drug Abuse Control Act.

73 "New Look at 'Consumer Protection'"? *Drug Trade News*, 1 May 1961, Box 221, Folder 07 "Drugs, Special Data, 1899-1966," AMA Papers.

74 Jeremy A. Greene and Scott H. Podolsky, "Reform, Regulation, and Pharmaceuticals—The Kefauver-Harris Amendments at 50," *New England Journal of Medicine* 367, no. 16 (2012): 1481-83.

75 *Illegal Narcotics Traffic*, 2715-16; *Part 12, Narcotic and Dangerous Drug Abuse in the State of California: Hearings Before the Subcomm. to Investigate Juvenile Delinquency of S. Comm. on the Judiciary*, 87th Cong. 2676, 2741, 2754, 2794, 2927-28, 2936, 3019-21, 3040 (1962); *Part 13, Illegal Narcotics Traffic and Its Effect on Juvenile and Young Adult Criminality: Hearings Before the Subcomm. to Investigate Juvenile Delinquency of S. Comm. on the Judiciary*, 87th Cong. 3056-57, 3119 (1962); *Agency Coordination Study: Hearings Before the Subcomm. on Reorganization and International Organizations of the S. Comm. on Government Operations*, 88th Cong. 1433-34 (1963).

76 "Irresponsible," Joel Fort in *Part 12*, 3019-21; "pill heads," Bernard Casselman in *Part 12*, 3040.

77 For the Commission, see Frydl, *Drug Wars in America*, 243-70; June, "Protecting Some and Policing Others."

78 An Act to . . . Establish Special Controls for Depressant and Stimulant Drugs and Counterfeit Drugs . . . , Pub. L. No. 89-74, 79 Stat. 226 (1965).

79 E. Keith Cannan to Dr. Jonathan O. Cole, 23 January 1968, Folder "D.Med.: CPDD: Barbiturate/Amphetamine Combs Study: Contract, 1967-1969," NAS-NRC Papers. The screening program was in place by 1975, as per Assembly of Life Sciences, Division of Medical Sciences, "Conference on evaluation of the dependence liability of amphetamines and barbiturates," 22-23 September 1975, Folder "ALS: D.Med:CPDD:Conf. Predic. Abuse Liab. Of Stim. & Depress. Drugs: ALSApproval," 1975-1977, NAS-NRC Papers.

80 Herzberg, *Happy Pills*.

81 June, "Protecting Some and Policing Others," is the definitive account of the BDAC.

82 *The Narcotic Rehabilitation Act of 1966, Hearings on S. Res. 199 Before the Special Subcomm. of the S. Comm. on the Judiciary*, 89th Cong. 343 (1966).

83 Frydl, *Drug Wars in America*; Schneider, *Smack*.

84 *Drug Addiction: Crime or Disease? Interim and Final Reports of the Joint Com-*

mittee of the American Bar Association and the American Medical Association on Narcotic Drugs (Bloomington: Indiana University Press, 1961); Musto, *American Disease*; Frydl, *Drug Wars in America*.

85   Schneider, *Smack*.

86   Herzberg, *Happy Pills*.

87   Musto, *American Disease*, chap. 11; Massing, *The Fix* (New York: Simon and Schuster, 1998); Schneider, *Smack*; Claire Clark, *The Recovery Revolution: The Battle over Addiction Treatment in the United States* (New York: Columbia University Press, 2017); Emily Dufton, *Grass Roots: The Rise and Fall and Rise of Marijuana in America* (New York: Basic, 2017).

88   *Hearings on Reorganization Plan No. 1 of 1968 (Drug Abuse and Narcotics) and H. Res. 1101 Before a Subcomm. of the H. Comm. on Government Operations*, 90th Cong. 1 (1968) (Lyndon Johnson, "Message").

89   *Reorganization Plan No. 1*; for liberal protests, see 31, 37–38, 79, 109–10.

90   Massing, *Fix*.

91   *Narcotics Legislation: Hearings on S. Res. 48, S. 1895, S. 2590, and S. 2637 Before the Subcomm. to Investigate Juvenile Delinquency of the S. Comm. on the Judiciary*, 91st Cong. 3 (1969).

92   *Narcotics Legislation*, 174–75; see also 172 for a witness from the Department of Health, Education, and Welfare noting that such views were "shared by the overwhelming majority of scientists and physicians."

93   *Drug Abuse Control Amendments—1970: Hearings on H.R. 11701 and H.R. 13743, Parts 1 and 2, Before the Subcomm. on Public Health and Welfare of the H. Comm. on Interstate and Foreign Commerce*, 91st Cong. 256, 265 (1970).

94   *Narcotics Legislation*, 640.

95   *Drug Abuse Control Amendments—1970*, 81 (statement of John Mitchell, Attorney General of the United States); *Controlled Dangerous Substances, Narcotics and Drug Control Laws: Hearings Before the H. Comm. on Ways and Means*, 91st Cong. 201–2 (1970).

96   *Narcotics Legislation*, 638–39.

97   *Drug Abuse Control Amendments—1970*, 62–63.

98   *Crime in America—Illicit and Dangerous Drugs: Hearings Before the H. Select Comm. on Crime*, 91st Cong. 45 (1965); see also 41–42, 53.

99   *Drug Abuse Control Amendments—1970*, 617, 619.

100   *Crime in America*, 330.

101   *Narcotics Legislation*, 317–18.

102   *Drug Abuse Control Amendments—1970*, 603; see also 504, 580.

103   See, e.g., *Drug Abuse Control Amendments—1970*, 233–38, 268–69, 466; *Narcotics Legislation*, 317, 354.

104   *Narcotics Legislation*, 621; "skittish patients," 953.

105   "Sanctity" in *Drug Abuse Control Amendments—1970*, 681–82; "subpoenaed" 386–87.

106   *Controlled Dangerous Substances*, 202; see also, e.g., *Narcotics Legislation*, 230.

107   *Drug Abuse Control Amendments—1970*, 121–22; see also 84–86, 134.

108   See Spillane, "Debating the Controlled Substances Act."

109   *Reorganization Plan No. 1*, 76.

110   See *Drug Abuse Control Amendments—1970*, 84; Comprehensive Drug Abuse Prevention and Control Act of 1970, Pub. L. No. 513, 84 Stat. 1245–46. Factors

affecting which schedule a drug would be placed in included actual or relative potential for abuse; scientific evidence of pharmacological effect; state of current scientific knowledge; history and current pattern of abuse; scope, duration, and significance of abuse; risk to public health; psychological and physiological dependence liability.

111 *Drug Abuse Control Amendments—1970*, 177-82.

112 *Drug Abuse Control Amendments—1970*, 209-10.

113 *Drug Abuse Control Amendments—1970*, 86.

114 Comprehensive Drug Abuse Prevention and Control Act of 1970, 84 Stat. 1245. For an earlier version with congressional action required, see *Reorganization Plan No. 1*, 663; this was still in the bill as late as July 1970, see *Controlled Dangerous Substances*, 25. This potential flexibility came with limits: any substance "required to be controlled by treaty" had to remain on the schedule (84 Stat. 1236). Thanks largely to the dozens of global drug control treaties America had led in creating over the twentieth century, this category included cocaine, all opioids, and marijuana; most sedatives and stimulants were added when the Convention on Psychotropic Substances was ratified in 1976 (McAllister, *Drug Diplomacy in the Twentieth Century*; Reiss, *We Sell Drugs*; Pembleton, *Containing Addiction*).

115 See Spillane, "Debating the Controlled Substances Act"; Courtwright, "Controlled Substances Act."

116 Courtwright, "Controlled Substances Act."

117 *Narcotics Legislation*, 1, 209. See also *Narcotics Legislation*, 2; *Drug Abuse Control Amendments—1970*, 600; *Controlled Dangerous Substances*, 365.

118 *Controlled Dangerous Substances*, 195.

119 Less-strict schedules still carried significant punishments for "pushers": five years and $15,000 for non-narcotics in Schedule I or II, or any Schedule III drug; three years and $10,000 for Schedule IV; and even for lowly Schedule V, one year and $5,000. Pub. L. No. 91-513, § 404, 84 Stat. 1264 (1970); § 401, 84 Stat. 1260-61. As June, "Protecting Some and Policing Others," notes, possession of "dangerous drugs" without a prescription was criminalized for the first time; however, as the next paragraph shows, the impact on white market consumers was actually quite limited.

120 *Controlled Dangerous Substances*, 484; see also 277.

121 John Ingersoll to Dr. Charles L. Dunham, 15 June 1970, Folder "D. Med: CPDD:U. of Michigan Screening Program Contract Correspondence, 1970-1972," NAS-NRC Papers.

Chapter Six

1 Hugh Parry, Mitchell Balter, Glen Mellinger, Ira Cisin, Dean Manheimer, "National Patterns of Psychotherapeutic Drug Use," *Archives of General Psychiatry* 28, no. 6 (1973): 769-83. See also Hugh Parry, "Use of Psychotropic Drugs by U.S. Adults," *Public Health Reports* 83, no. 10 (1968): 799-810.

2 Herzberg, *Happy Pills*, esp. chap. 4.

3 DAWN was begun as part of President Nixon's Special Action Office on Drug Abuse Prevention (SAODAP); in 1974, it was handed over to the new Alcohol, Drug Abuse, and Mental Health Administration (ADAMHA), which

included the National Institute on Drug Abuse (NIDA). *Monitoring the Future* was added in 1975 and the Community Epidemiology Work Group in 1976.

4   US Department of Justice, Drug Enforcement Administration, US Department of Health, Education and Welfare, and National Institute on Drug Abuse, *DAWN Quarterly Report July-September, 1976* (Washington, DC: Government Printing Office, August 1977).

5   An Act to . . . Establish Special Controls for Depressant and Stimulant Drugs and Counterfeit Drugs . . . , Pub. L. No. 89-74, 79 Stat. 226 (1965).

6   Comprehensive Drug Abuse Prevention and Control Act of 1970, Pub. L. No. 513, 84 Stat. 1258-60.

7   Jeremy A. Greene, "The Afterlife of the Prescription: The Sciences of Therapeutic Surveillance," in *Prescribed: Writing, Filling, Using, and Abusing the Prescription in Modern America*, ed. Jeremy A. Greene and Elizabeth Siegel Watkins (Baltimore: Johns Hopkins University Press, 2012), 232-56.

8   US Department of Justice, Drug Enforcement Administration, "Automation of Reports and Consolidated Orders System (ARCOS)," accessed July 27, 2019, https://www.deadiversion.usdoj.gov/arcos/#background.

9   David Courtwright, "Mr. ATOD's Wild Ride: What Do Alcohol, Tobacco, and Other Drugs Have in Common?" *SHAD* 20 (2005): 105-40. See, e.g., Peter G. Bourne, "Polydrug Abuse—Considerations in a National Strategy," *American Journal of Drug and Alcohol Abuse* 1, no. 2 (1974): 147-58; Lloyd Johnston, "Defining the Term 'Polydrug Abuse,'" *National Institute on Drug Abuse Research Monograph*, series 2, October 1975, 36-39. According to Google's Ngram viewer, use of the word "polydrug" leaped by a factor of five from 1970 to 1971. "Substance abuse" was virtually never used before 1970 and then saw a similar sharp increase. MEDLINE does not have any cite of "polydrug" before 1974.

10   Herzberg, *Happy Pills*, 100-102.

11   Everette May and Arthur Jacobson, "The Committee on Problems of Drug Dependence: A Legacy of the National Academy of Sciences. A Historical Account," *Drug and Alcohol Dependence* 23 (1989): 183-218.

12   Watkins, *On the Pill*; Cohen, *Consumers' Republic*; Glickman, *Buying Power*.

13   *Investigation of Juvenile Delinquency in the United States: Investigative and Legislative Hearings on Barbiturate Abuse, Pursuant to S. Res. 32, Section 12, and S. Res. 256 Before the Subcomm. to Investigate Juvenile Delinquency of the S. Comm. on the Judiciary*, 92d Cong. 200 (1971-1972).

14   Public Health Service, "For Release: Immediate," *HEW News*, 5 August 1970, Box 4528, Folder 511.07-511.09, 1971, FDA Papers.

15   Rasmussen, *On Speed*, 217-19.

16   Food and Drug Administration, Notice, "Amphetamines: Drugs for Human Use; Drug Efficacy Study Implementation; Amendment or Previous Notice and Opportunity for Hearing," 44 Fed. Reg. 41,552 (July 17, 1979), https://cdn.loc.gov/service/ll/fedreg/fr044/fr044138/fr044138.pdf.

17   Drug Enforcement Administration, "Title 21—Food and Drugs, Chapter II—Drug Enforcement Administration, Department of Justice, Part 1308—Schedules of Controlled Substances," 38 Fed. Reg. 31,310 (Nov. 13, 1973), https://cdn.loc.gov/service/ll/fedreg/fr038/fr038218/fr038218.pdf.

18 American Medical Association, "For A.M. Release Monday, June 11, 1973: Strict Control Urged for 'Love Drug' Pills," Box 221, Folder 08, AMA Papers.

19 Annual quotas posted in *Federal Register* (locate by searching for the drug name and the term "aggregate quota" in the *Federal Register*).

20 Courtwright, "'Big Tent' Reform."

21 The number rose to over 400 in the 1980s and to over 700 in the 1990s; DEA revocations published in *Federal Register*.

22 See E. B. Staats, [Comptroller General], *Retail Diversion of Legal Drugs: A Major Problem with no Easy Solution* (Washington, DC: General Accounting Office, 1978), 12–24; Drug Enforcement Agency, Office of Diversion Control, *Drug Diversion—A Historical Perspective* (Washington, DC: DEA, 1993), 10.

23 For the Uniform Controlled Substances Act see *Handbook of the National Conference of Commissioners on Uniform State Laws and Proceedings of the Annual Conference Meeting in its Seventy-Ninth Year* (Baltimore: Port City Press, 1970), 223–63; for state adoption statistic, see *Competitive Problems in the Drug Industry, Part 31: Hearings Before the Subcomm. on Monopoly of the S. Select Comm. on Small Business*, 94th Cong. 14, 903 (1976).

24 Controlled Substances Board, "Draft: Diversion Investigation Unit Proposal," April 27, 1977, Box 1, Folder 39 "Diversion Investigation Unit 1977," PEB Correspondence.

25 Controlled Substances Board, "Diversion Investigation Unit (DIU)," n.d., Box 1, Folder 39 "Diversion Investigation Unit 1977," PEB Correspondence. For an example of closer cooperation, see "Memorandum of Agreement [between Wisconsin and federal controlled substances agencies]," 23 May 23 1979, Box 4, Folder 6 "Controlled Substances Board 1979," SBME Correspondence.

26 See, e.g., "Controlled Substances Board, Minutes of Meeting, 15 August 1979," Box 4, Folder 6 "Controlled Substances Board 1979," SBME Correspondence.

27 David E. Joranson to Controlled Substances Board Members, "A Preliminary View of Amphetamines in Wisconsin: Review and Recommendations," 2 February 1977, Box 2, Folder 4 "Amphetamines—Legislative Documents 1976–1978," SBME Correspondence.

28 Joranson to Controlled Substances Board Members, "Preliminary View of Amphetamines in Wisconsin."

29 David Joranson, "Reducing Licit Amphetamine Supply: Results in Wisconsin," Box 1, Folder 6 "Amphetamine Rule 1978–1983," SBME Correspondence.

30 Joranson, "Reducing Licit Amphetamine Supply."

31 Joranson, "Reducing Licit Amphetamine Supply."

32 Dennis E. Curran, Chief Investigator, to John W. Rupel, 15 November 1977, enclosing "Summary of investigations into amphetamine practice of Wisconsin physicians," Box 1, Folder 5 "Amphetamine Rule 1977," SBME Correspondence; Jerome A. Flynn, Investigator to Donald Ausman, MD, 11 August 1977, Box 8, Folder 13 "Ausman, Donald/MEB 1976," SBME Investigations.

33 A. B. Kores, MD, to Medical Examining Board, 15 November 1977, Box 1, Folder 5 "Amphetamine Rule 1977," SBME Correspondence. Folder 5 also contains dozens of other physicians requesting special permission.

34 Warner Holzinger to Wisconsin Medical Examining Board, 15 February 1978, Box 2 Folder 7 "Amphetamines—Public Correspondence 1977–1978," SBME Correspondence.

35   An irate taxpayer to Whom it may concern, 15 December 1977, Box 2, Folder 7 "Amphetamines—Public Correspondence 1977–1978," SBME Correspondence.

36   Joranson, "Reducing Licit Amphetamine Supply."

37   Joranson, "Reducing Licit Amphetamine Supply."

38   See, e.g., Mrs. Delmar Rorison, Louisiana State Board of Medical Examiners to Wisconsin Medical Examining Board, 17 November 1977, Box 1, Folder 5 "Amphetamine Rule 1977," SBME Correspondence; J. I. Cacciatore, Inspectional Services Division, Tampa, FL, to Wisconsin State Board of Medical Examiners, 16 July 1979, and Heikki Leesment, New Jersey Department of Law and Public Safety, to Medical Examining Board, State of Wisconsin, 21 March 1979; both in Box 1, Folder 6 "Amphetamine Rule 1978–1983," SBME Correspondence; Controlled Substances Board Minutes of Meeting, 20 June 1979, Item 7 "State of Washington Amphetamine Regulation," Box 4, Folder 6 "Controlled Substances Board 1979," SBME Correspondence; Maryland, "10.03.44 Regulations governing the prescribing and dispensing of methadone, amphetamines, and methamphetamines," Box 4, Folder 15 "Amphetamines et al Prohibition 1977–1978," PEB Correspondence.

39   Dean Barringer, Director of Department of Regulation and Education et al., "Statement prepared for delivery before the Illinois Legislative Investigation Committee," 7 December 1973, Folder "Controlled Substances Section," DASA Admin.

40   Illinois Dangerous Drugs Advisory Council Meeting 26 September 1977, DASA Minutes.

41   Illinois State Medical Society memo to Illinois General Assembly, 30 October 1975, File "1975 HB 2692 Medical Disciplinary Board," DPR Admin.

42   Albert W. Ray Jr., MD, Illinois State Medical Society, 7 December 1973, "Statement to the Illinois Legislative Investigating Commission Regarding Misuse of Medical Prescriptions in response to House Resolution 285," Folder "Controlled Substances Section," DPR Admin.

43   Illinois State Medical Society memo to Illinois General Assembly, 30 October 1975. The Controlled Substances Act was also amended to close several loopholes; see Louis R. Fine to Thomas F. Howard, 20 February 1975, Folder "Controlled Substances Act—Enforcement," in DPR Admin.

44   Illinois Dangerous Drugs Advisory Council Meeting, 26 September 1977, DASA Minutes.

45   Ronald E. Stackler, DPR Director, "For immediate release," 5 November 1975, Folder "Discipline imposed upon licensees, File II," DASA Minutes.

46   Dangerous Drugs Advisory Council Meeting Minutes, 23 March 1976 and 29 June 1976, DASA Minutes.

47   For DIU, see David B. Selig to David Fogel, Director of IL Law Enforcement Commission, 12 July 1974, and "Testimony of Thomas B. Kirkpatrick, Jr., Executive Director of IL Dangerous Drug Commission, before the House Select Committee on Narcotics Abuse and Control, Oct 1, 1977," both in Folder "IDAP Task Force," DASA Admin. For state-level data, see "Task force on prescription drug abuse," 6 September 1979, in File "Medical marijuana - 1979: hearings, responses to inquiries; amphetamines, re: weight reduction; #1," DASA Admin.

48   Lawrence Slotnik to Bruce Brizzolara, Superintendent of DRE, 4 October 1979, in Folder "Medical Disciplinary," DPR Admin.

49   Food and Drug Administration, Notice, "Amphetamines: Drugs for Human Use . . . ," 41,567.

50   See, e.g., dozens of letters filed in Box 222, Folder 4, AMA Papers.

51   *Drug Abuse Control Amendments—1970*, 666.

52   Administrative Narcotics Division, "Six Month Report, January—June, 1976," Folder "Criminal Justice Council (Folder 2) 1973-1976," LA NDDC. For computerized system, see *Drug Abuse Control Amendments—1970*, 592.

53   Alfonso A. Narvez, "Task Force Seeks Power to Study Theft of Drugs and Makers' Level," *New York Times*, June 29, 1977, https://www.nytimes.com /1977/06/29/archives/task-force-seeks-power-to-study-theft-of-drugs-at -makers-level.html?_r=0.

54   John H. Lavin, "What Happens When a State Licensing Board Gets Tough," *Medical Economics*, June 14, 1976, 101.

55   See, e.g., Board Briefs, October 1975, in "Discipline imposed upon licensees, File II," DASA Minutes. This was issue 11, suggesting recent origins.

56   See, e.g., Jackson W. Riddle, Exec Secretary of New York's Medical Board, to Secretaries of all State Medical Boards, 17 February 1976, Folder "Medical Disciplinary Board," DASA Minutes; Raymond Reed, Executive Secretary of California Board of Medical Examiners to All medical examining boards, 22 October 1975, and Federation of State Medical Boards of the United States, Inc., "Board Action Report for October 1975," both in Folder "Discipline imposed upon licensees, File II," DASA Minutes.

57   Rasmussen, *On Speed*, 220.

58   Herzberg, *Happy Pills*, app. 2.

59   See Drug Abuse Warning Network, *Trends In Drug Abuse Related Hospital Emergency Room Episodes and Medical Examiner Cases for Selected Drugs, 1976-1985* (Bethesda, MD: National Institute on Drug Abuse, 1986).

60   "Inspection report, 7-8 February 1956," Box 2161, Folder 500.67 March-Dec 1956, FDA Papers.

61   Louis R. Fine to Thomas F. Howard, 20 February 1975, Folder "Discipline imposed upon licensees, I," DASA Minutes.

62   "Memo from Wayne Rusch," 17 February 1976, Box 8, Folder 16 "Balciunas, Vitaldas/MEB," SBME Investigations.

63   For "only for patients I know well" and "welfare" quotes, Timothy N. Fast to Dennis Curran, Investigator for Division of Consumer Complaints, "Interview with Vitoloas Balciunas," 12 January 1977; "cutting welfare benefits" from "In the matter of disciplinary proceedings against Vitoldas Balciunas, MD; Order," 21 January 1982; both in Box 8, Folder 16 "Balciunas, Vitaldas/ MEB," SBME Investigations.

64   Quote from "Memo from Wayne Rusch"; revocation order State of Wisconsin, "In the matter of disciplinary proceedings against Vitoldas Balciunas . . . Order," Box 8, Folder 16 "Balciunas, Vitaldas/MEB," SBME Investigations.

65   Jerome Flynn to Medical Examining Board, September 6, 1977, Box 23, Folder 2 "Theiler, Alvin 1976," SBME Investigations.

66   "In the matter of Alvin Theiler, M.D.," 11 January 1978, 24-28, 36, 43, 46-47, 77, Box 23, Folder 2 "Theiler, Alvin 1976," SBME Investigations.

67 "In the matter of disciplinary proceedings against Alvin C. Theiler, Findings of Fact, Conclusions of Law and Order," Box 23, Folder 2 "Theiler, Alvin 1976," SBME Investigations.

68 The next four paragraphs are drawn from David Herzberg, "Busted for Block-busters," in Greene and Watkins, *Prescribed*, 207-31.

69 *Methaqualone (Quaalude, Sopor) Traffic, Abuse, and Regulation, Legislative Hearings on the Methaqualone Control Act of 1978, S. 1252, Before the Subcomm. to Investigate Juvenile Delinquency of the S. Comm. on the Judiciary*, 93d Cong. 160-61 (1973) (testimony of Sherwin Gardiner).

70 Malthea Falco, *Methaqualone: A Study of Drug Control* (Washington, DC: Drug Abuse Council, 1975), 12-34.

71 Quaalude advertisement, *Archives of General Psychiatry* 25, no. 5 (1971): 30-32.

72 *Methaqualone Traffic, Abuse, and Regulation*, 191 (testimony of George Gay, MD, Haight-Ashbury Free Clinic).

73 Falco, *Methaqualone*, 12-34.

74 Pascarelli, "Methaqualone Abuse, The Quiet Epidemic," *JAMA* 224, no. 11 (1973): 1512-14; Ager, "Luding Out," *New England Journal of Medicine* 281, no. 1 (1972): 51; Zwerdling, "Methaqualone: The 'Safe' Drug That Isn't Very," *Washington Post*, November 12, 1972, in US Senate, *Methaqualone Traffic, Abuse, and Regulation*, 360-64. See also David Herzberg, "Blockbusters and Controlled Substances: Miltown, Quaalude, and Consumer Demand for Drugs in Postwar America," *Studies in the History and Philosophy of Biological and Biomedical Sciences* 42, no. 4 (2011): 415-26.

75 *Methaqualone Traffic, Abuse, and Regulation*, 94.

76 *Methaqualone Traffic, Abuse, and Regulation*, 246-47 (testimony of Parke-Davis); 265 (testimony of Rorer).

77 Drug Enforcement Administration, "Methaqualone and Its Salts," 37 Fed. Reg. 27,516 (Oct. 4, 1973). See also Herzberg, "Blockbusters and Controlled Substances." Quotas tracked in *Federal Register*; impact gauged by Crosby et al., "Drug Scheduling—What Effects?" in *Proceedings of the Annual Meeting of the American Pharmaceutical Association* (1978), cited in Spillane, "Debating the Controlled Substances Act," 26.

78 "Dr. Calloway, Longtime Civil Rights Leader, Dies," n.d., no newspaper title, and "The Real Dr. N. O. Calloway, Part 2," *Wisconsin State Journal*, 1 October 1978; both in Box 9, Folder 34 "Calloway Clippings & Publicity," SBME Investigations; and "Biographical data of N. O. Calloway, 2 April 1971," Box 10, Folder 2 "Calloway General 1978-1980," SBME Investigations.

79 "Biographical data of N. O. Calloway."

80 "Chronology of Events: Dr. Nathaniel Calloway Case," n.d., Box 10, Folder 2 "Calloway General 1978-1980," SBME Investigations.

81 Schlotthauer, Johnson & Mohs and Wayne Rusch, investigators, to State of Wisconsin Medical Examining Board, 24 April 1975, Box 10, Folder 1 "Calloway General 1975-1977," SBME Investigations; Nathaniel Calloway, "In Defense of Quaaludes," *UW Daily Cardinal*, 24 January 1975; all in Box 9, Folder 34 "Calloway—Clippings & Publicity," SBME Investigations. See also, e.g., Dennis Curran, Notes on Lecture by Dr. N. O. Calloway, 9 March 1977, Box 10, Folder 1 "Calloway General 1975-1977," SBME Investigations.

82 Charles Haig, "Let's Leave the Man Alone"; Mark Knickelbine, "Misin-

formed Reporter Libels Dr. Calloway?"; both in "Readers Are Riled: The Great Drug Story Debate," *Press Connections*, 8 March 1978, Box 9, Folder 34 "Calloway—Clippings & Publicity," SBME Investigations. See also Sarah Peisch, "Rap Drugs, Not Doctor," in "Readers Are Riled."

83   Deborah Williams to Mr. Dennis E. Curran, 20 January 1978, Box 10, Folder 2 "Calloway General 1978-1980," SBME Investigations.

84   For the whiteness of Calloway's clientele, see LeRoy Dalton to Patricia Fitzgerald, 25 October 1977, Box 10, Folder 2 "Calloway General 1978-1980," SBME Investigations; see also Dennis Curran to Medical Examining Board, 24 April 1975, Box 10, Folder 1 "Calloway General 1975-1977," SBME Investigations.

85   "N. O. Calloway, Comparison of Unit Doses October, 1975 and October, 1976, Filled at Schwartz and WSA Pharmacies," Box 9, Folder 35 "Calloway—Drug Research," SBME Investigations.

86   "Methaqualone—300 mg Sales"; see also untitled table, "Total # of Registrants Ordering Drug in 1976" etc.; both in Box 9, Folder 35 "Calloway—Drug Research," SBME Investigations.

87   For three pharmacies, see "Figure 3: 1975: Zip Code 537, Total Purchases by Retail Pharmacy, Source: ARCOS"; for percent written by Calloway, see untitled table "Pharmacy, Total # of schedule II Rx's," etc.; both in Box 9, Folder 35 "Calloway—Drug Research," SBME Investigations.

88   Dennis Curran, Investigative File, "Interview with Frances Breit," 3 October 1977, Box 10, Folder 1 "Calloway General 1975-1977," SBME Investigations.

89   KJL to CLC, Memorandum Re: State of Wisconsin v. Calloway, 24 August 1978, Box 9, Folder 35 "Calloway—Drug Research," SBME Investigations.

90   See, e.g., "Coroner's Inquisition, Drug Overdose-Self-Administered . . . ," 9 December 1977; "Coroner's Report," 4 July 1974; both in Box 9, Folder 33 "Calloway—Autopsies"; KJL to CLC, Memorandum: State of Wisconsin v. Calloway, 24 August 1978, Box 9 Folder 35, "Calloway—Drug Research," SBME Investigations.

91   "Chronology of Events: Dr. Nathaniel Calloway Case."

92   Dennis Curran to Jerry Flynn, 24 June 1977; Jerry Flynn, Investigative File, 12 September 1977; both in Box 10, Folder 1 "Calloway General 1975-1977," SBME Investigations.

93   Dan Allegretti, "Dr. Calloway May Lose License," *Capital Times*, n.d.; Michael Arndt, "Illegal Quaalude Rx's," *UW Daily Cardinal*, n.d.; Deanna Zychowski, "For immediate release," 19 July 1979; "A Tribute to Dr. N. O.," *UW Daily Cardinal*, 19 October 1979; all in Box 9, Folder 34 "Calloway—Clippings & Publicity," SBME Investigations.

94   This section is drawn from Herzberg, "Busted for Blockbusters," in Greene and Watkins, *Prescribed*.

95   Prosecutors' summation, *United States v. Witt*, court transcript from February 14, 1983, 15121, Box 10; Case File 82 Cr. 33-CSH, *Witt*.

96   Martin Siegel, Grand Jury Testimony, 6, Box 3, *Witt*; Siegel, September 30, 1982, 761-62, Box 3, *Witt*; Siegel, September 30, 1982, 316-17, Box 3, *Witt*.

97   Siegel, September 30, 1982, 154, Box 3, *Witt*.

98   Glass testimony, October 12, 1982, 2220-43, Box 7, *Witt*. Both physicians were DOs (Doctors of Osteopathy).

99   Glass testimony, October 12, 1982, 2216–18, 2234–36.

100 Glass testimony, October 12, 1982, 2262–71, 2274–2337.

101 Trial documents do not specify which pharmaceutical companies preceded Pfizer. Asherson, November 2, 1982, 4134–36, 6308, Box 12, *Witt*.

102 Asherson, November 2, 1982, 4134–52, 4496, 4157, 4411, 4519–24; DePietto, October 29, 1982, 3847; all in Box 12, *Witt*.

103 Dr. Emily Cole testimony, December 3, 1982, 7490, Box 13, *Witt*; Gregory Drezga testimony, January 14, 1983, 11294, Box 4, *Witt*; English, December 7, 1982, 7838–58, Box 4, *Witt*.

104 Statistical information about the clinic's employees in this paragraph come from "Information about Manhattan Center," n.d., Box 3, *Witt*.

105 Martin Siegel testimony, September 23, 1982, 214–19, Box 3, *Witt*; Ronald Asherson testimony, November 2, 1982, 4320, Box 12, *Witt*; Lawrence Glass testimony, October 12, 1982, 2220–21, Box 7, *Witt*.

106 Martin Siegel testimony, September 23, 1982, 214–19, Box 3, *Witt*; Ronald Asherson testimony, November 2, 1982, 4320, Box 12, *Witt*; Lawrence Glass testimony, October 12, 1982, 2220–21, Box 7, *Witt*; Asherson, November 2, 1982, 4411, Box 12, *Witt*; Prosecutor summation, February 14–17, 1983, 15077, Box 10, *Witt*.

107 See, e.g., Gordon Schauer testimony, October 12, 1982, 2110, Box 7, *Witt*.

108 Benjamin Rose testimony, December 8, 1982, 8043–47, Box 4, *Witt*; Jaimie Kahn testimony, October 4, 1982, 1102–3, Box 8, *Witt*; DePietto, October 29, 1982, 3843, Box 12, *Witt*.

109 Ben Rose Ex Parte Affidavit, 3–4, Box 7, *Witt*.

110 Siegel, September 30, 1982, 214–15, Box 3, *Witt*; Asherson, November 2, 1982, 4320, Box 12, *Witt*; Rose, December 8, 1982, 8627, Box 4, *Witt*; Kahn, October 4, 1982, 1112, Box 8, *Witt*.

111 This according to many witness reports, and evidence appears to back them up. For example, Dr. PS saw nine patients on his first day; six were in their early thirties, three in their late twenties; five claimed to be in sales; Sarosi, December 3, 1982, 7542–57, Box 13, *Witt*.

112 Defense opening arguments, September 22, 1982, 87, Box 3, *Witt*.

113 See, e.g., United States v. Betancourt, 734 F.2d 750 (11th Cir. 1984); United States v. Blanton, 730 F.2d 1425 (11th Cir. 1984); Lazarus v. Department of Professional Regulation of Florida, 481 So. 2d 22 (Fla. Dist. Ct. App. 1985); Apiau v. Florida Board of Medical Examiners, 473 So. 2d 775 (Fla. Dist. Ct. App. 1985); Federgo Discount Center v. Board of Pharmacy, 452 So. 2d 1063 (Fla. Dist. Ct. App. 1984); Cilento v. Florida, 377 So. 2d 663 (Fla. 1979); United States v. Jackson, 576 F.2d 46 (5th Cir. 1978); United States v. Dunbar, 591 F.2d 1190 (5th Cir. 1979); United States v. Doe, 711 F.2d 1187 (2d Cir. 1983); Ohio v. Sway, 472 N.E.2d 1065 (Ohio 1984).

114 Peter Bourne, "Polydrug Abuse—Considerations in a National Strategy," *American Journal of Drug and Alcohol Abuse* 1, no. 2 (1974): 152.

115 Herzberg, *Happy Pills*, chap. 4.

116 See Mark T. Hoekenga, VP-Medical Liaison, Merrell-National Laboratories to Dear Doctor, 13 December 1977, Box 2, Folder 5 "Amphetamines—Physician correspondence 1977–1978," SBME Correspondence, which warned that "there is a development in Wisconsin that threatens your prerogatives as a physician" and soliciting letters to the Board. Pennwalt sent a similar letter to all Wisconsin physicians (William Govier, VP of Research and Development to Dear Doctor, 4 January 1978, Box 2, Folder 6 "Amphetamines—Professional Correspondence 1976-1979," SBME Correspondence).

117   Robert T. Willis, MD, to Medical Examining Board, 9 January 1978, Box 2, Folder 5 "Amphetamines—Physician correspondence 1977-1978," SBME Correspondence; see also Robert T. Willis, MD, to Medical Examining Board, 14 November 1977, Box 1 Folder 5 "Amphetamine Rule 1977," SBME Correspondence.

118   Regina Royal Coats to Dear Sir, 16 November 1977, and Jack Schroeder, MD, to Department of Regulation & Licensing, 18 November 1977, both in Box 1, Folder 5 "Amphetamine Rule 1977," SBME Correspondence.

119   Joseph Gfroerer and Marc Brodsky, "The Incidence of Illicit Drug Use in the United States, 1962-1989," *British Journal of Addiction* 87 (1992): 1345-51.

120   Paul Gootenberg, *Andean Cocaine: The Making of a Global Drug* (Chapel Hill: University of North Carolina Press, 2008).

121   Courtwright, "'Big Tent' Reform"; Massing, *Fix*.

122   Clark, *Recovery Revolution*.

Chapter Seven

1   Vincent Dole and Marie Nyswander, "A Medical Treatment for Diacetylmorphine (Heroin) Addiction," *Journal of the American Medical Association* 193 (August 1965): 646-50; Vincent Dole, Marie Nyswander, and Alan Warner, "Successful Treatment of 750 Criminal Addicts," *JAMA* 206, no. 12 (1968): 2708.

2   Description of Dole and Nyswander taken from Claire Clark, "'Chemistry Is the New Hope': Therapeutic Communities and Methadone Maintenance," *Social History of Alcohol and Drugs* 26, no. 2 (2012): 192-216.

3   Schneider, *Smack*.

4   Clark "'Chemistry Is the New Hope.'"

5   Massing, *Fix*.

6   Mical Raz, Treating Addiction or Reducing Crime? Methadone Maintenance and Drug Policy under the Nixon Administration," *Journal of Policy History* 29, no. 1 (2017): 58-86.

7   Nancy Campbell and Anne M. Lovell, "The History of the Development of Buprenorphine as an Addiction Therapeutic," *Annals of the New York Academy of Sciences* 1248 (2012): 128.

8   Campbell and Lovell, "Development of Buprenorphine," 127.

9   Raz, "Treating Addiction or Reducing Crime?" 75-76.

10   Raz, "Treating Addiction or Reducing Crime?" 74-75. See also Campbell and Lovell, "Development of Buprenorphine," 130.

11   Clark, "'Chemistry Is the New Hope'"; Raz, "Treating Addiction or Reducing Crime?"; Schneider, *Smack*.

12   Archer et al., "Narcotic Antagonists as Analgesics," *Science*, August 1962, 541.

13   See Joseph G. Bird to Nathan B. Eddy, 9 March 1962; Bird to Eddy, 23 February 1962; Eddy to Bird, 19 February 1962; Bird to Dr. Everette L. May, 4 December 1961; Louis Harris to Eddy, 2 November 1961; Eddy to Bird, 26 Sep-

tember 1961; Eddy to Bird, 6 April 1961; Bird to Eddy, 16 March 1961. See also E. Keith Cannan to Henry Giordano, 1 April 1963. For press report, see Joseph Hixson, "Chemists May Have Non-habit-forming Drug," *Herald Tribune*, 8 September 1963. All in Folder "Sterling-Winthrop Research Inst 1961-1964," NAS-NRC Papers.

14   Joseph G. Bird to Dr. Marshall Gates, 4 September 1962; Fraser began study of 20,228 in spring 1962; Bird to Eddy, 9 March 1962. Both in Folder "Sterling-Winthrop Research Inst 1961-1964," NAS-NRC Papers.

15   Arthur S. Keats and Jane Telford, "Studies of Analgesic Drugs: VIII. Narcotic Antagonist Analgesic without Psychotomimetic Effects," *Journal of Pharmacology and Experimental Therapeutics* 143, no. 2 (1964): 157-64.

16   H. F. Fraser and D. E. Rosenberg, "Studies on Human Addiction Liability of 2'-hydroxy-5,9-dimethyl-2-(3,3-dimethylallyl)-6,7-benzomorphan (WIN 20,228): A Weak Narcotic Antagonist," *Journal of Pharmacology and Experimental Therapeutics* 143, no. 2 (1964): 149-56.

17   Nathan B. Eddy, to Joseph Bird, 2 January 1964, Folder "Sterling-Winthrop Research Inst 1961-1964," NAS-NRC Papers.

18   For FBN agreement, see John R. Enright, Acting Commissioner of Narcotics, to Nathan B. Eddy, 4 October 1965, Folder "Bureau of Narcotics, General 1961-1965," NAS-NRC Papers. For Eddy's assistance navigating FDA requirements, see also Nathan B. Eddy to Joseph G. Bird, 8 September 1966, Folder "Sterling-Winthrop Research Inst, 1965-1966," NAS-NRC Papers.

19   Robert Plumb, "Pain Drug Found Nonaddictive but as Powerful as Morphine," *New York Times*, September 11, 1963, 1.

20   Hixson, "Chemists May Have Non-habit-forming Drug." See also Faye Marley, "Substitute for Morphine," *Science News Letter*, September 21, 1963, 179; "God's Own," *Newsweek*, September 23, 1963, 71.

21   For popular media accounts, see, e.g., Jane Brody, "Pain-Killing Drug Approved by F.D.A.," *New York Times*, June 27, 1967, 41; "Relief without Addiction?" *Time*, July 7, 1967, 67. For medical media, see, e.g., Max Sadove, Reuben Balagot, and Faustino Pecora, "Pentazocine—A New Nonaddicting Analgesic," *JAMA* 189, no. 3 (1964): 197-202. Even the skeptical *Medical Letter on Drugs and Therapeutics* was not pushing back this time; see "Pentazocine (Talwin)," *Medical Letter on Drugs and Therapeutics* 9, no. 24 (1967): 95-96.

22   Nathan B. Eddy, "Analgesic and Dependence-Producing Properties of Drugs," *Research Publication of the Association of Research in Nervous and Mental Disease* 46 (1968): 6.

23   "What Makes It Great? Commentary by Lionel Trilling, Copyright 1970 Winthrop Laboratories"; see also Hereward Lester Cooke of the National Gallery of Art on Edgar Degas (Sterling Drug Papers doc P1020586) and Benjamin West (Sterling Drug Papers doc P1020691). All in Box 155, Folder 2-7 "Product Files S-T 1960s-1970s," Sterling Drug Papers.

24   "In Place of Morphine or Meperidine," 23 December 1968, Box 155, Folder 8, Box 156, Folder 1-2, "Product Files S-T 1960s," Sterling Drug Papers.

25   "Winthrop Proudly Announces . . . Talwin," n.d.; "Winthrop Proudly Announces . . . Talwin, Potent Non-narcotic Analgesic," 29 September 1967; both in Box 155, Folder 2-7 "Product Files S-T 1960s-1970s," Sterling Drug Papers.

26 "In Place of Morphine or Meperidine."

27 For published reports, see, e.g., Raynaldo Sandoval and Richard Wang, "Tolerance and Dependence on Pentazocine," *New England Journal of Medicine* 280 (1969): 1391–92; William Weber and Howard Rome, "Addiction to Pentazocine: Report of Two Cases," *JAMA* 212, no. 10 (1970): 1708.

28 James Inciardi and Carl Chambers, "Patterns of Pentazocine Abuse and Addiction," *New York State Journal of Medicine* 71, no. 14 (1971): 1727–33; Charles R. Schuster, B. Baddeley Smith, Jerome H. Jaffe, "Drug Abuse in Heroin Users: An Experimental Study of Self-Administration of Methadone, Codeine, and Pentazocine," *Archives of General Psychiatry* 24, no. 4 (1971): 359–62.

29 For AMA, see Council on Drugs, "The Misuse of Pentazocine: Its Dependence-Producing Potential," *JAMA* 209, no. 10 (1969): 1518–21. For FDA Advisory Committee recommendation, see *FDC Reports*, 29 April 1974, Box 1, Folder 18 "Controlled Substances Board, Pentazocine (Talwin), 1974," PEB Correspondence.

30 "What Makes It Great?"

31 The states were Maryland, South Dakota, Alabama, Kentucky, and Wisconsin; see Controlled Substances Board, Minutes of Talwin Hearing, 9 January 1974, Box 1, Folder 18 "Controlled Substances Board, Pentazocine (Talwin), 1974," PEB Correspondence. For battles between Sterling-Winthrop and Arkansas, Ohio, New York, and Wisconsin over regulating Talwin, see Box 4, Folder 43 "Controlled Substances Board, Pentazocine (Talwin), 1974–1975," PEB Correspondence.

32 Edward Senay, "Clinical Experience with T's and B's," *Drug and Alcohol Dependence* 14 (1985): 305–11.

33 Calvin Wadley and Gordon Stillie, "Pentazocine (Talwin) and Tripelennamine (Pyribenzamine): A New Drug Abuse Combination or Just a Revival?" *International Journal of Addiction* 15, no. 8 (1980): 1285–90.

34 Thomas B. Kirkpatrick, Public Announcement, Folder "Advisory Council Meeting—June 1, 1978"; Minutes of Executive Staff Meeting, 13 February 1979, Folder "1979 Exec. Staff Mtgs"; both in DASA Minutes. For data on addiction treatment intake, see K. K. Kaistha, Chief Toxicologist, "Talwin Update," Folder "Dangerous Drugs Advisory Council Meeting, 11/18/81 10a, Executive House Chicago," DASA Minutes. See also US Congress, House of Representatives, Select Committee on Narcotics Abuse and Control, *Abuse of Dangerous Licit and Illicit Drugs—Psychotropics, Phencyclidine (PCP), and Talwin: Hearings Before H. Select Comm. on Narcotics Abuse and Control*, 95th Cong. 335, 365–69 (1978).

35 *Abuse of Dangerous Licit and Illicit Drugs*, 412.

36 *Abuse of Dangerous Licit and Illicit Drugs*, 488.

37 Kirkpatrick, Public Announcement, DASA Minutes. Sterling-Winthrop sued the Commission, but it was not successful in preventing the move (see Folder "September 13, 1978," DASA Minutes).

38 *Abuse of Dangerous Licit and Illicit Drugs*, 368, 269.

39 For Talwin sales, see *Abuse of Dangerous Licit and Illicit Drugs*, 374.

40 "Petition of Sterling Drug Inc. for repeal of Rule Wis. Adm. Code, Section CSB 2.06(4m), Box 1, Folder 18 "Controlled Substances Board, Pentazocine

(Talwin), 1974," PEB Correspondence. For T's and Blues problems, see Controlled Substances Board, Agenda, 16 December 1981, Item 6, Box 4, Folder 8 "Controlled Substances Board 1981," SBME Correspondence.

41 "Advisory Council Meeting March 10, 1982, Room C-1, Stratton Bldg, Spfld, ILL 10am," DASA Minutes.

42 "Advisory Council Mtg—May 12, 1982, 6pm Springfield, ILL"; for Ohio, see "Mtg of dangerous drugs advisory council Sept 13, 1982—Chicago, IL (Marina 300 Rest.)," both in DASA Minutes.

43 Wisconsin law in "Advisory council mtg—May 12, 1982 6pm Springfield, ILL," DASA Minutes; effects in "The effects of Talwin control in Wisconsin," Box 4, Folder 8 "Controlled Substances Board 1981," SMBE Correspondence.

44 *Abuse of Dangerous Licit and Illicit Drugs*, 344-45.

45 *Abuse of Dangerous Licit and Illicit Drugs*, 383.

46 *Abuse of Dangerous Licit and Illicit Drugs*, 336.

47 Drug Enforcement Administration, "Placement of Pentazocine into Schedule IV," 44 Fed. Reg. 2169 (Jan. 10, 1979), https://cdn.loc.gov/service/ll/fedreg/fr044/fr044007/fr044007.pdf.

48 Controlled Substances Board, Minutes of Meeting, 14 July 1982, Box 4, Folder 9 "Controlled Substances Board, 1982," SBME Correspondence.

49 Julilly Kohler-Hausmann, *Getting Tough: Welfare and Imprisonment in 1970s America* (Princeton, NJ: Princeton University Press, 2017), chap. 1. See also Samuel K. Roberts, "'Rehabilitation' as a Boundary Object: Medicalization, Local Activism, and Narcotics Addiction Policy in New York City, 1951-1962," *Social History of Alcohol and Drugs* 26, no. 2 (2012): 147-69.

50 Quoted in Kohler-Hausmann, *Getting Tough*, 91.

51 Kohler-Hausmann, *Getting Tough*, 118-20

52 Massing, *Fix*; David Courtwright, *No Right Turn: Conservative Politics in a Liberal America* (Cambridge, MA: Harvard University Press, 2010), 83-84.

53 Dufton, *Grass Roots*.

54 Schneider, *Smack*; David Courtwright, "The Rise and Fall and Rise of Cocaine in the United States," in *Consuming Habits: Drugs in History and Anthropology*, ed. Jordan Goodman, Andrew Sherratt, and Paul Lovejoy (London: Routledge, 2007), chap. 11.

55 Michael J. Durfce, "Crack Era Reform: A Brief History of Crack and the Rise of the Carceral State, 1985-1992" (diss., University at Buffalo-SUNY, 2015); Noel Wolfe, "Battling Crack: A Study of the Northwest Bronx Community and Clergy Coalition's Tactics," *Journal of Urban History* 43, no. 1 (2017): 18-32; Donna Murch, "Crack in Los Angeles: Crisis, Militarization, and Black Response to the Late Twentieth Century War on Drugs," *Journal of American History* 102, no. 1 (2015): 162-73; David Farber, *Crack: Rock Cocaine: Street Capitalism, and the Decade of Greed* (Cambridge: Cambridge University Press, 2019).

56 Michelle Alexander, *The New Jim Crow: Mass Incarceration in the Age of Colorblindness* (New York: New Press, 2012); Craig Reinarman and Harry Levine, eds., *Crack in America: Demon Drugs and Social Justice* (Berkeley: University of California Press, 1997).

57 Massing, *Fix*; Clark, *Recovery Revolution*; Kohler-Hausmann, *Getting Tough*; Schneider, *Smack*.

58 Matthew Lassiter, "Impossible Criminals: The Suburban Imperatives of America's War on Drugs," *Journal of American History* 102, no. 1 (2015): 126–40.

59 Quoted in Daniel Carpenter, *Reputation and Power: Organizational Image and Pharmaceutical Regulation at the FDA* (Princeton, NJ: Princeton University Press, 2010), 389.

60 Carpenter, *Reputation and Power*; Lucas Richert, *A Prescription for Scandal: Conservatism, Consumer Choice, and the Food and Drug Administration during the Reagan Era* (Lanham, MD: Lexington, 2014); Tomes, *Remaking the American Patient*.

61 Richert, *Prescription for Scandal*, 45; for book series, see, e.g., John Vernon, *Regulation of Pharmaceuticals: Balancing the Benefits and Risks* (Washington, DC: AEI Press, 1983).

62 Richert, *Prescription for Scandal*, 65.

63 Richert, 82, 95.

64 Richert, 88–89.

65 Quoted in Carpenter, *Reputation and Power*, 368.

66 See, e.g., Richert, chaps. 4–6; Carpenter, chap. 6.

67 Richert, 183, Carpenter, 731.

68 Richert, 179–81; Carpenter, 734–50.

69 Tomes, *Remaking the American Patient*, 370–71.

70 Greene and Herzberg, "Hidden in Plain Sight."

71 Roma Valenzuela to Congressman John Rhodes, 25 July 1973; Box 4866 "511.09—515," Folder 228 "511.09—512 Vibramycin, 1973," FDA Papers.

72 John Simenstad to Medical Examining Board, 11 November 1977, Box 1, Folder 5 "Amphetamine Rule 1977," SBME Correspondence.

73 See, e.g., Elizabeth Rasche Gonzáles, "Where Are All the Tranquilizer Junkies?" *JAMA* 269, no. 19 (1983): 2603–4; Jonathan Gabe and Michael Bury, "Tranquilisers and Health Care in Crisis," *Social Science and Medicine* 32, no. 4 (1991): 449–54; Susan Speaker, "From 'Happiness Pills' to 'National Nightmare': Changing Cultural Assessment of Minor Tranquilizers in America, 1955–1980, *Journal of the History of Medicine*, July 1997, 38–76.

74 Allan Horwitz, *Creating Mental Illness* (Chicago: University of Chicago Press, 2003).

75 Horwitz, 73–74.

76 Horwitz, 79.

77 See Ray Moynihan and Alan Cassels, *Selling Sickness: How the World's Biggest Pharmaceutical Companies Are Turning Us All into Patients* (New York: Bold Type, 2009).

78 Herzberg, *Happy Pills*, chap. 5.

79 Keith Wailoo, *Pain: A Political History* (Baltimore: Johns Hopkins University Press, 2015).

80 Marcia Meldrum, "A Brief History of the Multidisciplinary Management of Chronic Pain," in *Chronic Pain Management: Guidelines for Multidisciplinary Program Development*, ed. Michael Schatman and Alexandra Campbell (New York: CRC Press, Taylor & Francis, 2007).

81 M.J. Schiffrin, *The Management of Pain in Cancer* (Chicago:L Year Book, 1956), 7–8, 13–33, cited in Marcia Meldrum, "A Capsule History of Pain Manage-

ment," *JAMA* 290, no. 18 (2003): 2470-75. See also Marcia Meldrum, "The Prescription as Stigma," in Greene and Watkins, *Prescribed*, 188-89.

82   Richard M. Marks and Edward J. Sachar, "Undertreatment of Medical Inpatients with Narcotic Analgesics," *Annals of Internal Medicine* 78 (1973): 173-81, cited in Meldrum, "Prescription as Stigma," 189.

83   Joanna Bourke, *The Story of Pain: From Prayer to Painkillers* (Oxford: Oxford University Press, 2014), 291-95; Wailoo, *Pain*.

84   Keith Wailoo, *Dying in the City of the Blues: Sickle Cell Anemia and the Politics of Race and Health* (Chapel Hill: University of North Carolina Press, 2001).

85   For Sloan Kettering study, see Raymond W. Houde, "Systematic Analgesics and Related Drugs; Narcotic Analgesics," in *International Symposium on Pain of Advanced Cancer*, ed. John J. Bonica and Vittorio Ventafridda, *Advances in Pain Research and Therapy*, vol. 2 (New York: Raven Press, 1979), 263-73; for St. Christopher study, see Robert G. Twycross, "Choice of Strong Analgesic in Terminal Cancer: Diamorphine or Morphine?" *Pain* 3 (1977): 93-104; Robert G. Twycross, "Overview of Analgesia," in Bonica and Ventafridda, *International Symposium on Pain*, 617-33, both cited in Meldrum, "Prescription as Stigma," 190-91.

86   Meldrum, "Capsule History." Note that some pushed for stronger social welfare assistance through the Social Security Act's disability program; see Wailoo, *Pain*.

87   See, e.g., National Institutes of Health, *The Interagency Committee on New Therapies for Pain and Discomfort: Report to the White House* (Washington, DC: Government Printing Office, 1979); *New Approaches to Treatment of Chronic Pain: A Review of Multidisciplinary Pain Clinics and Pain Centers*, ed. Korenz, K. Y. Ng, NIDA Research Monograph 36 (Washington, DC: Government Printing Office, 1981).

88   Kathleen M. Foley, "Current Issues in the Management of Cancer Pain: Memorial Sloan-Kettering Cancer Center," *New Approaches*, 170, 176, 178.

89   Foley, "Current Issues," 170, 178.

90   Jane Porter and Hershel Jick, "Addiction Rare in Patients Treated with Narcotics," *New England Journal of Medicine* 302, no. 2 (1980): 123.

91   Hershel Jick et al., "Comprehensive Drug Surveillance," *JAMA* 213, no. 9 (1970): 1455-60; Russel Miller and Hershel Jick, "Clinical Effects of Meperidine in Hospitalized Medical Patients," *Journal of Clinical Pharmacology* 18 (1978): 180-89; Ivan Borda, Dennis Slone, and Hershel Jick, "Assessment of Adverse Reactions within a Drug Surveillance Program," *JAMA* 205, no. 9 (1968): 646-47; Russell R. Miller and David J. Greenblatt, eds., *Drug Effects in Hospitalized Patients: Experiences of the Boston Collaborative Drug Surveillance Program 1966-1975* (New York: Wiley and Sons, 1976), 5-8; Russell R. Miller, "Clinical Effects of Parenteral Narcotics in Hospitalized Medical Patients," *Journal of Clinical Pharmacology* 20 (1980): 165-71.

92   Foley, "Current Issues," 176.

93   Russell Portenoy and Kathleen Foley, "Chronic Use of Opioid Analgesics in Non-malignant Pain: Report of 38 Cases," *Pain* 25, no. 2 (1986): "reasonable attempts," 183; "sharp contrast," 179; "more humane," 184.

94   Portenoy and Foley, 184.

95   Portenoy and Foley, 182.

96 D. E. Weissman and J. D. Haddox, "Opioid Pseudoaddiction—an Iatrogenic Syndrome," *Pain* 36, no. 3 (1989): 363-66. See also Barry Meier, *Painkiller: An Empire of Deceit and the Origin of America's Opioid Epidemic* (New York: Random House, 2003), 68-69.

97 See Anna Lembke, *Drug Dealer, MD: How Doctors Were Duped, Patients Got Hooked, and Why It's So Hard to Stop* (Baltimore: Johns Hopkins University Press, 2016), 59-62. For Foley's Purdue support, see Peter Whoriskey, "Rising Painkiller Addiction Shows Damage from Drugmakers' Role in Shaping Medical Opinion," Washington Post, December 30, 2012, https://www.washingtonpost.com/business/economy/2012/12/30/014205a6-4bc3-11e2-b709-667035ff9029_story.html?utm_term=.2827378a4ced. For Purdue's funding of the Kathleen M. Foley Chair in Pain and Palliative Care, see Matthew Perrone, Associated Press, "Federal Pain Panel Rife with Links to Pharma Companies," *Seattle Times*, January 27, 2016, https://www.seattletimes.com/business/federal-pain-panel-rife-with-links-to-pharma-companies/.

98 See, e.g., Portenoy's self-description in his written testimony to the US Senate, Committee on Health, Education, Labor and Pensions, "Oxycontin: Balancing Risks and Benefits," https://www.help.senate.gov/imo/media/doc/Portenoy.pdf; Meier, *Pain Killer*; Anna Lembke, *Drug Dealer, MD: How Doctors Were Duped, Patients Got Hooked, and Why It's So Hard to Stop* (Baltimore: Johns Hopkins University Press, 2016).

99 US Senate Homeland Security and Governmental Affairs Committee, Ranking Member's Office, *Fueling an Epidemic, Report Two: Exposing the Financial Ties between Opioid Manufacturers and Third Party Advocacy Groups; Minority Staff Report* (2017).

100 Wailoo, *Pain.*

101 Bonnie McNeal, Project Manager, to Purdue Pharma L.P., 12 December 1995, enclosing "11. Application summary, A. Annotated Package Insert (including Patient Instructions), Oxycodone Hydrochloride Controlled Release Tablets, OxyContin TM Tablets, Draft Package Insert," in (New Drug Application) NDA-20-553, supplied by request from FDA.

102 Wright's move to Purdue is reported in multiple places, e.g., https://www.marketplace.org/2017/12/13/opioid/.

103 OxyContin Marketing Budget, 1996, 9, 13, https://khn.org/news/purdue-and-the-oxycontin-files/ (hereafter cited as OCMB).

104 "Non-habit forming" in OCMB, 1996; and Caitlin Esch, "How One Sentence Helped Set Off the Opioid Crisis, December 13, 2017, in *Uncertain Hour*, produced by American Public Media, podcast, https://www.marketplace.org/2017/12/13/health-care/uncertain-hour/opioid.

105 Back pain through post-op pain: OCMB, 2000, 1-41; rheumatology through sports/rehab: OCMB, 2001, 268; primary care: OCMB, 2002, 320.

106 OCMB, 1998, 131. See also Purdue Pharma, "New Hope for Millions of Americans Suffering from Persistent Pain," press release, May 31, 1996, https://documents.latimes.com/oxycontin-press-release-1996/.

107 OCMB, 1996, 31.

108 J. David Haddox et al., "The Use of Opioids for the Treatment of Chronic Pain," *Clinical Journal of Pain* 13, no. 1 (1997): 6-8.

109 See, e.g., David Joranson and Aaron Gilson, "Policy Issues and Imperatives in the Use of Opioids to Treat Pain in Substance Abusers," *Journal of Law, Medicine & Ethics*, September 1, 1994, http://journals.sagepub.com/doi/abs/10 .1111/j.1748-720X.1994.tb01298.x.

110 John Fauber, "UW a Force in Pain Drug Growth," *Milwaukee Journal Sentinel*, April 2, 2011, http://archive.jsonline.com/watchdog/watchdogreports /119130114.html/.

111 David Joranson, Aaron Gilson, June Dahl, and J. David Haddox, "Pain Management, Controlled Substances, and State Medical Board Policy: A Decade of Change," *Journal of Pain and Symptom Management* 23, no. 2 (2002): 138-47.

112 See FSMB, "Model Policy for the Use of Controlled Substances for the Treatment of Pain," adopted May 2004, "Introduction," https://dprfiles.delaware .gov/medicalpractice/Model_Policy_Treatment_Pain.pdf.

113 FSMB, "Model Guidelines for the Use of Controlled Substances for the Treatment of Pain," adopted May 2, 1998.

114 See FSMB, "Model Policy," "Introduction."

115 David Baker, *The Joint Commission's Pain Standards: Origins and Evolution* (Outlook Terrance, IL: Joint Commission, 2017).

116 Baker, "Joint Commission's Pain Standards"; David Baker, "History of the Joint Commission's Pain Standards: Lessons for Today's Prescription Opioid Epidemic," *JAMA* 317, no. 11 (2017): 1117-18.

117 OCMB, 2001, 260.

118 OCMB, 2001, 267.

119 See, e.g., Elisabeth Rosenthal, "Patients in Pain Find Relief, Not Addiction, in Narcotics," *New York Times*, March 28, 1993, 1; "Pain Specialist Dr. Russell Portenoy on Pain Management," NBC News, *Sunday Today*, May 9, 1999, retrieved from Nexis Uni. See also US General Accounting Office, *Prescription Drugs: OxyContin Abuse and Diversion and Efforts to Address the Problem* (Washington, DC: Government Printing Office, 2013).

120 American Pain Foundation, *Treatment Options: A Guide for People Living with Pain*, n.d., 5, 10-11, https://ce4less.com/Tests/Materials/E019Materials.pdf.

121 Jules Netherland and Helena Hansen, "White Opioids: Pharmaceutical Race and the War on Drugs That Wasn't," *BioSocieties* 12, no. 2 (2017): 217-38.

122 *OxyContin: Its Use and Abuse: Hearings Before the Subcomm. on Oversite and Investigations of the H. Comm. on Energy and Commerce*, 107th Cong. 3 (2001); Meier, *Pain Killer*, 26.

123 Kelly Ray Knight, "Women on the Edge: Opioids, Benzodiazepines, and the Social Anxieties Surrounding Women's Reproduction in the U.S. 'Opioid Epidemic,'" *Contemporary Drug Problems*, December 2017.

124 See, e.g., Maia Szalavitz, "What the Media Gets Wrong about Opioids," *Columbia Journalism Review*, August 15, 2018, https://www.cjr.org/covering_the _health_care_fight/what-the-media-gets-wrong-about-opioids.php, citing Rachel Lipari and Arthur Hughes, "How People Obtain the Prescription Pain Relievers They Misuse," *CBHSQ Report* (Substance Abuse and Mental Health Services Administration), January 12, 2017, https://www.samhsa.gov /data/sites/default/files/report_2686/ShortReport-2686.html; T. J. Cicero, M. S. Ellis, and Z. A. Kasper, "Psychoactive Substance Use Prior to the Development of Iatrogenic Opioid Abuse," *Addictive Behaviors* 65 (February

2017): 242–44; Nora D. Volkow and A. Thomas McClellan, "Opioid Abuse in Chronic Pain—Misconceptions and Mitigation Strategies," *New England Journal of Medicine* 374 (2016): 1253–63.

125   See, e.g., Kathleen R. Merikangas and Vetisha L. McClair, "Epidemiology of Substance Use Disorders," *Human Genetics* 131, no. 6 (2012): 779–89; Bridget F. Grant, Tulshi D. Saha, and W. June Ruan, "Epidemiology of *DSM-5* Drug Use Disorder Results from the National Epidemiologic Survey on Alcohol and Related Conditions—III," *JAMA Psychiatry* 73, no. 1 (2016): 39–47.

126   See, e.g., Anne Case and Angus Deaton, *Deaths of Despair and the Future of Capitalism* (Princeton, NJ: Princeton University Press, forthcoming 2020).

127   Andrew Joseph, "'A Blizzard of Prescriptions': Documents Reveal New Details about Purdue's Marketing of OxyContin," *Stat News*, January 15, 2019, https://www.statnews.com/2019/01/15/massachusetts-purdue-lawsuit-new -details/.

128   *OxyContin: Its Use and Abuse*, 35–36, 41; see also Meier, *Painkiller*; Lembke, *Dope Doctor, M.D.*; Macy, *Dopesick*.

129   GAO, *OxyContin Abuse and Diversion*, 35.

130   GAO, *OxyContin Abuse and Diversion*, 37–39.

131   Stefan Kertesz and Adam Gordon, "A Crisis of Opioids and the Limits of Prescription Control: United States," *Addiction* 114, no. 1 (2019): 169–80; Silvia Martins et al., "Prescription Drug Monitoring Programs Operational Characteristics and Fatal Heroin Poisoning," *International Journal of Drug Policy* 74 (December 2019): 174–80.

132   Netherland and Hansen, "White Opioids."

133   Netherland and Hansen, "White Opioids"; Helena Hansen and Samuel K. Roberts, "Two Tiers of Biomedicalization: Buprenorphine, Methadone, and the Biopolitics of Addiction Stigma and Race," *Advances in Medical Sociology* 14 (2012): 79–102.

134   Hansen and Netherland, "White Opioids."

Conclusion

1   Nancy Campbell, *OD: Naloxone and the Politics of Overdose* (Cambridge, MA: MIT Press, 2020).

2   Samuel K. Roberts, "Drugs, Pariahs, and Politics: Toward a Harm Reduction of Color Approach" (presentation, Department of History, Princeton University, Princeton, NJ, December 1, 2017), https://history.princeton.edu /news-events/events/samuel-kelton-roberts-drugs-pariahs-and-politics -toward-harm-reduction-color; Kirsten West Savali, "The Scholar: Samuel K. Roberts Jr. on Drug Policy, Radical Recovery, and 'Capital Flight,'" *Root*, February 17, 2017, http://web.archive.org/web/20171220102408/https:// www.theroot.com/the-scholar-samuel-k-roberts-jr-on-drug-policy-radi -1792488258.

3   See, e.g., Robin Room, "The Monopoly Option: Obsolescent or a 'Best Buy' in Alcohol and Other Drug Control?" *Social History of Alcohol and Drugs* (forthcoming Fall 2020).

Index